# Administrative
# Action

PRENTICE-HALL INTERNATIONAL, INC., LONDON
PRENTICE-HALL OF AUSTRALIA, PTY., LTD., SYDNEY
PRENTICE-HALL OF CANADA, LTD., TORONTO
PRENTICE-HALL OF INDIA (PRIVATE) LTD., NEW DELHI
PRENTICE-HALL OF JAPAN, INC., TOKYO
PRENTICE-HALL DE MEXICO, S.A., MEXICO CITY

# Administrative
# Action

## THE TECHNIQUES OF ORGANIZATION AND MANAGEMENT

### WILLIAM H. NEWMAN

*Samuel Bronfman  Professor of Democratic Business Enterprise*
*Graduate School of Business, Columbia University*

*Second Edition*

PRENTICE-HALL, INC.
*Englewood Cliffs, N.J*

**to    C. B. N.**

Current printing (last digit):

13   12   11   10   9   8   7   6

© 1950, 1951, 1963, by

PRENTICE-HALL, INC.

*Englewood Cliffs, N.J.*

Library of Congress Catalog Card Number: 63-13843
Printed in the United States of America

C 00719

# Preface

Recognition of the essential role of administrators in modern society has increased greatly during recent years. Individual companies, to be sure, have long been concerned about the competence of their own executives. But now, virtually every country in the world encourages executive development as a vital component for its economic growth. Study of administration—or "management"—has, almost overnight, been identified as a necessity.

Widespread use of the first edition of *Administrative Action* indicates that its focus on basic elements of administration serves a helpful role in this upsurge of demand for better managers. Executive development programs, individual executives, and advanced university students have all welcomed its integrated treatment of the administrative process.

New features of the second edition deal with:

- *Building External Relationships.* A new chapter suggests how concepts of internal administration can also be useful in managing a flow of continuing relations with distributors, suppliers, financial institutions, and other external groups.
- *Over-all Control Structure.* The balancing and integrating of numerous controls throughout a company is the subject of another new chapter. Significant by itself, the idea of an over-all control structure also complements the concept of a planning structure and an organization structure discussed earlier in the book. Together, these three structures form the basic framework of a company's formal management.
- *Decision-Making.* In this second edition, two chapters are devoted to the *process* of making decisions—that is, establishing plans about action to be taken; and most of this material is new.
- *Logistics and Strategy.* Clearly, the *dynamic* administration of a firm, or a department, involves more attention to strategy than the existing literature implies. Consequently, this part of the book has been expanded.

Although these and other revisions have been made, the main approach to administration has not been changed in this edition. The book is still built around the underlying processes of planning, organizing, assembling resources, supervising, and controlling. With respect to each of these processes, the book seeks to (1) sift out from diverse sources basic knowledge about the process, (2) state these ideas in a practical and operation form, and (3) add new insights and interpretations that will assist executives in administering dynamic enterprises.

The ideas in this book come from many people, as well as from personal experience in various activities. My greatest debt is to those able executives I have worked with in an operating or consulting capacity. Among these, James O. McKinsey, formerly Chairman of Marshall Field & Company and an outstanding management consultant; L. S. Fish, Organization Counsel for Standard Oil Company (New Jersey); and Luther Gulick, President of the Institute of Public Administration, have been especially inspiring. My colleague, Professor Thomas L. Berg, has shared in the development of ideas on external relations and control structure, and Professor Charles E. Summer, Jr. has made many helpful suggestions.

In expressing appreciation to these men, I do not wish to imply that any one of them agrees with all that is said in this book. They all do share with me the conviction that a grasp of the principles and techniques of administration is vital to every executive who is to perform well his role in our increasingly complex society.

W.H.N.

# Contents

## II Organizing 141

# 1
# Administration—A Basic Social Technique

Skillful administrators are vital to every dynamic, successful enterprise. Other things, such as capital and technical knowledge, are also needed, but without competent executives no company can long hold a place of leadership. These men must plan, direct, and control the operations of the business.

The task of directing the cooperative efforts of individuals toward some common objective is as old as civilization. The Bible comments briefly upon the administrative problems of Moses as the leader of the children of Israel. The pyramids have borne witness through the centuries of the administrative, as well as the engineering, skills of the ancient Egyptians. In the church, in the government, in the army, as well as in business enterprises, administration plays a dominant role. To be sure, the specific activities of these various enterprises differ greatly. Yet in each there are problems of organizing, of selecting executives, of establishing plans, of measuring results, and of coordinating and controlling the activities to accomplish agreed-upon ends. It is with these basic processes, which are common to all cooperative effort, that we shall deal.

*Administration* is the guidance, leadership, and control of the efforts of a group of individuals toward some common goal. Clearly, the good administrator is one who enables the group to achieve its objectives with a minimum expenditure of resources and effort and the least interference with other worth-while activities.

**Crucial importance of improving administration**

Not only is the work of administrators vital to particular enterprises; it is also a crucial activating element in building strong na-

*1*

tions. In industrialized countries like the United States there is widespread expectation and insistence on rising standards of living for expanding populations. And less-developed countries throughout the world are facing a revolution in the aspirations of the common man. Political and social stability—perhaps international peace—is closely associated with fulfilling such aspirations.

The ability of nations to meet these rising expectations depends to a significant degree upon the competence of their managers. The initiative, the drive, the translation of idealistic goals into tangible results, the persistent concern with efficiency, the readjustment to new demands and new technologies are all typical of the qualities business leaders are expected to provide. Increasingly, the general public is looking to the administrators who guide the productive enterprises of a country to serve as the catalysts that convert resources into goods and services.

At the same time, administration is becoming more complex. Speedier transportation and communication have greatly expanded the events that may have a direct impact on a firm in, say, St. Louis. Interdependence of companies, and of nations, is increasing. Technology is changing at an accelerating pace. Meanwhile, employees from office boys to vice-presidents are becoming less tractable.

The combined pressures of achieving better results while dealing with more complex situations place a high premium on improvements in administrative ability. Whether we like it or not, business enterprise has become one of the most powerful social institutions in Western civilization. Our quest in this book for ways to improve administrative skill, then, has significance far beyond helping an individual win a promotion.

### Administration—a distinct skill

Administrators are often men who possess outstanding ability in the particular activity that they are directing. For example, the manager of a baseball club may have been a star player, the production vice-president of a radar company may be an expert electronics engineer, or the merchandise manager of a department store may be a canny buyer of women's gloves. Distinguished performance in such specialized jobs probably leads to promotion to broader responsibilities. Such intimate knowledge and firsthand experience with specific operations is of great value to an executive.

Yet, unusual operating skill alone is not enough. Ample evidence exists that a star performer on the sales force or at the drafting board does not necessarily make a good executive. On the other hand, a man with only average operating skill may prove to be a very capable manager. This suggests that administrative skill is something different from technical proficiency in the operations being managed.

In fact, this administrative skill is so important that capable executives can move from one post to another and do an outstanding job in each spot. One man, for example, has successfully held positions as sales manager of a cracker company, general manager of a hosiery mill, and president of a chemical concern; and this is no isolated case. Perhaps even clearer evidence that administrative ability is a distinct skill is found in the use of army and navy officers as executives in business firms. These ex-officers usually have no background in their new company or industry, but they do have a basic grasp of the processes of management.

In the present study we are interested in those skills that versatile executives are able to focus on entirely new and divergent administrative problems. If we can identify and understand the techniques used by such skillful executives, we shall have tools that will be highly valuable to the administrators of the future.

Whenever an administrator is given responsibility for an operation that is new to him, of course he must learn as much as he can about that operation and secure the counsel of men who know it intimately. The man who has *both* personal experience with the operations and administrative skill undoubtedly has a considerable advantage. The point being made here is that management talent and technique are something in addition to, and distinct from, the substantive aspects of the work.

**Objectives of this book**

This book explores the intangible and vital processes of administration. Its three primary purposes are to:

1. Bring together existing knowledge regarding the *basic processes of administration*. As we shall see, many sound ideas are already recognized by leaders in business, government, and military administration, but these ideas will be more useful when we treat them systematically as parts of an integrated whole.

2. State these ideas in a practical and *usable form*. Rather than stop with descriptions and observations regarding administrative

processes, effort is made to express the concepts in the form of general guides, or principles, for executive action. At many points, existing knowledge (and the complexity of administration) will not permit us to go very far with specific recommendations, but such concepts as we do have will be stated in a way that relates them directly to concrete management problems.

3. Add *new ideas* and interpretations. The summarizing and writing down of administrative concepts and the extensive experience that lies behind this book naturally result in some new interpretations and insights.

Implied in these three points is a fourth objective, namely, to give a balanced and integrated view of administration. This is the most difficult task of all. It calls for much judgment, and, since the importance of the several aspects of administration will vary from company to company, the view presented will be at best an approximation. Moreover, knowledge is more fully developed in some phases of management than in others. Under the circumstances, the most we can do is emphasize time and again the interdependence of administrative processes, and seek a balanced view of existing knowledge of administration.

## Basic processes of administration

Administration has been defined as the guidance, leadership, and control of the efforts of a group of individuals toward some common goal. This indicates the purpose or function of administration but tells us little about the nature of administrative processes, that is, how the administrator achieves these results. And, unless we can dig into the what and how of administration, it will remain an elusive ability acquired by the fortunate few through inheritance, intuition, or circumstance.

One way to analyze administration is to think in terms of what an administrator does. Using this approach, the work of any administrator can be divided into the following basic processes:

1. *Planning*—that is, determining what shall be done. As used here, planning covers a wide range of decisions, including the clarification of objectives, establishment of policies, mapping of programs and campaigns, determining specific methods and procedures, and fixing day-to-day schedules.

2. *Organizing*—that is, grouping into administrative units the

activities necessary to carry out the plans, and defining the relationships among the executives and workers in such units.

3. *Assembling resources*—that is, arranging for use by the enterprise the executive personnel, capital, facilities, and other things or services needed to execute the plans.

4. *Supervising*—that is, the day-to-day guidance of operations. This includes issuing instructions, motivating those who are to carry out the instructions, coordinating the detailed work, and also cultivating normal personal relationships between the "boss" and his subordinates.

5. *Controlling*—that is, seeing that operating results conform as nearly as possible to the plans. This involves the establishment of standards, comparison of actual results against the standard, and necessary corrective action when performance deviates from the plan.

A sixth group of activities takes more or less of the time of every administrator, namely, performing nondelegated activities. For instance, the sales manager may call on customers, or the production manager may spend some time in the designing of a new product. Even the administrators of very large enterprises are not able to delegate all actual performance to subordinates.

Important among nondelegated duties are the external contacts that the chief executive of a large enterprise must make personally; he must meet important customers, deal with union officials, appear before Congressional committees, and take part in certain civic activities. In fact, a detailed analysis of how two top-flight executives actually spent their time revealed that one spent over a third of his working hours on such outside contacts while the other spent approximately 20 per cent of his time in this manner.

Strictly speaking, the performance of nondelegated duties is not part of administration, and the activities involved are of almost infinite variety, depending upon the local situation and the particular interest and capacity of the executive concerned. Consequently, in this study we will do no more than recognize that nondelegated activities do limit the time an executive has to spend on administrative duties.

While all administrators engage in the five basic processes just listed, clearly the proportion of time they spend on each will vary from time to time and from one executive to another. For example, in day-to-day operations, especially at lower administrative levels, organizing and securing resources may receive very little attention, and the executive will spend his time planning, supervising, controlling, and performing nondelegated duties. On the other hand, certain executives who have one or two principal assistants to whom they delegate most of the operating responsibilities may spend the bulk of their time in planning. Nevertheless, the five processes are sufficiently universal in application, basic in nature, and comprehensive in scope to provide a useful framework for our analysis of administration.

### Relation of basic processes to other divisions of business

Administration cannot possibly take place all by itself; it is inextricably tied to actual operations.

*Relation to business functions.* The work of executives may be divided into subject fields, such as sales, production, or finance. It may also be divided into administrative processes; for example, planning, directing, and controlling. These are simply two different approaches to the same body of activities, as is shown in Figure 1. The sales manager must plan, organize, assemble resources, supervise, and control, just as any other executive. Administration, then, is not another of the so-called "functions" of business. It is a necessary part of the work found in any and all of the subject groups.

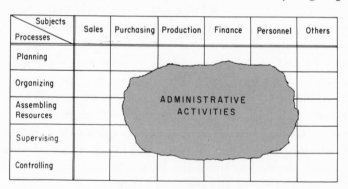

| Subjects<br>Processes | Sales | Purchasing | Production | Finance | Personnel | Others |
|---|---|---|---|---|---|---|
| Planning | | | | | | |
| Organizing | | | ADMINISTRATIVE | | | |
| Assembling Resources | | | ACTIVITIES | | | |
| Supervising | | | | | | |
| Controlling | | | | | | |

FIGURE 1. *Two Different Ways of Analyzing the Work of a Business Administrator.*

Most of the discussion of administration in the past has concentrated on some one subject-field. Emphasis has been on current issues in the particular field (union recognition, resale price maintenance, depreciation rates, and the like), with only secondary consideration of administrative processes. In this book, the emphasis is reversed. Major attention will be on the underlying problems faced by executives in any field, and the more specific issues will be of interest only as illustrations of the basic processes.

Of course, a top-management level in every enterprise is concerned with over-all administration rather than with a single field. Some of the problems at this level are distinctive, as will be noted especially in Chapter 17. Generally, however, the nature of administration is similar at all executive levels, and in this study no sharp line will be attempted between top, near top, and not so near top management. The words administrator, manager, and executive will be used interchangeably, and, except when narrowed by context, will apply to any executive from a first-line supervisor to the chief operating official.[1] Here, again, we are primarily interested in the basic management skills that every executive should possess.

*Human relations.* Throughout this book the theme of human relations will recur. Plans are made to guide human activity, and they should be formulated in light of their effects on many people. Organization deals with jobs for people and the established relationships between these people. Assembling executive personnel is 100 per cent human relations. Supervision is concerned with the daily interaction of executives and subordinates. Control is effective only if human behavior conforms to plans. In other words, human relations is not a separate issue, but an ever-present one.

Our viewpoint here is that of a manager; we are concerned with his tasks and what he can do about them. Consequently, it will be most helpful to tie human behavior to each of these tasks as we go along rather than discuss it separately. This is more than a convenience in writing; it is what the executive in fact does. He thinks of the human, economic, technological, and legal aspect of each problem as part of the operating situation in which he must work. The absence of separate chapters on human relations, then, in no way denies its importance. Instead, it reflects a deliberate plan to include human behavior as an integral part of each administrative process.

---

[1] Some writers separate the work of top administration from that of subordinates. Unfortunately, there is no agreement on whether the top level should be called management or administration or on what is covered by the term selected. In the present study, a distinction between administration and management serves no practical purpose.

### The development of principles of administration

Although administration has been essential in public, private, and eleemosynary enterprises for centuries, written discussion of the basic techniques used prior to 1900 are very few and far between.

Before the twentieth century, training of an administrator typically consisted of informal apprenticeship in a single enterprise. The young man, perhaps fourteen years old, was put to work without much thought of training beyond instruction in his immediate task. A general attitude of secrecy and high regard for tradition prevailed. Any discussion of one's own problems with men in other companies who faced similar difficulties was usually looked upon as a breach of confidence. If useful innovations were made, knowledge of these spread slowly.

Attitudes about administration have shifted, however, especially in the last few years. Techniques of management are now freely discussed by associations of businessmen and in professional schools. The volume of written material, usually descriptive in nature, is staggering. In this new development several, somewhat independent, currents of thought have strongly influenced our present ideas about administration.

Scientific management, personnel administration, accounting and budgeting, military administration, decision theorists, and operations researchers have all made major contributions. In addition, many other groups or schools of thought are concerned with administration. The public administrators, office managers, social anthropologists, purchasing agents—these and literally thousands of other organizations all deal to some extent with administrative problems.

Although there is now much talk about administration, two observations are pertinent here. First, most of these groups are interested in only some limited area of activity, and quite naturally they confine their attention to related subjects. Even those groups that broaden their scope to embrace administration generally are inclined to emphasize some one aspect, such as the budgeting process, a technique for analyzing managerial situations, or the treatment of people as individual personalities. The tendency is for each group to think it has the best—perhaps the only—road to salvation. For purposes of this study of the basic processes of administration, we shall have to draw ideas from many sources.

Second, many of the ideas with which we shall deal are new, or less than a generation old. Here, as in other fields, our knowledge of social relations lags far behind our understanding of the physical environment. Hardly surprising, then, are the gaps in the information we possess, the inconsistencies in other places, and frequently the hypotheses not substantiated by demonstrated facts. Nevertheless, the body of knowledge we do have is large enough so that the executive who has it at his command will be much more effective in his work.

## Summary

Administration is the guidance, leadership, and control of the efforts of a group of individuals toward some common goal. It is a very important and widespread activity, being essential to united human effort—in government, military, charitable, and business enterprises.

Skill as an administrator is quite different from ability to perform the work being directed. For this reason, successful executives are able to move from one job to another even though they have had no personal experience in the detailed operations involved. It is this distinct administrative skill that is discussed in this book.

Administrative skill involves mastery of five basic processes: (1) planning, (2) organizing, (3) assembling resources, (4) supervising, and (5) controlling. These processes are present to a greater or lesser extent in all executive jobs, that is, in jobs at different levels and in various fields. The subject matter will vary, but the underlying processes will be similar. Because of their fundamental character, a part of this book will be devoted to each of the five processes.

Information and ideas regarding sound administrative practice come from a variety of sources. Scientific management, personnel management, accounting, public administration, military administration, psychology and sociology, industrial engineering, operations research, and other disciplines, all have made contributions. Although this knowledge is still scattered and incomplete, a body of ideas does exist that can be highly valuable to every executive.

The purpose of the succeeding chapters in this book is to: (1) bring together existing knowledge regarding the basic processes of administration, and summarize this in a systematic and integrated manner; (2) state these ideas in a practical and usable form; and (3) add new ideas and interpretations.

### SELECTED REFERENCES

Mee, J. F., "Management Thought: Its Genesis and Historical Development," and E. J. Morrison, "The Nature and Role of the Management Process," in F. A. Shull and A. L. Delbecq, eds., *Selected Readings in Management*, Second Series, Richard D. Irwin, Inc., 1962, pp. 29-47.

Merrill, H. F., ed., *Classics in Management*, American Management Association, 1960.

Smiddy, H. F. and L. Naum, "Evaluation of a 'Science of Management' in America," *Management Science*, I, No. 1.

Tead, O., *Administration: Its Purpose and Performance*, Harper & Row, Publishers, 1959.

# *1*

# Planning

# 2

# Goals—The Guideposts
in Administration

**Questions the administrator wants answered**

Planning is a familiar, everyday activity. The results of planning, or the absence of it, may be seen all about us. For example, the writer recently had occasion to employ both a plumber and a paperhanger. The plumber started vigorously on his work but soon discovered that he needed a special wrench that, unfortunately, was back at the shop. After the old piping was torn out, he made some measurements and again returned to the shop to get the new pipe necessary. Most of the pipe he was able to cut and fit with the equipment he had brought along, but one place called for a special joint which he returned to the shop a third time to obtain. And so the job continued. The man worked industriously, but his output per hour was low because he had not sized up the total situation, anticipated the difficulties, and prepared to meet them before he commenced tearing things apart.

In contrast, the paperhanger got a slow start. He measured and estimated, he discussed colors, he considered furniture that had to be moved and special ladders that would be necessary to reach the ceiling over the stairwell. When he did get started, however, he proceeded without interruption. The materials he needed were at hand in the right quantity, and he had the necessary equipment. There was no question as to what was to be done, neither were there unanticipated emergencies.

The difference in output between the two workmen was striking, and it resulted not so much from a difference in the effort that the two men put forth or in their skill in actually performing the work itself. Instead, the difference clearly was that the paperhanger did a good job of planning ahead, whereas the plumber thought only of the next step.

The desirability of planning is now widely recognized, so much so that it is almost a fad to talk about planning even though the advocate may have only vague ideas of what is really needed and how to go about it. Thus, the Scout leader is urged to plan his meeting carefully so that he may move with dispatch from one activity to the other without a loss of attention. The followers of Frederick Taylor urge planning in considerable detail as an essential step to production operations. Any self-respecting municipal government now engages in some form of city planning. And on the national level, the need for a National Resources Planning Board is generally accepted. There is not, however, 100 per cent support for the "planners," and rightly so, because much that flies under the banner of planning is vague and visionary.

The effective administrator, then, must ask himself a series of practical questions:

1. What is really meant by planning, and how does it relate to other phases of administration?
2. What are the different kinds of plans that may be useful, and what are the advantages of each?
3. What are the practical limits on the extent and detail to which planning should be carried?
4. What basic steps are necessary in developing a plan?
5. Can executive planning be simplified?
6. How are strategic and logistic factors in formal planning recognized?

The discussion in this and the next six chapters will be organized around these key questions.

## Nature of Planning

**Working definition of planning**

Speaking generally, planning is deciding in advance what is to be done; that is, a plan is a projected course of action. Considered in this light, planning is a very widespread human behavior: the entrepreneur plans a new enterprise, a marketing vice-president plans a sales campaign, the lawyer plans the presentation of his case, the social worker plans relief for an unemployed man, the housewife plans lunch, the carpenter plans the repair of a screen door.

Executives make many judgments that are not plans. For instance, an executive may decide that Zip Zilch is honest, that wholesale prices probably will rise in the year, that existing wage data are an adequate sample of the market.[1] Such judgments as these are often necessary in arriving at plans, but they are not plans because they do not stipulate action to be taken.

**Relation of planning to other phases of administration**

Once a plan is adopted, that is, a decision has been made and approved, the administrator is free to move into other phases of his operation. Perhaps the plan requires modification in existing organization, or assembly of additional resources. If so, the executive must give attention to these. He then proceeds to issue instructions for the execution of the plan and, finally, checks to see whether any corrective action is necessary to secure fulfillment of the plan. This last control step provides information that may lead to a modification of the old plan or the adoption of new plans, which in turn starts a new cycle of planning, organization, assembly of resources, supervision, and control. (See Figure 2.)

In actual operation, administrative cycles are, of course, no more regular than the so-called business cycle. A merchant, for example, may lay out a program for all phases of his business, or he may decide to buy a given lot of clothing and put this part of his program into operation before he has planned the sales promotion to dispose of those articles. The demand for the products may be so active

---

[1] Judgments of this sort are often called *decisions,* but to avoid confusion we shall use *decision-making* in its narrower meaning—now popular in management discussions—as equivalent to planning.

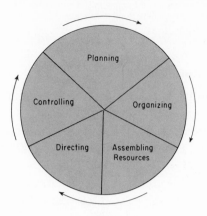

FIGURE 2. *Cycle of Administrative Duties. The proportion of time an administrator spends on each duty will vary widely; under some circumstances organizing and assembling resources may drop out entirely.*

that before he has sold all his stock he decides to reorder. Perhaps competitors' action is such that he must step up his sales-promotion campaign, cut his price, or even attempt to cancel part of the goods he has already ordered. In these situations what he does is to modify his original plan, issue a new set of directions, and then check up to see how the revised program is carrying out.

The period of time covered by the plan and the frequency of change differ greatly, for instance, with a mail-order house whose catalogue commits the enterprise for a period of several months and the small corner haberdashery that operates on a minimum of stock and virtually no price commitment. Nevertheless, each case has a cycle of planning, supervision, and control.

In some situations the administrative processes take place in fairly clear, separable steps. Thus, the engineering design and specifications of a building may be completed before the organization and schedule for actually erecting it are laid out; then arrangements are made for money, materials, and men needed at various stages in the future; direction actually to begin construction work may not be given until all the foregoing preparations have been completed; finally, the task of checking and controlling is undertaken.

Such a sharp separation of steps is more the exception than the rule, however. Even in construction operations, work on foundations may be started before detailed specifications for office space are completed, and delays in material deliveries or unseasonable weather may necessitate a revision of schedule. In fact, detailed schedules for wiring and for painting may not be prepared at all until the project is well underway. Thus, the planning, organizing, assembling of resources, supervising, and controlling are all going on at the same time. In other types of business where operating conditions are even less predictable, or activities more diversified, there is even greater intermingling of planning with other phases of administration. This intermingling may modify the extent of planning, but it does not change its nature or its importance.

Although the mail-order house, the corner haberdashery, the building-construction company, and the cigarette manufacturer all must plan, the types of plans that these companies employ differ greatly. Each administrator must decide what kinds of plans are practical for him to use. Should he limit his planning to his day-to-day activities, or should he attempt annual planning? How can he use policies to advantage; what use may be made of standard methods and procedures? Real administrative skill is required in answering such questions as these.

### Types of administrative plans

Planning is a broad concept; it embraces a wide range of ideas. In fact, much of the confusion concerning planning arises because people use the same words to cover quite different concepts. Thus, a clear understanding of the different kinds of plans that an administrator may use is helpful.

Plans may be divided into three broad groups:

1. Goals
2. Single-use Plans
3. Standing Plans

Within each of these groups there is quite a variety of plans, ranging from the broadest type of plans covering the operations of the entire enterprise for a considerable period down to detailed plans for the activities of a single individual on one day.

An executive responsible for planning should recognize clearly all the different types of plans he has at his disposal. For this purpose, the nature and advantages of goals and single-use and standing plans will be considered in this and the following chapter. The limitations on planning will then be discussed in Chapter 4. The main issue running through these chapters is, "What kind and how much planning is practical?"

The best way to develop sound plans is a different issue. This is a matter of planning technique, and it is examined in the last two chapters of this section, following the discussion of types of plans.

## GOALS AND THEIR ADVANTAGES

Sound admnistration starts with a statement or at least a clear recognition of goals to be achieved. Each executive, from the president to the first-line supervisor, should know the aims of his particular activities.

For this purpose, expressing plans in terms of the results to be accomplished is useful. The production manager, for instance, may say that he plans to increase output 20 per cent; the personnel manager plans to increase the proportion of women employees; or the controller plans to issue a readable annual report by February 15. Plans expressed as results to be achieved may be called *goals*. Used in this broad sense, goals would include such things as objectives, purposes, missions, deadlines, standards, targets, and quotas.

Goals serve a multiple purpose in administration. They are vital links in the planning process, they aid in decentralization, they provide a basis for voluntary coordination, they may become a focus for individual motivation, and they are also essential elements in the process of control. In this section we are primarily interested in goals as a type of planning; their pervasive influence in other phases of administration will be considered as these topics are discussed in later chapters.

### Objectives

*Significance of broad objectives.* Every enterprise needs a clear statement of its objectives as a basis for all of its planning. Plainly, for example, an airline must decide whether its primary objective is to carry passengers or freight before it can lay out its program, select equipment, hire personnel, and begin to operate in anything other than a haphazard manner.

Likewise, anyone entering a new field, such as frozen foods, must decide the extent to which he wishes to achieve nationwide distribution of a branded product, initiative and leadership in technological development, or economies in production through the manufacture of large quantities to be sold through diverse channels of distribution. Choice among these objectives will affect much of the planning on more specific matters.

The importance of objectives in planning is borne out by Gulick's observation, based on extensive experience in a wide variety of governmental operations:

> *A clear statement of purpose universally understood is the outstanding guarantee of effective administration.*
>
> Translated to military terms, this is "The mission must be defined . . ." This rule applies not only to the great purposes of national action, but to each specific activity as well. . . . On this point, military administration taught us a real lesson. With minor exception, no activity was initiated by the military without clear definition, a definition cast in terms of purpose, timing and resources; no organization unit was set up without a statement of its mission. . . . In administration, God helps those administrators who have a clearly defined mission. . . .[2]

*Multiple objectives.* Normally, an enterprise has several different objectives, and one of the tasks of the administrator is to bring a balance in the extent to which these various objectives are stressed. For example, in addition to dividends for stockholders, the business administrator is concerned with stable employment and satisfactory working arrangements for employees, with reliable service to customers, and with the relation of the enterprise to the general public. Thus, we find H. P. Hood and Sons, Inc. formally announcing the goals shown in Figure 3.

A somewhat similar, though briefer, statement has been prepared by the American Brake Shoe Company, as follows:

### OUR AIM

Our ambition is to make our Company—
A better place to work.
A better neighbor in our communities.
A better company to sell to.
A better company to buy from.
A better company to invest in.
Each of us can help in some way every day.

Statements of broad objectives can, of course, be mere pious words—carefully framed, hung on the office wall, and completely disregarded. However, many senior executives—especially those

[2] L. Gulick, *Administrative Reflections from World War II,* University of Alabama Press, 1948, pp. 77-78.

who provide dynamic leadership—attest to the benefit they have gained from a searching appraisal of what their economic purposes should be and what relationships they should seek with other institutions.

---

## H. P. HOOD AND SONS, INC.

### FUNDAMENTAL OBJECTIVES

Our over-all objective is to conduct our business so that all groups in the community will regard us as the best company in our industry and want us to prosper and grow.

In order to accomplish this, our direct goals are:

1. To make available to consumers a combination of price, quality, variety, and service through friendly and trustworthy people which will make our company the best in our industry from which to buy.
2. To provide farmers who sell to us a combination of money and worthwhile services which are greater than they can obtain by selling their products elsewhere.
3. To establish wages, working conditions, benefits, job security, opportunity, and personal recognition which combined will make our company the best in our industry with which to work.
4. To offer investors in company stocks and debentures a greater return on their money and greater security than they can obtain elsewhere in our industry.
5. To demonstrate that H. P. Hood and Sons is a good neighbor and citizen by our active support of good government, education, health programs, and other good works which benefit the entire community in which we operate. Our goal is to be a leader in our industry.

To reach these objectives, we must operate more efficiently than our competitors. We must also pioneer in developing adventurous programs and be willing to take risks, so long as the balance is in the best interest of attaining our over-all objective and goals.

---

FIGURE 3. *Broad Objectives of H. P. Hood and Sons, Inc.,*
*distributor of dairy products.*

To be most useful, objectives have to be more than words; they must have real meaning to the executive and involve personal commitment or dedication. A psychologist would say they must be "internalized."

*Translating broad objectives into tangible terms.* Important as broad objectives are, they do have to be translated into more specific sub-goals. A machinery manufacturer, for instance, decided it wanted to concentrate on its major product line and become a worldwide distributor in that field. To achieve this objective several subsidiary moves were necessary: acquire manufacturing facilities in the European Common Market and in Japan; dispose of a secondary product not closely related to the main line; strengthen sales representatives in Latin America, India, Australia, and other key locations; re-engineer some products to permit local production of bulky parts. These sub-goals were more operational—things upon which executives could act.

Another company examined its objective of being "a good citizen in communities in which it had plants" and decided this meant less dependence of several communities on the company. Sub-goals arising from this decision included attracting other kinds of industries to the community, selling company-owned houses, transferring a company recreation park to city supervision, and encouraging the employment of a city manager.

These examples indicate both (a) the way broad objectives promote and give validity to more specific actions, and (b) the need for concrete sub-goals to transform a general aim into action terms.

*Objectives for each department and division.* Good planning requires recognition of objectives for the several administrative divisions of an enterprise, as well as for the enterprise as a whole. Thus, the objective or mission of the printing department with respect to cost and to service should be clear to the manager of the department and to those responsible for general supervision over it. Likewise, the objective of the advertising department in securing direct orders, as contrasted with its objective in promoting wide acquaintanceship with the company's brand name, should be understood.

When the manufacturer of a well-known line of radio sets decided to enter the industrial phase of the electronics business, the manager of the new department needed to know whether he was expected to duplicate R.C.A.'s entire line of broadcasting, transmitting, and industrial communication equipment within, say, the next three years.

Of course, the missions of some departments are easier to define than others; for example, the warehouse department as compared with the public relations department. But, in every case a clear definition of purpose is of great assistance in administration.

### Budgets and deadlines

*Budgets.* A budget expresses in numerical terms, typically financial accounts, the anticipated results of operations in some future period. If budgets are well prepared, they will be more than mere predictions; instead, they will reflect the actual plans for each of the activities covered. Once prepared, they constitute a goal toward which activities are directed. They have a number of distinctive merits as planning devices, notably their specificness of expression, their ease of coordination between one department and another, and their ready adaptability as control standards. Budgets are such an important managerial device that an entire chapter will be devoted to them later. They are mentioned here so that they will be recognized as an important form that planned goals may take.

*Time goals.* Timing of activities is an essential element in administrative planning. One way to incorporate the "when" into a plan is to set up a deadline, or a series of deadlines, when certain events should be completed. These deadlines take many forms. The newspaper has deadlines for each edition; the engineering department may establish a date when new equipment is to be installed and ready to operate; the sales department may have a rule that all incoming inquiries are to be answered within two days of receipt of the letter; or the salesman may set a goal for himself of calling on at least five individuals on his new-prospect list each week.

Detailed planning may include a whole series of these deadlines. These should be related to each other so that preliminary steps are completed before succeeding steps must start, and all of the steps must be geared into the major or controlling date for the entire operation.

### Operating goals

A wide variety of operating standards may be set up that express the anticipated results of the more detailed plans. There probably will be expense standards; material costs being set at, say, 30 per cent of cost of goods sold, overhead at 160 per cent of direct labor, or office payroll at $1500 per month. Also, a variety of output standards may be expressed in physical terms; for example, three generators finished per week, thirty pieces per machine per hour, ten new prospects located per day. Other operating standards might deal with lost time due to accidents or the training of a substitute for every key position in the organization.

The executive who can say, with an assurance based on detailed planning, that he plans to produce $X$ number of products during the next month with a total of $A$ people on the payroll and a salary expense of $B$, that material used should be $C$ pounds, that the rate of spoilage will be $D$, and similarly states the results he plans to achieve in other phases of his operations is well on the road to success as an administrator of his department.

### Safe versus courageous goals

When an administrator sets any type of goal—company or departmental objective, budget, deadline, or operating standard—he always faces a question of how optimistic to be. Should he "ask for the moon" or seek only what he is sure can be accomplished? If he sets unattainable goals, sooner or later they will have to be disregarded, and they may actually create confusion about what will really happen. If he sets easy targets, resources may be wasted and his operations may become obsolete.

Four ways of dealing with this dilemma are:

1. *Distinguish clearly between hopes and expectations.* "World leadership in the optical business" or "highest pay in our industry" may be helpful statements of desired ends, but next year's budget had better reflect more modest expectations. When goals are really just hopes, they are values to be sought, and they provide useful guidance in this sense. For other purposes, however, we need realistic estimates of what can actually be accomplished; for example, integrated planning, personnel appraisals, and control standards should be based on attainable goals.

2. *Set realistic short-run goals as steps toward more ideal long-run ends.* One practical way to reconcile idealistic or optimistic aims with the hard facts of life is to decide how much progress along the way should be achieved in a month or a year. This permits us to retain the inspiration and guidance of the "big idea" while, at the same time, be working on doable sub-goals.

3. *Keep "allowances" in a separate reserve.* Experienced administrators know that unexpected difficulties and delays will in-

evitably occur, and plans should make some allowance for such events. However, all goals do not need a safety cushion. Instead, high standards can be set throughout the operation, and any necessary allowances for, say, time or expense can be bunched in a separate reserve. This arrangement has the advantages of stimulating high performance, bringing difficulties to light, and having a single total allowance that is smaller than the cumulation of many individual safety factors would be.

4. *Adjust short-run emphasis on sub-goals to secure balanced long-run results.* Few of us can work hard on numerous goals at the same time. But if we give top priority to one or two goals, we probably will get a distorted over-all result. So an administrator should assess his current situation and decide which sub-goals—for example, cost reduction, market position, executive development, new products, and the like need attention most; then as progress is made and conditions change, other goals can be stressed.

**Hierarchy of plans**

The preceding discussion has already suggested that the plans for a given enterprise should fall into a hierarchy; that is, as the decisions are pushed through successive steps to cover narrower and more detailed operations, there should be a clear recognition that one step is subordinate to the other. In other words, a general objective or major decision is accompanied by a whole series of successively more detailed plans, each designed to implement the general plan of which it is a part.

As an illustration of a hierarchy of plans, consider the issues arising in connection with "The Voice of America" radio program which the United States beamed to countries behind the Iron Curtain during the Cold War. The underlying question for Congress and the State Department was, of course, whether the United States should be concerned, at least at that time, with the political beliefs of foreign nationals. Given a positive answer to this issue, plans for influencing these beliefs had to be adopted—including the role radio was to play. Then, engineering plans regarding location, power, wave lengths, and similar matters had to be determined. At the same time the types of programs had to be settled; for example, news versus jazz music or other representations of American culture. Then, specific methods for station operators were needed, and before anything was broadcast a time schedule down to the fraction of a minute and a script specifying virtually every word had to be adopted. Here the planning ranged from foreign policy to changing needles on the phonograph-record player.

The idea of an order or a rank as between plans has been generally recognized by large, multi-unit enterprises. Because of the impracticability of attempting detailed planning at a central point, such enterprises develop a master plan and then allow the subordinate units considerable freedom of operation within those limits. In smaller establishments, organizational necessity may not force as sharp a distinction in the levels of planning, but as a device for orderly thinking it is just as applicable.

We see, then, that the concept of hierarchies in plans is useful, both to assure internal consistency and integration of the plans themselves, and also in the process of organization as an aid to successful decentralization.

### Relationship of goals to other types of plans

As already indicated by definition and by illustration, goals cannot be set up without regard to single-use and standing plans. Instead, they are an inseparable part of the whole planning process. The general objectives or missions give rise to a program, each part of which has some contribution to make to the achievement of the broad objectives. These parts may be expressed as sub-goals, and then a whole series of plans are developed to achieve them. These more detailed plans may be translated into a budget and a master schedule developed. The master schedule, in turn, may provide the deadlines that guide the detailed scheduling in individual departments. Likewise, the budgeted expenses for a given department should be correlated with output standards that are based on the specific methods and procedures planned for the individual operations.

This idea of goals and sub-goals supported by a program and standing plans all neatly dovetailed and contributing toward the over-all objective is not an easy thing to put into practice. In some instances, notably government operations, an enterprise may be trying to achieve several objectives simultaneously, and if steps toward these objectives conflict, it is necessary to decide which receives priority. Likewise, ethical concepts of desirable social behavior modify the unquestioned acceptance by all members of an enterprise of a single objective. This complicates the planning process (often to the point where the individual behavior is not fully consistent), but it does not change the essential need for goals and subsidiary goals in rational planning.

### Contributions of goals to the planning process

But why bother, a practical-minded executive may ask, to translate operating plans into anticipated results when those goals are already implied in the plans themselves? Among the benefits of expressing plans in terms of goals are the following:

1. Purposeful and integrated planning is made easier. The formulating and crystallizing of goals serve as a beacon light in directing the subsequent planning. Thus, when planning from a general objective to a specific operation, the major goal provides the mission toward which the subsidiary goals are directed; these subsidiary plans in turn provide objectives toward which the more detailed plans are directed, and so on until a hierarchy of goals is established. Without such relationships of major goals to minor goals, integrated planning is not possible.

2. Diverging and unproductive work is more likely to be avoided. The stressing of objectives, missions, and standards helps the executive or the operator to "keep his eye on the ball." Anyone heavily engrossed in some one activity naturally tends to attach great importance to the work itself without considering it from the viewpoint of some broader purpose. Planning in terms of goals contributes to the constant vigilance that is necessary to keep the enterprise pruned of unproductive or overgrown branches.

3. Operating goals or standards can be used as building blocks in developing programs. Rarely does the executive who is asked to prepare a program for the coming year or to lay out the steps in a new project have the time to make a completely original investigation, one that will determine the number of salesmen needed to cover a given territory, the quantity of materials needed to produce one thousand units of a product, the time that must be allowed between beginning production and actual delivery of products, and other such operating standards. Instead, he takes operating goals that have already been established, modifies them where necessary for changed operating conditions, and uses the revised standards as a basis for building the program. If the needed operating standards

have not already been determined, program development will be slow and expensive, or it will contain large elements of guesswork.

4. Goals are, of course, a *sine qua non* for administrative control, that is, the securing of results in accordance with plans. Problems of motivation and control are outside the scope of this chapter, but two connections between goals and subsequent operations may be emphasized in passing. In the recording and appraising of operating results, standards of some sort are vital if the appraisal is to have any validity. The goals serve as such standards. Also, the recognition and acceptance of objectives and standards play an important part in the motivation of individual effort.

SUMMARY

Planning, that is, deciding in advance what is to be done, is an essential duty of every executive. It provides the basis for organization, assembling resources, supervision, and control.

While every executive must do some planning, he has a wide choice in the types of plans he uses and the detail in which they are prepared. The nature and advantages of *goals* have been considered in this chapter. This, of course, is an incomplete picture since the executive must also consider other types of plans and the limitations on planning before he is in a position to decide how much planning is practical.

The next two chapters, then, will take up single-use and standing plans and the limits on planning.

We have noted that planning in terms of goals covers a wide variety of activities. Goals range, for example, from a company objective to make low-cost products to an objective of a clerk to keep his desk neat; or from the aim of a Federal Reserve Board to help stabilize prices to the aim of a bank teller to make accurate entries in depositors' passbooks. Like other types of plans, the goal may be precise or loosely defined; it may be broad in coverage or apply to only a limited part of an operation. Although these goals should fit together into an over-all plan, a department head or first-line supervisor can set up his own set of goals, even when no over-all plan exists.

Distinctive benefits of setting up goals include: (1) Purposeful and integrated planning is made easier. (2) Unproductive work is more likely to be avoided. (3) Operating goals, or standards, can be used as building blocks in developing programs. (4) Goals also serve as standards for purposes of control, and they play an important part in motivation. The other side of the story, limitations on the establishment of goals, is discussed in Chapter 4.

### SELECTED REFERENCES

Drucker, P. F., "Business Objectives and Survival Needs," *Journal of Business*, April 1958.

Levitt, T., *Innovation in Marketing, New Perspectives for Profit and Growth*, McGraw-Hill Book Co., Inc., 1962.

Schleh, E. C., *Management by Results*, McGraw-Hill Book Co., Inc., 1961.

Thompson, S., *Management Creeds and Philosophies*, American Management Association, 1958.

# 3
# Single-Use and Standing Plans

Once an objective of an enterprise, department, or section has been set forth, the executive in charge must then map out a course of action to fulfill this mission. In other words, he must plan how he is going to accomplish the task.

This planning often is no simple job. Thousands of man-hours, tons of materials, innumerable customer contacts, large financial resources, and many other factors may be involved. Even a simple assignment will require careful planning if it is to be done with maximum efficiency. The executive should consider: (1) what types of plans will be most useful to him, (2) how far it will pay to go in preparing such plans, and (3) what procedure he should follow in arriving at these decisions.

Broadly speaking, the executive may make single-use or standing plans; most likely he will use some combination of these. The *single-use* plans lay out a course of action to fit a specific situation and are finished when the goal is reached, whereas the *standing plans* are designed to be used over and over again. The purpose of this chapter is to examine various kinds of single-use and standing plans so that their nature and advantages will be clear. The choice and combination of these instruments decides the *form* planning will take. How far ahead and by what method these plans should be developed will be discussed in later chapters.

## Single-Use Plans and Their Advantages

Sooner or later almost every executive uses several kinds of single-use plans. Important in this regard are (1) major programs, (2) projects, (3) special programs, and (4) detailed plans. What is the character of each of these types, and when should it be used?

### Major programs

A major program shows the principal steps that need to be taken to accomplish an objective, who will be accountable for each step, and the approximate timing of each. Considerable effort is required to design a good, comprehensive program, and the administrator should understand its nature and benefits in order to decide whether its preparation is worth the trouble in his operations.

The character of a general program is illustrated by the over-all planning for a vegetable cannery that was recently purchased from the former owner-manager by an investment group, which installed a new man as president. Three members of the investment group also had interests in grocery wholesaling companies, and part of the general scheme was that the cannery would serve as a significant source of supply for these wholesale houses. The new president proceeded to map out a general program. The types of vegetables to be canned were decided first, and then a sales forecast was prepared showing estimated sales of each product to the associated grocery houses and to the general trade for the next three years. On the basis of these figures it was possible to ascertain the capacity of plant and equipment that would be needed and to make general plans for additions to the facilities.

Another feature of the cannery program was deciding what key, full-time personnel should be maintained. A plan was devised for additions and for dropping some of those already on the payroll. Inasmuch as canning is highly seasonal, estimates of fluctuations in the inventory that would be kept also had to be made. And finally, on the basis of the foregoing decisions and estimates of cost and selling prices, the financial requirements were determined, and a plan for financing the cannery was set up. By developing this comprehensive program, each part of which dovetailed into the other parts, the president was able to *anticipate possible trouble* or bottlenecks and arrange to meet these difficulties. Moreover, a basis was provided to *guide the more detailed planning* for the several phases of the cannery operations.

The idea of a major program may be useful not only for over-all operations of an enterprise but also for a major undertaking. For example, a metal-equipment manufacturing company decided to produce a power machine that could be used to reduce labor costs in the installing of woodwork in new houses. The company bought the patent rights from the inventor and knew that the equipment would have to be sold to large contractors, particularly those erecting twenty-five or more houses at a given location. Beyond that the question was, "Where do we go from here?"

It was important that the production department not manufacture the new product in quantities greater than the sales department could dispose of, and, on the other hand, it was necessary that the sales department not promise delivery for products that could not be produced. Moreover, it was essential that the sales and production departments combined not embark on an undertaking that could not be financed by the company. Consequently, a general program was developed that covered the following points:

1. Designing the product for manufacture.
2. Tooling and raw material purchasing.
3. Production.
4. Display at the National Home Builders Convention.
5. Preparing sales literature.
6. Selecting dealers and demonstrators.
7. Providing capital requirements.

The timing of each of these steps had to be established, and while some of the things could be done concurrently—for example, raw material purchasing at the same time that the sales literature was being created—other steps had to be done in sequence. Therefore, a master schedule was necessary. Incidentally, in this particular instance the key date in the master schedule was the Home Builders Convention. This occurred but once a year, and if the machine had not been ready for display at this convention, sales efforts would have been hampered significantly for an entire year. The company had a suitable organization and an adequate capacity to handle the new product. Still, considerable specialized and cooperative effort was necessary to *assure coordination* and effective launching of the new line.

Major programs were very useful in each of the instances just described. Nevertheless, a great many business enterprises and government bureaus do not set up such a plan in any clear-cut fashion. This may result from failure to appreciate the advantages of such planning, stability of operations that diminishes the need for programming, the limitations on planning discussed in the next chapter, or plain inertia and laziness. Good reasons may exist why an executive does not set up a major program covering his activities, but the burden of proof should be on him if he fails to do so.

### Projects

Frequently, parts of a general program are relatively separate and clear cut, and can be planned (and executed) as a distinct project.

In the general program just described for the development of the new woodworking machine, for example, the preparation of sales literature was set up as a separate project. The project, in turn, was divided into four major parts. (1) The advertising media had to be selected and appropriate advertising copy prepared. (2) A descriptive circular was needed to use in response to inquiries from the advertising and to be handed out by distributors in their contacts with potential customers. (3) Plans were made for answering written inquiries regarding the new product; this was done primarily by trying to anticipate the questions that would be asked and preparing standard paragraph answers to such questions. (4) Also included in the project was the preparation of specific though simple instructions for the use and maintenance of the product.

Considerable work was necessary before final decisions were made on each phase of the project. Those responsible for the sales literature had to work closely with the designers and also with those securing and training distributors and demonstrators. This cooperation involved both the content of the detailed subject matter and also the synchronization of timing; copy released for trade-paper advertising had to be geared to anticipated production, and the operating instructions had to be available for demonstrator models and early deliveries.

The administrator may, of course, wish to set up projects in almost any phase of his company operations. A large financial institution, for instance, decided that as part of its over-all personnel program, salary administration should be based on careful job evaluation, and the initial planning and work was assigned as a separate project. A plan had to be developed for each of the following steps:

1. Organizing and staffing. It was decided to have a policy committee, an evaluation committee, and a (full-time) job analyst committee, and the duties and membership of each group had to be settled.

2. Setting policies for the project. Guides were needed from the start on such matters as positions to be covered by the survey, treatment of wage changes while the survey was in progress, general technique to be used in evaluating jobs (factor comparison was selected), and assurances that could be given to the employees regarding the effect of the study on their existing pay, particularly if it was higher than the maximum rate determined by the study.

3. Preparing job descriptions. This involved deciding on the form, content, and terminology to be used in the descriptions; the training of analysts; and scheduling the actual interviews and studies of individual divisions.

4. Evaluating the jobs. Since factor comparison was the method employed, a group of key jobs had to be ranked and rated, and then all the remaining jobs had to be slotted in for each of five compensable characteristics.

5. Making a market survey of wage rates prevailing in the community for comparable positions.

6. Developing a company salary structure. This involved decision as to the level of wages in the company relative to the market, the number of salary grades that would be used, and the maximum and minimum pay for each salary grade.

7. Installing the plan. The time when the new plan would become effective and the treatment of individual employees whose salaries fell either above or below the agreed-upon ranges had to be decided.

8. Informing employees. During the entire study, employees were informed of the purpose of each step that was being taken, their participation in the work, and the way it would affect them.

While detailed plans were not necessary for each step in this project before starting on the first one, it was important to know what the steps would be so as to understand the importance of the activities at any given time, to plan the assignment of personnel to work on the project, and, perhaps most important, to be able to explain to employees and executives just how a particular part of the investigation was going to affect the final salary structure. The amount of money in the pay envelope is of major concern to every employee, and if projects such as this are not carefully planned, some part of it may misfire and cause serious damage to employee morale.

The project is a flexible type of planning, and may be adapted to a variety of situations. If operations can be divided easily into *separate parts with a clear termination point,* the project is a natural and effective planning device.

### Special programs

Another type of single-use plan deals with some one phase of company operations, but, unlike projects, it has no clear completion date or point. Instead, these special programs are likely to cover a problem that is continuing, with the result that plans have to be adjusted from time to time to take account of the situation as it develops.

Special programs may be illustrated by the planning a medium-sized company did with respect to replacing its executive and sales personnel. At the time of the initial analysis, the key executives and their respective ages were as follows: president, 53; vice-president 48; sales manager, 54; treasurer, 71; production manager, 66. All of these men were in good health except the sales manager who, six months earlier, had been in the hospital for a month with stomach ulcers. The sales force, which in this industry was a natural source for top executives, had been reduced by a death and a retirement from five to three; this posed an immediate problem because the company wished to expand its sales volume.

Even from this limited information we can see that the company needed to develop a program for the immediate replacement of the treasurer and production manager and for an increase in the sales force. The treasurer's retirement had been anticipated in selecting an accountant, so what was necessary here was to arrange the actual transfer of duties from the older man to the younger man and to make salary adjustments. A man from the plant was selected as the likely successor to the production manager, and placed in training for this position. However, the production manager was still active, and his proposed successor had not yet demonstrated completely his ability to fill the top post, so the plan was to have these two work together as a team for at least the next few years.

The sales manager and vice-president proceeded immediately to locate potential salesmen. They decided to seek fairly young men who had potential executive ability as well as sales ability. This was particularly important, inasmuch as none of the three older salesmen had shown ability to take over the sales manager's position should he suddenly drop out of the picture. After further consideration, they decided to take no more than two salesmen on at one time in view of the problem of training them and working them into the company's sales operations.

These steps met the immediate needs of the company, but the company also recognized that it would be unwise to wait for ten years before considering replacement for the other three top men. No immediate measures are being taken in this area, however, because the likely candidates are already embarked on an immediate training program or just taking over new duties. Nevertheless, these younger men are being watched closely, and the company anticipates that about three years hence additional steps will be taken to train the most likely candidates to take on senior executive responsibilities.

In Part III the general problem of executive personnel will be explored in more detail. This particular case is cited here merely to illustrate the importance of predicting changes that are likely to occur over a period of several years and deciding what steps should be taken before the events transpire. In this way a company can deal with changes with the least disruption to, and perhaps even to the benefit of, its operations. An alert administrator should be on the lookout for circumstances where this type of planning will be useful.

### Detail plans

For a great many situations, planning in even more detail than has been suggested in the preceding illustrations is highly desirable. In fact, the word *planning* is sometimes used to refer merely to the detailed arrangements necessary to carry out a major decision. Thus, the planning room in a production department frequently is concerned only with methods, instructions, material and tool requisition, scheduling, and routing of specific orders through the shop. In the tradition of Frederick W. Taylor, the aim of such planning is to foresee every step in a long series of operations, select the most efficient way of performing each step, and provide the necessary resources and information so that each step will occur in the right place at the right time.

A common example of this type of planning is found in scheduling in machine shops that do varied work. Here the capacity of each machine and the time required to perform each operation have been determined. As each order is received the necessary operations are noted, and the work is assigned to individual machines. By keeping track of the work thus assigned and the work completed, it is possible to schedule the jobs that are to be done on individual machines and, with the aid of standard times, to know when jobs can be completed. In this manner a detailed schedule for shop operations is prepared, showing what jobs are to be performed on each machine each day, the time at which the various steps will be taken on a given order, and, therefore, when the order will be completed. Gantt charts and similar devices have been used for years for such scheduling; more recently linear programming has been used for very complex situations.

An essential part of such planning is, of course, keeping track of what actually does happen and adjusting the plan if, for some reason, the work either moves faster or more slowly than originally projected. When such scheduling is properly done, the equipment is used to the optimum and jobs are completed when promised. The possibility of getting rush orders through the plant can be ascertained, and the effect of such orders on work already scheduled is also readily shown.

Detailed scheduling, such as just described, is made possible through the standardization of methods and operating conditions in the shop. In other situations, particularly in those where several different people are involved, exercising such close control is not feasible. Nevertheless, where the results are highly important, as in a real estate negotiation or a labor negotiation, planning very carefully what is to be said, what is to be done, the manner in which it is to be done, and who is to do it is desirable. Since the behavior of the other individuals involved may not be just as anticipated, such plans frequently have to be modified on the spot. Even so, the performance is probably much more effective than it would be if no such detailed planning had been done in advance.

This detailed planning sooner or later reaches a point of diminishing returns, so the administrator must decide in what areas, to what detail, and how far ahead formal plans of this sort pay.

**Hierarchy among single-use plans**

These various single-use plans—major programs, projects, special programs, and detailed plans—should fit together into a consistent whole. The idea of a hierarchy of such plans is a simple and intriguing idea. A major program normally consists of a series of steps, and each of these steps becomes a project or special program in itself. The projects, in turn, are further subdivided into more specific assignments, and this process of narrowing the range as segments of the plan become more and more detailed continues until specific actions of each individual are decided.

True, in actual practice proceeding in just this way may not be practical. For one thing, some of the more detailed plans may be so crucial that they are settled first, and the broader plans adjusted to them. The capacities of existing equipment or a union contract that must be signed promptly to avoid a strike are examples of this. In other words, planning may come up from the bottom as well as down from the top.

Moreover, in a company of any size planning is done by many people, and they may work simultaneously and somewhat independently. If each person waited until the broader plans of those above him were settled, the time required to go from a general program to specific actions would be long indeed. So what often happens is that separate divisions go ahead with the preparation of their own programs, and later these are—or should be—fitted together into a master plan.

The concept of a hierarchy among single-use plans is extremely useful, nevertheless. Regardless of the order in which the plans are prepared, they should fit together as parts and subparts of an integrated scheme of operation. Their purpose, nature, and timing should be dovetailed so that coordination results. The planner who does not make sure that his decisions fit into the broader course of action, and are also consistent with more detailed plans of those who will do the actual work, may well be a "bull in the china shop."

**Benefits of preparing single-use plans in advance**

Before leaving this discussion of single-use plans, the advantages resulting from their advance preparation should be reviewed. Most of these benefits have been referred to in the various illustrations, but to be sure that they are fully recognized the more important ones are summarized on the next page:

1. Integrated and purposeful action is more readily achieved. When plans are made on the spur of the moment, expediency is the rule and action taken today is likely to hamper work of tomorrow. Moreover, if action takes place in several places at the same time, action in one spot may interfere or undermine the work initiated at another point. Advance planning provides an opportunity for review to see that each part fits in with the others and is directed toward the over-all purpose.

2. Crises can be anticipated and delays avoided. When bottlenecks or weak spots are uncovered by careful and realistic advance planning, time often is available to find a remedy before the event occurs, whereas expensive and lengthy shutdowns may be unavoidable if corrective action is not initiated until the crisis is present. Moreover, as Machiavelli observed centuries ago, trouble is often more easily corrected in its early stages than after a crisis has developed:

> Thus it happens in matters of state; for known afar off (which it is only given to the prudent man to do) the evils that are brewing, they are easily cured. But when for want of such knowledge they are allowed to grow so everyone can recognize them, there is no longer any remedy to be found.[1]

3. More efficient methods and procedures can be developed. Time is usually required for the systematic and thorough investigation of alternative methods. Decisions made in a hurry may possibly hit upon the most efficient methods, but they are more likely to rely on custom or any possible method that "gets by."

4. Delegation of authority to act is facilitated. Communication of plans to subordinates takes time; explanations and interpretations are often required, and sometimes formal training is needed (this is more likely in the case of standing plans than single-use plans). In a small enterprise the decision-maker may have ready access to the men who are to carry out the plans, but as supervision becomes more remote, advance plans become more necessary.

5. The groundwork for control standards is laid. These operating plans, when translated into anticipated results, become standards of performance. The nature and importance of such *goals* has already been discussed in the preceding chater, and will be considered again in the analysis of control in Chapter 24.

[1] Niccolò Machiavelli, *The Prince*, Modern Library, p. 11.

## Standing Plans and Their Advantages

If an administrator had to prepare a complete set of plans each time he wished to initiate action or a change occurred in operating conditions, he would be faced with an impossible task. The time and energy required for planning might well exceed that devoted to the execution of the plans, and this could be justified only under unusual conditions. Instead, every enterprise develops a wide variety of standing plans which are followed every time a given situation is encountered.

The distinctive characteristic of a standing plan is that the same decision is used to guide action over and over again. Thus, a policy to sell only for cash may be applied to hundreds of inquiries regarding credit terms; a standard procedure for the requisition and purchase of supplies may be used in all departments for a wide variety of needs; a standard method for shipping products may be followed by a whole group of packers almost every day in the year.[2]

Such standing plans greatly simplify the task of the administrator. They establish a pattern of action that the planner assumes as normal, and he can then concentrate his attention on the changes he wishes to make in this customary pattern for abnormal circumstances.

Of course, many work habits or business customs just grow without any deliberate planning on the part of executives. Sometimes these behavior patterns simply reflect the way the first employee found it convenient to work, and this method was copied with minor modifications by subsequent employees. In other cases an executive may have been confronted with a specific problem on which he made a decision, and then when the problem came up again he remembered that his original decision worked satisfactorily and so he decided in the second instance to follow the same behavior. After four or five decisions applying to the same situation, this solution becomes, perhaps unconsciously, the standard answer to that kind of a question. If such policies and methods are accepted by the management to the extent that new employees are deliberately trained to follow them and all employees are subject to censure if

---

[2] Some standing plans may not, in fact, be used over and over again. For example, plans for meeting a disaster such as a fire may rarely be put into action. Nevertheless, such stand-by plans are designed so that they can be used time and again if occasion warrants.

they deviate from them without good reason or permission, they then become part of the standing plans of the enterprise.

Experience has demonstrated, however, that the administrator can profitably give careful attention to the standing plans he expects to be followed by those under his direction. Gilbreth, Taylor, and other pioneers in the scientific management movement found that even skilled craftsmen following customary methods frequently are not very efficient. Many progressive companies now recognize the value of having good standing plans and make special provision in their organization for the careful study of policies and of methods and procedures.

In considering standing plans it is often helpful for the administrator to give separate attention to: (1) policies, (2) procedures, (3) methods. Each of these will be examined briefly in this section to see how they may be used and what benefits result. Organization structure can also be thought of as a standing plan, inasmuch as the assignment of duties and the relationships established provide a continuing frame of reference to guide employees in their daily activities; this aspect of administration is given detailed consideration in Part II.

**Policies**

A *policy* is a general plan of action that guides members of the enterprise in the conduct of its operation.

An illustration of the need for policy is found in the recurring question faced by every executive responsible for machinery of when and how much money should be spent for maintenance. Where repairs are easily made and delays caused by breakdowns are not costly, it may be wise to postpone activity until something goes wrong. In many other situations a policy of preventive maintenance is the wiser course. The commercial airlines, for example, overhaul an airplane motor after a certain number of hours of service, even though it may be running satisfactorily at the time. Sales divisions typically require that salesmen's automobiles be serviced regularly and may, in fact, provide for complete replacement before the need for expensive maintenance arises.

In production operations preventive maintenance provides for the periodic replacement of parts that may break or wear out, regular inspection to detect weaknesses or poor adjustment that may cause trouble at a later time if not taken care of immediately, and similar efforts to anticipate trouble. Once a company has a clear-cut policy as to the extent to which it will engage in preventive maintenance, then the operating executive and the maintenance division itself have a guide that may be used time and again in deciding what action should be taken with respect to a given piece of equipment. This results in considerable economy of the executive's time.

Policies are also helpful in securing consistency of action. For instance, the day is past when layoffs could be made according to the personal inclinations of several different foremen. Union or no union, having one foreman lay off on the basis of seniority, another on the basis of quality of work during the last week, still another on the basis of nationality, with perhaps a fourth using a "good guy" standard is well recognized as a bad practice. Instead, most companies now have a clear-cut policy stipulating the basis for selection of men to lay off when a reduction in staff is necessary. Such a policy can be explained to employees in advance, and when applied throughout the enterprise, it goes a long way toward establishing a sense of fair play in the entire group.

Some policies deal with the fundamental nature of a company's operations. A large New York store, for example, had followed a policy for years of catering to well-to-do women of mature years who wish to buy high-quality, conservatively styled, and, frequently, custom-made apparel. This policy on customers affected the type of salespeople who were employed, the type of training that they received, the pricing policies of the company, the services it rendered, the collection of bills, and many other aspects of the operation. After a decline in sales volume, a new general manager was employed whose background had been in the selling of popular-priced apparel to women of all ages and tastes. A period of confusion followed during which it was not clear whether the store was going to maintain its former customer policy or shift over to a policy similar to that of stores in which the general manager had had his previous experience. During this interval the older customers were sometimes annoyed at the styles and the lower-quality merchandise they found in some departments, new customers attracted by the more flashy advertising found themselves getting personal service that could not be justified in terms of their potential purchases, and considerable difference of opinion arose as to the selection and training of new salespeople. This difficulty was not eliminated until the board of directors made a clear-cut decision as to the type of customer the store was going to try to serve.

Virtually every enterprise should establish a wide range of policies covering its more important operations. A suggestive outline of the subjects that might well be considered in this connection by almost any business establishment is given in Figure 4.[3]

The administrator of a given enterprise will have to decide which activities should be closely governed by specific policies and which can be better managed on a more flexible basis. He will have to weigh the benefits of clear-cut and detailed policies against the disadvantages of such planning. These disadvantages are discussed in the next chapter.

**Standard procedures**

The distinction between policies and methods or procedures is useful although it is not clear cut. A *policy* typically covers a broad area or a basic issue, whereas *method* normally deals with the way a policy is carried out. This distinction between the broader aspects of an operating situation and the more detailed and specific considerations is useful in planning because it emphasizes a different viewpoint. Some executives have a tendency to become involved in methods and procedures to the exclusion of policies, whereas others have just the opposite tendency; effective administration gives ample consideration to both policies and methods. Also, the distinction between policies and methods is sometimes helpful in the process of delegation, as will be explained in Chapter 11.

This distinction is useful but not fundamental since what is policy and what is method depends upon the position from which the operation is viewed. For instance, the board of directors may regard the choice of advertising media as method of sales promotion, but to the sales manager the use of daily newspapers is a basic policy; similarly, the choice of type font is method to the sales manager, but it may be policy to the layout man. From any given point of view, however, policy is clearly much broader in scope than either method or procedure.

---

[3] For a discussion of each topic in this outline, see W. H. Newman and J. P. Logan, *Business Policies and Management*, 4th ed., South-Western Publishing Co., 1959.

While in common usage *methods* and *procedures* are frequently used interchangeably, in the present study *procedure* will imply a series of steps, often taken by different individuals, whereas *method* is concerned only with a single operation or work place.

In many types of business activity it is highly important to be sure that certain steps are taken and that the work is done accurately. Consequently, a detailed standing plan—in army parlance standing operating procedure, or just S.O.P.—is established. One bank, for example, has established the following standard procedure for the cutting of coupons on bonds that it holds for its own account or for customers' accounts:

> A list, called "Withdrawal of Securities" is prepared from the Cross Index record of bonds. The customers' names, quantity, and title of bonds that have coupons attached, falling due in the next period, are listed. Coupon envelopes are prepared, as well as ownership certificates (see Coupon Dept.). The coupon envelopes are prepared from the Collateral Loan cards and Safekeeping Book, thus acting as a check against the Cross Index record. The securities are then withdrawn from the Vault and Collateral Truck by an officer and clerk, counted and checked to the list, the list signed by both representatives of the bank. The officer retains this list of securities. After the coupons are detached, counted, and placed in the envelopes, the securities are again returned to their respective compartments in the Vault and the customers' accounts, in which case, duplicate credit slips are executed. One copy represents the credit to the account, and the other serves as a mailed notice to the customer.

A standard procedure should make sure that pertinent information flows to the people needing such data and that each person involved in the process understands just what he is to do. By making such steps established routine, the task of administration is significantly simplified.

Many procedures call for the transfer of information in written form. When this is so, the preparation of standard forms to be used is an essential aspect of the procedure. No end of confusion would result from the practice of recording information on sheets of paper of different sizes, to say nothing of the organization of the information on the paper. A well-designed form with lines for all of the essential information facilitates accuracy and completeness of information, permits rapid use, and also standardizes the record storage facilities.

*Does Your Company Have Sound Policies Covering These Points?*

I. Sales Policies
  A. Products or services to be sold
      1. Type of products
      2. Number and variety of products
      3. Quality of products
  B. Customers to whom products will be sold
      1. Channels of distribution
      2. Type of customers
      3. Size of customers
      4. Location of customers
  C. Prices at which products will be sold
      1. Relation to prices of competing products
      2. Relation to costs of production and distribution
      3. Relation to prices of individual items
      4. Quantity and trade discounts
      5. Frequency of price changes
      6. Resale price maintenance
  D. Sales promotion
      1. Sales appeals emphasized
      2. Types and media of advertising
      3. Use of personal solicitation
II. Procurement Policies
  A. Producing versus buying goods needed
      1. Buying goods for resale
      2. Producing main items, buying others
      3. Producing own raw materials
      4. Producing own services
  B. When and in what quantities to procure goods
      1. Procurement for stock, budgeted needs, or customer's order
      2. Minimum inventories required
      3. Size of production run or purchase order
      4. Stabilization of production
      5. Anticipation of price changes
  C. Selection of vendors
      1. Number of vendors
      2. Type of vendors
  D. Production processes
      1. Basic process to be used
      2. Extent of specialization
      3. Extent of automation
III. Personnel Policies
  A. Selection
      1. Hiring new employees

FIGURE 4. *Policy Outline for Typical Business Enterprise.*

2. Promotion of present employees
3. Discharge of present employees

B. Training
1. Purposes of training
2. Use of on-the-job training
3. Use of organized training

C. Compensation
1. Relation to market rates
2. Internal alignment
3. Use of financial incentives

D. Arrangements for work
1. Hours of work
2. Vacations
3. Working conditions

E. Employee services
1. Social and recreational activities
2. Safety and health
3. Pensions
4. Group insurance

F. Industrial relations
1. Companywide and industrywide bargaining
2. Grievances and arbitration
3. Union-management cooperation
4. Other means of communication

IV. Financial Policies

A. Uses of capital
1. Extent of investment in fixed assets
2. Restrictions on inventories
3. Extension of credit to customers
4. Use of capital not needed immediately for operations

B. Sources of capital
1. Owners
2. Long-term creditors
3. Short-term creditors

C. Protection of capital
1. Reduction of risks
2. Insurance
3. Hedging
4. Accounting reserves

D. Distribution of earnings
1. Plowing back earnings
2. Stable dividend rate
3. Adequacy of retained earnings

FIGURE 4. *Policy Outline for Typical Business Enterprise (Continued).*

**Standard methods**

Standard methods have received considerable attention, especially in manufacturing enterprises, ever since Frederick Taylor and his associates insisted that there was "one best way" to perform any operation. Much study may be necessary to ascertain just what the best method is, and management has a responsibility for maintaining standard operating conditions and for training the workers. Once these conditions are met, however, each worker performing the operation is expected to do it in accordance with the approved method. The net result usually is a substantial improvement in efficiency. There are also collateral benefits in making planning and control significantly easier. The description of a standard method for a simple operation is given in Figure 5.

The use of a standard method contributes not only to the efficiency but often to the quality of work and the uniformity of the products produced. For instance, the larger commercial laundries do not permit the girls ironing shirts to follow any method they choose. The order in which the parts of a shirt are pressed, the machine on which each operation is performed, and the portions of the shirt that are to be hand-ironed are carefully specified. Likewise, the folding and the wrapping of the shirt is standardized. If each presser were permitted to follow her own inclinations in handling the work, some shirts would be done with meticulous care while others would come through with wrinkled collars and buttons off; the customer would be particularly aware of the variations in quality because some shirts would be folded one way and others another way. Obviously, the laundry attempts to establish a standard method that will give quality of product consistent with its pricing and customer policies.

Although standard methods have been developed in the most detail and applied most extensively in production operations, the general concept is applicable to some degree in every field of purposeful activity. Thus, the retail store that accepts telephone orders for its merchandise may well standardize (1) the conversation of the order-taker, at least to the extent of the expressions used in answering the phone, closing the conversation, quoting prices, suggesting substitutions, and the like, (2) order writing, including the way the pad is held, the type of pencil used, the inserting of carbons, the tearing out of completed orders, and the order form itself, (3) checking prices and inventory on hand, often through the use of stock lists fully indexed for ready reference. When such methods are carefully developed and a salesperson is properly selected and trained, the time required to handle a call often can be cut in half; moreover, the customers receive more satisfactory service and the amount of sales per call is increased. Contrast this with the results when the salespersons are permitted to take telephone orders on a "catch as catch can" basis.

FIGURE 5. *Description of a Standard Method with Corresponding Output Standard. Courtesy, American Greetings Corporation.*

**STANDARD RATE & METHOD AUTHORITY**

*American Greetings Corporation*

PAGE 1 OF 4 PAGES

STANDARD NUMBER: 807-12  MACHINE NAMES: Corley-Miller Sheeter Gluer

ASSEMBLY INSTRUCTIONS: Sheet and apply solvent to acetate film by machine, overwrap one interleaved card by hand and package 6/K-bag.

CREW SIZE: 3  STANDARD HRS. PER M UNITS: 9.540  STANDARD UNITS PER HR: 314  UNIT OF MEASUREMENT: 1 K-bag

ALLOWANCES: PERSONAL: 10 %  MACHINE DELAY: 5 %  OTHER: %  TOTAL: 15 %  DATE: 4/26/62

DEVELOPED BY: J. M. Rosenstein  APPROVED: R. C. Swilik  REVIEWED: E. V. Koris

| ELEMENT NUMBER | ELEMENT TITLE AND METHOD DESCRIPTION | NORMAL MINUTES | OCCURRENCE PER UNIT | NORMAL MINUTES | SOURCE |
|---|---|---|---|---|---|
| 1. | Get 25 cards to workplace from C-box: Reach 28" to left, move down in box, grasp stack of cards on one end, grasp stack on other end, squeeze to hold, move 28" to stock shelf, LH. Grasp cards at half point and reverse to face all one way, RH. Jog twice on shelf, move to shelf and release face down, BH. | .1063 | 1/25 | .0043 | 710 |
| 2. | Get one interleaved card, open & position on acetate sheet: LH reach to card on stock shelf. Contact env. edge and move up to open card while reaching into card. Grasp card, move to film, and position left edge to film, while RH reaches to far edge of film. (Applies to cards which can be opened with one hand) | (.0220) | 1/1 | (.0220) | MTM #1 |
|  | OR |  |  |  |  |
| 2A. | Get one interleaved card, open & position on acetate sheet: BH reach to card on stock shelf. Contact env. edge and move up to open card reaching into card, LH while reaching to top of card, contacting and moving up to open card, RH. Grasp card and move to film, LH, while RH moves along, grasps & regrasps to open card & reaches away. LH positions left edge of env. to film while RH reaches to far edge of film. (Applies to cards which must be opened with both hands.) | .0244 | 1/1 | .0244 | MTM #1A |
| 3. | Wrap film around card on sheeter-gluer conveyor: RH grasp far edge of film. LH regrasp card to get thumb out while RH moves film over card. LH releases card, reaches to near edge of film & grasps with fingers. LH moves film over card while RH reaches to film with thumb. RH contacts film to hold down while LH regrasps film to press down. BH wipe outward to seal film. | .0262 | 1/1 | .0262 | MTM #2 |
| 4. | Fill out tally heading. | .3697 | 1/8x1/314 | .0001 |  |
| 5. | Fill out job change on tally. | .3775 | 1/1250 | .0003 |  |
|  |  |  |  | .0553 | / Card |
|  |  |  |  | .3318 | /K-bag |

THIS STANDARD IS GUARANTEED AS LONG AS CONDITIONS REMAIN AS DESCRIBED ON THIS AND ACCOMPANYING PAGES. IF THERE IS A CHANGE IN METHOD, MATERIAL, QUALITY REQUIREMENTS OR EQUIPMENT RESULTING IN A CHANGE OF 5% OR MORE, THIS STANDARD WILL BE CANCELLED AND A TEMPORARY OR A NEW STANDARD WILL BE ISSUED AS SOON AS PRACTICABLE.

**Flexibility of plans**

Both single-use and standing plans, by their very nature, restrict freedom of action. Men carrying out the plans may object to such restriction, partly because they dislike restrictions of any sort, but more significantly because they believe that the plans are not well suited to the specific problems they face. So exceptions are made; that is, the plan is not carried out in all respects.

If plans are simply disregarded, they obviously fail to serve the purposes we have been discussing in this chapter. On the other hand, some provision for flexibility may be warranted. Fortunately, several ways exist to achieve flexibility without, at the same time, sacrificing the benefits of planning. Three possible ways of securing flexibility are:

1. *Provide for prompt exceptions.* For instance, a company may have standing policies and procedures covering the extension of credit to customers. Most shipments will fit within these plans, but if a special case arises when an exception seems warranted, the credit manager or assistant treasurer is empowered to grant credit beyond the established limits. This kind of arrangement for avoiding rigid application of rules is often called *the exception principle.* It is used most often with standing plans.

To provide real flexibility, the executive who can make an exception to established plans should be available to say "yes" or "no" quickly enough to secure the full benefit of the special concession. Sometimes a pattern develops among the exceptions, and when this occurs, the plans may be elaborated to include the treatment of unusual cases within the regular structure. However, if an executive makes exceptions so often and with no clear and consistent reason for doing so, the stability plans are designed to provide will be dissipated.

2. *Consider possible revisions regularly.* Flexibility is often needed to deal with new conditions that were not anticipated when the plans were formulated. Consequently, many companies provide for periodic review of progress to date and of new information; plans are then revised to the extent that seems strategic.

This revision technique is well suited to single-use plans. It should be used with restraint on standing plans, however, because policies, procedures, and the like serve as a basis for habitual behavior and social structure. Frequent changes in the "rules of the game" are often disconcerting to employees. In fact, in times of rapid change the behavior patterns may become so unstable that little work gets done. Occasional review of standing plans is, indeed, wise; but if changes are to be made, the need for full understanding by the people affected (preferably through their participation in the revision process) and for a retraining period should be recognized.

3. *Distinguish between rules and guides.* Close examination of the actual operation of many companies, including highly successful ones, reveals that plans are often not strictly observed. Local executives or operators make their own exceptions, especially when goals have been clearly established and decentralization is favored. In effect, the policies, methods, programs, and other plans are treated as *guides*—recommended practice—but not as rules which must be obeyed. Obviously, such behavior introduces considerable flexibility into company activities.

In all companies certain plans are strictly enforced. For example, pricing and services to customers may have to be uniform, deviations from quality standards will not be tolerated, accounting classifications must be kept uniform. On such matters the need for consistency and/or the reliance one department places on another requires close adherence to plans. In other matters such as public relations, production methods, or purely internal operations of a department, occasional local variations may give better results.

Flexibility can be enhanced by publicly recognizing this distinction between rules and guides. Instead of letting each employee discover for himself where exceptions will be tolerated, the administrator should be explicit about the matter. By removing uncertainty about when and how much deviation, if any, will be permitted two ends are served: flexibility is introduced where practical, and close observance of the remaining plans is more likely to occur.

### Integration of standing plans

The standing plans of any single enterprise are inevitably related to one another and care should be exercised to see that the plans are properly integrated.

As with single-use plans, there is a hierarchy aspect about standing plans. This is reflected in the fairly common division of policies into basic, general, and departmental. Again it is reflected in the concept that policies are general plans of action, whereas methods and procedures cover the particular manner in which these policies will be executed.

This idea of status among the standing plans was clearly indicated when a large oil company decided that the purchase of crude oil in the field was an expensive way to acquire control over raw material and that in the future the company would also engage in scientific prospecting. The basic policy to engage in prospecting led to the adoption of a number of subsidiary policies, such as the geographical limits within which the company will support exploration, the use of seismograph technique in seeking new fields, the encouragement of joint ventures with other oil companies when drilling exploratory wells, and the practice of employing geologists familiar with a particular locality when leasing or drilling in that area is under consideration. These subsidiary policies, in turn, led to the adoption of some standard methods. For example, the seismograph crews have a standard routine they follow when "shooting" a given area.

Clearly, whenever such a hierarchy of standing plans exists, the broader the plan the more dominant it is, and any other plan directly subordinate to it contributes toward the achievement of the broader course of action. This does not mean, however, that every broad policy will necessarily have a whole group of subordinate standing plans, because the subordinate activities may not be repetitive enough to justify this type of planning.

Entirely aside from any concept of relative status or hierarchy, the standing plans should be consistent one with another. For instance, a management consulting firm that seeks work from a large number of small companies should make sure that its various standing plans dovetail. Its services will probably be somewhat standardized in order to lower costs and fees; several offices in different centers will be needed to gain ready access to small businesses; considerable decentralization of authority will be necessary; the length and expense of staff training will have to be kept low; and so forth. These personnel policies, organization and location plans, and standardization of services fit into an over-all concept of operation. Without such consistency among plans, inefficiency—if not outright conflict—is likely to develop.

Furthermore, single-use plans must be integrated with standing plans, inasmuch as programs, projects, and schedules typically are prepared on the assumption that standing plans will continue in effect. Thus, the development of a program for new woodworking equipment, described briefly at the beginning of this chapter, was done within a whole framework of existing policy with respect to personnel, production technique, finance, and organization structure. Likewise, the new program assumed the continuance of the established methods of machine operation and procedures for procurement and accounting. Insofar as the new woodworking program could utilize the existing standing plans, the integration of the program into over-all company activities was easy. Nevertheless, care was necessary to make sure that the standing plans were appropriate since it would have been much wiser to make a specific exception for the program or to modify a standing plan itself than to jeopardize the new undertaking.

Therefore, a standing plan or a single-use plan, while it is often the subject of intensive study and discussion by itself, must be considered as a part of the total plans of the enterprise.

**Advantages of using standing plans**

Most administrators recognize that policies and standard methods and procedures have a place in management planning, but the practical questions are: When should they be used? How specific and detailed should they be? The answers to these questions rest on a careful consideration of the advantages and disadvantages of standing plans as they apply to the specific situation. Among the benefits that an administrator may expect to obtain from the use of standing plans are the following:

1. Executive effort is economized. Once the standing plan is established it is unnecessary for the executive to redecide the same issue. The plan is applicable, of course, only under a given set of conditions. Someone must ascertain that these conditions prevail in the case at hand, but if this is true, no further decision by the executive is required. Moreover, less time is needed for instructions and explanations of what is to be done.

2. Delegation of authority to act is greatly facilitated. Often the exception principle is utilized, under which subordinates are expected to proceed with action so long as the situation is covered by standing plans, but when exceptional problems arise to bring these to the attention of the supervisor. If this arrangement is care-

fully observed, an administrator can maintain close control over a large volume of operations with relative ease. He knows that consistent action is being taken on similar cases; he can predict what the action will be; and he knows that the action is in accordance with his best judgment.

3. Widespread use of "the one best way" is possible. If an operation is to be repeated a large number of times, considerable effort to ascertain the most efficient way of performing it is warranted. And, having discovered this method, it is made standard practice for all those who perform that activity. Of course, standing plans may be far from the most efficient; this is likely to happen when plans are not currently adjusted to changing conditions or when traditional behavior is adopted as the standard without critical examination. In such cases, the other advantages of standing plans are still obtainable, but a significant source of economy is being overlooked.

4. Significant personnel economies are possible. The establishment of standing plans for a large part of the duties of a given position allow such positions to be filled with persons of less experience and all-round ability than would be needed if the incumbent made the plans himself. The training of persons to fill such positions is made easier by the existence of recognized policies and procedures, and the transfer of employees from one position to another in the same organization is likewise eased.

5. Control is made easier. Standing plans, especially standard methods and procedures, lead to uniformity of action, and relatively definite performance standards can be established for such activities.

6. Coordination of activities is greatly aided by a preliminary coordination of plans. The clear statement of both single-use and standing plans permits a check of one with another, and opens the way for greater consistency and synchronization.

### Summary

Good planning depends in part upon choosing the best forms or types of plans for the specific operation. There are several types that should be part of the tools of every executive. He should know the nature, benefits, and limitations of each type of plan so that he can be adept and flexible in laying out his work.

Operating plans fall into two broad groups, single-use and standing plans. In the single-use group are general programs, projects, detailed schedules, specifications, and methods. Standing plans, which are used over and over again, include policies, organization structure, standard procedures, and standard methods. In both groups broad plans cover a wide range of activities and often a long period of time, and detailed plans deal with the action of a single individual for a short interval.

This range of possible operating plans is indicated, along with goals, in Figure 6. The diagram suggests an over-all concept of planning that can be adapted to many managerial jobs.

In addition to the selection of the proper types of plans, the executive should seek *integration* of his plans. The various plans should be consistent with each other. Also, it is usually helpful to recognize a *hierarchy* among the plans, in which the more specific plans are subordinate to and within the limits of the broader, controlling plans. This does not necessarily mean that all detailed planning should be deferred until broad plans are settled, nor does it dictate the degree of centralization in the organization; but whatever the sequence or place of their preparation a sound relationship between the plans should be secured.

| SCOPE | GOALS | COURSES OF ACTION | |
|---|---|---|---|
| | | Single-Use Plans | Standing Plans |
| Broad Plans | Objectives (Missions) | General Programs | Policies |
| | Budgets and Deadlines | Projects | Organization Structure |
| | Performance Standards for Expense, Quality, Quantity, etc. | Personnel Assignments | Standard Procedures |
| Detailed Plans | | Detailed Schedules, Specifications, Methods, etc. | Standard Methods |

FIGURE 6. *Types of Administrative Plans. This concept of plans may be adapted to any administrative unit, that is, to an entire enterprise, a department, or a small section.*

A number of benefits resulting from the advance preparation of operating plans have been stressed. Among these are: (1) Integrated and purposeful action is more readily achieved. (2) Crises can be anticipated and delays avoided. (3) More efficient methods and procedures can be developed, especially for standing plans which will be used time and again. (4) Delegation of authority to act is facilitated. (5) The groundwork for control standards is laid. (6) Executive effort is economized where standing plans can be used. (7) Coordination of activities is aided by preliminary coordination of plans.

But, thus far we have looked at only the positive side of the picture. There remain two very practical aspects of planning to be examined: (1) the factors that limit the period and detail in which it pays to plan, and (2) the techniques to use to arrive at wise planning decisions. After these issues have been considered in the next five chapters, we will be ready to move on into matters of organization and other steps necessary to carry out the plans.

### SELECTED REFERENCES

Branch, M. C., *The Corporate Planning Process*, American Management Association, 1962.

Koontz, H. and C. O'Donnell, *Principles of Management* (2nd ed.) McGraw-Hill Book Co., Inc., 1959, Part V.

LeBreton, P. P. and D. A. Henning, *Planning Theory*, Prentice-Hall, Inc., 1961, Chaps. 2 and 12.

Neuschel, R. F., *Management by System*, McGraw-Hill Book Co., Inc., 1960.

Terry, G. R., *Principles of Management* (3rd ed.) Richard D. Irwin, Inc., 1960, Chap. 10.

# 4

# The Limits of Planning

In the preceding discussion, the benefits an administrator may receive from planning have been emphasized. Among other things we noted that planning promotes consistent, integrated, and purposeful action; crises are more likely to be anticipated and mistakes avoided through careful planning; economy is secured through purposeful action and the avoidance of difficulty; time is available to determine the most effective methods, and once identified these methods may be used again and again; with plans established, executives are able to delegate authority to act with less risk that the authority will be abused; moreover, the plans form a basis for reasonable and effective control.

This is a potent list of advantages, and on the face of it one might conclude that the effective administrator should insist that every action of members of the enterprise be planned in detail for a long period in advance. There are, of course, some very practical limitations on the use of planning, and one of the important duties of an administrator is to decide in light of these limitations just how far his particular enterprise or department can carry the planning concept.

Virtually all work must be planned, at least informally and a few minutes ahead. Even our unsystematic plumber who is installing a new water connection makes a decision (a plan) to cut and thread the pipe, and with this plan in mind proceeds to obtain the pipe and get the necessary tools. The question, then, is not whether there shall be planning, for it is inevitable that on-the-spot plans be made by someone. The crucial issue is how far in advance and in what detail these plans should be made. (A related question as to who should make the plan is considered at some length in the chapters on organization.)

What are the things that make extensive planning impractical for long periods in advance? What can an administrator desiring to secure the benefits of planning do to overcome at least partially these limiting factors? We now turn our attention to the answers to these questions.

RELIABILITY OF FORECASTS

**Need for accurate forecasts**

Most business plans are based on a whole set of assumed conditions—involving the market, raw material supply, governmental controls, available personnel, operating efficiencies, competitors' behavior, price levels, and numerous other factors. A plan is useful only as long as the assumptions on which it is based prove substantially correct. An engineer dealing with inanimate materials can predict their behavior with considerable, though not complete, accuracy. A military commander bases his campaign on a great mass of data secured by his intelligence division. Many of the assumptions of the administrator, however, deal with social conditions and human behavior, which are to a large degree unpredictable. If the operating conditions change significantly, the plans lose much of their value. To the extent that future conditions cannot be reliably forecast, the usefulness of planning may be questioned.

The effect upon practical planning of the inability to forecast accurately may be illustrated in the instance of the American Independent Oil Company. This company obtained a drilling concession from the Sheik of Kuwait in the oil-rich Persian Gulf. Since almost all of its stockholders were domestic oil companies that operated refineries in the United States, plans might have been made immediately for the distribution of the crude oil that was to be secured from this concession. While oil most likely would be produced in the area, still considerable time would elapse before the discoveries could be made, wells and pipe lines completed, and the oil made available for the stockholders. During the interim the quantities and grades of crude oil needed by the various United

States refineries might change, and plans made when the concession was obtained would have no particular value when the oil became available. In fact, the numerous technical and political difficulties that had to be overcome before even test wells could be drilled made the planning of production, well-drilling, and transportation premature at the time the concession was obtained.

Accurate forecasting may be difficult for an established enterprise in a purely domestic situation. Few retail stores, for example, feel confident enough of their ability to predict consumer demand, supply conditions, and other market factors to make detailed advertising plans three months ahead. The broad characteristics of the advertising campaign may be mapped out, but the items to be featured, the stress to be laid on price, the attempt to counteract competitors' advertising are all so unpredictable that the actual copy is prepared only a few weeks in advance of its publication. Such unpredictability is characteristic of many areas of human activity.

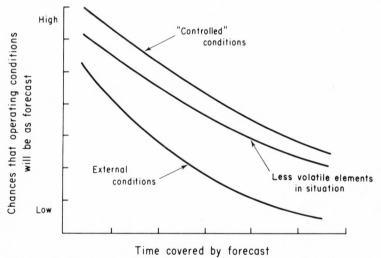

FIGURE 7. *Effect of Time on Accuracy of Forecasts.*

The reliability of most forecasts diminishes rapidly as they are projected further into the future. Wage rates, material prices, nature of competition, and many other things normally may be predicted with reasonable confidence for two or three months; it is possible to make an informed guess about them for a year hence; but a forecast for three or four years is hazardous and must be couched in terms of general trends. Except for a few things like the weather, which may be predicted more accurately for a month than for any particular day in that month, the longer the period covered by the prediction, the more likely are unanticipated events to upset the calculations. This inverse relationship between time and accuracy of forecasts is diagrammed in Figure 7.

The eroding effect of time on predictability is one of the primary reasons why it is practical to plan in considerable detail for activities in the relatively near future, but impractical to make detailed plans for several years in advance. Moreover, if we wait to see how things work out, we have that much more additional information upon which to make our forecasts for a subsequent period.

### Overcoming unreliable forecasts

Administrators who wish to enjoy the benefits of planning can at least partially overcome the limits imposed by unreliable forecasting in two ways. First, they may make studied attempts to *improve* their *forecasts*. Thousands of companies subscribe to one or more forecasting services or employ some economic consultant to advise them. Many companies have made great strides in the compilation of data upon which to base predictions; for example, the automobile companies receive from week to week the sales, automobiles on hand, used car prices, and other market information from all of their dealers throughout the country. Several of the larger companies have a separate division whose sole mission is to prepare business forecasts. Of course, if the uncertainty relates to internal conditions, forecasting can often be improved by exercising closer control—as will be discussed in later paragraphs.

A second way to deal with unreliable predictions is to *detour* around the areas of greatest uncertainty. For instance, if securing an objective within a definite time is of sufficient importance, as it often is in military operations, alternative programs may be developed and started in operation; then, when the actual operating conditions become apparent, the most effective alternative is followed to its conclusion. Obviously, it would be more economical to follow only the one alternative finally used, and in most business enterprises the pressure for economy dictates that a single course be followed even though it is admittedly more risky.[1]

[1] The danger of following a single, though risky course may sometimes be partly offset by insurance. As a rule, however, insurance is practical only for catastrophes that are quite unlikely to occur, and hence are not covered in the regular planning.

In a few situations unreliable forecasting may be counteracted by *hedging;* that is, by arranging operations so that losses in one area will be offset by gains in another, or vice versa. In a narrow sense, hedging is applicable only to protection against price changes for a limited number of commodities; the general principle, however, is sometimes applicable in other situations, such as offering two or more styles of products with the expectation that if one does not appeal to customers the other will, or locating plants in both the United States and abroad so as to be able to serve the foreign market regardless of the changes in foreign exchange rates.

The most common way to detour around unreliable forecasts is to separate those parts of the operation that will not be affected by the uncertain factor—volume, style, weather, or whatever it may be—and then making a tentative plan for the remaining segment in considerable detail. When the uncertain factor is finally settled, it is, relatively, a simple job to pull the various parts of the program together. It is quite possible, for example, to do the design work and develop engineering specifications for a product before it is practical to decide when, and perhaps in what plant, it will be produced. Many an advertising campaign has been mapped out, copy prepared, media selected, and all completed except for the timing, which depended upon factors difficult to appraise when the planning was initiated.

These means of overcoming unreliable forecasts are at best only partial remedies. Improved forecasting technique may push forward the time span of confidence, but the practical limits are soon reached for most enterprises. The detours around unpredictable elements are only applicable in certain circumstances, and even then apply only to part of the operations of the enterprise. Consequently, the inability to forecast accurately remains one of the factors that limit the period and the detail in which planning is practical.

## RECURRENCE OF SIMILAR PROBLEMS

### Repetitive operations essential to standing plans

Standing plans by their very nature are useful only to the extent that an operating situation is repeated again and again. They are not well suited to such actions as the negotiation of a labor agreement, the tearing down of an old building, or the manufacture of an experimental airplane. The special needs of specific customers, personnel, equipment, competition, and the like may justify special treatment. Sometimes such a large part of the activities under the direction of an executive deal with these special situations that standing plans have very limited use to him; the activities in question may be rarely repeated, if at all, or the situation in which they take place may be so dynamic that each problem calls for its own treatment. Single-use plans and goals may, of course, be used to considerable advantage, but standing plans appear to be ruled out under such conditions.

### Seek out and maintain standard operations

The administrative job is tougher if, because of an ever-changing operating situation, standing plans cannot be used. Standing plans are an important device for relieving the pressure on an executive and for securing efficiency in operation. Naturally, therefore, an executive should seek to obtain at least some of these benefits, even though the activities seem to call for individualized treatment. Two important ways in which this may be accomplished are: (1) isolating repetitive aspects of the situation and standardizing the treatment of these, and (2) controlling the operating situation so that greater repetitiveness is present.

Many operations that vary from one time to another in certain characteristics are, nevertheless, similar in other respects. While standing plans for the entire operation would be a mistake, they still may be very helpful for parts of it. For example, often policies can be established to advantage, even though more detailed standard methods may be inappropriate. Thus, a company may have policies with respect to the size, location, and type of customer it will solicit and the basic sales appeals it will use, but not have a standardized sales approach for its salesmen. Likewise, there may be a policy of promotion from within the company, but no standardized path that an employee in the maintenance department or the insurance department must follow if he is to obtain a higher-paying job. In fact, it is a rare enterprise that does not have sufficient similarity in some of the issues facing the executive to make the use of policies a desirable administrative tool.

Also *part*, though not all, of the method may be standardized. For example, in selling, the writing of sales orders, the physical handling of display material, or the writing of the omnipresent daily report on calls made may be standardized, even though most of the selling activity is left to the discretion of salesmen. In the machine shop a "one best way" of operating machines can be developed even when the dimensions of the parts being made and the final product that will be assembled vary widely. In fact, careful analysis shows that a great many operations have repetitive aspects about them, and the operators will develop customary and habitual methods of performing these aspects even through the executives of the department take no initiative in the matter. So, the area over which the concept of standing plans may be applied beneficially is much wider than appears at first glance.

Another way the administrator may increase the applicability of standing plans is deliberately to *regulate the operating situation* so that conditions will remain approximately the same each time an operation is performed. This was an essential feature of Frederick Taylor's *Shop Management,* for he laid great stress on uniformity of raw materials, maintenance of tools and equipment in top operating condition, avoidance of waiting for materials or new work assignment, and objective standards of satisfactory work. As long as these things were permitted to vary, insisting on standard methods and standard output time was difficult and unreasonable, but once management brought them under control, the use of standard methods became very practical.

Similar actions designed to create stability and uniformity in operating conditions are possible in a variety of activities. The insistence on the use of standard forms and procedures throughout an enterprise makes it possible to routinize a great deal of the work of the accounting department. The adoption of recognized material specifications and establishment of a material requisition procedure permits a certain degree of standardized procedure within the purchasing department.

This standardization, however, is very largely confined to activities within the enterprise. When dealing with outsiders, such as customers, vendors, or trade association officials, such control is much more difficult, and the enterprise must adapt itself to the wide variety of situations that naturally arise.

And so, in dealing with the lack of recurrence of similar conditions, the administrator can extend the limits of practical planning to some degree. He may seek out repetitive aspects of what appear to be different operations, and he may be able to establish some uniformity of working conditions at least within the four walls of the company. Nevertheless, every administrative situation is more or less dynamic, and most external factors are not subject to managerial control; to the extent that this is true, we find a very real limitation on the use of standing plans.

TENDENCY TOWARD INFLEXIBILITY

**Reluctance to change**

The establishment of advanced plans tends to make administration inflexible; the more detailed and widespread the plans, the greater the inflexibility. Theoretically this need not be so, for the man who makes the plans obviously has the right to modify them; the tendency exists, nevertheless. In a large chemical company, for example, a new management placed great stress on laying out general programs for at least a year in advance and very specific programs for a six-month period. This worked very well until there was a sudden downturn in the prices of chemical products to which the company made relatively slow adjustment. Perhaps the detail of the plans made the executive feel too secure and thus inattentive to changes in marketing conditions; no doubt the tendency existed, having once prepared a plan, to make it work. Looking back on the experience, a number of the executives feel that their enthusiasm for planning seriously interfered with the readjustment and cost the company thousands of dollars.

This is no isolated case of inflexibility. Any college professor who has sought to have a change made in the schedule of courses or the assignment of rooms once these plans have been completed is fully aware of the difficulty of making a change even for good reasons. A shop foreman who has once made up his mind to a course of action is likewise slow to make room for a rush order or a shift to another product.

This inflexibility is partly a *psychological reluctance* to change a decision; planning is hard work and there is not much fun in going over the same ground two or three times; a mind-set has been established, and maintaining a fresh and objective viewpoint is difficult; there may well be a sense of "loss of face" when first guesses have to be modified.

Moreover, a well-developed program is likely to lead executives throughout the enterprise to *make commitments*—for materials, to employees, to customers—well in advance. Then, if subsequent conditions make a revision of the plans desirable, the man who has a well-developed program may be at a disadvantage in relation to the man who crosses his bridges when he comes to them. This suggests that the man with a program to guide his actions but who delays commitments until the time to make them is opportune is following a wise course; such good judgment and self-discipline, however, are not always achieved. Chester I. Barnard, formerly president of New Jersey Bell Telephone Company, has observed in his classic analysis of administration:

> The fine art of executive decision consists in not deciding questions that are not pertinent, in not deciding prematurely, in not making decisions that cannot be effective, and in not making decisions that others should make.[2]

Standing plans are often more inflexible than the single-use plans just discussed. The inflexibility of military and governmental procedures is all too prevalent; many an officer has put through an action he knew was not best rather than run the gamut of an exception. The author remembers sitting for three hours in the office of a trust company while the officials of that renowned institution and the Philadelphia Electric Company quibbled over who would modify their customary procedure so as to permit the installation of an electric range (in which neither of them had any financial interest), and the reader can undoubtedly supply his own grotesque examples of red tape interfering with effective action.

Standing plans soon take on the aspects of habit and tradition, and for ease of supervision it is desirable that they should. Still, as any reformer knows, people are loath to change their customary manner of behavior unless present conditions are clearly unsatisfactory and/or the proposed change offers definite benefits. This natural conservatism of both executives and operators means that the danger is ever-present that standing plans will be outmoded and that exceptions will be made reluctantly.

### Revising plans

A number of ways an executive can counteract this tendency toward inflexibility have been noted in the previous chapters. He can make provision for *regular review* of existing plans for the purpose of changing them when necessary in light of experience

[2] *The Functions of the Executive,* Harvard University Press, 1938, page 194.

and the current situation. He can provide for *exceptions* to the standing plan, perhaps by authorizing the man on the firing line to make such exceptions and report the reason therefor later, or at least by providing for ready access to some person authorized to make such exceptions. Finally, he can try to create a psychological *attitude that favors adaptation* rather than inflexibility. This attitude is, in part, a willingness to make changes, but perhaps more important it is a stressing of objectives and goals so that members of the organization will accept and even urge a change when a particular plan is not furthering the purpose of the enterprise.

Clearly, revisions and exceptions detract from the benefits of planning, and if they are too numerous, a point may be reached where planning is "a lot of work and nobody follows it anyhow." The longer the duration and the more detailed the plan, the more likely are revisions and exceptions to be necessary. And the very real danger always exists that inflexibility rather than exceptions will dominate. Some degree of inflexibility is part of the price of planning, and the administrator must decide at what point the price becomes greater than the benefit.

## EXPENSE OF PLANNING

**Balancing expense and benefits**

Planning is expensive and the advantages may not warrant the required expenditure. Well-developed plans usually call for considerable gathering and analysis of facts, exchange of ideas by operating executives, and attention by the top administrator. If the plans will have to be revised later, or if the activity studied is not very important, then the effort devoted to planning might better be spent in some other way.

Since standing plans are intended for repeated use, it often pays to carry them into much greater detail than is justified for single-use plans. For example, pipe-fitting in ship construction is essentially an unplanned activity. It would be possible through detailed plans and specifications to determine in advance the exact length and shape of each piece of pipe needed, but this would be a difficult task because there are very few 90° angles and many obstructions, which makes almost every piece of pipe a special item. Aside from a few wartime exceptions, such as Liberty ships, almost every vessel constructed is a special job, and the detailed plumbing plans for one ship would not be applicable to another. In this situation the cost of planning would far outweigh the benefits secured, and the practice is almost universal to rely on skilled pipe fitters to measure, cut, and try as they go along.

On the other hand, we know that Frederick Taylor and his associates devoted years of work and used up thousands of pounds of metal in determining methods to be followed in machine shops. In this instance, however, the standard plans that finally resulted from the studies could be used over and over again, and the economies obtained from these repeated operations soon paid for the high expense of the original study. Generally, the cost of preparing plans does not increase proportionately with the expansion of an activity, so the volume of repetitive work is a significant factor in appraising expense.

The expense of preparing plans and the benefits derived from their use, though very real, are both difficult to measure. Consequently, considerable judgment is required in deciding when planning no longer pays its way. The expense of special planning departments such as engineering, market research, or production methods can, of course, be isolated, but as a general rule in business establishments the total expense of these departments can be justified if their work is effectively utilized by operating personnel. The time and energy that the operating personnel devote to planning, however, is hard to measure expense-wise. As planning is pushed farther ahead in time and further down in detail, a point is reached where these executives might better be devoting their time to some other administrative activity.

This balancing of expense and benefits of planning should be done on an *incremental* basis. Just because engineering, for example, is essential to good operations does not mean the time and expense devoted to engineering should be unlimited. Instead, the pertinent question is whether the *additional* (incremental) *expense* of more engineering will be greater or less than the *additional benefits* secured.

## TIME REQUIRED

### Speed versus accuracy

Planning is time-consuming, and under some circumstances prompt action is more important than the advantages of advance planning. The influence of the time available on the detail to which planning was carried was dramatically illustrated in World War II; first in the retreat from Dunkirk, and second in the invasion of Normandy. When time is of the essence as it was at Dunkirk, detailed planning often goes in the discard. Likewise, occasions occur in business when prompt action following a change in operating conditions or receipt of additional information is more important than detailed planning. In a competitive market situation, in emergencies, in the process of negotiations, and similar situations little doubt exists that careful planning would improve the decision, but the fact that action taken a week or a month hence would be too late makes such planning impossible.

The need for prompt action is not a limiting factor, of course, on standing plans; even though a week or a month may be required to prepare them, they will still be useful the following month and the next and the next.

**Anticipating emergencies**

Although emergencies and other needs for prompt action cannot be avoided, the executive need not sit back and wait for the lightning to strike. He can predict, say, a month in advance that there is a fifty-fifty chance that the emergency will occur; then if the matter is serious enough, he can prepare tentative plans to be put in effect when and if they are needed. If the emergency does not occur, the expense of preparing the tentative plans is regarded as an insurance premium.

Another approach is to develop policies, standard methods, and procedures that may be quickly brought into effect at the appropriate time. Not only fire departments and hospitals, but also many companies faced with irregular demand for their product or calls for special customer service, are set up to operate on this basis. The executive faced with emergency still has to take prompt action, but this action can be better planned because of the thinking that has been done in advance.

EFFECT ON INDIVIDUAL INITIATIVE

**Detailed conformity**

When planning is comprehensive in scope and extends down to detailed activities, it tends to stifle the initiative of individual operators and supervisors, especially in those large enterprises where many standard methods and procedures are set centrally. Danger exists that men may be regarded as automatons. As one army colonel who was recently assigned to a large university for graduate study remarked, "I've been following S.O.P. [standing operating procedure] so long I no longer can think for myself."

The current discussion of foremen's unions also reflects a change in opportunity to exercise initiative. Advocates of foremen's unionization contend that the man who fifty years ago was an independent boss of his department is now little more than a messenger and a lead man. Plans as to what work is to be done, how it is to be done, the machines to be used, the people assigned to his department, their training, the pay they will receive, the disciplinary action that may be taken, the checking on quality, the safety measures to be followed, the reasons for unfavorable costs, and the steps to be taken to correct them are now, they contend, all decided by someone else. The planners, so runs the argument, have taken over, and virtually nothing is left to the judgment and initiative of the foreman, let alone the operator himself.

Note that the fundamental issue is who does the planning, the worker and the foreman or someone else? This is a matter of organization and will be discussed in more detail in later chapters. Generally true, however, is that with the increasing emphasis on better planning, the tendency has been to shift some of the planning work to special planning divisions and to establish policies, programs, and standard procedure, all of which tend to circumscribe the discretion of the man on the firing line. Thus, usually with more extensive planning a large group of employees have less freedom in the exercise of their own judgment. Conformity, rather than originality, is expected of them. This restriction in initiative not only tends to snuff out the creative spark that is so essential in successful enterprise, but it also has a bad effect on morale.

**Participation in planning**

What can the executive do to overcome this disadvantage of extensive planning? First, it is desirable and in some situations essential, that the operator himself be *consulted* regarding many of the decisions affecting his work. He has intimate knowledge of operating conditions that both the planning division and the higher executive lack. Consequently, a wise practice, and an increasingly prevalent one, is to seek the ideas and opinions of the people who have to carry out the plans. Second, whenever feasible, plans can be designated as recommended guides rather than strict rules. Third, special care can be taken to identify those individuals who have initiative, originality, and sound judgment and then *transfer* those people to spots where these abilities can be used. Emphasis on planning and the establishment of special planning divisions have increased the number of positions where just such talents are needed.

Extensive planning does affect the opportunities for individuals who demonstrate initiative. However, if steps such as those just suggested are taken, this can be a change in where and how initiative is expressed rather than a reduction in opportunity. Consequently, the administrator should rarely refrain from extensive planning because of the effect upon individual initiative. Instead, he should take steps to make sure that the effect is not undesirable.

## SUMMARY

No enterprise can exist without some planning. The real question is, "How much?"—that is, how far ahead and in what detail should planning be carried?

The chief limits on the extent of planning are: (1) inability to forecast accurately, (2) absence of repetitive operations, (3) tendency toward inflexibility, (4) expense of planning, and (5) time required for planning. Ways have been suggested for overcoming these limiting factors, but the remedies can be only partially effective at best, and a point will be reached where further planning is not justified.

These limitations on planning should, of course, be balanced against the benefits that can be expected. The chief benefits of using different types of plans have already been discussed in the preceding chapters, and in the next chapter the way in which the pros and cons of planning worked out in a specific company will be described. Following this review, we will turn to the question of how management decisions may best be made.

SELECTED REFERENCES

Barnard, C. I., *The Functions of the Executive*, Harvard University Press, 1938, Chap. 13.

Dimock, M. E., *A Philosophy of Administration*, Harper & Row, Publishers, 1958, Chaps. 14 and 15.

Marx, F. M., ed., *Elements of Public Administration* (2nd ed.), Prentice-Hall, Inc., 1959, Chap. 17.

Thompson, S., *How Companies Plan*, American Management Association, 1962, pp. 13-49.

Worthy, J. C., *Big Business and Free Men*, Harper & Row, Publishers, 1959, Part II.

# 5

# Structure of Planning in an Enterprise

## Need for balance

There is no formula to tell an administrator how far ahead and in what detail to plan the activities under his direction, nor will a single answer apply throughout an enterprise. Instead, for each activity various types of plans that might be helpful should be recognized, and the limits that have just been discussed should be carefully appraised and weighed against the benefits that can be expected from the extensive use of each type of plan.

Thus, we should expect that some companies or departments will lay great stress on standard methods and procedures and on output standards because of the repetitive nature of their operations; in other departments perhaps making long-range plans and carefully scheduling activities will be more important because of the unusual importance of being right the first time; and so forth.

The preceding discussion has stressed the benefits and the limitations of various types of plans in order to assist an administrator in choosing those that will be useful to him. Figure 8 gives a list of questions that will help bring to mind the more common of these advantages and disadvantages of different types of plans.

Just because the plans for each activity deserve individual consideration does not mean, however, that each should be treated separately. As has been stressed, there is considerable interdependence among plans, and it is often necessary to move forward on several fronts together. For example, detailed scheduling is difficult without output standards, and output standards in turn are not very reliable unless standard methods have been established.

Piecemeal planning may be a lot better than none at all, but if it is not coordinated with other planning then the extent to which it can be carried out profitably is probably restricted. A single department, for instance, may have its own budget, but without over-all company budgeting, the lack of data regarding related activities will probably place severe limits on the span of time it will be practical to cover.

In connection with this matter of interdependence, we should note the tendency for benefits to accelerate or snowball. Planning in one department helps both that department and the related activities; the planning of these related activities makes plans for still other work easier and more dependable; and if the plans are built one upon the other, the tendency is to compound the benefits derived from the original planning effort.

Insofar as plans are dependent one upon the other, a balance in the extent to which each is carried should be observed. Thus, if forecasting difficulties limit the extent of sales planning, a corresponding limit may well exist on the details to which financial plans are carried. As Russell Robb has so ably pointed out, we can carry one phase of our planning to such detail that it is really wasted effort when considered in light of the possibilities of refinements in other related phases of planning. He stressed:

> . . . most final results [plans] are not single measurements but are the result of a combination of several quantities of different kinds and of a more or less complex computation. . . . We were taught . . . to determine in advance what influence each of these factors had in the result. We were urged then to learn our limitations in the determination of each of these factors so that we should not waste time in fruitless refinement [of some factors when corresponding refinement was not possible for other important factors]. This seems a perfectly obvious procedure, that the exercise of common sense would always lead us to follow; but in reality we are not likely to follow it unless we make a studied attempt to do so.[1]

**Case illustrating the varied extent of planning**

A brief description of the extent to which planning was used in a specific company will illustrate the mosaic pattern that planning

---

[1] *Lectures on Organization,* privately printed, pp. 25-27.

takes and will also summarize the more important factors involved in deciding the extent of planning.

The Rocklyn Corporation, which will be used as an illustration, is a relatively small company with two hundred to three hundred employees. It manufactures replacement parts for automobiles and sells these through parts jobbers located throughout the United States. The president, who founded the company, is intimately familiar with all of the activities, but in recent years he has taken steps to

---

### Key Questions Guiding the Extent of Planning

*Single-Use Plans* (Programs, projects, detailed specifications, schedules, and the like)
1. Will the plan help get the right man at the right place at the right time, adequately supplied with instructions, materials, and equipment; instead of "too little, too late"?
2. Will the plan improve coordination of several activities?
3. Will planning lower costs or increase effectiveness of the activity, through (a) anticipating trouble, and (b) developing more efficient methods?
4. Will planning ease the load on hard-worked executives by (a) permitting more decentralization of authority to act, and (b) providing guides for use in control?
5. To what extent is detailed planning warranted by the reliability of forecasts of operating conditions?
6. Will planning in advance lead to unwise commitments?
7. Will executives continue to be alert to new conditions and quick to adapt their actions to them?
8. Is the activity important enough to warrant formal planning? Will the improvement in results be worth more than the added expense involved in additional planning?
9. Is there time for detailed planning, or is prompt action more important?
10. Will the planning capitalize on the abilities and ideas of individuals throughout the enterprise and build morale?

*Standing Plans* (Policies, standard methods, standard procedures, and the like)

1. Can administrative work be simplified by adoption of plans that will be used over and over again?
2. Will efficiency be improved by intensive study to discover the "one best way," and by insistence on the use of such standard methods and procedures?

---

FIGURE 8. *Questions an Executive Should Ask Himself About Planning.*

*Key Questions (Continued)*

3. Is uniformity of action important, and will standing plans help to achieve it?
4. Will standing plans ease the load on hard-worked executives by (a) permitting more decentralization of authority to act, and (b) providing an established behavior pattern to use in appraising action of subordinates?
5. Will use of standard methods simplify training and permit use of less experienced workers?
6. Is the repetition in operations significant enough to justify the effort involved in making standing plans?
7. Can operating conditions be controlled closely enough to make detailed standard methods feasible?
8. Will the expense of preparing the plans and enforcing them more than offset the benefits?
9. How serious is the inflexibility that will arise? Can provision be made for prompt modifications and exceptions when they are needed?
10. Will insistence on standing plans have a bad effect on individual initiative?

*Goals* (Objectives, missions, deadlines, performance standards, and the like)

1. Are the efforts of executives ineffective due to lack of clear-cut objectives?
2. Can plans be dovetailed more easily by identifying goals, sub-goals, and sub-sub-goals?
3. Will the planning process be made easier and more reliable by development of many detailed standards which can serve as building blocks in programming?
4. Will activities that do not contribute significantly to basic objectives be recognized and curtailed?
5. Will personal incentive be improved by providing standards of achievement?
6. Will control activities be more realistic and effective by closely relating planning with control standards?
7. Will prediction and internal control be reliable enough to make the goals really valid?
8. Will the benefits of having clear goals be greater than the added expense of preparing them?
9. Will the goals have to be changed so often that confusion and frustration will result, rather than improved morale?
10. Will the statement of detailed goals lead to unwarranted advanced preparation and reluctance to change?

FIGURE 8 (*Continued*).

decentralize authority so as to end one-man management. Other key executives include a production manager, sales manager, secretary-treasurer, and chief engineer. The company is well known in a narrow field and has been financially successful.[2]

*Objectives.* The Rocklyn Corporation has a clear objective of offering to the trade a top-quality product and the best delivery service available. It makes a narrow line of products for replacement sale only, but seeks to fill this particular niche well. In other words, it does not seek volume sales of a low-priced product, nor has it aspired to great expansion through product diversification. Production facilities are not fully used, so the company is seeking a second product line; but here again the objective will be specialization and distinctiveness.

This basic objective has been very helpful as a guide to further planning and a means of integrating policies and programs. At one time or another the production department has urged mass production of only the fast-selling items, the sales department has suggested a wider variety of products, the treasurer has wanted to be stringent on credit terms. But the general objective has brought the various departments back into line and has promoted consistency of action. The objective also highlights a desirable accomplishment, and the executives of the company take considerable pride in the extent to which they have achieved it.

*Policies.* Policies also constitute an important part of the company's plans. General rules exist regarding the types and location of customers that will be solicited, the general level and the frequency of price changes, the types of parts or materials that will be purchased rather than manufactured, the credit terms that will be granted, the sources from which capital will be obtained, and other similar matters.

These policies save the president and the other executives a great deal of time because they do not have to decide similar issues over and over again. They are important to the decentralization that has taken place because the president can authorize other executives to proceed with action and know that they will follow a path he approves. They are also helpful in assuring consistency of action,

[2] A more complete description of the Rocklyn Corporation is given as one of several comprehensive cases in W. H. Newman and J. P. Logan, *Business Policies and Management,* 4th ed., South-Western Publishing Co., 1959.

which is particularly important when dealing with customers or employees, because each of them resents any favoring of the other man.

Although general policies exist, no attempt has been made to set up detailed policies or to incorporate these standing plans into a manual. For example, in dealing with employees or dealing with material vendors the company has sought to be flexible, meeting each situation on its particular merit. In other areas similar problems have not come often enough to call for a clear-cut policy. Inasmuch as this is a relatively small company where communication between the executives is informal and prompt and where the executives have time to give considerable attention to individual situations, the absence of detailed policy has not been serious.

*Over-all programming.* A third major component of planning in the Rocklyn Corporation is its budget program. Each year a budget is prepared showing month by month the anticipated income and expense and the cash position, along with a projected balance sheet at the end of the year. In practice it has been found desirable to revise this budget at the end of the first six months.

The budget has been a very helpful device in anticipating problems and laying plans to meet them. It has provided a basis for planning production to meet seasonal needs, for determining the number of employees to be hired, temporarily laid off, or discharged, for arranging of bank loans, and for similar activities. Moreover, it has provided a base from which to make either upward or downward adjustments when the level of business activity has changed sharply. Although the budget has not been used as a restrictive device (as are Congressional appropriations), it has increased the president's willingness to delegate authority to other executives because its preparation led to a general understanding as to the course of action that would be followed. The budget also is useful as a standard of performance, and thereby aids in the control process.

Budgeting in the Rocklyn Corporation is not carried beyond one year because of the difficulty of forecasting the demand for products and the supply situation, including labor conditions, availability and prices of raw materials, and similar factors. Detailed departmental budgets are not prepared because the effect of action in the respective departments is relatively easy to trace to the company profit and loss statement; the company feels that the expense of preparing detailed programs for the different departments would not produce a corresponding benefit.

*Projects.* The company makes effective use of the project concept in dealing with special problems. For example, it has set up a special project for the study of pensions for its employees, a new method of inventory control, and possible sale of its products to truck and tractor manufacturers as original equipment (instead of replacement parts). In each of these projects two or more departments were involved, a variety of data was desired from different sources, and the abilities and available time of various individuals had to be considered.

The planning of these investigations on a project basis meant that each phase was assigned to one person and that he knew what the other man was going to do and how his findings would fit into the total picture. Thus, the actual work was delegated to several individuals, and yet the total effort was coordinated and comprehensive enough to lead to a sound decision. With a few exceptions, such as the installation of the inventory control plan, the project planning was rarely carried beyond the assignment of particular parts to individuals. Mapping out in detail just what each person was to do did not offer any great benefits, and in a number of instances would have taken time that could be used better in arriving at a decision promptly.

*Standard methods and procedures.* The departments of the Rocklyn Corporation differ in the extent to which they use standard methods and procedures. The production department has a standard method for the operation of each of the major pieces of equipment. The existence of such standard assures that work will be performed with reasonable efficiency; output standards can be established, and quality is generally maintained; also, the existence of a standard method makes the training of new employees easy.

Significant, however, is that these standard methods reflect primarily the best-known industrial practice and are not the result of detailed motion study by Rocklyn Corporation itself. Consequently, the standard method is not as specific as is found in some shops. Executives of the Rocklyn Corporation point out that a considerable part of the work is paced by existing machinery, so that detailed motion study would increase output by a relatively small percentage; in addition, few operators perform any single job, and the expense of a detailed motion study could not be spread over a large number of machines or activities. Ideas gleaned from equipment manufacturers, trade magazines, and contacts with other manufacturers enable the company to keep up with the best practice but not to originate a change.

The office has established standard procedures for accounting and credit work as well as for the receipt and disbursement of cash. These procedures assure that the necessary action will be taken and that it will be uniform on similar transactions. Also, relatively inexperienced clerks can perform most of the work, even though they do not understand the system well enough to handle unusual transactions. No attempt has been made to establish standard methods for operating office equipment because of the lack of volume of any one type of operation. Girls who operate typewriters and calculating machines are presumed to have learned a standard method in high school or business college, but the company allows them to follow any method they wish so long as a reasonable amount of work is accomplished.

In the sales department even less attention has been given to standard methods and procedures. Most of the sales are made by sales agents who often sell two or three other lines of products and are not technically employees of Rocklyn Corporation. One result of this arrangement is that the company has less control over the activities of its sales representatives. Sales techniques that the company would like to make standard have been suggested, but recent analysis of the actual practice indicates that frequently these suggestions are ignored. Until the company can devise some better means of controlling the individuals concerned, there is little point in developing standard selling methods.

*Detailed single-use plans.* Production scheduling is the only detailed planning for nonrepetitive operations that is done formally. A majority of the employees and most of the company equipment are used for production, and delay in this department would cause a considerable loss of both man-hours and machine-hours. Therefore, the quantity needed of each style and size of product is worked out in advance, and then the operations necessary to manufacture those lots are determined. With these data in hand, work is assigned to individual machines for approximately a month in advance. If some particular job lot is delayed or if a rush order is received, the schedule must, of course, be adjusted, but this can be

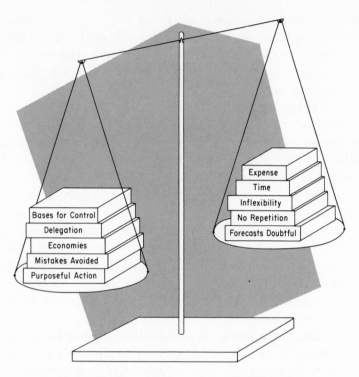

Figure 9. *Pros and Cons of Detailed Planning.*

done with some knowledge of its effect on other work that is already scheduled. As a result of this detailed planning, most delays can be avoided, the personnel needed to operate the equipment can be scheduled in advance, and plans made for either layoffs or special maintenance work during the slack time. This careful scheduling also reduces the inventories that need be on hand in order to insure prompt deliveries to customers. Incidentally, such close scheduling would not be possible if the company did not have output standards based on standard methods.

Of course, considerable planning of nonrepetitive operations is done by various individuals in laying out their own work, but the company has made no systematic effort to influence the extent to which this is done. Outside of the shop the work is quite varied and the staff relatively small, so the executives do not feel that it is worth their time to plan just how each individual should perform each operation. Instead, they allow the employees to use their own initiative, and then if supervision indicates that help is needed, informal contacts permit suggestions by the executive as the work progresses.

*Goals and performance standards.* Clear-cut performance standards have been established only for the operating men in the shop. Here output standards have been given careful attention, inasmuch as the company has an individual and group incentive plan based on a comparison of actual output with standard output. These output standards are also useful in estimating costs and in production scheduling. In addition, there are clearly defined quality standards, which, of course, are necessary in view of the company's over-all objective of selling a top-quality product.

Mention has already been made of the budget and of the production schedule, which can be readily translated into goals. Aside from these and the performance standards of the shop, however, the Rocklyn Corporation made very little use of the goal concept in its planning. A discussion of the basis upon which to distribute a year-end bonus recently brought to light a lack of goals for most of the employees outside of the production department. The company recognized that the comparison of the actual results with the budget was inadequate because sometimes the forecasting was unsatisfactory and for most employees the budget does not reflect their entire performance. For example, the budget does not show promptly the effects of a poor service to customers or bad relations with other outsiders. Much more important than the absence of a basis upon which to distribute bonus is the loss of a positive direction and incentive that goals can provide for the individual. The executives of Rocklyn Corporation are aware that considerable improvement in their planning can be made in this particular area.

The planning of the Rocklyn Corporation has been presented not as an ideal but as representative of a typical, successful, small corporation. To attempt to follow this or any other single enterprise as a model might well be disastrous. Each enterprise must determine the type and the extent of planning that fits its particular needs. The description of Rocklyn Corporation planning does provide a review of some of the types of planning that may be used and some of the advantages and limitations that may result. Perhaps it has also served to emphasize that these planning concepts are practical working tools of the administrator, and not merely abstractions regarding the social processes of group living.

## Good planning—a practical goal

One further point may be in order. A person who contemplates all the planning that is necessary to administer an enterprise of any size may be overwhelmed at the variety and complexity of decisions and interrelations that are present. Fortunately, these decisions can usually be made over a period of time. Almost invariably a number of individuals take part. We have noted that the use of standing plans (policies, standards, methods and procedures, and the like) greatly simplifies the process, and experience frequently provides a useful guide in developing single-use plans.

Also, once a program is developed that will accomplish a given mission, the executive can give most of his attention to those phases of actual operations that may deviate from the plan. In other words, it may be desirable to take a large range of factors into account in formulating plans, but it is unnecessary to review all this information every day the plan is in the process of execution. Wallace Clark has pointed out:

> . . . If an executive must analyze the whole situation and take all of these things into consideration whenever he receives a new figure or report, the task becomes burdensome and is sure to be neglected, although he knows he cannot afford to lose sight of any of the factors.
> . . . The most effective method is for him to lay out a plan which, if adhered to, will produce the results at which he aims. All the variables which could be foreseen have been noted, so when actual progress differs from what was planned, it is evident that something has happened which was not expected and which, therefore, requires attention. . . . . The executive is thus relieved of the necessity for spending time on those phases of his business which are making satisfactory progress and is left free to concentrate his attention on those things which are not moving at the desired rate. . . . He watches the rate of flow of the forces which are beyond his influence and manipulates those which are within his power to control, aiming at the balance which will be to the best interests of his company.[3]

## SUMMARY

Every administrator, from the top executive of an enterprise to the supervisor of a small department, must do some planning. He will do a better job of planning if he understands clearly the different types of plans that he might use, the situations in which each

---

[3] *Executive Planning*, Wallace Clark & Company, p. 9.

type of plan is likely to contribute to the efficiency of the enterprise, and how such plans will enable him as an individual to be a better, and probably less hard-worked, administrator.

The purpose of the last four chapters has been to describe and illustrate a range of plans that have proven to be useful in a variety of situations, and also to indicate the advantages and the limitations that an administrator may expect if he employs them. These are basically simple concepts, and yet in practice thousands of executives have fumbled their planning work because they were not aware of the alternatives available to them.

# 6
# Logistics and Strategy

Two aspects of planning, logistics and strategy, often receive inadequate attention in formal decision-making. They are likely to be troublesome, and yet any experienced executive is keenly aware that a good idea may fail to produce results if its timing and its introduction are not carefully suited to the specific situation. Under some circumstances basic plans can be established first, and then consideration can be given to logistics and strategy. But this sequence is hard to maintain. A more generally useful approach is to think of logistics and strategy as permeating the entire planning structure. Normally, we should include logistics and strategy as factors to be incorporated into goals, policy, programs, and other types of plans.

## LOGISTICS

*Logistics* are concerned with having the right *resources* available at the right *place* at the right *time*. Resources is a broad concept here, including the necessary number of people with the needed knowledge and capabilities, as well as necessary materials, equipment, buildings, supplies, and cash. Thus, a branch sales manager, an office manager, and a building contractor, all have to think about logistics even though the specific resources they deal with differ.

Some logistics problems can be easily resolved—assuming someone in the administrative organization thinks through requirements of the situation in detail and makes sure that resources will be available as needed. Often, however, availability of resources is a limiting factor on plans that can be seriously considered; logistic analysis may show that one plan is feasible while another is not. An East Coast equipment manufacturer, for example, was planning to open a California branch when an opportunity arose to enter the European Common Market. The company desired to expand in both directions, but analysis showed that available technical staff would be sorely needed in California during the same period that expert advice was vital at the European plant. Also, senior executives would have been hard pressed to give close guidance to both expansions. So, opening a California branch was deferred for two years. In fact, a year later a licensee arrangement was negotiated, and plans for a company-owned California branch have been abandoned. A less fortunate illustration of the importance of logistics occurred when a television company failed, because of production changes and delays, to get its highly advertised color sets into the hands of dealers when demands for this model was at its peak. By the time the sets became available, competitors had a firm grasp on a major share of the market.

**Steps in logistics analysis**

There may be several unknowns, and corresponding uncertainty, in the logistics of a situation, but the basic steps of analysis are well known.

1. *Break the activities necessary to achieve the objective into steps or parts.* This involves thinking through in considerable detail just what actions will be necessary. For complex operations major steps may be first identified, and then each of these further subdivided.

2. *Note the relationships between each of these parts.* Especially important are any necessary sequences. In a sales promotion campaign, for example, usually the package must be fully designed before art work for advertising can be completed, and the advertising themes have to be settled before counter displays can be designed. Similarly, in opening a new department at least the underlying organization and work structure should be decided before large numbers of people are employed.

3. *Determine the resources that will be needed for each step.* What are the requirements for specific raw materials, skilled personnel, instruction books, inventories of finished goods, telephone service, delivery trucks, or any other resource? Planning at this stage

cannot be in terms of general averages or financial accounts. A barrelful of half-inch bolts won't help if a single three-inch bolt is necessary, nor will an extra lawyer fill the place of an electrical engineer.

4. *Find out when each resource will be available.* Materials may be in tight supply, or the lead-time for special-purpose machinery may be long. Perhaps key personnel have been assigned to other work. If it becomes apparent that necessary resources will not be available when needed, immediate attention should be given to the possibilities of substitution, subcontracting, or other alternate sources.

5. *Estimate processing time for each step.* How long will it take to complete the step once it is started? For example, what will be the elapsed time between the placement of an order and the receipt of goods; how long will it take to train salesmen once they have reported for the job; how much engineering time will be required after customer specifications have been agreed upon? For some steps these elapsed times may be quite short, whereas for others, such as clinical tests of pharmaceuticals or S.E.C. approval of a new security issue, the period may extend over many months.

6. *Assign definite dates to each step.* These times will, of course, be based on the sequences, the availabilities, and the elapsed times identified by the preceding analysis. The resulting schedule should show both the starting date and the completion date for each part of the operation.

Adjustments are often necessary. For example, if one necessary resource will be unavailable for, say, six months, there may be little advantage in pushing for fast action on other parts of the program. Possibly, difficulties with logistics may be so serious that the entire project will be abandoned. In other instances, the critical items will have been identified, and attention can be focused on speeding these up.

The logistics of a plan can be summarized in a table showing amounts, places, dates, and the like; or in a chart, such as Figure 10. For highly complex logistic problems, such as designing and building a new military weapon system, a PERT sequence analysis may be warranted.[1]

---

[1] For a nontechnical description of this technique, see R. W. Miller, "How to Plan and Control with PERT," *Harvard Business Review*, March, 1962, pp. 93-104.

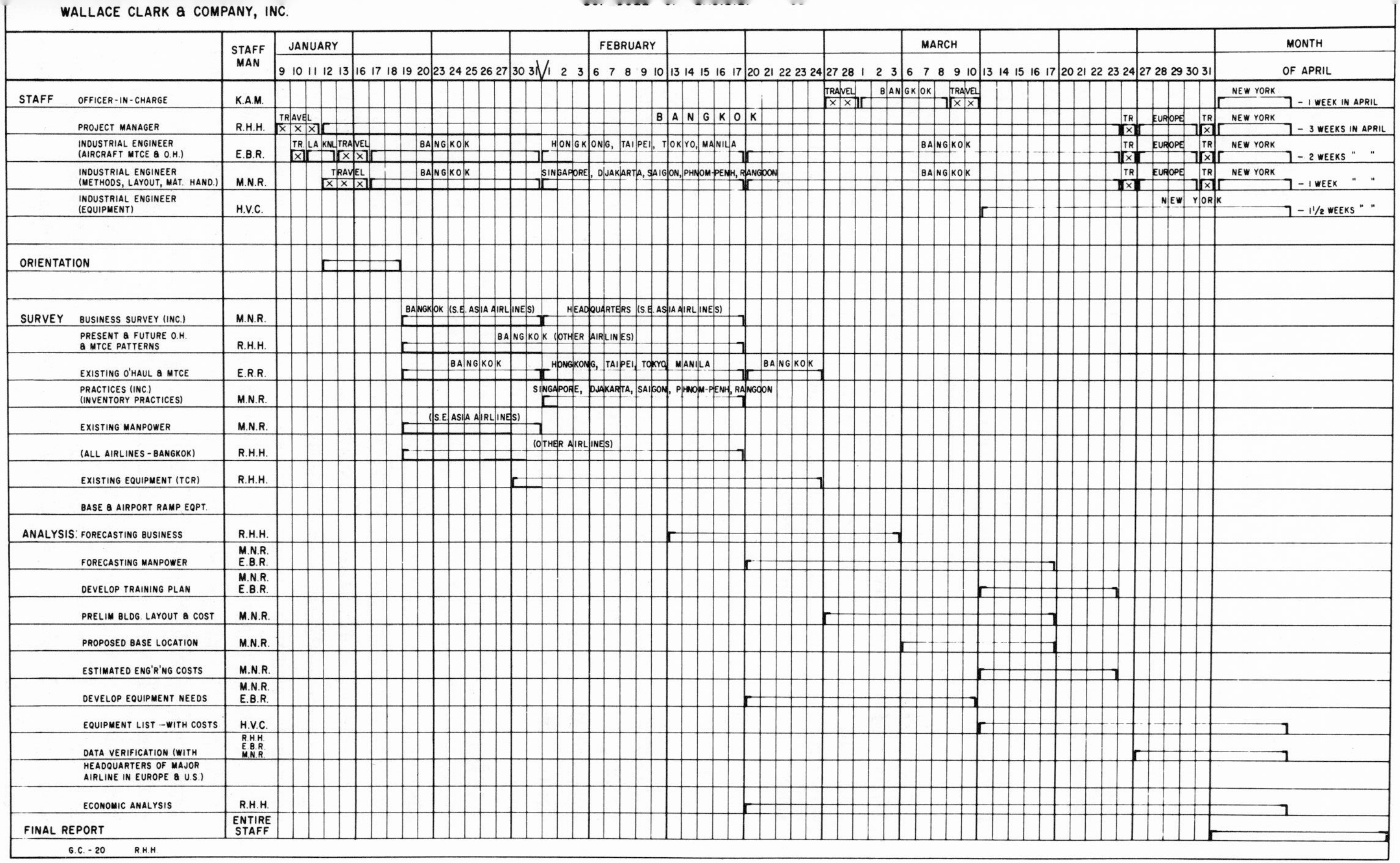

FIGURE 10. *Gantt Chart Showing Job Assignments for Far East Facility Study.*
Courtesy of Wallace Clark & Company Incorporated.

Logistics always involve some degree of uncertainty. An unknown part of the resources will be lost before the operation is completed, and unexpected delays will occur. This uncertainty can be met by (a) including margins of safety in the program, and (b) periodic revisions. Safety margins are expensive, so whenever feasible we put in a single allowance to cover a whole group of risks. For instance, instead of adding a safety margin to each time estimate, a single (and smaller in total) allowance is made at the end on the assumption that not all the estimates will be understated. The undesirability of safety margins at each step was dramatically illustrated during World War II when the Army discovered that it possessed or had on order more pup-tents than total men in service—even though only a small portion of the force would be using pup-tents at any one time. Safety factor had been added upon safety factor in the process of estimating requirements. In logistic planning we want some allowance for uncertainty, but the wise manager will want to know where margins have been introduced and to be sure that they are not pyramided one on top of the other.

### STRATEGIC CONSIDERATIONS IN PLANNING

Logistics deals largely with numerical matters—time, quantities, places, and the like. Subjective judgments regarding risks and values are also involved, to be sure, but hopefully the final plan will be quite specific, perhaps neatly expressed in a Gantt chart. Strategy, by contrast, deals primarily with the interactions of people. It is much more tenuous and responsive than logistics.

*Strategy* is used here to mean the adjustment of a plan to the anticipated reactions of those who will be affected by the plans. Many a plan will run into difficulty if attention is not given to the responses of competitors, customers, material suppliers, fellow executives, and others associated within the enterprise. Whom to advise first, whom to notify, how to say it, when and in what setting to act—these are what Henry Dennison calls "political" questions.

Although strategy has been recognized for centuries as a vital aspect of administration in business, government, and military operations, it has received little systematic attention except in connection with military operations. And the military meaning of strategy has serious limitations for our purposes because there are numerous strategies of cooperation where the idea of "my gain is your loss" has no place.

Many executives rely on intuition and habit in picking a strategy. But strategy is too important to be left entirely to unconscious choice. At a minimum the skillful executive should:

(a) Be aware of alternative strategies he might use (or be subjected to);

(b) Recognize key factors in choosing a particular strategy for a specific situation.

The strategies described below are not necessarily recommended, nor is any moral judgment intended. They may be good or bad, depending upon the situation and the purpose for which they are used, just like any other phase of administration. The list is in no sense complete. Nevertheless, it does suggest possibilities, and it also serves to show the nature and importance of strategy.

**Strategies for initiating change**

*Mass concentrated offensive.* When Marshall Field & Company decided to liquidate most of its $35,000,000 wholesale business, action was taken in all departments at once, inventories liquidated rapidly, and employees discharged promptly with liberal termination pay. The liquidation was costly, but was virtually completed within a year's time. Mr. McKinsey, chairman of the board, recognized that higher prices for some of the inventory might have been secured if it had been worked off over a period of two or three years, but he believed that these higher prices would have been more than offset by the uncertainty and poor morale that would have been inevitable during that period, and by the delay in starting a positive program for the manufacturing activities that were to be retained. Other examples of this strategy include the major reorganization of both General Electric Company and IBM; in each instance, action was fast, uncompromising, and backed by vigorous support of the senior executives.

*Fabianism—avoid decisive engagement.* This strategy, which recommends gradual rather than revolutionary changes, is in sharp contrast to the one just discussed. It was well illustrated by an executive who was brought into a company that manufactured several distinct lines of products and had been coasting along without many new ideas for well over a decade. The new man was slated to become general manager and might well have insisted that the heads of each of the product departments follow his ideas immediately. Instead, he took a newly created position called Sales Promotion Manager which provided him an opportunity to learn the business and to make suggestions to the experienced men for improvement within their departments. If his ideas were not immediately accepted, he did not try to force them through; he waited until they could be put into effect without a sharp clash with the "old guard." Progress on specific projects was slowed down as a result of this strategy, but internal dissension and lack of cooperation were avoided, and the services of men who had important product knowledge were retained.

*Make quick showing.* When there is skepticism, though not necessarily opposition, to a change, a prompt and favorable showing on a minor problem may open the way for more extended study of a knotty problem. For instance, proponents of electronic computers often are able to justify an initial installation on the basis of economies in handling payroll or accounts receivable records. Then having demonstrated merit on such routine operations, they can gain acceptance of more elaborate programming tactics, which may take two years of preparatory work.

Industrial engineers, both consultant and company-employed, have long recognized this strategy: "First find some savings that will cover your salary (or fee), then go to work on the tough problems." In fact, Frederick W. Taylor probably would not have been permitted to continue his years of study on "the art of cutting metals" if he had not also developed patents and other changes which provided more immediate benefits.

*Camel's head in the tent.* Sometimes a small beginning can be made when a total program would be unacceptable. For example, when the central purchasing office at the New York headquarters of a shoe company made virtually all purchases for the company, the manager of a new southern plant asked for permission to buy miscellaneous supplies locally. The request was granted, to reduce paper work and to speed up procurement. This arrangement worked well, and a few months later, on the manager's request, repair parts for machinery were added to the items bought locally. The next year new equipment was being obtained for the plant, and the manager pointed out that since engineers at the plant knew most about what was needed and a local purchasing unit was already operating strongly, orders for the equipment could best be handled by his organization. This, too, was done.

At a later date when pressure was being put on the plant manager to lower his costs, he proposed that he be permitted to purchase his raw materials (except for a few items where quantity purchases were clearly advantageous). Reasons advanced for this change were that raw material inventory could be more closely tied to production schedules, responsibility for quality would rest in one place, contact between suppliers and the plants would be simplified, and the ability of the plant to purchase efficiently had been demonstrated. The request was granted—over the protest of the central purchasing office. Had the plant manager asked for the right to buy all his requirements in the first instance, he would undoubtedly have been turned down; whereas the step-by-step approach finally achieved the result.

*Boring from within.* This strategy, perhaps best known in the operation of a Communist cell, may be used when some executive has an emotional antagonism toward a project or program. The production manager of one company, for instance, had no use for these "new-fangled personnel ideas." The personnel director, however, did borrow one of the outstanding young executives in the production department for a special project, and during the period when the young man was on loan thoroughly indoctrinated him and enthused him regarding modern personnel practice. Some time after the junior executive returned to his former job, a bad situation developed because a man clearly unqualified had been placed in a foreman position. The junior executive took the opportunity to suggest that they might study the foremen who were successful and those who were not in order to determine what to look for when a new man was to be appointed, and thus he began laying the basis for the use of personnel specifications.

At another time considerable argument arose regarding the rate of pay for the maintenance man in one division because he was receiving substantially less than the maintenance man in another division. This provided an opportunity for the junior executive to point out to several different members in the department that a job evaluation program might be helpful. By the end of two years the groundwork had been prepared for the beginning of a really sound personnel program.

These strategies, ranging from mass-concentrated-offensive to boring-from-within, are suggestive of approaches to get something done. Others of the same category might be the Trojan horse, Achilles' heel, sowing seed on fertile ground.

### Joint action strategies

*Strength in unity.* Some executives make a practice of seeking allies to work with them in promoting a change. Thus, if a department head wishes to get salary increases for his employees, he will try to get other department heads to join with him in a general request for higher wages; or if a company wishes to oppose or support legislation pending in Congress, it will seek to get other members of the industry to join together so that their representation may be more effective. The rugged individualist, on the other hand, prefers to play a lone hand.

*Unwilling ally.* Often an individual who is far from enthusiastic about some plan can be made an active ally by assigning him some important role in connection with its execution. Unless he wants to oppose the whole program, he then finds himself a member of the team promoting it. For example, when some consultants recommended basic changes in the organization of a company, a procedures' analyst within the company was asked to work out the detail and assist in the installation of the change. Although he was lukewarm to the basic proposals, he soon found that he was regarded by other employees as a major proponent and that the effectiveness of his work was going to be judged in a large measure by how well the changes worked out. The power-behind-the-throne strategy is sometimes associated with this unwilling-ally technique.

*You scratch my back, I'll scratch yours.* This strategy is well known in the form of *reciprocity* in purchasing and as *log-rolling* in legislative bodies. Actually, the reciprocal exchange of favors is a natural human relationship found in pioneer societies and in political alliances over the ages. Such coalitions usually involve commitments that restrict one's actions to some degree, as well as benefits. Obviously, the question always arises whether the benefits outweigh the restrictions. In reciprocal purchasing, for instance, if the quality, delivery, price, and service of several suppliers is equal, then buying from a firm that is also a good customer imposes no serious sacrifice; but if, say, inferior materials must be accepted, then the restriction imposed by reciprocity may be a great burden. Reciprocal alliances are likely to be stable when each part of the total arrangement is mutually advantageous. If a company or a person finds himself subjected to an onerous restriction, he is apt to press for a better bargain at every opportunity and be open to proposals for new coalitions with different members.

### Defensive strategies

*Keep on sawing wood* or *By their works ye shall know them.* This technique is used by an administrator who wishes to disregard criticism coming his direction. While dramatically illustrated by Galileo and Pasteur who persisted in their experiments despite the criticism of their associates, the technique has been used by countless other people who have faith in what they are doing and put their efforts into doing it well.

*Red herring across the trail.* This strategy consists of a deliberate attempt to divert attention and confuse the issue. It is commonly used in politics; for example, the injection of the race question into discussions where it has no bearing. A salesman who, when being questioned about his expense account, tries to shift the conversation to the danger that competitors may steal a large account is following a similar tack. Here, again, the strategy is not often desirable for operations within an enterprise where it is usually better to lay the cards on the table and deal with issues frankly. However, at times, such as when evading the questions of a man who is being considered for a transfer, deliberately confusing the issue may be appropriate.

*Counter-invasion.* This strategy is seen almost daily in competitive sales promotion. If one company offers a rose bush for a jar top and a five-cent stamp, its competitor is likely to respond by selling his peanut butter in a cocktail glass. Essentially the same thing happened in a company that was having difficulty getting its shipments made promptly and correctly. The manufacturing department, after emphasizing the difficulty, suggested that the shipping department be transferred to it from the sales department, thus giving the manufacturing department control over the physical handling of goods up to receipt by the customer. The sales department, agreeing fully as to the present confusion, countered with the request that warehousing be transferred from the manufacturing department to the sales department so that the sales department would have full control over all activities after the goods were in finished form.

*Divide and rule.* This well-known political strategy has been applied in government situations ranging from city council control fights to England's balance of power in Europe. It has also been used within business enterprises, though usually with serious loss of teamwork and coordination. The chief engineer of one company, for example, hoping to strengthen his position by being the person with the balance of power among the senior executives, deliberately stirred up rivalry between the manufacturing and the sales departments. Obviously, if such a strategy were widely used within an enterprise, it could quickly injure cooperation.

### Cautious strategies

*Passing the buck.* Rightly or wrongly, this technique of transferring blame to someone else is reported to be common practice among army officers. The alacrity with which the Army agreed that the War Production Board should handle the delicate matter of approving the locations and firms to be affected by cutbacks in military programs after World War II suggests that at least someone in that regime recognizes a disagreeable job when it comes along. As collective bargaining between the unions and the large corporations becomes an increasingly public issue, frequent attempts are made to maneuver the negotiations so that the public will believe that the other side is responsible for disagreement and strikes.

*Let someone else pull your chestnuts out of the fire.* While at first glance this strategy suggests cowardice, occasionally its use is quite legitimate. For example, a sales manager may have strong suspicion that the difficulty in quality of a certain product is due to the faulty procedures in the manufacturing department. If he presses the matter with the production manager or the president, he may well be accused of interfering with the other man's affairs. However, if the company has an organization analysis or industrial engineering department, the sales manager may urge this division to look into the matter. In other words, at times a desirable action can be more appropriately taken by someone other than the individual who will benefit from the action.

*Conserve your gunpowder.* In applying incentives, general recognition is given to the wisdom of exercising no more motivation than necessary to accomplish a result and conserving the stronger pressures and tactics until the desired action can be secured only through their use. The same thing is true in other areas. Overselling may not only be wasteful, but it may make later promotions more difficult. The top executive of a company may be deliberately kept out of negotiations with labor unions or material suppliers until a critical point is reached; if he enters at that point, his presence will carry greater prestige and weight.

### Negotiating strategies

*Haggling.* In several Middle Eastern countries prices are normally set by haggling. The seller asks for more than he expects to get, and the buyer offers less than he expects to pay; then the dickering starts. In the United States, despite a one-price tradition, real estate, automobiles, and even household appliances are often sold in the same way. Some people enjoy the process of haggling; perhaps each party feels that he has made a good bargain when the deal is finally closed.

Haggling is widely practiced in many other kinds of negotiations. It is so traditional in union collective bargaining, for instance, that each party commonly thinks up extra "demands" so that he will have something to concede. While often very real differences of opinion have to be resolved before action can be taken, haggling does invite insincerity and prolonged negotiations.

*Lay all cards on the table.* This strategy is the opposite of haggling. It is based on a frank disclosure of strengths, needs, and what the company or individual is prepared to do. The General Electric Company, for example, has been trying to follow this strategy in its union negotiations, incidentally making its position widely known to all employees in advance of bargaining sessions. (The General Electric unions contend that the practice eliminates not only minor haggling but also opportunity to find creative solutions to genuine differences.)

Within companies, or whenever substantial agreement exists on objectives to be sought, the full disclosure strategy is more widely used than when negotiating parties have sharply different goals. Typical plans for supervisory counseling with subordinates, for instance, rest on the assumption that both boss and subordinate are prepared to be completely frank with each other *because* they share the same objectives. When these conditions do not hold, the counseling techniques tend to break down.

*Surprise.* A cardinal feature of military strategy is surprise—catching the enemy off-guard by an unexpected maneuver and by bluffing. If the battle analogy is valid, then surprise may be a good strategy in business. But most relationships within a company and between companies are quite the opposite of a battle. Instead, mutual dependence is essential, and this requires predictable behavior. Under these conditions a strategy of *stability and consistency*—not surprise—is needed. Negotiations about one problem lay a foundation for later negotiations on other problems. If a change in objective occurs, this is explained in advance so as to avoid surprise. As illustrations, consider the difference in the U.S.S.R. and the British approach to negotiating with the U.S.A.

### Timing strategies

*Strike while the iron is hot.* This strategy calls for prompt action while the situation is propitious. Thus, a manufacturer of products depending upon a style or fad, such as hula hoops or beehive wigs, must get his goods on the market before public fancy changes. To cite another example in quite a different area, one wise executive who was being promoted to a vice-presidency because of the inefficiency of his predecessor immediately asked for and got more clear-cut authority than probably would have been granted to him after the current difficulties had been corrected. Similarly, a company wishing to change its channel of distribution from wholesalers to direct sales to retailers made the change promptly when demand was on the upswing so there would be a minimum of sales loss during the transition.

*Things must get worse before they get better.* If the need for a change is not generally recognized, delay is sometimes wise even though the executive is convinced of the need for the action. A controller followed this strategy when he delayed institution of budgets even though he strongly believed they would benefit his company. Other executives disliked new controls, and they would have considered budgets merely as more nuisance with accounting. So the controller waited until the company got into a very tight squeeze with high expenses and low sales; then the idea of budgetary control was welcomed as a device for maintaining a balance between expenses and sales volume. Likewise, the sales manager of a nationally known hosiery company recognized the need of decentralizing to his district manager authority to change prices, but delayed making the change until the desirability of such a move was clearly recognized by the president and other executives of the firm.

*Time is a great healer.* Some actions may be wisely delayed until there is a cooling-off period. In fact, one executive observed after returning from his vacation that he was surprised how many of the things that had been sent to his desk had taken care of themselves apparently quite satisfactorily before he returned. Another executive reports that he postpones, if at all possible, important personnel action for at least a month. During that period it may develop that a man who was scheduled for discharge can be advantageously transferred to another position, or that a clash in personalities which appeared to call for reassignment of duties has been mitigated to the point where no change is necessary.

*Keep one jump ahead.* Attempts to follow this strategy are clearly apparent in the annual change in models of automobiles; for example, in the introduction of economy models, power brakes, air-conditioning, and various body designs. From time to time some of the large industrial companies have attempted to secure favor with their employees by taking the lead in granting wage increases, union-shop provisions, company-financed pensions, or other benefits.

Of course, attempting to lead the parade involves a risk because sometimes the would-be leader finds himself alone on Grand Avenue when the rest of the parade has turned up Broad Street. For example, in the scramble of oil refineries to control their crude oil supply in the years immediately following World War II, the companies that first advanced their buying price usually obtained an advantage while the other companies were making up their minds to follow suit. One autumn, however, a company seeking this advantage was jolted when other companies did not follow it; the supply situation had adjusted itself, so instead of having an advantage, the company found that it was paying well above the market price for its principal raw material.

Timing is one of the most important elements in strategy. It is a factor not only in situations such as those just illustrated, but also in several of the examples to be discussed under other headings.

The variety of possible strategies an administrator might adopt has been indicated, though by no means completely, in the illustrations given in the preceding pages. Clearly, no single strategy is always the right one to follow. Instead, an administrator should choose one, or some combination, that is well suited to the immediate situation. This choice can be made intuitively, but usually strategy is too important to the success of a plan to be left to hunch. How, then, does an executive select an appropriate strategy?

No magic formula or moral code dictates the choice of strategy. We can, however, identify factors that are often important in making a wise choice. The following list is at least suggestive. Not all these factors in this list will be significant in any specific situation, and others may have to be added. But conscious review of these considerations will stimulate the kind of thinking an administrator should do about the strategies he selects.

### 1. Nature of objectives

*Urgency.* The need for prompt results often precludes the use of, say, a Fabian or camel's-head-in-the-tent strategy, and suggests mass-concentrated-offensive. Contrariwise, when immediate results are not so vital, an executive may decide to let-someone-else-pull-his-chestnuts-out-of-the-fire.

*Agreement on objectives.* When the persons affected by a proposed plan agree on desired results, it is feasible to lay-all-cards-on-the-table; any differences of opinion arise from judgment regarding probable results of the proposed action. Quite another situation exists when the persons affected want different results. Then boring-from-within to change objectives, or some strategy that focuses on the particular action, such as haggling or you-scratch-my-back-and-I'll-scratch-yours, is more appropriate.

*Desire for continuing cooperation.* In most business relationships we expect to deal with the same people over and over again. Consequently, today's strategy becomes part of tomorrow's experience. Thus, counter-invasion or passing the buck may haunt us, whereas stability and consistency may facilitate the subsequent actions. Clearly, the time span that needs to be considered affects the choice of strategy.

### 2. Present situation

*Resources available.* A firm with a relatively strong reserve of manpower and capital can give serious attention to a mass-concentrated-offensive, whereas a weaker firm may find strategies such as in-union-there-is-strength or conserve-your-gunpowder more suitable. Even the strong firm—or individual—may not wish to engage in a counter-invasion or to try to keep-one-step-ahead if it is committed to other, more attractive use of its resources.

*Temperament of executives.* Any executive can carry out better a strategy suited to his temperament. Some men, for example, are short on patience and find a Fabian or things-must-get-worse-before-they-get-better strategy hard to live with. Other executives are impressed with facts and try to be entirely logical in their conscious behavior; for them haggling and red-herring-across-the-trail are difficult strategies. Of course, each of us does many things that do not exactly fit our temperament, but the chances of success are better if the action comes naturally.

*Accepted mores.* The acceptance or the resentment to a particular strategy depends partly upon the prevailing mores of the company, industry, and country where it is used. As already noted, haggling is expected in some situations and frowned upon in others. Marked differences will also be found in responses to divide-and-rule, passing-the-buck, and many other strategies. Typically, an executive should operate within the accepted mores; at least any decision to break with tradition should be a conscious choice.

### 3. Chances of success

*Future environment.* An administrator's prediction of future conditions may indicate that a plan will become easier—or more difficult—to put into effect as time passes. This prediction affects strategy. When events are running in our favor, we may adopt such strategies as time-is-a-great-healer or keep-on-sawing-wood. But when we face a now-or-never situation, strike-while-the-iron-is-hot or mass-concentrated-offensive are more appropriate.

*Expected responses.* The administrator must also predict how specific people will respond to a given strategy. All the factors in this list can be considered from the viewpoint of each key person affected by a contemplated action, and then *his* counter-strategy predicted. His objectives, his present situation, his expectations, and his costs will all bear on the way he is likely to respond. Such an analysis may indicate that strategy *A* will have clear sailing, whereas strategy *B* will foment considerable resistance. Or, the analysis may indicate that all strategies will encounter some resistance by at least some people; in this case, the chances of overcoming the resistances have to be compared.

### 4. Costs

*Disruption.* Strategies vary in the amount of disruption they cause to established routines of the company, to informal social relationships, and to personal habits and self-concepts. Perhaps industry and other external behavior may be upset. Some disruption is inevitable, but generally one is wise to keep disruption low.

*Incentives dissipated.* Some strategies may call for large expenditures of energy, out-of-pocket expenses, or even loyalty and goodwill. These are scarce resources useful for many purposes. So one consideration in selecting a particular strategy is dissipating incentives only to the degree necessary to achieve the desired result.

*Blocking other strategies.* A particular course of action may require such a commitment of resources or create so much antagonism that it leaves no good alternatives and no easy retreat. Since outcomes are never certain, such a blocking of alternatives creates a risk—or cost. For example, to keep-on-sawing-wood normally leaves more alternatives open than does counter-invasion; a Fabian approach retains greater flexibility than a mass-concentrated-offensive. The more aggressive strategy may be justified for other reasons, but in the total balance should be weighed the sacrificing of opportunity to resort to alternative strategies.

*Side effects.* Sometimes a strategy will achieve its main objective but have undesirable side effects. For example, a textile company— acting with surprise and at a propitious moment—closed down its New England mill over the protests of both workers and community. The immediate object was accomplished, but part of the cost was union trouble in other plants and reluctance of several financial institutions to extend long-term credit because of the way the action was taken.

Most of the considerations in choosing a strategy in the preceding list cannot be measured accurately; subjective judgment is the main source of data. Nevertheless, analytical, perceptive thinking about the suitability of alternative strategies can pay high dividends in results achieved.

### SUMMARY

When to act, how to get results with the least resistance, what safety factors to allow, how aggressively to move—these are typical issues in logistic and strategic planning. Every administrator should incorporate such considerations into his decisions before initiating action.

Logistics—the provision of the right resources at the right place at the right time—can frequently be expressed in a clear-cut program. Uncertainties and subjective judgments are involved, to be sure, but the final logistic plan is often summarized on a crisp table or Gantt chart. Preparation of such a plan involves: dividing the total operation into steps, noting sequences and other relationships between such steps, determining resources needed, ascertaining when resources will be available and how long each move will take, and then assigning starting and completion dates for each step.

Many managerial actions, however, require a much more subtle analysis than is implied by logistic calculations. The response of people—inside and outside the company—is strongly influenced by the strategy employed. And many strategies are available. The way a change is introduced, the use of allies, the manner of negotiation, timing, defense—all permit a variety of strategies.

In making a choice among these alternative strategies, the administrator should temper his intuition with a consideration of: (a) the nature of his objectives—their urgency, mutual acceptance, and time span; (b) the present situation—resources available, prevailing mores, and temperaments of people involved; (c) the chances of success—as affected by the trend of events and possible counteractions; and (d) the costs—in terms of disruption, incentives dissipated, alternatives foregone, and side effects. Both the short-run and long-run effectiveness of an executive depend, to a significant degree, upon his skill in incorporating such factors into his plans.

SELECTED REFERENCES

Dimock, M. E., A Philosophy of Administration, Harper & Row, Publishers, 1958, Chaps. 2, 17, and 18.

Ginzberg, E. and E. W. Reilley, Effecting Change in Large Organizations, Columbia University Press, 1957, Chap. 3.

Hardwick, C. T. and B. F. Landuyt, Administrative Strategy, Simmons-Boardman Books, 1961.

Liddell Hart, B. H., Strategy, Frederick A. Praeger, Inc., 1954.

Moore, D. G., "Managerial Strategies," in W. L. Warner and N. H. Martin, eds., Industrial Man, Harper & Row, Publishers, 1959, pp. 219-226.

# 7

# The Process of Decision-Making

The preceding discussion has stressed types of plans available to the administrator. In addition to careful thought as to the structure of plans that will be useful, a sound process of arriving at those decisions is also vital. This and the next chapter are concerned with the *how* (decision-making) aspect of planning.

A number of activities have a considerable body of literature dealing with the *how* of planning. Motion study, systems analysis, plant and office layout, market research, advertising-copy testing, employee-attitude surveys, cost studies, and the like, all have their body of literature on how to do it. Generally, these discussions contain an elaboration on the basic analytical approach to business problems, checklists of points to be considered in the particular area, and special techniques for developing useful data (flow charts, statistical analysis, interviews, and the like). They may be exceedingly helpful to the person who is facing a managerial problem in the particular area covered.

Inasmuch as we are concerned here with the administrative process as a whole, these various techniques serve more as case studies from which to develop general principles regarding the process of making plans. This approach has two distinct advantages, even for those who are already familiar with one or more of the specific planning techniques. First, danger always exists that one will become so intrigued with the ratios or charts or formulas used in specific techniques that other, more general aspects of decision-making will be overlooked. Second, many areas of administrative decisions have no appropriate guidebook. A basic technique for arriving at a plan is, then, another of the important tools in the kit of every good administrator.

Discussion of the decision-making (planning) process will be divided into two parts. This chapter deals with the analytical-creative approach to decision-making, an approach which is applicable to virtually every type of administration. Chapter 8 then considers several ways of facilitating decision-making—through simplification, use of organization, operations research, and testing a preliminary choice.

## Traditional approaches to decision-making

Probably the easiest way to make plans is simply to follow previous experience or to copy the actions of someone else. Using this approach, the administrator goes back into his experience or that of his company and finds out what action was taken in a somewhat similar circumstance. If the result was satisfactory, the same course of action is followed; if the result was unsatisfactory, some other plan will be sought. This is done with little regard to the reason why the past action was successful or unsuccessful and no particular thought as to changes in the operating situation. Obviously, such a technique has little of the creative element in it; it may result in the rejection of good ideas that were not given a fair trial; and, since operating situations do change, sooner or later, the enterprise will run into difficulty.

In the follow-the-leader type of planning, an executive attempts to have someone else do his thinking for him. Some apparently successful individual—or enterprise—is singled out, and if he raises his prices, reduces his inventory, establishes a public relation department, fights with the labor union, or installs new equipment, then the executive tries to do likewise. This technique when blindly followed also leads to difficulty; the leader may not always be right, and even if his action is desirable for him, it may not fit your situation.

Both of these approaches to planning tend toward management by tradition and are contrary to the best practice of the present day. Past experience within the enterprise and the experience of other individuals should, of course, be given very careful consideration;

but this information should be subjected to analysis and included with other evidence before major decisions are made.

### Examples of analytical-creative planning

*Taylor, the pioneer.* Among the men who ushered in a new approach to administration, one of the most striking and influential was Frederick W. Taylor (1856-1915). Some knowledge about the man helps to emphasize the ideas for which he stood.

From his boyhood on Taylor demonstrated a bent for devising more efficient ways of doing things. For example, he designed a special tennis racquet for himself. Being small of build, he figured that tall opponents had a distinct advantage over him, and to overcome this handicap he made a racquet which was longer than normal and had a special curve in the throat. It was odd looking, indeed, and no such racquets are on the market today, but it must not have been too bad because he and his partner won the national doubles championship one year.

In his golf, however, Taylor really let himself go. He created a wide assortment of clubs, many of them novel in design, to overcome various playing difficulties on the course. One such club was a Y-shaped putter which was suspended from the shoulders and swung between the legs. By holding his shoulders steady, he was sure of the direction in which the ball would go and could then concentrate on how hard he would hit it. Incidentally, this particular club was so novel (and good) that it was ruled off the course. When one pictures Taylor leaving the clubhouse, that citadel of conservatism, with perhaps an extra caddy or two to carry his paraphernalia, we see a man who certainly wasn't tied down by tradition. He also experimented with the care of golf greens, and before he was done, he probably knew more about taking care of golf greens than any other man in the country. In his avocations as well as in his work, he was challenging, measuring, and inventing.

Taylor was forced to give up the study of law because of difficulty with his eyesight, and he became an apprentice machinist and patternmaker. As long as he was employed as an apprentice and journeyman, he made no special effort to reform shop methods. But shortly after he was made foreman, and thus responsible for seeing that the men under him did a fair day's work, he started to make changes in shop management that were as novel as his putter on the golf course.

Taylor knew that the men were soldiering on the job; he tried with typical success the then customary methods of ordering, pleading, badgering, and threatening to get the men to turn out more work. Unsatisfied with the results, he tried a new plan, namely, a task-and-bonus scheme. Simply stated, the idea was that if the men would turn out a fair day's work, they would be paid a 20 per cent bonus and a proportionately larger sum for any output above the standard. But this required knowing what a fair day's work was, and Taylor was not willing to accept past experience as the standard.

The amount of work a man could reasonably be expected to turn out depended upon the materials with which he worked, and this led to material standardization and quality control; it depended upon the way a man performed his work, and this after years of investigation led to the classic study on the art of cutting metals; it depended upon having new work immediately available for the workman as soon as he finished the job he was on, and this led to careful scheduling and internal transportation; it depended upon having the right man selected and properly trained, and this led to certain phases of personnel work; it depended upon having machinery in proper running condition, and this led to programs of preventive maintenance; it depended upon having the proper tools in good condition, and this led not only to a centralized toolroom but eventually to the invention of a high speed cutting steel (the patent for which Bethlehem Steel Company later paid $100,000).

Once management brought these conditions under control, the worker who cooperated with the plan could double or treble his daily output to the benefit of both himself and his employer. We see in Taylor a man whose unwillingness to accept the customary way of doing things led him by successive steps from his original problem of supervision into such things as the invention of a new steel.

His mechanical inventions first won fame for Frederick Taylor. Following a demonstration at an exposition in Paris in 1900, visitors came from all over the world to the Bethlehem shops where he served as superintendent (until his revolutionary ideas and uncompromising insistence upon them brought on a clash with top management). Taylor, however, insisted that these were but specific illustrations of a more basic approach to management problems. The important thing, he said, was not the particular techniques that happen to apply in a machine shop, but the attitude of mind of the executives. That attitude, that approach, which has been

---

### Commander's Estimate of Situation

1. *Mission*

   A statement of the task and its purpose. If the mission is general in nature, determine by analysis what task must be performed to insure that the mission is accomplished. State multiple tasks in the sequence in which they are to be accomplished.

2. *The Situation and Courses of Action*

   a. Determine all facts or in the absence of facts logical assumptions which have a bearing on the situation and which contribute to or influence the ultimate choice or a course of action. Analyze available facts and/or assumptions and arrive at deductions from these as to their favorable or adverse influence or effect on the accomplishment of the mission.

   b. Determine and list significant difficulties or difficulty patterns which are anticipated and which could adversely affect the accomplishment of the mission.

   c. Determine and list all feasible courses of action which will accomplish the mission if successful.

3. *Analysis of Opposing Courses of Action*

   Determine through analysis the probable outcome of each course of action listed in paragraph 2c when opposed by each significant difficulty enumerated in paragraph 2b. This may be done in two steps—

   a. Determine and state those anticipated difficulties or difficulty patterns which have an approximately equal effect on all courses of action.

   b. Analyze each course of action against each significant difficulty or difficulty pattern (except those stated in paragraph 3a above) to determine strength and weaknesses inherent in each course of action.

4. *Comparison of Own Courses of Action*

   Compare courses of action in terms of significant advantages and disadvantages which emerged during analysis (par. 3 above). Decide which course of action promises to be most successful in accomplishing the mission.

5. *Decision*

   Translate the course of action selected into a complete statement, showing *who, what, when, where, how,* and *why* as appropriate.

---

Source: War Department, *Staff Officers' Field Manual, FM 101-5,* U.S. Government Printing Office, 1960, p. 142.

FIGURE 11. *Army Method for Estimating the Situation.*

called scientific management, can well be applied to problems of administration in any field.

*Army doctrine of planning.* The analytical approach to planning is universal in its application, just as Taylor predicted. Turning to an entirely different field of activity we find Army men talking of the *estimate of the situation.* This is the mental process the officers are expected to go through in arriving at a plan of action. The recommended steps in making an estimate of the situation are briefly summarized in Figure 11, which is taken from a basic Army manual.

Although expressed in Army language and referring to a military situation, the steps recommended have general applicability. These ideas—clarifying the purpose or objective, assembling all pertinent information, identifying possible alternative courses of action, weighing the probable consequences of each alternative, and, finally, deciding what is to be done—are as applicable to running an insurance company or a Y.M.C.A. as they are to an Army.

## BASIC PHASES IN DECISION-MAKING

Decision-making involves four basic phases: Each phase has its own requirement that must be met if that part of the planning process is done well. For an executive to make a wise decision rationally, he must:

- Diagnose the problem properly.
- Conceive of one or more good solutions.
- Project and compare the consequences of such alternatives.
- Evaluate these different sets of consequences and select a course of action.

### Diagnosis

Decision-making techniques have no practical value until someone has answered the question, "What is the problem?" Typically, a problem originates when an executive becomes acutely conscious of an unsatisfied need. A variety of circumstances may give rise to such a felt need. Internal reports may indicate poor operation; pressure may arise from customers, bankers, or other outside interests to modify or improve the services rendered; the executive may want to emulate other well-managed companies; or, preferably, the smart executive may forecast a social or technological change and see new opportunities in adapting to it.

*Sharpening the objective.* A felt need, however, is only the beginning of good diagnosis. The typical administrator is confronted with a vast array of facts and forecasts as well as pressures to devote energies to problems that are already clearly recognized. He will secure attention to new problems only if he is able to single out from this miscellaneous array of facts and influences certain objectives—"results to be achieved."

This new objective should be related to other aims of the enterprise. We have already noted that every going enterprise has a whole structure of objectives, policies, programs, and other types of plans. How does the new goal fit in with this established structure? It should be either compatible with the existing structure, or if a change is contemplated, this should be clearly recognized.

Moreover, there is a question of how specifically to define the objective. The president of a firm making printing presses, for example, became concerned about improving delivery to his customers. In exploring this problem, the question was raised about defining the objective as quicker deliveries, or building finished goods inventory which would permit quicker deliveries, or standardizing products and subassemblies so that higher finished inventory would be economically feasible, or the forecast of future customer demands which would provide specifications for standardized products. The more specific the objective the easier it will be to tackle. On the other hand, narrowing problems too far is risky; perhaps some of the broader steps in the means-end chain will have ruled out possibilities that warrant careful consideration. In the previous illustration, for instance, if the printing press company could have devised some practical way of getting customers to place their orders farther in advance, this might meet the president's desire for improved deliveries and also retain greater flexibility in the design of its products.

Time spent on thinking through just what is desired often saves enormous expenditures of energy in later phases of the decision-making process.

*Identify obstacles.* Good diagnosis not only specifies results desired; it also identifies obstacles that must be overcome to reach these ends. That is, what stands in the way of getting from where we are to where we would like to be?

The identification of key obstacles calls for keen insight. For example, for years people believed that food left in tin cans would cause ptomaine poisoning. Can manufacturers spent large sums trying to find a lining that would overcome this disadvantage of their product. *Then* further diagnosis showed that the real obstacle to food preservation was care of the food, not the can itself. In this instance, the objective was sharp enough but the key obstacle was far from clear.

Too often *symptoms* are mistaken for real causes of a problem. The directors of a small insurance company, for example, were much concerned that the ratios of office and administrative expenses were high in relation to the company's volume of business. They exerted considerable pressure to reduce these expenses. In fact, the office expenses could not be significantly reduced because cutting the payroll would have forced the use of inefficient procedures. The real difficulty was a lack of sales volume large enough to support an economic office system.

The difficulty of identifying the key obstacle showed up in a department store that was having trouble with its merchandising department. Improved organization was considered the main hurdle to better performance; much attention was given to job definitions and then redefinitions, and relationships between personnel were studied in detail. The real difficulty was the merchandising manager himself. When a successor was appointed—a man of quite different temperament and perhaps better merchandising sense—marked improvement occurred within a few months.

The distinction between a key obstacle and a symptom is this: When a symptom is removed, the trouble persists; but when a key obstacle is overcome, the situation improves. Just as a medical doctor looks for the cause of a fever rather than treating the fever itself, so a business administrator should look for key obstacles to a stated goal.

*Recognized limits within which the solution must fall.* Thorough examination of a problem often reveals a number of conditions which must be met for a solution to be acceptable. The available *resources* may be limited. A closely held U.S. firm, for instance, wished to expand in the European market but had only limited capital that could be devoted to the expansion. This precluded building a new plant or buying a large going concern; instead, attention was focused on licensing arrangements, subcontracting production work, and the like. A manufacturer of power plant equipment, to cite another case, wished to expand in the electronic control field but soon recognized that the size of its engineering staff would permit only applications of known techniques; it had neither the personnel nor the office space to undertake completely new kinds of control work.

Another common limitation is *time*. If your president is asked to testify before Congress two weeks hence, there probably will not be time to compile a lot of original data. Or, the desire to beat competitors in marketing a new type of product will impose significant time limitations on development work.

Existing company *policies and activities* may be so important that an acceptable solution to a new problem will have to conform to them. The maintenance of the reputation of a clothing store for high-style merchandise, for instance, may be so valuable that any expansion which tended to undermine this public image would be unacceptable. Some companies have to place such stress on pension rights and stability of employment that they are very reluctant to undertake activities which have high seasonal or cyclical fluctuations.

Care must be taken not to place too many restrictions on acceptable solutions since this may arbitrarily rule out major innovations. The distinction should be made between essential and desired characteristics. Nevertheless, a recognition of acceptable boundaries, if any important ones exist, adds to the clarity of the diagnosis.

Diagnosis, then, is considerably more than an uneasy feeling that some activity might be performed better. It should be forward-looking and specify: (a) a result that is desired, (b) the key obstacle(s) to achieving this result, and (c) any boundaries imposed on acceptable solutions. One further comment is important. Rarely does an initial diagnosis remain unchanged. As we search for possible alternatives, new aspects of the problem often occur to us. Projecting the consequences of various alternatives may lead us to revise our objectives or introduce new limits. To keep problem-solving dynamic and to take full advantage of new ideas, we should remain ready to reconsider, and if necessary restate, the problem. Any restatement, however, should contain the three attributes of good diagnosis that have been discussed above.

**Conceiving good alternatives**

Once a problem has been well stated, the decision-maker must find possible solutions. Often good alternatives are quickly identi-fied: past experience, practice of competitors or other firms, suggestions by interested parties, such as equipment manufacturers, employees, or customers, are normal and highly useful sources of ideas. In fact, the initial recognition of a problem may have resulted from a suggestion of a specific action made by one of these interested parties.

*Need for creativity.* Helpful as such ideas are, the executive who relies entirely on such sources is headed for trouble. Obviously, an executive can never lead the parade if he relies upon a "me too" approach to his problems. Even more significant is the fact that each operating situation is unique in at least some respects, and even a ready-made proposal must be adapted to the local situation. The Wright brothers may have made the first flight in a heavier-than-air machine, but many modifications were necessary before a dependable aircraft was developed. Similarly, the modern supermarket is a far cry from the case-lot warehouses that sprang up during the depression of the '30s, and the end is not yet in sight.

These adaptations, made one upon another, often are as important in terms of a total innovation as a single dramatic discovery of, say, Salk vaccine. The point is, conceiving of creative solutions to problems occurs in many places and in many degrees. Some degree of creativity should be an integral part of millions of managerial decisions. With accelerated change in our social and technological environment, conceiving of creative alternatives is becoming even more important than it has been in the past.

Important as creativity is, surprisingly little systematic study has been done on how to encourage it. In the broad field of business, only advertising and product and process development have been explored with any rigor to find out what contributes to a man's creativity. In fact, the usual emphasis on logic and scientific validation may well have reduced the creative abilities of many executives. Nevertheless, some useful generalizations can be drawn about creativity by individuals and within groups.

*Personal search for novel ideas.* Probably the first requisite for an individual to have creative ideas is a willingness to entertain novel ideas. He has to be prepared to give up old ways of thought, to think differently and independently of other people, and to let what may appear to be "screwball" ideas flow from the unconscious to the conscious level of his mind. He must not be so preoccupied with always being right that all novel ideas are screened out—the good ones along with the silly ones.

Also, the creative person works hard in priming the mental pumps. This entails an active interest in a wide variety of subjects, familiarity with various aspects of the particular problem involved, along with an intensity and persistence in the search for new possibilities. Generating useful ideas is hard work; it is not merely a matter of lucky inspiration.

Assuming a person has these qualities—tolerance for novel ideas and intense curiosity about the problem as well as the world in general—several devices may stimulate a mental leap from the known to the new. One suggestion is to change attributes. A particular attribute of the problem is singled out, for example, appearance, raw material, personal motivation, financing, or the like; then all sorts of modifications of this attribute are imagined. This may or may not generate some useful possibilities. Then, another attribute is similarly explored, and so on with still other attributes. Numerous combinations are, of course, possible, and hopefully out of this effervescence one or more useful alternatives will emerge.

Another suggestion is to think in terms of analogies or metaphors. Suppose the treasurer is concerned about the use of capital in his company. He might say the flow of capital is like the circulation of blood in the human body. The rate of blood circulation depends not only on the heart action itself but also on gland secretions and nervous responses influencing the heartbeat. These thoughts, in turn, suggest a flexible regulation in capital flow based upon stimulation and retarding influences at different spots in the company, and from this some ideas for new control mechanisms may emerge.

Obviously, some individuals will be more adept in creative thinking than others, but almost any of us can increase the creative ideas we have if we seriously try to do so.

*Permissive atmosphere.* Creative ideas are more likely to be suggested in a permissive atmosphere. If a novel suggestion is greeted by: "What evidence do you have that it will work?" "Oh, we tried that ten years ago." "Where do you go to think up crazy ideas like that, George?"—the man with the idea will soon learn to keep his thoughts to himself. He probably will stop giving attention to novel ideas which occur to him, and opportunity for stimulating exchange of unusual thoughts with other members of the company will be lost.

A permissive atmosphere needs systematic cultivation. In this connection, *permissive atmosphere* means that members of the organization feel free to make proposals even though these ideas are at variance with past practices, group norms, or the views of influential executives; that supervisors and associates give positive encouragement to a person who wants to do something different; and that mutual respect for individuality is strong enough so that a person does not lose caste if he expresses an "off-base" idea.

This kind of atmosphere is difficult to maintain throughout an enterprise. In nearly every company there are departments where the technology dictates disciplined, dependable, standardized work. Other departments may have such irregular employment or high turnover that feelings of mutual respect and openness do not have time to develop. A highly permissive atmosphere is simply unsuited to such departments.

The real difficulty arises because we are wont to worship the idol of consistency—perhaps even conformity. Our democratic tradition that all men are equal and our fear of the abuse of power put pressure on a manager to treat everybody alike. This pressure creates a tendency to extend the management attitudes and practices necessary for large operating departments to all divisions of a company. If a highly permissive atmosphere is not well adapted to the major departments, we find a tendency to rule it out all over the organization.

The issue then becomes where, when, and how to introduce a permissive atmosphere within a total organization. Very large companies such as A. T. & T. and Standard Oil (New Jersey) may create physically and legally separate entities to do their basic research work; the academic atmosphere of the Bell Labs is renowned. Many smaller companies also do administer their research divisions or advertising divisions differently than their large operating departments. Occasionally, a "longhair" is given special treatment within, say, a controller's division. But frictions are apt to develop when people who have frequent interaction are guided by different styles of management.

So, even though we recognize that a permissive atmosphere is desirable for men with creative jobs, we have much to learn about how to provide this encouragement for some men and not for others within the same department.

A related issue is how much we can vary the degree of permissiveness for various activities of a single individual. Judging from the Russian successes in the physical sciences, one can be highly permissive with respect to some subjects and quite authoritarian with respect to others. Can we also turn permissiveness on and off in different periods of time? More specifically, can we expect subordinates to feel free to make creative suggestions during the early planning stages of a project and then switch to enthusiastic execution of an officially approved program even though it is at variance with their earlier suggestions? We will have a much better chance of making this switch successfully if (a) we all recognize how creative ideas are generated, and (b) we clearly announce when tentative proposals are wanted and when discerning judgment is expected.

**Projecting consequences of various alternatives**

After a problem has been diagnosed and several good alternative solutions have been identified, the decision-maker must forecast the consequences of following each alternative. This third phase of decision-making involves: (a) picking the crucial factors on which to concentrate attention in making projections, (b) actually forecasting a set of consequences of each alternative, and (c) since some uncertainty will inevitably exist, attaching subjective probabilities that the predicted consequences will occur.

*Pick key factors to forecast.* When predicting the results of a proposed action, we naturally consider its expected contribution toward the objective defined in our diagnosis of the problem. *In addition,* most alternatives have effects which are not related to the stated objective. Costs will probably be affected. And other consequences (the classic example is the labor relations result of a proposed technological change) may be quite important in appraising a particular course of action.

From a practical viewpoint, the decision-maker cannot attempt to forecast everything that bears on the desirability of each alternative. Too many factors can quickly push the analysis beyond human comprehension. Consequently, one must pick crucial factors and concentrate on these. The issue is how to think about the total environment so that the insignificant aspects are dropped from consideration and careful attention is focused on the crucial aspects. For example, what factors should an accounting firm consider in deciding whether to open its own office in Malaya or Peru? Or, what factors should be considered in appointing a Negro as advertising manager?

*Make the forecasts.* This is easier said than done. The outcome of an alternative will be affected by what other people do as well as by our own action. So, we must think of *both* the operating conditions over which we have little or no influence, and the probable results of action we can initiate. Among the operating conditions often important in business decisions are industry sales volume and prices, labor supply (skill, strikes, turnover, wages, and the like), availability and price of raw materials, actions of competitors, government regulations, interest rates and availability of capital, and technological changes in both production and marketing. The consequences resulting directly from our own action are as diverse as the alternatives we may be considering.

Much attention has been given to broad economic forecasting and within a firm to predicting operating costs. Figure 12 suggests an approach to appraising the outlook for sales and profits of a company. But for many factors involved in managerial decisions, we lack adequate forecasting techniques or underlying theories. And without a theory as to why the particular factor behaves as it does, forecasting is hazardous indeed. While we are waiting for a full array of forecasting theories—and the necessary facts to use them effectively—we shall have to rely in many areas upon the intuitive hunches of experienced businessmen.

Emotional bias is apt to slip into forecasts, especially when they lack a firm, practical base. Most of us dislike unpleasant conclusions and tend to err in underestimating costs and difficulties. Sound decisions are more likely to emerge if we *consciously guard against such bias*—being as objective and realistic as possible in our forecasts and then taking a calculated risk if we wish to do so.

*Attach subjective probabilities.* Since our ability to forecast accurately is severely limited, all projections are more or less uncertain. The executive needs some idea of how large such uncertainty is for each critical factor in a decision—he needs some feel for the magnitude of the risk. Statistical probability theory helps in a few types of situations, but usually the decision-maker must think in terms of the odds—or chances—that a particular event might happen. He makes a subjective appraisal of the probabilities. For instance, if he is concerned about foreign competition, he estimates the chances of a tariff reduction on the main product of the company; or, perhaps he thinks about the odds that a key executive will resign.

For many major factors we should not be satisfied with a simple statement that, say, the chances are six out of ten that company-

FACTORS IN APPRAISING OUTLOOK FOR A COMPANY

I. Outlook for the Industry

  A. Demand for Products or Services of the Industry
    1. Usefulness of and desire for products
    2. Stability of desire for products
    3. Ability of customers to pay for products

  B. Supply of Products or Services
    1. Capacity of the industry
    2. Labor costs and availability
    3. Material costs
    4. Taxes and other operating costs

  C. Competitive Conditions in the Industry
    1. Size, strength, attitudes of companies
    2. Organization of the industry
    3. Government regulation and support

  Conclusions:
  Volume and profit outlook
  Crucial factors to achieving future success in industry

II. Position of the Company in the Industry

  A. Market Position of the Company
    1. Relation of company sales to those of industry and leading competitors
    2. Standing of company products
    3. Reputation of company in major markets
    4. Strength of distribution system

  B. Supply Position of the Company
    1. Comparative location
    2. Relative efficiency of plants
    3. Relative engineering and research strength
    4. Access to materials

  C. Special Competitive Considerations
    1. Relative financial strength
    2. Ability of company management

  Conclusions:
  Relative strengths compared with crucial industry success factors
  Distinctive niche
  Integrated management structure for this niche

FIGURE 12. *Scheme for Forecasting Company Outlook. Use as background forecast when deciding a specific problem, or as an early step in an over-all appraisal of a company.*

owned distributors would increase sales twenty per cent. Such an estimate may represent the best informed projection that can be made, but the decision-maker will probably also want to know something about the deviations above and below the twenty per cent. For instance, if we know that the sales increase is unlikely to be less than fifteen per cent or more than twenty-five per cent, we face quite a different situation than one in which a possibility exists that sales may actually fall ten per cent or rise as much as fifty per cent. In other words, we need a subjective judgment about the standard deviation as well as about the most likely single value.

### Making the choice

With a problem well defined, good alternatives identified, and the likely consequences of each alternative forecast as best we can, one might assume that the final choice of action to be taken would be easy, if not obvious. Such is not the case. Typically, each alternative will lead to a whole set of consequences, and these outcomes may occur in varying degrees at different times, with different probabilities attached to each degree. A complex system of values is needed to make a choice between these various sets of consequences.

*Valuation of projected results.* In abstract theory, and in folklore, a business executive simply picks the alternative that will yield maximum profit to his company. Unfortunately, this is a gross oversimplification; it is unworkable and probably unsound. While many projected consequences can be expressed in dollar terms, and if they occur at different times, they can be reduced to present values by a discounting procedure, other consequences are more difficult to appraise. The importance of market position, animosity of government officials, engineering experience with a little-known process, reputation as a good place to work, morale of older employees, and numerous other intangibles are hard to measure. We have no *practical* way of converting many such factors into long-range profits for the firm, and consequently we must deal with these items in their intangible form rather than in terms of some convenient common denominator.

Moreover, there is doubt that focusing on profits alone will lead to the wisest decisions. Additional short-run profits are often sacrificed for greater continuity of the enterprise, stability of employment, assistance in defense work, attractiveness of the local community, fair treatment of suppliers and customers, consideration of loyal employees, and similar ends. Some people argue that such goals are valid only insofar as they contribute to the long-run profitability of an enterprise, at least indirectly by creating a good climate in which to conduct business. But this line of reasoning is not very useful because we have no clear-cut way to translate, say, company stability into an equivalent amount of current profits. When making concrete decisions, we simply have to deal with an array of goals which sometimes supplement and sometimes compete with each other. Profits are a major consideration in making a final choice, but not the only factor.

*Sharpening the comparison.* Fortunately, the decision-maker does not need a complete system of values in an absolute sense. His task, at this stage of the process, is merely to decide that one set of consequences is preferable to another set.[1] Such a comparative evaluation may be sharpened in the following ways:

(1) We should utilize the economists' notion of *marginal* value. Rarely do we face a simple choice between, say, high profits and security of employment. Instead, the choice is usually between a little more profit or a little more stability, and the values attached to these increments of profit or stability depend in part on how much we already have. If our bank is about to foreclose our mortgage, a little more profit is highly significant, whereas if we are in good financial condition and earning a rate of return on investment that is more than the industry average, then the additional profit will have less importance to us. Similarly, the importance of stable employment will be greater if we are talking about retaining a core of highly skilled employees than it will be for new workers if the normal turnover is high anyway.

(2) Abrupt shifts in marginal value may permit us to use the *satisfying* concept. For some types of result, we may desire a given degree of achievement, but attach little value to anything beyond that degree. We simply concentrate on a satisfactory achievement for that particular factor. For example, black smoke pouring out of our factory chimney may be very objectionable to the local community, but once we have cut the carbon content to a stipulated level, there may be little gain in proceeding further.

---

[1] This assumes that the alternatives being considered fall within the limits set forth in the diagnosis. Incidentally, maintaining that *status quo* may be such an alternative.

(3) The size of the *maximum risk* that will be tolerated deserves attention. When thinking about adding new product lines, for instance, a particular company may reject all proposals which have more than a ten per cent chance of seriously injuring the existing business. Or, another firm may say that it will not consider any product unless there is at least one chance in four that the new line will double company sales volume in five years.

The most the three preceding suggestions do is to simplify the task of making a choice. The executive still must decide what results he considers good and what results he considers undesirable, and he must have some sense of the *relative* importance as they present themselves in operating problems. The administrator, being a man of action, cannot evade making value judgments.

## Summary

Unlike Topsy who "just growed," good plans call for a lot of conscious, deliberate nurturing. The various forms plans may take—policies, programs, and the like—were explored in previous chapters, but the administrator is still left with the question, "By what mental process do I select good plans?"

This process of decision-making can be divided into four phases: diagnosing a problem, finding good alternative solutions, projecting the likely consequences of each alternative, and selecting the one that on balance promises the greatest advantages. Each of these phases poses its own difficulties and opportunities for exercise of executive skill.

A challenging conclusion emerging from a careful look at the decision-making process is that quite different mental attitudes and abilities are needed. Sensitive perception coupled with logical analysis are especially important in diagnosis and in projection; originality and imagination play a larger part in the creative search for alternatives; and subjective valuations are unavoidable in final selection.

Executives possess these abilities in varying degrees, and they tend to overemphasize those aspects of decision-making where they excel. Consequently, an important benefit of a full grasp of each phase of the decision-making process is a personal awareness of where one is likely to fall short—that is, where skill should be cultivated and/or counsel from others sought.

## SELECTED REFERENCES

Gordon, W. J. J., *Synectics: The Development of Creative Capacity*, Harper & Row, Publishers, 1961.

Jones, M. H., *Executive Decision Making* (Rev. ed.) Richard D. Irwin, Inc., 1962.

Newman, W. H., and C. E. Summer, *The Process of Management*, Prentice-Hall, Inc., 1961, Part III.

Osborn, A., *Applied Imagination* (Rev. ed.) Charles Scribner's Sons, 1961.

Simon, H. A., "Theories of Decision-Making in Economics and Behavioral Sciences," *American Economic Review*, June 1959, pp. 253-283.

Stein, M. I. and S. J. Heinze, *Creativity and the Individual*, Free Press of Glencoe, Inc., 1960.

# *8*

# Aids in Decision-Making

The variety of factors that arise in administrative decision-making are legion, especially in dynamic situations and in large firms. Nevertheless, several basic issues appear again and again in different planning situations. And, concepts exist to help an executive deal with these general issues. A review of these concepts will suggest how the basic decision-making process, just described in Chapter 7, can be more effectively applied in a complex organizational setting.

These ways of facilitating the making of decisions include: simplifying the task of planning, organization for planning, logical aids in choice, operations research, and testing a choice.

## SIMPLIFYING THE TASK OF PLANNING

The process of making a plan outlined in the preceding chapter—diagnosis, creative search for alternatives, projection of each alternative, and making the choice—imposes a very heavy burden on the administrator. If each time he laid out a course of action, he personally had to consider all alternatives of each particular act and compile information on the wide variety of factors that might affect a choice among these alternatives, the task would be staggering. In practical application some means of simplifying the task must be found.

### Use standard parts

Just as the use of standard parts greatly simplifies manufacturing operations (in fact, is prerequisite to modern production), so, too, can standard parts simplify planning. The decision-maker takes predetermined standards, such as output per man-hour, pounds of material per unit of product, sales calls per day, advertising expense per month, percentage of bad-debt loss, normal seasonal fluctuation in sales, plant and equipment required per thousand units of output, investment in accounts receivable per dollar of sales, and uses these standards in preparing his new plan. B. E. Goetz calls these the "building blocks of managerial planning and control." [1] In making a particular plan the administrator often uses a variety of these standards and simply assumes that they are correct.

In a similar way the administrator assumes that standard methods and standard procedures will be followed. This is a very important aspect of military planning where standing operating procedure is developed and practiced for years ahead of time; then, in an actual maneuver, the commander concentrates on the strength of his various forces and the place and time he will use them, assuming all the while that the detailed action will be governed by the standing plans (and indoctrination). Likewise, the sales manager and production manager assume a customary behavior pattern as they lay out their plans. Clearly, the more an administrator can use such performance and operating standards, the easier is his planning task.

The use of standard parts does not preclude a very thorough examination from time to time of the parts themselves. While at a given moment the practical procedure for an administrator is to assume that the output standards and operating standards are correct, he may find himself in serious difficulty if this assumption is not true. Therefore, these detailed plans should be developed by careful analysis prior to the time that they are used as building blocks in a broader plan. Thus, we find support for those who believe planning should be approached "from the bottom up," as is strongly advocated in the following statement by Wallace Clark:

> Experience has shown us that it is far better to begin at the bottom in installing methods of management. For example, in planning it is not wise to start with general programs for the plant and move down to the schedules for the individual shops, because that method becomes too theoretical and does not win the understanding and support of the shop foremen. It brings more effective and lasting results to begin the installation of planning methods down in the shops themselves, starting

[1] *Managerial Planning and Control*, McGraw-Hill Book Company, 1949, chapter 5.

with the foremen and helping them plan the work to be done on their machines the following day. A few well qualified men are trained to do the planning there, where they learn accurately the capacity of the machines, the capabilities of workmen and see at firsthand the difficulties which face the foremen.[2]

It may not be practical to start at the bottom and work up when a plan is needed before there is time to complete the numerous detailed studies, or when operating conditions cannot be controlled, as they can be in a production shop such as the one discussed by Mr. Clark. Nevertheless, if it has not been practical to develop the operating standards ahead of time by careful analysis, then the administrator must either accept the possibility of error in his planning, or give up the benefits of this simplifying method.

**Plan within recognized limits**

Another way to simplify the planning task is to work within certain recognized limits or frames of reference. Commonly used devices of this sort are:

1. *Limits set up in diagnosis of the problem.* We have already noted that restrictions may be placed on resources to be used, time action is to occur, results to be achieved or avoided, and the like.
2. *Planning premises.* Especially when activities of departments are interdependent, assumptions about volume of work, price changes, availability of labor or other future conditions may be defined for the enterprise as a whole—and all plans built on these same premises.
3. *Company objectives and policies.* For most decisions the objectives and policies already established by the company are simply accepted as guides for more specific plans.
4. *Intermediate goals.* Rather than think about a broad scope of long-range plans, often a specific, intermediate result to be achieved within, say, a year's time is used as the focus for current decisions.

Thus, the executive accepts the mission or objective set for him by his superior; he accepts the companywide policies in accordance with which he is expected to operate. He may also be told to make certain basic assumptions regarding the sales volume, price and availability of materials, labor conditions, and installation of new equipment. These objectives, policies, and basic assumptions clearly limit the plans he may adopt, and to that extent his planning task is simplified.

[2] *Reserved-Time Planning for Production,* Wallace Clark & Company, pp. 5-6.

An executive in the middle or lower ranks of management should seek to obtain such limits on his planning as a practical means of simplifying the task. It is entirely proper for him to discuss the validity of the limits at the appropriate time, but once they are established, they should be regarded as fixed points as far as his planning is concerned. Even the top-level executive should make use of this same simplifying device. Objectives, policies, major forecasts should be subject to periodic review; but, as a means of conserving time and promoting orderly thinking, once a decision has been made on such matters, it should be used as a fixed frame of reference until new evidence indicates a need for a significant change.

### Identify satisfying levels of attainment

In discussing marginal values in the preceding chapter, we noted that after a satisfactory level of achievement has been attained, the value of even better performance may not be great. For instance, a life insurance company might consider two weeks a satisfactory speed for settlement of death claims, or a personnel manager might regard a turnover rate of five per cent as satisfactory. In fact, many administrators have fairly clear ideas about satisfactory levels of costs (often equal to the best competitor) or percentage share of the market they should obtain.

If such acceptable levels of performance are recognized, planning is simplified. An executive does not have to continue his search for alternatives once he has found at least one solution that will give satisfactory results. In other words, he is relieved of the pressure to create and investigate many alternatives so as to be sure he has the *best* one. Or, to state the idea in milder terms, he would be glad to do better than just meet the acceptable level, but he doesn't lie awake nights thinking about it.

Obviously, this practice can lead to mediocre performance if the acceptable level of results is set too low. On the other hand, it is a means of establishing some sort of practical limit to the energy devoted to planning.

### Consider major factors first

Most planning problems involve a variety of considerations, and this naturally raises the question of where to begin. A logical approach is to analyze first those major factors that may dominate or control the entire decision; the study of these major factors may indicate that one or two alternatives should be immediately abandoned. With this knowledge in hand, irrelevant study can often be avoided.

The desirability of such an approach is illustrated in the experiences of a new company that developed a typesetting machine, called Castype. The new machine made slugs like a Linotype, but could be operated by an office typist using an ordinary typewriter keyboard. The new company spent much time and effort on engineering, patent protection, and even located subcontractors to make the parts. However, when bankers were approached to finance actual production, they asked about the *size* of the market. This crucial factor had never been studied carefully, and market research revealed only a very narrow market—too small to permit economical production runs or adequate repair service. Obviously, the market should have, and could have, been studied before incurring engineering and other development costs.

The study of major factors first in order to determine where detailed planning should be conducted is helpful in a variety of planning situations. Just as the artilleryman may "bracket his target" or the statistician may follow the method of "successive approximation," the administrator may use one or two key factors to narrow down the area for detailed planning.

Thus, one woolen-textile mill in scheduling production for a season first obtains a market forecast of the demand for each of several major types of fabric, and prepares a general schedule by departments to meet this demand. Potential bottlenecks are brought to the attention of management, and either production changes are made or the sales department is requested to modify its sales program. A revised production plan is then prepared, but the scheduling of specific patterns and colors is not done until the beginning of each month. This monthly plan provides the basis for detailed scheduling of machines within each department, although revisions of these detailed schedules are often made from week to week. Specific commitments for delivery to customers must, of course, be tied in with the detailed schedules. The point of interest to us here is that a department manager should not prepare the detailed schedule until after the analysis of general market conditions, coordination of production and sales plans, and the specific sales forecast have been completed.

Simplification of planning by the means just suggested—use of standard parts, planning within recognized limits, use of satisfying levels, and considering major factors first—is common practice in some companies. In other companies, however, adoption of these devices requires a real change in traditional ways of resolving problems.

**Dispersion of planning**

The planning necessary in a medium- or large-size enterprise far exceeds the capacity of any single executive. This planning task obviously must be shared by several people. One of the main functions of organization is to deal with this division of planning among executives and other employees.

The whole process of organizing is analyzed at length in Part II. The need for special provisions for planning will be examined as well as some of the pitfalls and limitations of these arrangements. We need not repeat that discussion in the present chapter, but a review of the chief arrangements for planning may be helpful so that the relationship between the planning process, discussed here, and organization will be clear. Important in this regard are (1) delegation and decentralization, (2) use of staff assistants and divisions, and (3) joint participation in planning.

*Delegation and decentralization.* The simplest way for an executive to spread the task of planning is by delegation to his operating subordinates. These men are already involved in carrying out the work, and it is natural to turn to them for help with the planning.

An operating subordinate may take part in planning in several ways. At the least he can help his boss clarify the problem, think of alternatives, or gather facts needed to make a decision. This may start as *consultative direction* (see Chapter 21), and later be formalized as a regular part of the job. At the other extreme, large segments of the planning may be assigned *in toto* to the subordinate, and he in turn may redelegate part of this work to men under his direction. Under this arrangement the senior executive usually sets the objectives, establishes major policies, and reserves final approval of major programs; the more detailed planning within these limits is done by men down the line.

Just how far this delegation and redelegation of planning should be carried is the big issue in decentralization, which is discussed in

Chapter 13. The degree of decentralization does not have to be uniform for all departments or for all subjects. A sales manager, for example, may himself decide on the time and prices at which a new product will be offered but delegate all advertising planning to his sales-promotion assistant and planning for direct selling to his branch managers. At the same time, the treasurer may insist that credit can be granted to purchasers of the new product only if he gives his personal approval. In each instance the optimum degree of decentralization must be decided.

When planning is shared by means of delegation to operating subordinates, no special divisions are created. The departments and divisions responsible for "doing" are also used for some of the planning. The major questions are where in the chain of command should the various kinds of decisions be made, and what help in this decision-making should be provided by subordinates and superiors. At least some planning is done at every level.

*Use of staff assistants and divisions.* Under some conditions, an executive with heavy planning responsibilities may not wish to delegate these to operating subordinates. He may believe that the planning is too important, that it calls for special knowledge, or that a broad perspective is required. Perhaps some plans such as accounting procedure or personnel policy should be consistent throughout the enterprise, and hence should be decided at one point for all departments. For reasons such as these, he decides to centralize a large segment of the planning; but, he cannot do all this planning work himself.

Staff is used to help the executive in such situations. A staff assistant can greatly simplify the planning task of an executive. He may help locate problems, draw tentative conclusions, prepare letters and instructions; in fact, he may do all of the planning on a particular problem except the final approval. The conditions favoring such use of staff and the staff's inherent weaknesses are examined in Chapter 12.

In large enterprises or departments with complex planning problems the staff idea is expanded to the establishment of a number of divisions, each of which works on plans in a special area. Thus, a market-research division, a sales-promotion unit, a product-development section, an industrial-engineering group, and other specialized units may be doing staff work. These units may have some direction and control duties, too, but their major function is to help in one way or another with the planning of operations related to their specialty. They can provide the concentrated attention, special knowledge, and skill that the busy operating executives cannot give.

One of the best ways to regard staff assistants and staff divisions is as extensions of the capacity of the executives they serve. They do planning work that the executive might do himself if he had the time. In order to secure an integration of planning, which has been stressed in earlier chapters, the findings and recommendations from the staff typically flow through the executive who is authorized to make the final decision. He can then quickly make a plan that is based on a thorough study by his aides.

*Joint participation.* Rarely are plans made by a single individual working alone. The executive or staff man who is developing the plan almost always consults with a number of other people. He gets advice on what might be done, seeks facts from many sources, checks his tentative plan with those who will be affected, and before he is done, probably will modify his initial idea considerably.

This joint participation in planning is so benefical that the organization may require it. For example, an operating executive may be required to consult the personnel officer before promoting a man in his department. Or the personnel officer, in turn, may be required to discuss any proposed payroll announcement with key operating men before it is issued. Perhaps committees charged with review of plans will be formed. Once an organization has functioned for a time, these consultations take place as a matter of course and are supplemented by many informal contacts. Joint participation in one form or another is vital to sound planning.

**The institutional mind**

Supplementing the dispersion of planning among many people is what H. S. Person calls "the institutional mind." A business concern has a memory in the form of its records, its traditions, and its lore. Also it has communication systems, both formal and informal. The communication systems enable an executive to draw on the memory, and in this way the executive can utilize a wide range of past experience. Even though personnel changes have occurred, the institutional mind permits a new executive to profit from what was learned in the past.

The communication system and the memory devices will never work perfectly, of course. Some information will be lost; the retrieval may be ineffective; distortions in communication will occur. One aspect of organizing is setting up records and procedures which will be useful to planners—the larger and the more complex the company, the more important is a good system for putting past experience at the disposal of present decision-makers.

Another feature of the institutional mind is uncertainty absorption. This means simply that various individuals in an organization are actually uncertain about, say, next year's sales, development costs of a new product, or risk of litigation—but they pass on to other planners a single prediction of what will happen. For instance, the production manager does not worry about capital to finance a new plant because the treasurer says he believes new loans can be obtained (that is, the treasurer absorbs the uncertainty surrounding the acquisition of new capital). To a significant extent we can stipulate in our organization design who absorbs which uncertainties; the planning procedures specify who will provide various pieces of information that will then be used by other people in their work on a particular decision.

By recognizing these features of the institutional mind in building our organization, we can help reconcile the heavy demands of rational decision-making with the complexities of administering a modern enterprise.

## LOGICAL AIDS IN CHOICE

Much of the academic writing about business decision-making deals with *logical* choice among alternatives. Often the discussion is theoretical, or it centers on a particular type of problem. However, four basic concepts are met frequently enough by administrators to deserve mention here.

### Concentrate on differences between alternatives

In choosing between several alternative courses of action, those factors that remain the same in all instances may be disregarded and attention focused on those that vary. This procedure sharpens the real issues and avoids those that are irrelevant. For example, a men's wear shop had to move, and its manager found two possible new locations for which the rent was the same and the space and fixtures, for all practical purposes, were alike. Since these were the only two real possibilities in the locality in which the store operated, discussion of the reasonableness of the rent or the adequacy of the space was irrelevant. Instead, the points deserving attention were the difference in buyer traffic passing the door, convenience for former clientele, possibilities for expansion, cooperativeness of landlord, and similar factors that were not the same for the two locations.

To cite another illustration, a traffic manager had to decide whether to ship his product to an area three to five hundred miles distant by truck or by rail. He discussed the problem with a number of associates in the accounting, production, and sales departments and was faced with a variety of issues touching on almost everything he did. An examination revealed, however, that while changes might have been desirable in the warehousing, billing, and packaging of the product, they had no direct bearing on the choice of carrier. The real issue in this situation was a balancing between convenience of delivery, frequency of service, and traffic rates. To have associated the choice of carriers with a change in the accounting system or in the packaging would have confused the issue and possibly have led to an erroneous conclusion.

Mentally setting aside the constant factors is often difficult. The writer remembers how aggravated his wife was with a notice either to pay a $10 fine for making an illegal left-hand turn or, if there was any question of fact, to appear for a hearing before a police judge a week hence. Unfortunately, there was no doubt as to what took place, and other points—the sign was hard to see, left-hand turns should be permitted at that corner, it was the middle of the morning when it didn't make any difference anyway, other towns charged only $3 for a first offense—may well have been true but didn't affect the available courses of action since apparently the $10 fine would be levied in any event. The only real choice was between paying it immediately or devoting a morning a week hence telling the police officials how unreasonable they were and then paying it. Had there been a fifty-fifty chance of avoiding the fine at the hearing, then the question would have been whether a morning's time was worth more or less than $5. In any case, discussion of the fairness of the legal system was irrelevant to the decision that had to be made.

**Disregard sunk costs**

In other words, concentrate on present and future sacrifice. This principle is simply illustrated by a trader on the New York Stock Exchange who owns a hundred shares of U.S. Steel stock. He has a choice of selling the stock at the current price, say, $75 per share, or holding it in anticipation of a price rise and dividends. It makes no difference whether he paid $100 per share or $50 per share (except as this may affect his personal income tax situation); the significant factor is the present price because this is what he sacrifices if he chooses to hold the stock.

Sunk costs are past expenses and investments, or parts thereof, that cannot be retrieved by resale. Sunk costs are most commonly encountered in equipment that becomes obsolete, in buildings that were erected in times of high construction costs, and in special-purpose facilities and equipment that have comparatively little value except for the particular use for which they were designed. The concept of sunk costs also applies to inventory, the market value of which has changed since it was purchased, or to an advertising campaign or personnel course that has already been completed.

If these past expenditures have created assets that can be sold in the present or future market, then that present value should be considered an expense of using them; but the balance of the expenditure is water over the dam as far as current planning is concerned. The sunk costs will not be changed by any alternative course of action, and, in line with the principle previously discussed, may be set aside in our thinking because they are not variable factors.

Naturally, it is desirable to recover through operations as much of the sunk costs as possible, and the use of only the present resale value in laying out plans favors continued employment of the asset. Any new asset should provide economies or other benefits sufficient to cover interest and depreciation on the total investment (present sacrifice), whereas the old equipment should be charged with interest and depreciation on only the resale value (present sacrifice).[3] Incidentally, the valuation of assets for bal-

[3] Possibly the resale price may be higher than the original cost. Even so, it is the resale price that is significant for planning considerations. The enterprise must decide whether it would be better off to sell at the high price or hold the asset for its own use.

ance sheet and profit and loss accounting purposes follows quite a different set of rules, inasmuch as these records are designed primarily for financial and historical purposes, rather than as planning tools.

### Discount uncertainty and time

Administrative planning is necessarily based on forecasts and estimates, and it is frankly recognized that unforeseen events may upset even the best of these. Consequently, one must often think in terms of probability or calculated risk. The underlying assumption is that during its existence, a company will face so many risks that the law of averages will work out.

This approach poses difficulties when certainties, high probabilities, and long shots are all involved in the same problem. If only a few clear-cut probabilities are involved, one can multiply the income or expense by a fraction representing the probability of its occurrence; a sure income of $100 would then be considered equal to a one-out-of-five chance of an income of $500. When a variety of uncertainties are present and even the probabilities are hard to estimate, it is more practical to complete the analysis with the best figures and forecasts available and then make an over-all adjustment for uncertainty. Thus, we find engineers following the rule of thumb that new investment in equipment should pay for itself in two or perhaps three years. While the rate of discount usually rests on subjective judgment, discounting is an entirely logical manner for dealing with such situations.

A similar, though less troublesome, adjustment is for differences in the time when income or expenses may occur. A thousand-dollar income ten years from now clearly is not worth as much as a thousand dollars today, nor is a necessary two-hundred-dollar expenditure five years from now quite as onerous as two hundred dollars a year from now. When relatively large sums are involved in the analysis, they may be placed on a comparable basis by discounting each on a compound interest basis, using the value of capital to the enterprise as the interest rate. Numerous minor adjustments of this nature are usually not worth the trouble because probable errors in forecasts and the uncertainty involved overshadow the improved accuracy from such minor adjustments for time. Nevertheless, in some planning situations the concept of discounting is highly useful.

### Separate measurable and intangible factors

Most planning decisions involve both measurable and intangible factors. It is desirable, if possible, to separate measurable items, reduce them to some common denominator (usually dollars), and compute the net gain or cost and the net investment. This gives only one or two items which can be balanced more easily with the remaining intangible factors.

For example, a company enjoying increased sales had to have additional warehouse space. Preliminary investigation reduced the possibilities to two alternatives: an addition to the present warehouse, or the erection of a new district warehouse that would also serve as a district sales office. A number of the factors could be computed with reasonable accuracy. These included differences in shipping cost arising from bulk shipment to the district warehouse, the expense of operating the district warehouse minus the savings in central warehouse expense resulting from the transfer of stock to the district warehouse, and differences in traveling and communication expense of salesmen and executives. Also the net investment was computed, that is, the excess of investment in the new warehouse and office over the additional investment that would be needed for the addition to the old plant. Office space at the home plant was not a factor, as it would remain constant in either alternative.

While some economies in freight would be realized, the total calculations showed a net increase in annual expenses of $15,000 and a net additional investment of $60,000 for the district office and warehouse operation. To simplify the problem further, the depreciation and interest on the net investment was estimated at about $5,000 a year, bringing the net increase in expenses to $20,000 per year. On the other hand, it was recognized that the district sales office should result in increased sales inasmuch as customer service would be improved, closer supervision of salesmen would be possible, and a district sales executive located close to the scene would facilitate adjustments to the local conditions.

The problem was thus reduced to the fairly sharp issue of whether enough increased sales would result from the intangible factors to justify an increase of expense of $20,000 per year. Sales volume was important to the company because of its relatively high fixed manufacturing cost, and it believed that increased competition would make service and effective salesmanship important in securing sales. Consequently, the company decided to go ahead with the new district warehouse and sales office.

An analysis such as the above helps planning by sharpening the issues. Tangible and intangible factors are not mixed together so that in effect the entire decision is made on an appraisal of the intangibles; only those factors that are different for the several alternatives receive attention; all the measurable factors are consolidated into a single net figure, thus reducing the complexity of the final decision.

## OPERATIONS RESEARCH

In resolving certain kinds of problems *operations research* may be of great assistance. While the term is sometimes loosely used to embrace all sorts of analysis of managerial situations, the distinctive aspects of operations research include: expression of problems in mathematical formulas (or models), quantitative measurement of the factors affecting the results, and a quantitative scale for evaluating results. Electronic computers make possible the use of this mathematical approach for highly complex problems.

The best-known applications of operations research have dealt with inventory levels and allocation, production scheduling, capacity of facilities needed for varying demand, and other problems in which physical goods or equipment were important—though not the only—facets. A variety of ingenious studies have also been made in marketing and finance, and explorations are under way in other areas.

Generally speaking, the situations where operations research has paid off have these characteristics: (1) A problem is so complicated or involves such a sheer mass of data that it cannot be fully grasped by one single person's mind, and yet its parts are so interrelated that dividing it into comprehensible units would not necessarily yield the best answer. (2) The relationships are known, clear-cut, and of a type that can be expressed by available mathematical formulae. (3) Statistical data are available for all important variables. The first of these requirements makes the study worth the trouble, the second is necessary to build a satisfactory model, and the third is a requisite for practical application.

If an executive faces an important problem having the above

characteristics, he clearly should seek help from someone familiar with operations research techniques. The vast majority of managerial problems, of course, do not meet these qualifications; for them there is serious doubt whether an operations research study would be worth its expense.

There is no magic about operations research, and we should be clear about what it does *not* do as well as what it does. Before the mathematical tools can be used effectively, (a) the problem has to be recognized and defined, (b) good alternatives have to be identified or created, and (c) a simplified value structure has to be accepted. Mathematics *per se* makes no contribution to these vital phases of decision-making. To be sure, sophisticated operations research people often have been of great help in diagnosis, creating alternatives, and clarifying values, but use of mathematical models is no assurance of such contributions; fundamentally, these aspects of decision-making can and should be shared by all people working on the problem.

TESTING A CHOICE [4]

Can an executive tell whether his tentative decision is a wise one? Unfortunately, the most he can do is to reduce the chance of serious error. Over the years, several different ways of checking the soundness of a decision have proved useful. Every manager should be familiar with these techniques so that he can pick those that are appropriate for each specific decision. Urgency of action, what is at stake, and degree of doubt will determine how many checks to use and how far to press them.

### Re-examining the analysis and the evidence

Most people prefer to stick to a line of thinking once it is well drawn in their minds, especially if ideas are familiar, accepted, and attractive. Consequently, a comfortable decision—right or wrong—tends to go unchallenged. To catch errors in such thinking, the following devices are helpful.

*Listen to the "devil's advocate."* For centuries, the Jesuits and other groups in the Catholic Church have used the institution of the "devil's advocate" as a way of testing decisions. A specific in-

---

[4] Adapted from W. H. Newman and C. E. Summer, *The Process of Management*, Prentice-Hall, Inc., 1961, chap. xv.

dividual is assigned the task of pointing out weaknesses and errors in proposed action. He assembles the best negative arguments he can. If a proposal cannot withstand such an attack, action is postponed.

In business, a decision-maker himself often makes a deliberate effort to stand aside and think of all the reasons why a proposed action won't work. Before an executive says, "Go ahead," he should take time to calculate everything that may go wrong. But this negative approach may be difficult and unpleasant for an aggressive executive, and if a problem is complicated or involves strong emotions, he should perhaps assign the task to someone else. The role is likely to be unpopular, so a manager should insure that everyone recognizes that the devil's advocate is not passing judgment on a matter, but simply seeing to it that all adverse points are considered.

A decision may be challenged on the basis of evidence, logic, values, or other grounds. At the time of the devil's advocate's cross-examination, all sorts of embarrassing questions are raised. For example, "If officers need the proposed three-week vacation, why not all employees?" Or, "True, our annual reports do show a high correlation of sales volume and advertising expense, but does this mean that more advertising will increase sales? Maybe the causation runs the other way or does not exist. Remember, the United States leads India in heart disease and baths per capita, but it does not follow therefore that baths cause heart trouble." A decision is sound only if it can be defended by good answers to such challenges as these.

*Project a decision into detailed plans.* Often we can check on the wisdom and practicability of a decision by spelling out its consequences in more detail. A very large manufacturing company, for example, tested its tentative decision to decentralize into product divisions by using this approach of projecting consequences. It allocated customers, outlined a proposed divisional organization, devised a tentative placement of executives, and estimated the administrative cost of the new setup. This analysis uncovered so many weaknesses and difficulties that the original decentralization plan was abandoned. Not until a year later was a substantially modified reorganization put into effect.

Thinking through the implementation of a decision is, of course, just an elaborate projection that, conceivably, could be part of an early analysis of alternatives. But since an elaborate projection for each alternative is often impractical, an executive can make a tentative decision and then test it in detail. Failure to think through a decision and what it entails has led to many an executive mistake that might have been avoided.

*Reconsider assumptions.* Every executive decision is based on assumptions—or planning premises. They may be assumptions supported by sketchy data about future demands for company products or availability of raw materials; assumptions about the attitudes and future behavior of employees, perhaps based on reports of staff men or hearsay evidence; or assumptions about company values that are as much a reflection of personal desires as of company goals. In checking a decision, a manager should ask himself just which assumptions are crucial to the success of a proposed action and try to obtain further clarification on these pivotal premises.

All assumptions cannot be verified, of course. There will always remain incomplete data, errors in perception of facts, and distortion in communication with which to contend. But an executive should reconsider assumptions so that he at least knows what risks he is taking rather than proceed naively.

**Securing Consensus**

A director of the Standard Oil Company (New Jersey) has observed, "When a proposal comes before our Board for decision, there is rarely sharp difference of opinion. We try to anticipate problems, and then we discuss possible solutions with everyone directly affected and those who might have useful views. These discussions often seem slow, but by the time we are ready to act a clear consensus backing the proposal has usually developed."

Most of us use this technique, at least occasionally. We make a tentative decision—about, say, accepting a job—but before taking action we get the frank opinion of one or two friends. In so doing, we are testing the decision.

Formal arrangements are sometimes made to get consensus on important decisions. The U.S. Supreme Court is a notable example. Boards of directors and some company committees presumably provide group review and endorsement of key plans. But the use of consensus to test decisions need not be limited to such formal bodies. Informal advice from individuals may contribute just as much to the wisdom of a decision.

If the assent or dissent of others is to be meaningful, the advisor should be both well informed about a situation and seriously concerned about the soundness of the decision. Neither polite agreement nor log-rolling politics nor cavalier advice is desirable.

### Pilot runs

The surest way to test a decision is to try it out. A test will not tell us whether some other decision might not work better, but it will tell us whether a proposed plan is at least promising. Sometimes a new product or process can be tried out on a limited scale with custom-made models or equipment. Automobile companies give their new chassis and new engines severe road-tests before the products are put into mass production and sold to the public. A chemical company with a new detergent may have its laboratory make up limited quantities for market tests in a restricted area. A large chain-store company is experimenting with extending credit in only a few of its outlets before modifying its "cash only" policy. As these cases show, even if a tentative decision looks good on paper or in the laboratory, a further test under more nearly normal operating conditions is desirable.

Pilot operations have their limitations, of course. They are often costly; they may consume valuable time; and they may not be feasible for some actions (such as floating a bond issue while interest rates are low). Consequently, this test is appropriate for only a few major decisions an executive must make.

### Sequential decisions

Occasionally, we can make a decision one part at a time; when the results of the first part are known, we can use them in deciding the second part; the results of the second part help to shape our decision on the third part; and so on with each succeeding part. Thus, we make a series of decisions to solve one main problem.

This form of decision is often used for executive promotions. Suppose a company president has his eye on a salesman named John Pollack as a likely replacement for the Sales Manager who will retire in three years. The president's first step might be to bring Pollack into the home office as Sales Promotion Director. If Pollack does that job well, he may be put in charge of sales planning. If his work continues to be effective, he may be named Assistant Sales Manager six months before he is moved into the key spot. These successive assignments serve a double purpose. Pollack gets experience and learns about home office operations, and the company can make a *series* of appraisals of this capability to be Sales Manager. The results of each move provide data used in deciding what the next move should be.

The sequence of decisions a pharmaceutical company commonly makes in bringing a new product to the market also illustrates the process. A new product typically goes through several stages: laboratory discovery or idea gleaned from nontechnical sources; clinical tests for effectiveness; production-process engineering; market analysis to decide packaging, pricing, and distribution channels; approval by Public Health authorities; sales promotion and quantity production. Each stage provides new evidence for deciding whether to drop the product, proceed to the next stage, or try a new tack.

Sequential decisions are in sharp contrast with bear-by-the-tail decisions familiar in sales promotion campaigns, where it is difficult to discontinue a project after it is launched. Sequential decisions should also be distinguished from the proverbial British habit of "muddling through," whereby one step is taken with simple faith that some way will open up for the next move. In sequential decisions a tentative plan or a new alternative for dealing with a major problem is in mind from the beginning. The plan is then tested against newly acquired evidence and perhaps revised at each stage.

All these proposed devices for testing decisions have their usefulness. Some fit one situation better than others. But in general, they may be applied in the following order: (1) checking our own thinking by the "devil's advocate" approach, projecting detailed plans for implementation, and reconsidering assumptions; (2) securing consensus from other competent people; and then, where suitable, (3) making test runs either by pilot operation or by sequential decision.

## SUMMARY

Decision-making in a modern business firm is so complex that ways of facilitating the process are essential. One approach is to simplify the planning itself by use of standard parts, recognized limits, and satisfying levels of achievement, and by focusing on major factors first. Organization is another aid; delegation, staff assistance, and formalizing the institutional mind are all means for sharing the total decision-making tasks.

Also, an executive can simplify his projections and choices by concentrating on differences, disregarding sunk costs, discounting, and separating measurable and intangible factors. Operations research can help with certain types of complex choices. And, after a tentative decision is made, the choice can be tested by rechecking one's thinking, securing a consensus, and perhaps making test runs. There is no royal road to wise decisions, but these aids make the creative analysis recommended in Chapter 7 feasible even in large enterprises.

This chapter concludes Part I on planning. The discussion has centered around two broad management problems: (1) what forms plans should take, and (2) how planning decisions should be made.

The structure of plans in a company typically is made up of several types. Objectives, budgets, deadlines, standards and other *goals* set the sights for company and departmental executives; and they play a key role in integration and control of operations. *Single-use* plans—such as programs, projects, and specific methods—map out action to be followed in an ever-changing environment. Many parts of every company's activities are repetitive, however, and for these *standing plans*—including policies, standard methods, and standard procedures—greatly simplify the planning task and provide stability.

An inevitable question is how far ahead and to what detail the planning should be carried. Inaccurate forecasts, expense, time, danger of inflexibility, and absence of repetitive operations, all place limits on how much planning is practical. Also, logistic and strategic considerations should be woven into the fabric of plans. These and related questions have been discussed in Chapters 2 through 6.

The last two chapters have dealt with the process of decision-making, the *how* of planning. The quality of decisions can be improved by assuring that *all* phases of the process receive careful attention—diagnosis, creative search for alternatives, projection of alternatives, and choice. Finally, since this process requires a lot of effort, a variety of aids for practical application have been suggested.

A good pattern of well-conceived plans, however, is only a first step in administration. The administrator must also create an organization to formulate and carry out such plans; resources must be assembled; supervision of actual operations is necessary; and before the executive's task is completed, he must exercise control. Upon these further processes of administration hinge the success of even the best-conceived plans.

## SELECTED REFERENCES

Cooper, J. D., *The Art of Decision-Making*, Doubleday & Company, Inc., 1961.

Dubin, R., *Human Relations in Administration* (2nd ed.) Prentice-Hall, Inc., 1961, Part V.

Goetz, B. E., *Management Planning and Control*, McGraw-Hill Book Co., Inc., 1949.

March, J. G. and H. A. Simon, *Organizations*, John Wiley & Sons, Inc., 1958.

Miller, D. W. and M. K. Starr, *Executive Decisions and Operations Research*, Prentice-Hall, Inc., 1960.

# II
# Organizing

# *9*

# Departmentation

## Major issues in administrative organization

The numerous plans in an enterprise, which have been discussed in Part I, call for a variety of activities, and if these activities are to be administered effectively, some form of organization is essential. Just as soon as two or more people contribute their efforts to a joint enterprise, an understanding as to "who does what" is necessary. The operating and administrative activities must be partitioned into bundles of duties that can be assigned to specific individuals, and relationships must be established between these individuals to assure that their efforts are coordinated toward a basic objective. In other words, the team must be organized.

The administrative process of *organizing* an enterprise or any of its parts consists of (1) *dividing and grouping the work* that should be done (including administration) into individual jobs, and (2) defining the established *relationships* between individuals filling these jobs. There will be, of course, other informal and social relationships over which the administrator has little influence; they are part of the setting in which the administrative organization operates. Since we are concerned in this book with principles or guides for executive action, attention will be focused on the organizing an executive can and should do, and the social structure will be considered simply as an important part of the situation in which the executive works.

Organization is essential in small as well as large enterprises. The small country newspaper, for example, may have only a half-dozen employees full- or part-time, and yet the paper will not meet its weekly deadline unless each person understands his part in the total operation. Are reporters expected to get photographs along with the stories and have the necessary cuts made? Is the business manager responsible for purchasing paper, as well as soliciting and designing advertisements and promoting circulation? Who is supposed to help the printer read proof? Can anyone besides the editor make changes in the copy or cut the length of a story to fit the space available? And who is responsible for omitting Mrs. Fibbs Snyder's name from the list of the program committee of the Parent-Teachers Association? These are only a few of the organization questions that the manager of the paper must answer. The organization of a large metropolitan daily newspaper is, of course, much more elaborate with its separate sports editors, circulation managers, proofreading department, and other specialized divisions. Here there are problems of organization *within* the several departments as well as for the paper as a whole.

The principal issues that arise in organizing a small enterprise, a large enterprise, or a department within an enterprise are the following:

1. How should activities be divided into groups for purposes of administration?
   a. What guides should be used in assigning activities to departments?
   b. What service divisions should be created?
2. What relationships between individuals should be formally established?
   a. How may authority and duties be delegated?
   b. What use should be made of "staff" and "functional authority"?
   c. How much decentralization is desirable?
3. Are special provisions needed to knit the enterprise into a working unit?
   a. What role should be assigned to committees?
   b. What functions should the board of directors perform?

4. What should be the over-all organization structure?
   a. Have limits on span of supervision been recognized?
   b. Is the over-all structure balanced and workable?

Although these questions are expressed from the point of view of a top executive, they are of major interest to executives throughout the enterprise. Junior executives as well as senior executives have problems of adjusting organization in their own departments; they frequently advise regarding changes in the organization of related activities, and their daily activities are conducted within an organization structure the nature of which they should thoroughly understand.

This chapter deals with the first question on departmentation. The other questions listed above will be considered in the following chapters.

### COMMON WAYS OF GROUPING ACTIVITIES

Departmentation is the process of grouping activities into units for purposes of administration. This process takes place at all levels in an enterprise. The president groups activities into major divisions under the senior executives who report directly to him; the sales manager may divide his work among an advertising department, customer service department, market research department, and three or four sales districts; the credit manager, who directs one of the groups under the treasurer, may divide his work among a group of credit men, each of whom handles a specific group of customers; the shop superintendent appoints foremen to look after each step in the production process; and the activities in the bookkeeping office are grouped into jobs for individual bookkeepers. The common question faced by all executives from the president down to the first-line supervisor is, "How should duties be combined into jobs so as to promote the most effective results?" The administrative units created may be called divisions, bureaus, branches, units, offices, or some other name; whatever the name of the unit created, this process of partitioning is generally called departmentation.

### Typical patterns used in departmentation

Several typical patterns are found in the departmentation of many enterprises, and an administrator will find it useful to be thoroughly familiar with these different alternatives. In business enterprises the

patterns most commonly found are groupings by products, territories, time, customers, and functions. In government enterprises
Gulick has found similar groupings, which he designates as purpose,
place, person or thing, and process. Other students of organization
have reported a somewhat similar list of patterns. A few very brief
examples will illustrate the meaning of these terms and call attention to the benefits often secured by using the particular pattern.

*Grouping by products or services.* Activities directly associated
with a product (or service) are often combined. Thus, the corner
grocery store may have divisions for meat, groceries, and fresh
produce. On a grander scale we find in General Motors separate
divisions for Chevrolet, Buick, Cadillac, Frigidaire, Diesel engines,
and other major product lines. Sometimes this product division
occurs only within a department; for example, the work of the
purchasing department may be divided according to different types
of products to be secured. Such grouping by product takes advantage of specialized product knowledge, promotes coordination
of the various activities connected with the product (purchase,
production, storage, sales, and the like), and often makes it easier
to place responsibility for the results achieved.

*Grouping by locations.* When activities are widely dispersed, it
is frequently desirable to provide local administration. Instances
of this arrangement are found in the territorial sales divisions of a
company distributing its products in several states, and in the self-
contained operations of branch plants. Even within a building we
may find a department store floorwalker assigned to a particular
floor or the maintenance man to a given section of the building.
Among the advantages of this form of departmentation is the more
intimate knowledge executives should have regarding local conditions. This permits adaptation to local needs and also helps in
getting prompt action. Likewise, the activities within the area are
more easily coordinated, and it is often possible to exercise more
direct and immediate control.

*Grouping by time.* When operations during a day or week extend
far beyond the normal work period of an individual, a "second
shift" is often added. Public utilities, restaurants, continuous-process
industries, and many other enterprises have divisions distinguished
on the basis of time as a normal arrangement. Other companies
wishing to provide quick deliveries or obtain greater output from
limited facilities may use this device. Typically, the "second shift"

performs operations that are very similar to those done in the normal working hours, but at least first-line supervisors are needed to provide adequate supervision and control. The more difficult organizational questions are how fully serviced and self-contained each shift should be, and what relationships should be set up between specialized executives who work only normal hours and the men who perform similar duties during the off hours.

*Grouping by customers.* This pattern, which is naturally found most often in sales operations, is sometimes reflected throughout the enterprise. The bargain basements of department stores, for example, often cater to a different group of customers than those served by the upstairs store, call for different buying and service activities, and may follow somewhat different personnel policies. Customer grouping is sometimes a dominant factor in the organization of brokerage houses. In government operations we find separate bureaus for immigrants, veterans, Indians, children, farmers, and small business. Again, the advantages of such grouping are to be found in the use of specialized and detailed knowledge, the coordination of activities related to the customers, and, by no means unimportant here, the assurance of adequate attention.

*Grouping by processes.* Under some circumstances it is desirable to place all or most of the people using a given kind of equipment in one department; for example, stenographers, painters, or operators of heat-treating furnaces. In other cases, notably in manufacturing, the division may be based on clearly defined steps in a sequence of operations. Thus, a sweater mill may have separate units for knitting, steaming, cutting, sewing, trimming, pressing, inspection, and boxing and shipping. Among the advantages of such departmentation are the expertness that comes with concentration on the single process, a tendency to avoid investment in duplicate facilities, and, when the process is performed in one place, the possible improvement in supervision.

*Grouping by functions.* With the growing complexity of administration of almost all types of enterprises—business, government, military, and eleemosynary—functional departmentation has become increasingly popular. Just what is recognized as a function, however, differs greatly in actual practice. Some functional departments deal with a particular aspect of management, such as scheduling or inspection. Others are built around a similarity in work, as in a clerical department; or they may be based on a similarity in ability required to supervise them, as in the case of research. In other instances, the distinguishing characteristic of a functional division is its singleness of purpose or objective. The public relations department is a fairly recent example of this type, while the time-honored separation of sales, production, and finance has made functional grouping one of the dominant patterns in business enterprise. The chief characteristic and benefit of such grouping is specialization. By concentrating on some single phase or similar group of activities, specialized knowledge and skill can be fully utilized. Functional divisions are also established to assure that adequate attention is given to the activities concerned.

A familiarity with these typical ways of grouping activities is important background for the executive who is designing or modifying an organization. They are significant, not so much as patterns to be copied, but more as suggestive approaches in the development of an organization structure adapted to the specific needs of the enterprise.

### Inadequacy of patterns

*Difficult questions not answered.* Unfortunately, an executive cannot settle his departmentation questions simply by casting a vote for some one of the typical patterns just discussed. Even if a decision is made to follow, say, a product pattern, numerous questions will remain of just what activities belong in each division. For example, a retail store may decide to adopt a product pattern, but this still leaves unanswered the question of whether each department is free to do its own credit work, whether delivery will be centralized, what kind of accounting records should be maintained and who will keep them, and so forth.

Likewise, the decision to establish branch sales offices does not determine who will do the advertising, the extent to which personnel activities will be performed by the home office, or the matter of local storage of merchandise. A decision to establish a controller's division does not provide automatic answers as to who should be responsible for corporate and real estate taxes, insurance, cost accounting, economic forecasting, and market research, nor does it answer the even more fundamental question of whether the controller is expected really to control or merely to provide data and analyses that will be helpful to operating executives in controlling their respective departments.

In other words, these so-called patterns of departmentation at best emphasize the dominant characteristic of a division or department. Important as this characteristic may be, it provides no formula for determining just what is to be included in a particular department—be it functional, customer, territorial, process, or product. And these questions of content and border line are often the most troublesome to resolve.

FIGURE 13. *Departmentation of a Commercial Bank.*

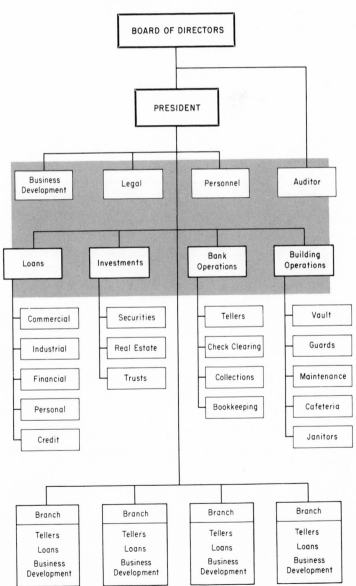

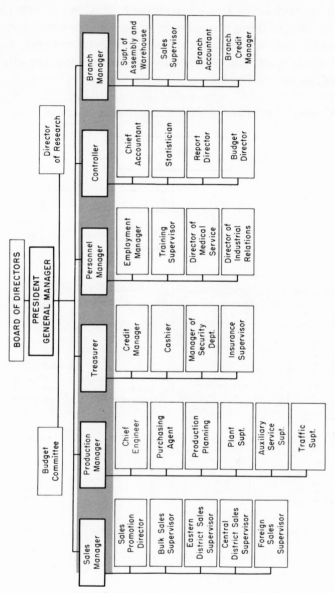

FIGURE 14. *Organization of a Manufacturing Concern.*

*Most organizations are composite.* We should also note that very few organizations follow any one pattern of grouping. From the point of view of structure the subdivisions under any single executive should be based on a single pattern, and where similar activities are performed in several different locations a parallel form of organization should be followed. Even this is not essential, however, and there certainly is no need to follow, say, a territorial pattern at all levels in the organization just because it is the dominant characteristic of the major departments.

The use of several different patterns is illustrated in the chart of departmentation of a commercial bank, shown in Figure 13. While the organization of this, and most other commercial banks, is predominantly functional, the branches have been established on a territorial basis and the loaning activity, except for a centralized credit department, is divided according to types of customers. The detailed organization within the check-clearing department (not shown in the chart) is on a process basis.

The departmentation of a manufacturing concern, indicated in Figure 14, again shows that several different patterns were used. The predominantly functional pattern was modified to provide for a branch manager because of the difference in location of the branch plant. Also, the subdivision under the sales manager is primarily on a territorial basis. Both the commercial bank and the manufacturing concern have relatively simple organization structure, and yet no single pattern would have been adequate for the grouping of their activities.

## Basic Factors in Grouping Activities

What activities should be included within a department, section, or other organizational unit? Where is it practical to draw a dividing line between the responsibilities of two closely related sections? What relationships between organizational units should be formalized, and what delegations of authority should be made?

Clarification of points such as these is essential if the organization is to function smoothly. In actual operations, the administrator will face questions of clarification and refinement of his organization many more times than he will have occasions to consider changes in major characteristics of the organization structure. Shifts in volume or in operating conditions are occurring all the time, and

minor organization adjustments to these changes are often necessary. For practical purposes, then, we need some guidance, not
only in deciding on the basic organization pattern, but also for
spelling out that pattern and resolving borderline issues.

The effective answers to these questions, unfortunately, are not
simple. Experience demonstrates that no formula or mechanical
application of rules provides a satisfactory answer. Instead, the
particular arrangement will be influenced by the purpose of the
enterprise, its size, people involved, stability and maturity, technology employed, major obstacles faced, and similar factors.

A practical way to design such an individualistic organization is
to identify the vital operational factors and then make combinations of activities that give optimum results in terms of these factors. Thus, the firm that seeks to give prompt delivery to distinctive
customers may find that coordination is a dominant factor; whereas,
the company emphasizing mass production at low cost may stress
economies from functional specialization.

A number of guiding considerations operate in almost every
departmentation problem. Although their relative importance varies
from one situation to another, they are prevalent enough to warrant the administrator's at least considering them when shifting and
grouping activities. In most situations appropriate attention to
these factors will be all that is necessary to secure a sound and workable arrangement of activities. These key considerations in departmentation are:

1. Take advantage of specialization
2. Facilitate control
3. Aid in coordination
4. Secure adequate attention
5. Recognize local conditions
6. Reduce expense

Because of the significance of these considerations, it will be helpful
to examine in more detail typical situations to which they apply.

### Take advantage of specialization

*Functional specialists.* Specialization is such a widely recognized
characteristic of modern enterprise that it needs little emphasis
here. The use of specialization in organization is illustrated by the
familiar division of a business concern into sales, production, finance,
and accounting departments, and the division of an accounting

department into units such as accounts receivable, cost accounting, and analysis of reports.

The advantages of this "division of labor" include the fuller use of the distinctive abilities of individuals. Each person has strong points and weaknesses, and by assigning work in accordance with these different abilities greater efficiency can be secured. Moreover, through concentrated attention on a limited type of work, an individual develops skill that enables him to increase his output even more. Frederick Taylor's discussion of functional foremen emphasized the benefits of specialization in managerial tasks and helped to promote the concept of division of labor for executives as well as for manual workers.[1]

In accordance with this concept of specialization, grouping together in one administrative unit all persons performing the same kind of work (typing, carpentry, drafting), or all people doing work requiring similar abilities (engineering, sales promotion, machine maintenance) may be desirable. In each instance the activities are grouped so that the work of the operators and/or the executive is specialized.

*Other types of specialization.* Besides functional specialization, just discussed, expertness in some other important body of knowledge may be desirable. For instance, one company dealing in industrial polishing supplies divided a major part of its activities on a product basis because it was not reasonable to expect a man to have technical and commercial knowledge regarding pumice, steel wool, chamois skins, sponges, and felt-polishing wheels. The company had a number of highly specialized men, but the basis of specialization was on product rather than on function.

Similarly, the work within purchasing departments is frequently specialized by products rather than functions. On the other hand, the work of a sales department may be divided between export, industrial, and residential sales, with experts in each type of work. In fact, it may well be argued that a legal division or traffic division represents as much a specialization on a body of knowledge as it does on type of ability.

Since specialization may take a number of forms, an ever-present problem arises of what kind of specialists to seek. In general, we try to minimize the range of abilities or knowledge required of the specialist. Thus, a company dealing with quite different products,

[1] See *Shop Management*, Harper & Brothers, 1911, pp. 98 ff.

each of which requires technical knowledge, may find product specialization practical; whereas another company whose products are all made by the same process and go to the same type of customer may find shifting from one product to another an easier transition than going from production to sales, and thus will have its activities specialized by functions. The way in which executives have been trained, both in academic institutions and within the company, may affect the form of specialization that appears to be most practical.

Where the choice of specialization is not clear-cut, other organization factors, such as ease of control or need for adequate attention, may throw the balance one way or the other. The fact that there is choice as to the basis of specialization, however, does not lessen the desirability of some form of concentration, and the more homogeneous these groupings can be, the greater the skill that is likely to be developed.

**Facilitate control**

One of the basic tasks of administration is controlling, that is, assuring that performance conforms as nearly as possible to plans. Controlling is discussed in detail in Part V, but we should note here that the grouping of activities may either complicate or simplify the executive's task of control. Departmentation may have a direct bearing on independence of checks, clear-cut accountability, telling comparison of results, or ease of supervision.

*Independent checks.* As a general rule one activity intended to serve as a check on another should be under a separate executive. Quality inspection cannot serve its purpose well if it is under the direction of a foreman who is also being pressed for volume output. In the same way, where accounting records are being used as a control over the flow of cash, it is desirable to separate record-keeping from cashiering. How far up the executive pyramid this separation should be maintained is another question that we will discuss later.

To cite another case of the need for independence where checking is involved, it is neither fair nor realistic to expect a man to report on the unfavorable performance of an individual who at the same time serves as his boss.

*Deadly parallel.* In some situations control can be added by establishing two or more operating units in "deadly parallel." Thus, chain stores or consumer finance companies with many somewhat similar outlets may establish zones or districts of comparable size and characteristics. Then sales, expenses, and other results may be easily compared, and the executive with an unfavorable result has a hard time showing that "it can't be done." While such comparisons do not do the entire job of providing control standards—for example, all divisions may have high operating costs—they can be very helpful in this regard.

This particular arrangement is applicable, of course, only to those enterprises that have comparable activities in two or more locations, plants, or products. Even in railroad operations some of the lines lay out their divisions so as to permit one superintendent to concentrate on metropolitan areas, another on mountainous regions, and perhaps a third on level plains; other lines, however, have made very effective use of the "deadly parallel" concept.

*Clean break.* Another way that departmentation can assist control is by providing a "clean break" between operating responsibilities. A clear and natural division between the work of one department and that of another makes it easy to decide which executive is accountable for results, but when the work of two divisions or sections is interrelated, placing responsibility is much more difficult. For instance, traffic and warehousing are often placed under the same executive, certainly not because of similarity of work, but to have a single executive fully accountable for the movement of finished goods to the consumer.

A clean break between activities that are actually performed together, or by the same individual, is very difficult to achieve. Thus, if salesmen of a furniture company handle all of its products, the duties and responsibilities of a bedroom furniture section, a living-room furniture section, and a dining-room furniture section are difficult to define. Likewise, one of the major drawbacks to the establishment of a public relations department is that, aside from relatively minor publicity activities, public relations cannot be separated from other operations.

The possibility of setting up planning and advisory units for such functions as public relations and personnel while leaving the execution of the plans to the operating people will be considered in Chapter 12. Under such an arrangement at least the operating responsibility can be assigned to cleanly separated divisions; there still remains the question of whether the activities of the planning units can be defined clearly enough to avoid confusion and dual responsibility. Often a compromise must be reached between the desire for specialization and concentrated attention on the one hand, and a clean break that will facilitate control on the other.

*Ease of supervision.* Physical convenience of supervision is another aspect of control that should be considered when grouping activities. For instance, when accounting and warehousing activities are performed at a district office, they may be placed under the supervision of the district sales manager rather than assigned to the controller and production manager some hundreds of miles away. Likewise, all selling activities on, say, the first floor of a department store may be placed under one executive, or all the production activities performed in a particular building may be placed under a superintendent. Such arrangements may be made even where local coordination is not a significant factor simply because the executive on the spot can supervise and control the operations so much more effectively than even a more skilled person some distance away.

The effect on executive control, then, is clearly one of the factors to be considered in grouping activities into divisions, sections, or other organizational units. A clean break between responsibilities, perhaps the "deadly parallel," or independence for checking, and occasionally the physical convenience for supervision are all practical considerations in departmentation.

### Aid in coordination

*Interrelated activities.* Quite different activities may be grouped under a single executive because they need to be closely coordinated. One of the principal reasons why many stores place the purchase and the sale of style merchandise such as women's dresses under a single executive is the need for synchronizing the time of purchase and selling effort and for relating customer preferences to the selection of merchandise. In manufacturing enterprises often raw material inventory control and purchasing are under the same executive, even though the nature of the work is quite different; here a knowledge of stock on hand and rate of use must be related to the ordering of new supplies. To cite still another example, a man in charge of a construction project may have under his direction such diverse activities as the purchase of sand and cement, the installation of air-conditioning equipment, and the selection of color harmony to be used in the foyer. Here, as in the other illustrations cited, the need for coordination becomes a dominant factor in the grouping of activities.

*Common objective.* Sometimes a particular objective or purpose guides the grouping of activities. Within a personnel department, for instance, may be found such diverse activities as cafeteria operation and employee counseling. They are related because they are two parts of a more general program that seeks to provide the enterprise with effective and enthusiastic employees.

Similarly, electrical appliance companies typically make repair service an integral part of the sales department even though the nature of repair work is much more akin to production. The primary purpose of the repair service is to help in making sales and in developing satisfied customers who will boost the product to their friends. Sensitiveness to consumer needs and desires is much more likely when the activity is made a part of the department that is selling goods to consumers.

Unity of purpose plays an important part in smooth relationships and voluntary coordination. Departmentation may seek to capitalize on this force.

*Most-use criterion.* When grouping activities into organizational units, the administrator often finds a number of "orphan" operations. For example, service activities such as messengers, central files, or purchase of supplies in a financial enterprise certainly do not deserve status as major operating divisions, and there is no compelling reason for placing them in any specific spot in the organization structure.

In such circumstances the "most-use" criterion may be useful. Thus, if the sales department, or the accounting department, makes the most use of central files, the filing operation is attached to that department. Likewise, the reception desk may be made a part of the purchasing department, sales department, or personnel department, depending upon which has the most callers and relies most frequently upon the receptionist to provide initial information and advice. Fundamentally this most-use idea is one of coordination because the greatest need for coordination will arise between the so-called orphan activity and the major department that makes the most use of its service.

Departmentation is only one of the means for securing coordination, as will be explained more fully in Chapter 23. Consequently, if grouping activities together to get coordination involves heavy sacrifice of other benefits, alternative ways of obtaining united effort should be considered at the same time. Nevertheless, when coordination is crucial or difficult, organizational arrangement is likely to be one of the most practical ways of achieving it.

**Secure adequate attention**

If a particular activity is unusually important to the success of an enterprise, it may deserve special recognition in the organization. Not only is the activity likely to be placed in a separate division, but the more important the activity, the higher in the administrative hierarchy is the division attached.

This principle is illustrated by the position of inspection in various companies. In a broom factory the production foreman himself may do the inspection; in a textile mill, where quality control is more important, the inspection may be done by a separate section reporting to the mill superintendent; in an aircraft plant, where reliable quality is vital to the success of the enterprise, the inspector may report to the general manager, or certainly to a vice-president in charge of production.

The same tendency exists in other fields; for example, when advertising is relatively unimportant it may be a section under the sales-promotion manager, whereas in a department store where the president considers advertising the key to success, it may be a major department reporting directly to the chief executive. Again, the position of purchasing may range all the way from local operating managers to the president, depending upon its importance to the enterprise. In this area a distinction is sometimes made between the type of product purchased; relatively unimportant operating supplies may be purchased locally, whereas the principal raw material, such as tobacco for cigarette manufacturers, cotton for a textile mill, or crude oil for a refinery, is purchased by a unit reporting directly to the chief executive, if not by the executive himself.

The adequate-attention criterion is important because of two natural human tendencies. An executive or an operator with a variety of duties cannot give first consideration to each of them, and through pressure of work or lack of interest one or more of the duties may be slighted. If the activity—for example, advertising, purchasing, traffic, or industrial relations—is made the sole or primary duty of a particular division, it is sure to receive the attention of at least this unit in the organization. We may note in passing that this reason, along with the benefits of specialization, are the chief justifications for many service, advisory, and other auxiliary divisions.

A second consideration is the difficulty of communication through several layers of supervision, a characteristic of human association which is discussed more fully in Chapter 15. If an executive considers a particular matter of such importance that he personally wants to review the facts and participate in the decision with respect to it, then an organization that provides for direct access between this executive and the division handling the matter simplifies the communication. The facts and recommendations may be presented directly to the executive with less risk of omissions and misinterpretation than occurs when an intermediate executive presents the case; and the executive has more assurance that his plans will be properly understood and carried out.

The executive can rarely apply the adage, "If you want a thing done right, do it yourself," but he can secure adequate attention by placing the important activities in separate organizational units and then tying these units in at a relatively high place in the administrative hierarchy.

Before leaving this point of adequate attention, we should note that this criterion often clashes with other considerations and may call for some compromise to secure the optimum arrangement. For example, the separation of an activity and "moving it upstairs" may create problems of coordination at the operating level. Certainly when an activity like negotiating a contract with the labor union gets far removed from the location where the work takes place, real danger exists that the agreement will not be adapted to actual operating conditions. Also, the adequate-attention criterion tends to break up a basic pattern in the organization structure; thus, where the major operating divisions are based on products, the segregation of a particular function makes a rift in the pattern; or, the establishment of a separate product division in a predominantly functional organization may cause confusion. In such circumstances one must weigh the benefits of more adequate attention against the difficulties of coordination or confusion that may result.

### Recognize local conditions

Perhaps this consideration should not be listed at all because the tendency is to give it too much rather than too little attention. From a practical standpoint, however, the adaptation of the departmentation to the personnel available and to the operating conditions makes a lot of difference in the effectiveness obtained.

*Adjustments to available personnel.* Important in this connection are the personalities of the executives who will staff the organization. For example, a careful review of the organization structure of one hosiery company showed a need for a single sales executive who would be responsible for advertising, sales promotion, direction of the salesmen, active participation in line building, pricing, control over finished-goods inventory, and related problems. However, the company had a sales-promotion man who was original and creative but lacked the stability and analytical ability to regulate inventory, set prices, and administer a large group of people. And, on the other hand, it had a sales supervisor who did an excellent job of directing the salesmen and making contacts with customers, but had very little originality or sense of design. Neither man was qualified for the top position, each was too valuable to dismiss, and the introduction of an additional executive above them would have been both expensive and disruptive to morale. Consequently, the company decided to have both men report to the general manager, recognizing that he would have an additional burden of coordinating sales activities.

Astute observers of organization have repeated time and again that organization should decide the need for personnel rather than have personalities dictate the form of organization. An organization built around personalities is likely to give too much emphasis to some activities and not enough to others, and a major reshuffling of duties is needed each time an executive retires or is promoted. The best practice is to design an organization that will best serve the purposes of the enterprise, and then select executives who are qualified for the positions created.

Desirable though this sequence may be, it may not be practical, particularly in a small company. Executives with the required abilities may not be available, except at great expense of money and morale, as in the instance cited above; or there may be men of unusual ability who can carry more duties than contemplated in the theoretical organization. In such circumstances a modification of the original plan to fit the men available may be the best arrangement. The least damage will be done if these adaptations are recognized as temporary provisions and plans laid for a return to a more logical pattern when replacements are necessary.

*Recognize informal groups.* Another local factor to which adjustment may be wise is the pattern of informal relationships that exist among employees. The sociologists lay great stress on what is sometimes called "informal organization"; that is, the social grouping and relationships that inevitably arise when people are associated together. These informal groups may arise from a common interest in baseball, similar family backgrounds, racial or religious factors, age, moral code, political beliefs, or any factor that promotes friendly association; and because of their informality a single individual will belong to several such groups and may drift in and out of still others. Since these social relationships have an important influence on the effectiveness with which the people work, they should be recognized in the establishment, and particularly in the staffing of an organization.

Just as on a ball team there are certain combinations that click, so too will a given arrangement of duties work well or poorly with particular combinations of people. The now classic Western Electric Company experiment showed that the mere change of seating arrangement of five girls reduced their combined output by 20 per cent; and there is no reason to suppose that the social relationships do not have as strong an influence on the behavior of executives. Here again it is desirable to set up the organization structure and then insist that positions be filled by individuals who are congenial with one another; but, in a given situation and with a limited number of candidates to choose from, sometimes more effective results will be achieved if the organizational pattern is adapted to these existing social groups. We should note, however, that just as certain abilities may be developed within an individual by training, likewise social groupings may be modified at least to some extent.

Where a closely knit, informal group is present, an organization change that upsets this group may cause considerable dissatisfaction. In such situations the advantages of making the shift should be substantial, and special effort should be made to get the group to see why the change was necessary.

*Full-time jobs.* Still another inherently local consideration is the need to combine activities into full-time jobs. For instance, in a small company the duties of chief accountant and treasurer may be consolidated because there are not enough duties to keep a high-calibre man busy in either position unless he spends a large portion of his time on routine work that can easily be done by a clerk. Sometimes one will find such miscellaneous responsibilities as supervision of telephones or messengers assigned to a given executive for no other reason than that he was carrying a relatively light load.

In still other situations it may be desirable to centralize the activities of some production or office operation so as to justify the investment in special equipment, or to utilize raw materials effectively and get quantity discounts. In all of these situations the organizational pattern that otherwise appears desirable is adapted to meet the local conditions.

**Reduce expense**

By no means unimportant in the process of departmentation is the consideration of expense. The creation of a public relations department, a separate purchasing division, duplicate accounting units in each of several plants, a number of self-sufficient product divisions, or other elaborations of the organization pattern all cost money. Additional executives may be required and with them more office space, secretarial help, and other services. So, when two or more arrangements are possible, one of the things to think about is the number of executives and operating personnel required, and their respective salaries. The least expensive arrangement is not necessarily the best one if it is relatively ineffective. But if a more elaborate arrangement is adopted, its additional benefits should very clearly exceed the additional expense.

This matter of expense may influence organization at all levels. For example, in retailing milk and providing residential laundry service, it is almost universal practice to combine both selling and credit work because the expense of having specialists in each field contact the customer for relatively small amounts would far outweigh the benefits that might be secured. Similarly, simplification in office procedure can often be obtained by assigning two or more operations to a single individual. Such combinations of duties may require the employment of more versatile and higher paid personnel, but significant economies are secured in getting the work to the employee, and the improved coordination with respect to a particular transaction is likely to offset any lack of specialization.

At higher levels the expense is often a major factor in the decision to establish a service unit. For some divisions such as purchasing, the financial savings obtained by the central unit may be estimated with some degree of accuracy and balanced against the direct expense; unfortunately, the burden of additional red tape and inflexibility, which should be included as part of the expense, is almost impossible to measure in financial terms. The benefits of other specialized divisions, such as employee training or public relations, defy accurate measurement; and here the expense of the proposed division must be balanced against an intangible benefit. One of the most difficult decisions of the administrator is to determine to what extent, if at all, his enterprise or department is warranted in setting up a more elaborate and specialized form of organization.

---

*When*
*Grouping and Reassigning Activities*
*into Administrative Units,*
*Seek the Optimum Combination of the Following Benefits:*

1. Take advantage of specialization
   Functional specialists
   Other kinds of specialists
   Special equipment

2. Facilitate control
   Independent check
   Deadly parallel
   Clean break
   Ease of supervision

3. Aid in coordination
   Interrelated activities
   Common objectives
   Most-use criterion

4. Secure adequate attention

5. Recognize local conditions
   Available personnel
   Informal groups
   Full-time jobs

6. Reduce expense

The importance of each point must be determined for the specific situation at the given time.

---

FIGURE 15. *Basic Factors in Departmentation.*

## SUMMARY

In every enterprise of any size, activities must be grouped together into divisions, departments, or other units for purposes of administration. Experience has indicated that this *departmentation* can often be based on products, location, time, customers, processes, or functions.

These common patterns are highly suggestive, but they provide no complete answer because they can be used in numerous combinations, and there is no clear-cut guide as to just what should be included in each category. Therefore, an administrator must build an organization suited to his own particular circumstance, and in so doing he must weigh one possibility against another.

An organization must continually adapt to current operating conditions. The people who fill the positions may be promoted or transferred to another job. Shifts in competitive conditions may make functions such as purchasing or advertising more, or less, important. Changes in volume, technology, or other conditions take place frequently. The executive must be continuously alert to such changes and decide whether they call for at least minor adjustments in his organizational arrangements.

In this balancing and refining process, a number of underlying factors deserve careful consideration in almost every instance. The administrator should take advantage of specialization, facilitate control, aid in coordination, secure adequate attention, recognize local conditions, and reduce expense. (See Figure 15.) All of these factors cannot be achieved to a maximum degree at the same time; so the wise administrator seeks an optimum arrangement in terms of his particular objectives and the particular situation in which he operates.

Departmentation is also influenced by the use of staff and functional authority relationships, the decentralization of authority, the span of supervision, and a desire for a consistent or symmetrical organization structure. These aspects of organization will be taken up in succeeding chapters.

## SELECTED REFERENCES

Albers, H. H., *Organized Executive Action*, John Wiley & Sons, Inc., 1961, Chap. 5.

Peterson, E., E. G. Plowman, and J. M. Trickett, *Business Organization and Management* (5th ed.) Richard D. Irwin, Inc., 1962, Chap. 9.

Pfiffner, J. M. and F. P. Sherwood, *Administrative Organization*, Prentice-Hall, Inc., 1960, Chaps. 7 and 8.

White, L. D., *Introduction to the Study of Public Administration* (4th ed.) The Macmillan Co., 1955, Chap. 3.

# 10
# Service Divisions

In setting up and refining an organization it is helpful to distinguish between those departments, sections, or units that are responsible for the performance of major operations and those auxiliary units that are established to aid and facilitate the work of the first group. The auxiliary divisions are essentially service units; their existence is justified only if they assist the operating departments to work more economically or effectively.

A great variety of such service divisions may be found in business enterprises. For instance, a manufacturing concern often has a traffic division so that the production and marketing departments will not have to be concerned with problems of moving goods to and from the plant. In financial establishments, the purchasing division typically functions as an auxiliary service for all other departments. Companies often have a legal division that handles the bulk of the corporate legal problems and works with outside legal counsel on special issues; these are technical matters that the operating departments are rarely qualified to handle.

A market research division may provide information and advice to district sales managers, the advertising manager, or the engineer designing a new product. Warehousing sections are found in most distribution and manufacturing establishments. Separate office-service sections to provide duplicating, telephone, messenger, mail, filing, and similar services are very common. A separate unit to provide maintenance and janitorial service is likewise a typical arrangement. These examples, by no means a complete list, indicate how prevalent is the use of auxiliary divisions.

The size and nature of activities of an enterprise will determine the extent of its needs for separate auxiliary divisions. Numerous articles and books can be found in the management literature extolling the benefits of a separate division for one or another of the auxiliary services. Frequently the writer of such an article is employed in a division such as he is advocating, and he quite naturally cites illustrations of enterprises where this particular form of organization has been beneficial. If all such advice were accepted by a single company, an array of specialized helpers would far outnumber the actual doers. In practice there is no categorical answer to the most desirable duties and position of a purchasing division, legal office, warehousing section, or other auxiliary unit. Each company should establish such divisions in accordance with its own needs.

Three fundamental issues that arise in this connection are the following:

1. Can the particular activity be separated advantageously from basic operations?
2. Should the segregated activity be combined into a single division, and, if so, where should it be attached in the organization structure?
3. What should be the relationship between the auxiliary unit and other parts of the organization?

### Separation of service activities

The desirability of separating service activities from basic operations is really a special case of departmentation. This topic has already been discussed in the previous chapter, and the factors that typically decide such questions were considered in some detail.

*Advantages of service divisions.* Generally, the reasons for segregating service activities focus on the advantages of specialization and the need to secure adequate attention. Special skills and knowledge are clearly a factor in the establishment of a statistical, traffic, real estate, legal, or engineering division. In most situations, problems of this sort do not occur often enough to warrant the employment of operating men with technical competence in these specialized areas.

In addition to the matter of technical competence, it is likely that the sales, production, or other operating executive will be so involved with his major activity that the minor activities and those that occur infrequently will receive scant attention. This is not necessarily a criticism of the executive, since it would not be efficient for him to spend a high proportion of his time on such matters as office services, purchases of supplies, warehousing, or routine traffic. In other words, the operating executive who is relieved of responsibility for auxiliary activities can often perform his primary task more effectively.

*Disadvantages of separating services from operations.* The reasons for not separating the service activities usually center around problems of coordination and of overhead expense. Some service activities, such as janitor service, warehousing, and traffic, present no particular difficulties of coordination if separated from basic operations. However, statistical computations, internal transportation, legal review of activities, and a large part of personnel work typically are very closely related to day-to-day operations; the performance of such work by a separate division creates additional problems. Where the need for consistent and synchronized action is frequent, one may be wiser to sacrifice some skill in performance to secure greater harmony.

In this connection, one danger of functional specialization, such as is found in most service divisions, is that it leads to provincial thinking. The functional specialist (like the urban New Yorker) permits his sophistication in one area to delude him into a misconception of and disinterest in other areas. In his zeal to perform his particular specialty well, he becomes careless about the effect of his action (or lack of action) on related activities. This danger of provincial thinking is particularly serious when (1) the service division is attached high in the executive hierarchy and arrogance of men in the service unit can be checked only by a top official who has little time to consider detailed operations, and (2) when the number of so-called service divisions is large and the operating executive lacks time and energy to check up and negotiate with a variety of "helpers."

Service divisions cost money in terms of salaries, office space, and the like. They often produce substantial economies so that this expense is offset by a comfortable margin, but this is not always the case. The returns from such activities as market research, engineering, and personnel relations are often difficult to measure, and these and similar activities can be expanded to a point where additional savings are not equal to additional expense. More likely is a failure to adjust service activities to reduced opportunities for making savings. The operation of such departments tends to be a fixed over-head item which is not reduced with a drop in volume of operations. Or, a division that originally served a useful purpose may be continued long after its usefulness has passed. This danger of an inflexible expense item should be watched when setting up special auxiliary units of the organization.

Establishment of service units, then, requires careful examination in each particular situation. Most enterprises of any size have several such units, but the desirability of a particular type of service unit should rarely be taken as a foregone conclusion, and the extent of the service is almost always a topic calling for a considerable amount of judgment. At least one generalization should be borne in mind when dealing with such issues. The burden of proof should always rest on the separation of service from basic operations. Every step in this direction increases to some extent the complexity of the organization; therefore, unless a strong case can be made for the separation, leave the activity as a basic part of the operation.

**Place of service unit in organization**

A decision to separate a particular activity from basic operations inevitably raises the issue of where this activity should be placed in the organization structure. Sometimes the activity is centralized in a single department that serves all other parts of the enterprise, but in other circumstances, such as warehousing in a company with a number of plants, several service units are established. The choice between one unit or several depends primarily upon a balance between the economies of a single unit and the need for providing the service in close proximity to the major operations. However, as we shall see, the matter of control sometimes enters into the decision.

*Single versus duplicate units.* A single service unit is often able to secure the maximum economy, particularly in the medium- or small-size enterprises, through concentrated attention, standardization of routine, specialized technical knowledge, and distinctive skill of personnel in the centralized unit. Moreover, the volume of work may only be large enough to justify the employment of a single set of experts in, say, insurance or traffic, or a single installation of expensive equipment, as in the case of punch-card tabulation or printing. The pressure of economy of overhead may dictate a single division.

Important as these considerations of efficiency and cost may be,

(A) Organization with no service division; each operating
section performs its own auxiliary activities.

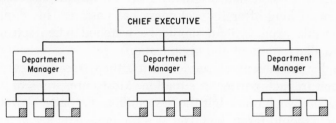

(B) Organization with service units in each operating department.

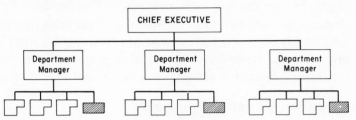

(C) Organization with separate service division.

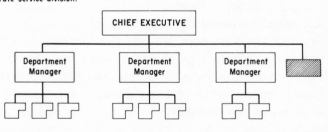

(D) Organization with multiple service units.

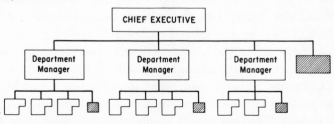

FIGURE 16. *Diagram Showing Alternative Arrangements of Service Divisions.*
*Shaded area represents any particular auxiliary activity being studied.*

one should always bear in mind that the service units must be closely coordinated with the main stream of operation. The farther removed the auxiliary unit is from the operations it serves, the greater are the problems of coordination. To cite an extreme case, secretarial work is rarely performed by executives themselves, yet the importance of coordination with respect to timing of the service, familiarity with the local situation, and particular needs of the individual executive results in a wide number of secretarial units attached to the particular operation they serve. Only where considerable standardization of secretarial service is feasible and/or where there is wide fluctuation in the need for such service are centralized secretarial pools likely to be found.

The need for coordination between the service division and operations often results in the establishment of several matériel storerooms adjacent to actual fabrication, separate purchasing offices at each plant in a multi-plant company to procure at least some of the requirements, and localized accounting units. Moreover, if the volume of service work needed in a particular location or by a single department is large enough to provide the principal benefits of specialization, then several service units may be established to secure easier coordination with operations without sacrificing efficiency. For example, some large manufacturing concerns are able to provide engineering service in each of their operating divisions; they then either have no central engineering department at all, or limit its activities to research and special laboratory work.

*Location in organization structure.* Related to the choice of one versus several service units is the question of where such units should be attached in the organization structure. Some people have argued that any service unit that serves several operating departments should report to the executive who supervises these departments, thus assuring fair treatment to each department. The executives of the service itself are likely to support this view because it tends to place them directly under a top executive, which gives them more status and more independence of action relative to subordinate executives.

However, this approach followed to its logical conclusion would place a large number of divisions directly under the chief executive. Thus, the directors of statistical, purchasing, real estate, legal, office, maintenance, or janitor services could lay claim to a position, perhaps minor, at the "head table." In a similar manner there might be pressure to put several service units directly under the sales vice-president or production vice-president.

As will be discussed in Chapter 15, there are definite limits on the span of supervision of any executive, and for this reason it may not be practical to have the service units report directly to a top official. Occasionally, the service units are collected together under a single service executive, but more often each minor service unit is placed under that executive whose department makes the *most use* of the service. It is understood, of course, that the unit will continue to serve other departments, even though it is supervised by an executive who otherwise has no direct concern with their operations.

In a manufacturing firm, for example, the maintenance and janitor service may be placed under the production executive because the bulk of these activities are concerned with production facilities. On the other hand, duplicating, telephone, messenger, and similar office-service activities may be placed under the sales vice-president or the controller. Similarly, a single purchasing division may be found within the production department, even though it is also responsible for the procurement of office supplies. Where there is no sharp competition for a service, this arrangement may work fully as well as having the service unit report to a higher executive.

In general, then, once a single service unit has been decided upon, this unit will be supervised by the operating executive of the department making most use of the service (or by a general service executive if there be one) unless the activity is of sufficient importance to justify immediate supervision by a top-ranking official or by the chief executive himself.

*Duties of central and of local units.* A large enterprise may have both a central division under a chief executive and subsidiary units in the operating departments, provided the service in question is of major importance. For example, a company of ten thousand employees often has a top personnel executive and also personnel officers stationed in the major operating departments. Likewise, a manufacturing company with several plants may have a central purchasing office as well as purchasing agents located in each of the plants.

Under this arrangement the central, or headquarters, office typically (1) performs a limited number of readily separated activities for the entire enterprise and (2) guides, through a staff relationship or functional authority,[1] the activities of the subsidiary units in the operating divisions.

In the case of purchasing, for example, the local purchasing agent may be authorized to buy all items used in small quantities, to make purchases to meet emergencies, to watch inventories and incoming shipments so as to prevent production delays owing to lack of materials, to secure realistic estimates of requirements from local operating executives, and to work with these executives on the coordination of purchasing with actual operations. The central purchasing office, on the other hand, may: undertake to buy or contract for the delivery of all materials used in large quantities, especially when quantity discounts, reciprocities, or other benefits of unified action are involved; establish general purchasing policies with respect to size of inventories, relationships with vendors, and the like; and give technical advice and instruction to the local agents. Likewise, where there are both centralized and decentralized personnel units, the functions of each must be defined. The local personnel officers may cover all rank-and-file personnel within the local departments while the central division concentrates on executive personnel, companywide dealings with unions, personnel research, and similar activities.

Occasionally, these local outposts are under the direct supervision of the central office, their only distinction from the central unit itself being their physical location in an operating department. Where independence from operations is desired, as in the case of auditors, this may be a practical arrangement. Usually, however, it is preferable to have the local unit a part of the "team" under the local operating executive, with only indirect supervision from the central unit.

*Dangers in multiple unit setup.* Since this arrangement of a central service unit plus corresponding outposts in operating divisions has the beguiling appeal of providing the benefits of both a single division and of units closely associated with operations, it is well to be fully aware of the implications of the arrangement. Usually, the central unit is expected to do some of the planning for the local units. The desirability of centralization of planning, contrasted with decentralization, will be discussed in Chapter 13; it is sufficient to note here that there is real danger of too great a degree of centralization, particularly if the headquarters unit has excess personnel.

[1] Staff and functional relationships are explained in Chapter 12.

Also, conflict of loyalty on the part of the service unit in the operating department almost inevitably arises. Often the real burden of selecting men for these posts rests with the central unit, and the chances of favorable transfer and promotion are determined primarily by the central unit. The local-unit man receives many of his instructions from headquarters and may well receive more sympathy and understanding of his problems from this source. As a result, he may feel more loyalty toward his central staff unit than toward his immediate boss in the operating department he is supposed to serve. This "loyalty to profession"—or in the military service, loyalty to corps—may assume serious proportions, and occasionally the service unit becomes so strong that it usurps the power of the operating officials. A more likely danger is that the local servicing unit will fail to provide the assistance to the operating unit that was contemplated in the original plan.

A further question arises as to whether the enterprise can afford to have both a headquarters unit and local operating units since this tends to increase the overhead expense. For distinctly local services, such as warehousing, telephone service, and the like, a voluntary exchange of ideas and experiences among several local units may provide as much pooling of ideas as is practical.

The place of the service unit in the organization structure depends, then, on the number of units established, the importance of the service to the total operation, the ease or difficulty of coordinating the service with actual operations, and, for large enterprises, the desirability of having both a central unit and local units.

### Relation of service units with other departments

When a service unit performs a clearly separable and subsidiary activity, its relationships with other departments are relatively simple. Thus, there need be no problems with respect to janitor service, duplicating service, or arranging for the transportation of goods. Once a clear understanding has been established of what services are to be performed in the separate unit, there is continuing need only for ascertaining requirements and checking to be sure that services are performed on time and in a satisfactory manner. As already indicated, the operating executives are often glad to be relieved of the responsibility of directing these somewhat specialized activities.

The relationships are more complicated, however, when the service unit also takes on a control function, and when it undertakes to set up a plan that is to be executed by the operating department. Each of these types of relations will be explored briefly.

*Use of concurring authority for control.* Sometimes the role of the service division extends beyond assistance that is requested by the operating department. The service division may be asked by a top executive to approve the desirability of proposed actions by operating executives. For example, the printing division may not only process the material requested, but also advise and *approve* the wording, format, paper, color of ink used, and similar features of the proposed documents. Here the printing division is attempting to secure uniformity in presentation, perhaps improvement in quality, and certainly economy in printing costs.

A similar situation arises when the purchasing department not only does the actual procurement of the goods needed but also joins in the decision that the goods requested are actually necessary in the particular quality specified. Such situations may, at first glance, appear to be a lack of clearly defined responsibilities, and this all too often is the fact. The arrangement, however, may be created intentionally. The service unit is given an added responsibility for control, and for this purpose is given *concurring* authority. Both the operating department and the service division must concur on the desirability of the action before the service division proceeds with its function.

The need for an inspector's approval before goods are shipped or moved on to a further stage of processing is familiar in manufacturing and distribution enterprises. But, the grounds on which approval may be withheld must be defined. Can a man who approves the printing of new forms, for example, refuse to give his O.K. because he is not in favor of the activity for which the form is designed, or is he merely to confine his attention to format? Does a procedure requiring "legal approval" of all new contracts empower the company lawyer to pass judgment upon the strategic and economic soundness of the transaction being recorded? Should the personnel department's authority to approve all transfers and promotions enable it to hamstring a change in organization? Let he who hath not experienced thwarting interference from such sources as these take heed and beware of concurring authority.

The use of service divisions for control purposes often leads to delay since difference in opinions must be resolved, either by negotiation or by appeal to higher authority. If several levels of supervision are involved, this may mean a series of negotiations and sometimes difficulty in securing the necessary time from the final arbiter, the common executive. Also, there is confusion of responsibility, not for action taken, since both the operating department and the control unit have concurred in such a decision, but for failure to take action. Without agreement often nothing happens. And yet, it is difficult to place responsibility for this failure of agreement.

Consequently, a service division should be given a control duty only when it is very important to guard against mistakes. The grounds upon which approval may be withheld should be carefully specified, and the arrangement should probably apply only to actions where some delay will not seriously hamper operations. The authority of a personnel department to approve the transfer, promotion, or discharge of an employee, the authority of a legal department to approve each contract from a legal (not substantive) point of view, the approval by a controller of major capital expenditures from the point of view of adequacy of approved budget—these are examples of situations that normally would meet these tests. Of course, to the extent that the service divisions are placed within the operating department and the operating executive has authority to override their veto, both effectiveness of the control and the dangers of its abuse are reduced.

*Combination of service and staff activities.* A somewhat different complication arises when a service unit prepares plans to be executed by the operating or other divisions of the company. Here we find that the service division assumes the role of staff, which will be discussed in Chapter 12. As is noted there, the recommendations of the staff become effective either because the operating executive voluntarily accepts them or because they are issued by (or in the name of) a senior operating executive. Occasionally the staff unit may be given functional authority although for reasons to be explained, this should be restricted to highly technical and relatively unimportant subjects.

Some service units, such as engineering, market research, or personnel, can easily and naturally expand their function from one of providing a purely auxiliary or supplementary service to one of giving of advice; and as this advisory activity increases, particularly if it is backed up from time to time with orders from the "big boss," the service unit becomes increasingly staff in nature. In theory it is relatively simple to draw a distinction between purely service activities and the staff work of assisting the operating executive in planning and supervising activities under his direction. In actual practice the dividing line between the two may be difficult to find because some service units perform both functions.

A personnel division exemplifies the composite role that some service units play. The cafeteria, recreation, and company magazine activities represent a group of clearly auxiliary services. Activities in connection with job analysis, wage and salary administration, and union relations are primarily service, and they also contain an element of control. Training, handling of grievances, and other executive behavior that builds morale can be separated from the operating executives only in minor phases, and the personnel director functions here more in a planning and advising capacity. In certain limited areas, such as medical examinations, safety work, and recruitment procedure, the personnel director may exercise functional authority.

Thus, this single division renders auxiliary service, controls, plans and advises, and exercises functional authority. Unless special effort is made to inform all employees of the responsibility of the personnel department with regard to *each* of its activities, confusion will prevail.

This diversity of relationships is also illustrated by a controller who, in addition to performing a large body of accounting activity within his own department, often works on budget, expense control, and perhaps economic forecasting. In some concerns, engineering is still another example.

While such composite relationships are always open to misunderstanding and simplicity in organization is highly desirable, practical considerations may dictate that the service unit be assigned a multiple task.

## SUMMARY

The separation of service or auxiliary activities from basic operations often adds to the efficiency of an enterprise. Although such an arrangement increases the complexity of the organization structure, it also permits specialized and concentrated attention on particular activities that may be poorly executed if left combined with major operations.

This segregation of an activity raises the issue of whether there should be a single service unit or several such units attached to various departments of the enterprise; and a related question is where these units should be attached in the executive hierarchy. The solution of this issue appears to hinge largely on the volume of work encountered, the importance of the activity to the enterprise, the people and traditions within the company, the difficulty and importance of securing coordination between the service and operating departments, and the desirability of giving the unit control as well as service responsibilities.

A further issue that frequently presents itself is just what relation the service unit is expected to have with the operating departments. The dominant characteristic of a service unit is, of course, the performance of activities that are useful in assisting the operating departments in their major tasks. In addition, for purposes of control, the units are sometimes given concurring authority with respect to what should be done. Not infrequently, a major service of a division is to advise the operating executive, and to this extent the service department becomes staff in nature.

Throughout the discussion of service units there has been a recurring theme of the danger that service units will become overly large, bureaucratic and inflexible in operation, and unresponsive to operating needs, and that they will add unduly to the complexity of the organization structure. This means that in their creation and administration care must be exercised to preserve the service aspects of their existence. In football terminology, we must remember who is running interference and who is carrying the ball; both have essential contributions to make, but unless the interference sticks to its facilitating role, we'll come out at the small end of the score.

### SELECTED REFERENCES

Allen, L. A., *Organization of Staff Functions*, National Industrial Conference Board, Studies in Personnel Policy, No. 165.

Holden, P. E., L. S. Fish, and H. Smith, *Top-Management Organization and Control*, McGraw-Hill Book Co., Inc., 1951, pp. 36-58.

Koontz, H. and C. O'Donnell, *Principles of Management* (2nd ed.) McGraw-Hill Book Co., Inc., 1959, Chap. 10.

*Shaping a New Concept of Administrative Management: Administrative Services as a Top-Level Corporate Function*, American Management Association, 1961.

# 11

# The Process of Delegation

Administrative organization, by its very nature, creates executive-subordinate relationships, and it also creates a variety of departments and divisions that frequently are intimately related. It is vital to good administration that these relationships be wisely defined and clearly understood.

*Need for clear relationships.* The confusion that arises when relationships are fuzzy can be suggested by two brief examples. A medium-size manufacturing company employed a new office manager. In addition to supervising the office force, the man was assigned the duties of modernizing the accounting system, introducing mechanical office equipment where appropriate, preparing reports regarding various divisions of the business, and making recommendations for improvement in operations based on his analysis of the accounting and statistical data. He was "given authority" over these activities, and proceeded not only to make rapid changes in operations under his direct supervision but, in his reports on other divisions, to recommend as drastic changes in their activities.

Within a few months he found that members of his own division were not complying with his instructions and, in fact, threatened to resign rather than comply with certain "unreasonable" demands. These employees were encouraged in their defiance by workers in other divisions who were greatly annoyed by the presumptuous criticism of their work. Actually, the president had no intention that the office manager should proceed in this manner, and soon the confusion over authority reached a point where the office manager had to be removed.

A large multi-unit company, to cite another example of confused relationships, decided to decentralize authority to its various plant managers, while at the same time retaining a number of service units, including a purchasing office, for the entire company. The manager of one of the plants was interested in improved packaging for his product, and in cooperation with a package manufacturer developed a distinctive new container. The local purchasing agent was arranging for manufacturer's delivery of the new package when the central purchasing office raised a question about the authority of the local plant to purchase such material without approval from headquarters. Before long, the authority of the central sales promotion department was also involved, and six months elapsed before the new package was finally approved. In the meantime, the packing, warehousing, and sales divisions were all uncertain as to how to proceed, particularly since the jurisdictional issues overshadowed the minor differences regarding the proper design of the new package.

The major issues arising in connection with organizational relationships can be grouped under three broad questions:

1. What happens to authority and responsibility in the process of delegation?
2. How can the ideas of staff and functional authority be used to advantage?
3. Under what conditions is decentralization desirable?

In this chapter, the underlying principles of delegation will be reviewed—what does delegation do to authority and responsibility, what are the limits on delegation, and what guides should we observe to keep the boss-subordinate relationships clear and simple? These concepts, important in themselves, also provide a basis for examining—in the next two chapters—the effective use of staff and the inevitable question of decentralization.

### DIFFERENT MEANINGS OF AUTHORITY

Probably no word in the field of administration is subject to more double-talk than is *authority*. The lawyers speak of legal authority, the maintenance engineers suggest calling in an authority on heat exchangers, the shop superintendent complains about the union usurping his authority, and the controller authorizes the chief accountant to set up a new account for deferred maintenance—yet each means something different by the word authority. So, before discussing the delegation of authority, we must understand what we do, and do not, mean by this word.

### Legal authority

Authority is often thought of in a legal sense, that is, whether an individual is legally permitted to take an action. With respect to enterprises, both public and private, a large body of law deals with the authority of individuals to act on behalf of the enterprise. Primary attention centers on some member of the enterprise—president, purchasing agent, salesman—in his relations with outsiders. Who is authorized to represent the enterprise, when is a contract binding, and similar legal questions are involved.

In private business, legal authority usually is not of particular concern in the administrative process. Legal authority is assumed to follow administrative authority. In fact, if any question arises on this point, a man is often given far more legal authority than he is permitted to exercise in actual operation. For example, the board of directors may pass a resolution giving several individuals legal authority to sign checks on the company bank account, and then proceed to set up a variety of internal controls that seriously restrict the exercise of this legal authority.

In dealing with organization problems within private business, then, delegations of authority should be made in terms of administrative feasibility; and whatever legal authorizations may be necessary should conform to, and certainly not confine, approved administrative action.

### Technical authority

The word authority is also commonly used to refer to a person who is a recognized expert in some particular field; for example, we speak of a man as an authority on banking, and another man as an authority on internal combustion engines. In fact, a personal secretary may be an authority on when to ask the boss for a raise. Such acceptance of one's opinion may be called technical authority. Advice of a person with technical authority is followed, not because of the position he holds, but because he presumably knows the right answer on a particular issue.

Technical authority adheres to the individual; it goes with the individual as he moves from position to position and is not something that an executive can assign and reassign. Obviously, when filling a vacancy in an executive position, it is desirable to select an individual who is an authority on the operation involved, for then the newly appointed executive will have both administrative authority and technical authority. This is not always possible, however, particularly when the executive position covers a variety of activities.

With respect to a particular subject, an old employee, an outsider such as a union official, or an equipment salesman may have more technical authority than the executive in charge of the activity. Where this is the case, the wise executive will consult the man with technical authority and frequently will follow his advice; or if this is not possible, he will try to make clear to the employees who normally would follow the man they consider the expert that sound and compelling reasons exist for adopting a different course.

**Ultimate authority**

Still another type of authority, for want of a better term, may be called *ultimate authority*. It deals with the original source from which one derives the right to take certain actions. Thus, we find the Pharisees asking Jesus: "By what authority doest thou these things?" And in more modern times we have the basic philosophical questions over the divine rights of kings, the underlying dominance of a national state, or authority derived from the expressed will of the people.

In this regard, sociologists point out that, whatever the philosophical concept, only as a vast majority of people in a particular nation or state consent to be governed by a set of rulers or a system of laws do government agencies (or business corporations) obtain authority to use social resources and direct individual action.

Thus, in any type of society some form of government and group of leaders must be generally accepted before we can begin to discuss administrative organization and the delegation of authority from one executive to another. Far-reaching as this concept of authority may be, in a practical discussion of administrative processes we must assume that the social structure has located authority within certain administrative enterprises. The assumption is made that society as a whole expects these business and governmental enterprises to perform definite services and has granted at least minimum authority for the excutives of these enterprises to carry out their respective missions.

### Operational authority

Having set aside legal, technical, and ultimate authority, what, then, are we concerned with when delegating authority and responsibility?

Simply stated, delegation of authority is giving someone *permission* to do certain things. For instance, the foreman gives a worker permission to run a machine and to use materials; the president gives the sales vice-president permission to place a certain amount of advertising with local newspapers; or the sales manager gives a salesman permission to call on customers in a given area and to enter into contracts for the delivery of merchandise. Assuming the executive making the delegation is himself authorized to take such action, he merely extends this permission to people working for him.

In practice, an executive rarely delegates operational authority without also indicating how the permission is to be used. In other words, delegation of authority is tied in with duties and obligations, as will be explained in the next section.

NATURE OF DELEGATION

### Simple delegation

Delegation takes place even in the smallest of administrative organizations. As soon as the plumber, the farmer, the manager of a corner grocery, or a real estate agent finds that he cannot perform all of the activities of his enterprise and hires an assistant, delegation takes place. In a large enterprise not only are delegations made from the president to the vice-president, but also redelegations are made by the vice-presidents to managers, managers to supervisors, and so on down the executive pyramid.

When the manager of the corner grocery store first employs an assistant, he probably assigns to the assistant a number of the more routine duties, explaining in some detail just what he wants done. The manager continues to make decisions regarding methods, schedules, and other phases of the operation, but he has relieved himself of at least part of the actual performance that is required. This is not all net gain, however, because the manager now has additional duties of directing and controlling the activities of his assistant. Even in this simple case the manager probably does not do all of the planning for the work of his assistant. He may specify when deliveries are to be made and in what order, and he will probably be very specific about the position of merchandise on the shelves but will leave to the assistant decisions as to how to operate the delivery truck and how to unload and unpack incoming merchandise.

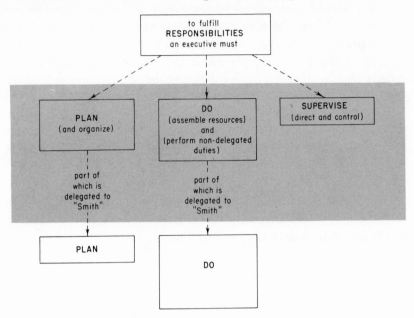

FIGURE 17. *Nature of Delegation.*

The simple delegation that has just been described may be generalized and diagrammed as in Figure 17. In this chart the activities of the executive have been divided into three parts: planning, doing (which is used here to include assembling resources and performing nondelegated duties), and supervising (which includes both direction and control). Using this terminology, delegation normally starts by assigning part of the doing and at least a minimum of the associated planning to a subordinate.

As the volume of the corner grocery store grows, this process of delegation is repeated. Each new assistant is assigned a certain part of the doing and part of the planning related to *his* activity. Some of the activities that the original assistant performed will probably be reassigned to new men, and the manager will delegate more of the duties that he himself formerly performed, bookkeeping and selling, for example. These additional delegations are indicated in Figure 18. Note that as the manager increases the number of his subordinates, he spends a smaller proportion of his time in actually doing and a larger proportion in supervision.

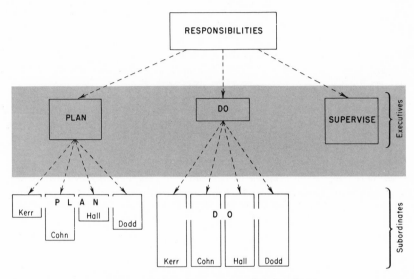

Figure 18. *Delegation to Several Subordinates.*

In making these delegations the manager must decide how the work is to be apportioned among his several subordinates. This is the problem of departmentation, already discussed in Chapter 9. A second, and perhaps more troublesome, issue is how much of the planning should be delegated along with the doing. For example, should the bookkeeper be permitted to establish his own system of accounts; should the delivery man decide the timing and nature of repairs on the delivery truck; should the fruit salesman decide when to reduce the price on peaches in order to move the stock before it becomes overripe? Who should do the planning is perhaps the most complex question in administrative organization; it is the key question in decentralization, which is discussed in Chapter 13.

**Relationships created by delegation**

The process of delegation has three aspects:

1. The assignment by an executive of *duties* (planning and doing of specified activities) to his immediate subordinates;

2. The granting of *permission* (authority) to make commitments, use resources, and take other actions necessary to perform the duties;
3. The creation of an *obligation* (responsibility) on the part of each subordinate to the executive for the satisfactory performance of the duties.

In a large enterprise there is, of course, a whole series of redelegations down to the point where the duties can be performed by the subordinate without further assistance. Where this occurs, a whole series of assignments and authorizations run down the "channel of command" and a corresponding series of obligations run up the channel.

In theory at least, the three aspects of delegation are inseparable, and a change in any one of them normally implies a corresponding adjustment in the other two. For example, if a man is given greater authority to make commitments in the name of a company, his duties with respect to planning are increased as is his responsibility for final results. Likewise, when a man is assigned additional duties, the actions he is permitted to take should be increased correspondingly, and he should be held accountable for the new activity.

### NEED FOR UNDERSTANDING LIMITS OF AUTHORITY

One of the chief difficulties with respect to authority is a failure to recognize the limitations, either expressed or implied, that surround almost every delegation. Too often, an executive gives the necessary authority to perform a vague group of activities without seriously considering the matter at all. In other cases, the executive has fairly definite ideas in mind but fails to make these clear to his subordinate and others affected.

#### General limits implied

The most common restriction on authority is the requirement that action be taken in accordance with company policies, procedures, and programs. Thus, we find one carefully worded statement of duties and authority contains the following provision:

> The duties prescribed in this regulation, and such others as may be assigned from time to time by the board of directors, the executive committee, or the president shall be performed in compliance with the company's policies and procedures relating to accounting and auditing, purchasing, engineering, organization planning, budgetary control, the legal requirements, and the company's employee, public, and governmental

relations, and in full cooperation with the staff and service department responsible for these functions.

Unfortunately, the requirement that action be taken only in accordance with company policies and procedures usually is merely implied. A man appointed to a new position is often left to discover for himself how much of his predecessor's action was dictated by departmental or companywide standing plans and how much can be changed on his own volition.

Rarely is giving an executive completely free rein wise. However, if he is expected to observe general rules, then the duty of his senior is to make sure he fully understands these limitations.

### Specific limits should be clear

In addition to such general restrictions, it is customary to place limits on the actions a man in a particular position may take with respect to specific types of transactions. All too often these restrictions are vague and become a source of friction within an enterprise. These specific limitations can be spelled out as is done in the following list of authority granted to a sales manager.

On Capital Expenditures—Full authority for individual items up to $2,500.

On Operating Expenditures—Full authority to authorize and approve all normal expenditures, standing fully accountable for the over-all total cost of selling.

On Maintenance of Facilities—Full authority to maintain equipment in safe and operable condition.

On Operating Features—Full authority to approve the type of operation of sales branches by salaried labor, through distributorships or through commission agents.

On Financial Aid to Distributors—Full authority to lend sums up to $5,000, where the amount is to be repaid within a five-year period.

On Commission Rates—Full authority to increase or decrease within an established schedule of maximum rates.

On Sales Aid Material—Full authority to expend up to $5,000 for any one sales division or sales district during a calendar year.

On Sales Promotional Plans—Full authority to expend up to $3,000 annually for each district. Such monies to be expended for sales prizes, dinners, and other incentives to stimulate sales promotional interest and to improve morale.

On Policy Adjustments—Full authority to make policy adjustments arising from the sale of products from such causes as contamination, improper application, improper recommendation, or to correct or adjust complaints up to the sum of $2,500.

On Organization Changes—Changes in the basic plan of organization require the approval of the Vice-President in Charge of Sales.

On Wages and Salaries—Full authority to adjust wages and salaries up to $400 per month for promotions. Merit increases or changes in established schedules require approval of a Vice-President and the salary review committee.

On Credit Administration—Full authority to approve the extension of credit to any customer up to $10,000 within established terms for payment.[1]

### Inherent limits on authority over employees

Another source of trouble arises in connection with the authority an executive *can* exercise over employees. Some executives assume that since employees have agreed to give their services to the enterprise, authority over them can be delegated in the same way as over materials and machines. A very essential difference exists, however, between inanimate objects and employees. Of course, both materials and employees must have the qualities and characteristics that the job requires, otherwise permission to use them is of no avail; but, in addition, employees must be *willing* to do the job.

Authority to deal with people outside the enterprise works reasonably because it is at least implied that the authority granted is only permission to negotiate and offer inducements and that it does not embrace the "right of command." Authority over employees within the company, however, is usually regarded in quite a different light; instead of permission to negotiate and offer inducements, the internal relationship is one of command. The crucial question is just what this right of command covers and whether it is something that can be delegated and redelegated in the same way as permission to use equipment.

It is entirely possible and practical to delegate authority to issue instructions on behalf of the enterprise to one or more of its employees. The employee, however, reserves the right to accept or reject such orders. If he doesn't like the instructions, he can always resign; or, what is far more prevalent practice, he can malinger and go through the motions of complying but not put forth the effort needed to achieve the desired results. Faced with such a situation, the executive begins to wonder just what is the significance of permission to issue instructions.

What authority, that is permission, can the enterprise grant to

[1] L. V. Bedell, "Organizing Planning," *Modern Management*, October, 1947, p. 4.

enable the executive to secure compliance with his instructions? He will, of course, be permitted to use various means of stimulating genuine interest in the work to be done. If this fails, he may be permitted to resort to a number of sanctions or pressures that the enterprise can bring to bear on the employee, notably withholding pay increases or promotion in responsibility, transfer to less desirable work, demotions to positions carrying lower rates of pay, temporary layoff without pay, and finally discharge. In many situations perhaps only the first of these actually can be made available to the executive. When an employee gives nominal compliance to instructions, building a case strong enough to justify demotion, layoff, or discharge is difficult; and if the insubordination is not clear-cut, the effect of drastic action on the morale of other employees may be bad.

Particularly with long-service employees, some overt action is usually necessary to warrant discharge (except in those relatively few occupations, such as professional baseball, where outstanding performance is widely recognized as necessary for continued employment). Most companies today use the authority to fire only in extreme cases and as a last resort; with the increasing attention to security and fair treatment of employees, this right is becoming even more circumscribed. In other words, in most situations only a very restricted authority to secure compliance is delegated.

Fortunately, most employees expect to do some work in their jobs. In the United States, particularly, a strong urge exists to "get ahead," many take pride in their work, and most are very sensitive to the social pressures of their fellow employees. Typically, they welcome and respond to leadership. As a result of these attitudes, the typical employee has a rather wide *zone of acceptance* for directions received from the designated spokesman of his employer. The sanctions that the employer places at the disposal of the executive, limited though they may be, widen his zone of acceptance.[2]

Summarizing: When an executive is delegated authority over other employees, he is given permission to issue directions to them

---

[2] In later discussions of supervision and motivation a number of measures that have the effect of increasing the zone of acceptance will be considered. Just how wide the zone of acceptance is, or can be made, will depend upon the cultural patterns, the traditions within the particular enterprise, the availability of alternative employment, the policies of the enterprise regarding the use of sanctions, and the attitudes and personal relationships of the individual employees.

and to exercise to a greater or lesser degree such sanctions as the company has at its disposal. This is a very significant right, but, as every experienced executive knows, it certainly is not unlimited power over behavior of subordinates. Every individual has a number of activities that, because of pride, fear, or hearty dislike, he will refuse to do and a much wider range of activities that he will do only half-heartedly. As Chester Barnard and others have observed, the only authority an executive really has is that which his subordinates are willing for him to exercise.

Unless this inherent limitation on authority over employees is recognized, delegations of authority and responsibility will get snarled up.

<h2 style="text-align:center">RECOGNIZED PRINCIPLES RELATED TO DELEGATION</h2>

Although the basic ideas on delegation appear simple, a number of difficulties have occurred enough times in the past to call for some general warnings. In addition to the points already made about the need for recognizing and defining the limits on authority, specific mention should be made of three others:

1. Responsibility cannot be delegated.
2. Dual subordination should be avoided.
3. Authority and responsibility should be coextensive.

Each of these needs some interpretation and qualification.

### Responsibility cannot be delegated

Occasionally an executive will be found who thinks that once he has delegated a duty to a subordinate, he no longer has an obligation (responsibility) for its proper performance. Looking at the same attitude from another view, a subordinate may feel that once his boss has delegated a duty to him, the boss should no longer be concerned with it.

This false notion confuses two separate delegations, the one a top official $A$ makes to executive $B$, and the one executive $B$ makes in turn to subordinate $C$. The redelegation by executive $B$ does not alter or relieve him of his obligation to his senior, $A$; he still has the same authority he had before although he may voluntarily restrict his actions so as to keep the work flowing to $C$, and he still is accountable for the results achieved.

The redelegation, it is true, has created an additional set of relationships between executive B and his subordinate C. The flow of obligation then becomes C to B and B to A; but executive B can't duck out.

The same reasoning holds in other kinds of responsibility. If Mr. Davis borrows money from the First National Bank and then re-loans it to his son-in-law, the transaction with the son-in-law in no way reduces the money Mr. Davis received from the bank or his obligation to repay it.

While an executive is responsible for the actions of his subordi-nates, for reasons just explained, in practice some recognition must be given to the operating situation. A sales manager, for example, cannot be sure that each of his salesmen uses the best judgment in dealing with each customer. Allowance must be made for human error, and when delegations and redelegations are necessary to ac-complish a large task, this possibility of error is increased. This, how-ever, is more a matter of standards of performance than one of responsibility. The accountability has not been removed by delega-tion; rather, appraisal of results will be tempered somewhat by the extent to which an executive must rely on subordinates to do the work.

### Avoid dual subordination

*A man cannot serve two masters well.* One of the most widely recognized principles of organization is that a member of an enter-prise should normally have only one line supervisor. The more obvious violations of this principle occur in those loosely knit or-ganizations where an employee is not sure who his boss is and at-tempts to adjust his behavior to please everyone who presumably is in a higher status (this is something like the hierarchy of peck-rights that zoologists observe among chickens in a single pen).

Aside from the fact that an employee is probably in a poor posi-tion to decide which orders should be postponed and which obeyed promptly, dual subordination is likely to lead to poor morale because the conscientious employee will feel frustrated if he cannot live up to what is expected of him, the indifferent employee will stop trying since he obviously cannot do all that has been requested, and all of them will sooner or later be reprimanded for failing to comply with instructions. The Bible says that a man cannot serve two masters well, and this same general idea leads to a condemnation of dual subordination in modern administration.

This apparently simple concept raises some difficult questions. Among the more ticklish ones are:

1. Does the use of staff create dual subordination?
2. Does by-passing always result in dual subordination?
3. How can the use of a grievance procedure be reconciled with the concept of a single-line supervisor?

*Subsidiary role of staff.* In the next chapter we shall observe that a staff man not only advises his immediate supervisor but often advises, interprets directions, and checks the work of the operating subordinates of that executive. Whether the staff man merely gives advice, speaks in the name of his boss, or, possibly, has functional authority, he unquestionably influences the decisions and the behavior of many people who are under someone else's line supervision.

Does this create dual subordination? The answer is no. If doubt exists whether the staff advice should be accepted, the decision of a line executive is controlling; he has the last word. And, it is the line executive who uses such sanctions as may be permitted and necessary. As long as all persons concerned recognize that the primary function of a staff man is to assist the operating executives (those in the channel of command) to do a more effective job, trouble can be averted.

*By-passing.* Dual subordination may also be created by by-passing. Thus, if a sales manager deals directly with a salesman, instead of working through the field supervisor, the salesman finds himself with two bosses. In such a situation the employee usually gives preference to the instructions from the senior executive and, finding the way open, may seek an increasing number of contacts with the "big boss." This tends to make the employee independent or indifferent to the wishes of the man who is nominally his immediate supervisor, and it certainly places the supervisor in a difficult position, inasmuch as he may not be fully informed as to the directions given to, or the accomplishments of, the employee.

Warning against by-passing is not intended to condemn all direct contacts between top executives and employees in the lower ranks. For the purpose of building morale and to secure first-hand information, executives should, at least occasionally, make contact with members of the enterprise two, three, or sometimes more levels below them. But, exchanging information and ideas is quite a different matter from giving directions. When issuing orders, good practice requires that the executive send them through the established channel of command, except in emergencies. The breaking of this rule leads to dual subordination, confused responsibility, and undermining of the executive who has been by-passed.

*Right of Appeal.* But what of an employee's right of appeal? The typical grievance procedure, formal or informal, permits an employee to carry a complaint over the head of his immediate supervisor if it cannot be satisfactorily resolved by direct negotiation with the supervisor. The employee's hope, of course, is to get the decision of the supervisor reversed or at least modified. Some industrial psychologists place considerable emphasis on the importance of a free and open right of appeal, even though the arrangement has all the characteristics of by-passing.

On this point we should distinguish between two types of situations. In one there may be what the employee considers to be a violation of the employment contract, the contract including or often consisting entirely of the informal customs and mores surrounding employment in a particular situation. The second broad type of situation is one in which the employee questions the wisdom of his supervisor's instructions, and it is quite aside from the conditions of employment. The grievance procedure deals only with the first of these, and, while it is admittedly a form of by-passing, the desirability of assuring employees of equitable treatment makes this an appropriate exception to the general rule.

On the other hand, the grievance procedure certainly does not contemplate that each employee may appeal any decision the wisdom of which he questions. Under consultative supervision and suggestion systems his opinions may be sought, but unity and efficiency in administration cannot permit an employee to challenge any or all directions he may receive. Except for questions involving a violation of the employment agreement, the integrity of channel of command should be maintained.

**Authority should equal responsibility**

The idea that authority and responsibility should be coextensive is another of the most widely recognized principles of organization. It recognizes, on the one hand, the unfairness of holding a man accountable for results that he is not permitted to guide according to his own best judgment; on the other hand, it recognizes that if a man is given considerable latitude of action, he should be held accountable for the wise use of this permission.

The principle is mischievous, however, in the misunderstandings it can create. One type of mistake is assuming that authority is the same thing as power, instead of being only permission, as already noted. It is often stated, for example, that a sales manager is responsible for obtaining the budgeted sales volume. He obviously cannot be given power to compel customers to purchase the stipulated quantity of goods; general economic conditions, expansion or contraction of the company customers, action of competitors, and other similar factors will have a major influence on sales volume. The sales manager can be given authority (permission) to promote, negotiate, perhaps adjust prices, or even modify the characteristics of the products; but these are only part of the influences that determine sales. Likewise, when we say that the personnel manager is responsible for relations with the union, or that the purchasing agent is responsible for delivery of raw materials on schedule at the budgeted price, we do not mean that they have absolute power over their respective fields of responsibility. We have also noted that authority over employees, while usually more potent than over outsiders, is still subject to limitations.

Moreover, the authority that can be granted wisely is usually circumscribed by operating rules and limitations. The sales manager will probably find that he cannot hire anybody he wishes nor change rates of pay without the approval of the personnel department. He is not at liberty to engage in advertising campaigns and other forms of sales promotion, except within the approved budget. He is not free to add new lines of products. Company policy may dictate the location and type of customer he can cultivate. And so with all the other executives; they are given authority within limits.

With authority thus watered down by external conditions and internal restrictions, what then happens to responsibility? Strictly speaking, the responsibility is correspondingly reduced. This is widely recognized in practice because a man is held specifically accountable for taking reasonable action "under the circumstances." His responsibility is, in fact, not nearly so sweeping as a careless or naive statement of it suggests.

In another and a more important sense, we expect a man to have a feeling of responsibility that far exceeds any authority he has been granted. The concept of civic responsibility, or being "my brother's keeper," places a heavy responsibility on an individual without giving him permission to run the local government or direct the actions of his brother. And so in business, a man may have responsibility for sales promotion, plant safety, expense reduction, public relations, or development of new products, but only very limited authority over the use of materials or the actions of other people. Results are to be achieved through presentation of facts, suggestion, and persuasion. As Chester Barnard observed:

> In any kind of organization good executives know how to get action for which they cannot be given authority of command. Nothing is more important to teach the beginner than this . . . in most organizations many members of high and low degree, who have little or no authority to command, are properly held accountable and responsible.[3]

This sense of responsibility involves a moral concern with conditions and results, an urge to devise ways and means of improving present conditions, a zeal to convince others of action that should be taken, patient persistence if desired action cannot be secured immediately, and a relentless watchfulness over a period of time. Such a concept of responsibility is very real and very potent, and it may operate even though an individual has no more authority than to get the facts and communicate with people whose action is involved.

In summary, then, the rule that authority and responsibility should be equal is sound, provided we recognize that: (1) the authority that can and should be delegated is often limited and, consequently, an individual can be held strictly accountable only to the extent that actions are really subject to his control, and (2) a person can be expected to feel a sense of responsibility even though his authority is confined to studying present conditions and promoting improvements, and he can be held accountable for sensing trouble and trying to get it corrected.

## SUMMARY

Administrative organization is not primarily concerned with legal, technical, or ultimate authority; the operational authority relationships that may be created by organization are, however, of major significance.

[3] Review of Mr. Urwick's book, *Elements of Administration*, in *Personnel*, Vol. 21, No. 4.

Delegation of such authority involves three aspects: assignment of duties, granting of permissions, and creation of obligations or responsibilities. As a practical matter, delegations are almost always restricted by standing plans, by specific limits on permission granted, and by the limited authority over employees that can be delegated. Confusion will be avoided by clearly recognizing such limitations. Also, the ideas that responsibility cannot be delegated, dual subordination should be avoided, and authority and responsibility should be coextensive are useful provided they are properly interpreted.

In delegations to operating subordinates, authority to "do" exceeds authority to "plan," inasmuch as the executive typically reserves some of the planning for himself. The role of staff in helping the executive plan and supervise is discussed in the next chapter. The degree to which planning should or should not be reserved by the executive—that is, centralized—is considered in Chapter 13.

### SELECTED REFERENCES

Allen, L. A., *Management and Organization*, McGraw-Hill Book Co., Inc., 1958, Chaps. 6 and 9.

Dubin, R., *Human Relations in Administration* (2nd ed.) Prentice-Hall, Inc., 1961, Part IV.

Koontz, H. and C. O'Donnell, *Principles of Management* (2nd ed.) McGraw-Hill Book Co., Inc., 1959, Chap. 6.

Newman, W. H., "Overcoming Obstacles to Effective Delegation," *Management Review*, January 1956.

# 12

# The Role of Staff

One of the distinctive features of modern military organization is the use of staff. A similar type of organization can be found in both religious and business organizations, but the idea is not so clearly developed. Many business executives would probably make better use of the staff concept if they and other members of their enterprise understood the nature and requisites for its successful use. Consequently, the purpose of this chapter is to:

1. Describe the basic role of staff.
2. Consider when staff may be used effectively.
3. Examine the requisites for successful staff work.
4. Explain the meaning of "functional authority," which may be regarded as an extension of the staff concept.
5. Note some of the special ways in which staff may be employed.

## THE CONCEPT OF STAFF

### Duties of a staff assistant

The nature of staff can be illustrated in the relationship between the president of a medium-size manufacturing company and his assistant, Jim Hull. The president was extremely busy and so he selected Hull, who had demonstrated considerable versatility in the four years he had been with the company, as his assistant.

At first, the president gave Hull only *routine tasks*, such as analyzing the telephone bills to determine which departments were responsible for the increase in long-distance charges, scanning current newspapers and four trade journals for items of interest, and similar miscellaneous duties. By turning these things over to Hull, the president found that he had more time for major problems, and that many of the minor issues received more adequate attention than they would if he had attempted to do them himself.

After Hull had demonstrated both his dependability and his discretion in dealing with others, the president asked him to get pertinent facts bearing on a proposed change in the firm's sales-compensation plan from the sales manager, controller, and personnel manager, as well as from other companies. The information Hull assembled and summarized enabled the president to deal intelligently and promptly with an issue that had a significant bearing on the company's future sales. As time went on, the president depended more and more on his assistant to *assemble and digest* facts relating to tough problems that had come to him for decision.

The next year, when a further question regarding sales compensation arose, the president enlarged the request he made of Hull. He wanted not only a digest of the pertinent facts, but also Hull's *personal recommendation* as to what should be done. And, before presenting his report, Hull was asked to find out whether the other executives interested in the decision agreed with the recommendation. Thus, instead of a baffling problem, the president had before him the pertinent facts sifted and sorted, a proposed course of action from a man who was already familiar with the president's views, along with either the endorsement or the exceptions, with reasons therefor, of the key individuals in the situation. The president could proceed immediately to his own appraisal of the proposal and consideration of the points of disagreement among his subordinates.

With this sort of groundwork laid, the president was able to dispose of a troublesome issue after a half-hour's conference, whereas without the groundwork he personally might have had to spend considerable time discussing opinions with several individuals, sifting the facts, and reviewing his plan of action with the men who would have to execute it.

A natural addition to Hull's duties was the preparation of any correspondence, bulletins, or other documents that the president had to issue to put a decision into effect. Sometimes this was done after the president had made the basic decision, but often Hull could *prepare the necessary documents* before the report was presented to the president. Then, if the president agreed with the recommendation, all he had to do was sign the papers.

In addition, on any important or controversial matter the president asked Hull to meet with the individuals directly affected by a decision and *explain* the reasons for the decision and just what was expected. As questions arose from time to time over the application of the decision to a particular situation, it was usually Hull who made the *interpretation* because, as the president was frank to admit, Hull knew more about the detail than he did. When the people throughout the company found that Hull was always consulted on such matters, and incidentally that he was usually easier to see, they raised their questions first with Hull and went to the president only if serious disagreement arose over the interpretation, or they wished to urge a change in the major decision. In the latter case, if Hull agreed that a change was needed, the president usually did not hear of the matter until he was presented with a complete proposal for a new decision.

The president took one further step: "Jim, you've been right in the middle of this sales-compensation problem and know my views on the matter. I wish you would *keep an eye on what happens*. Unless I hear from you, I'll assume things are going along satisfactorily. In other words, so far as sales compensation is concerned, I'm going to let you do my worrying for me." As the president was able to make an increasing number of delegations of this sort, he received a very substantial relief from the pressures on his time.

### Increasing the number of assistants

Before leaving this illustration, let us note two things that are likely to happen when an assistant is as effective as the one just described. If the president continues to lack time to do all the things that need his attention, he is likely to seek additional men to assist him as Jim Hull does. When there are several such assistants, it is natural to divide work among them in accordance with their abilities and experience. Thus, one assistant may be assigned problems having to do with production, physical facilities, and related matters. Another may be assigned duties in connection with legislation, tax, sales contracts, and so forth. Perhaps the third deals with problems of executive personnel, industrial relations, and training programs. Since the relationship is predominantly a personal one between the executive and his assistants, the manner in which the work will be divided among the assistants will depend upon the kinds of help the executive most needs and the capacities of those assisting him.

Beside increasing the number of assistants, one or more of these men may establish small staffs of their own. Their work may be quite time-consuming, particularly if they are expected to maintain contacts with widely dispersed operations or to conduct intensive research on particular subjects. A man cannot be available immediately at the call of the president and at the same time be making a tour of the branch offices to interpret a new sales-compensation plan. Consequently, in a large enterprise, often "Mr. Hull's office" consists of perhaps half a dozen individuals.

### The role staff can play

From this extended example we see that staff work consists of helping an executive plan and/or supervise the activity of others. It is work the executive would do himself if he had the time and the specialized knowledge. In a sense the staff assistants act as an extension of the executive's personality.

The duties assigned to a staff assistant may include part or all of the following:

1. Assembling facts;
2. Summarizing and interpreting facts;
3. Recommending courses of action;
4. Discussing proposed plans with various other executives and obtaining their concurrence or reasons for objection;
5. Preparing written orders and other documents necessary to put a plan into action;
6. Explaining and interpreting orders that have been issued;
7. Watching actual operations to ascertain if the orders issued are achieving the desired results;
8. On the basis of operating experience and anticipated conditions, initiating new plans;
9. Promoting an exchange of information among operating officials to increase voluntary coordination;
10. Developing enthusiasm among operating people for established policies and program;
11. Providing information and advice to operating people regarding performance of duties that have been delegated to them.

These are all phases of the planning, direction, and control that, if not assigned to a staff assistant, would normally be performed by the executive himself.

In actual practice a single staff assistant is not usually expected to perform all of the phases of the executive duties; he may be concerned primarily with assistance on planning or with assistance on supervision, or if the assistant is relatively inexperienced, his work may be confined to only certain aspects of these functions. More-over, the typical staff man will concentrate on only a limited number of subject fields. *"Staff" work has no clear meaning until the subjects covered and the action to be taken with respect to each subject are defined.*

## WHEN IS THE USE OF STAFF DESIRABLE?

The use of staff creates somewhat complex relationships within an organization. Simple delegation provides for the assignment of duties to subordinates; the planning of these activities may be as-signed to the subordinate along with the doing or be retained by the executive. But a staff man who participates in the planning, and perhaps some aspects of supervision, is a third party having relation-ships with both the executive and the executive's subordinate. This raises many of the implications of the old adage "While two is com-pany, three is a crowd." Therefore, the administrator should give careful consideration to the situations in which this more complex arrangement will have an over-all net benefit to operations.

### Special staff

The benefits of staff are most commonly acknowledged when the staff assistant has technical knowledge and skill not possessed by the executive or his subordinates. Legal counsel, for example, is found in a great many enterprises. Both the executive and his sub-ordinates recognize that legal aspects of a company's operations are technical and important enough to call for special advice. A ticklish question may arise, however, if the legal counsel becomes active in the direction and control of operations. A well-trained lawyer has little difficulty showing that almost everything a company does has legal implications, and consequently, if the role of the legal counsel is to be extended beyond giving advice, he should be an individual who has a good sense of technical operations.

The desirability of an independent auditor is also widely accepted. Since the auditor deals with one aspect of supervision, this activity cannot be delegated to operating subordinates; and, on the other hand, it is time-consuming and often so technical that the executive himself cannot perform the work. Many small companies, of course, rely entirely upon annual audits by a public accountant. Insofar as the executive regards these outside audits as an aid in his super-vision, the public accountant acts temporarily as a staff man.

This use of *special staff* has been highly developed in the army where a commanding officer is likely to have special assistants dealing with communications, medical work, legal work, engineering, chemical warfare, artillery, ordnance, quartermaster supplies, religious and moral activities, or other specialties. In government almost every agency or department head has an assistant on "information" who watches over the dissemination of information to the public, and in recent years a number of business corporations have added a public relations man to their staff. The particular types of specialized assistants that are needed by a top executive or one of the major operating executives depend, of course, on the operations they direct.

### General staff

Assistants need not be confined to narrow specialties. As was seen in the illustration of Jim Hull, they sometimes serve in an over-all capacity, dealing with those problems on which the executive needs help most at the particular moment. In an intermediate category would be those staff assistants who are continuously involved with the main stream of administration although they concentrate on only one phase of it. In this group would be an assistant who works on the budget, particularly if he works on substantive rather than procedural aspects. In a similar category would be an assistant who works on long-range programs, and sometimes we find an assistant who concentrates on expense control. Also within this group would be a man who works on executive personnel, personnel policies, and industrial relations. All such men work closely with and in the name of the executive they serve. They are extensions of his personality in the sense that they supplement his seeing and hearing, his imagination and cogitation, his specialized knowledge, his time for patient explanation and interpretation of plans, his coordinating influence, his frank appraisal, and his inspiration.

Although many of the foregoing illustrations of staff apply particularly to the top executive of an enterprise, the same idea often is useful for other executives. A production manager, for example, may well have an assistant working on plant engineering and another on production methods. In the same way, a sales manager may have staff assistants for sales methods, training, or market research. Any major executive may find the use of staff a practical way of avoiding an additional stratum of supervision, while at the same time providing good direction and supervision of operating people.

**Pros and cons on the use of staff**

A study of these various examples suggests that the use of staff is desirable when:

1. The duties of an executive exceed his capacity to fulfill them well, either because he lacks the necessary time and energy or because they require specialized knowledge that he does not possess; *and*

2. Relieving this load by delegation to operating personnel is not feasible because (a) uniformity or coordination of action in several operating units is particularly important, (b) economy or effectiveness can be increased by assigning the work to a specialist, or (c) operating subordinates lack the capacity (time or ability) to do more of their own planning or to work effectively with less supervision.

We should bear in mind, however, that the use of staff has its drawbacks. First, it often increases administrative expense. In this connection we should remember that the operating executive and personnel naturally have a keen interest in the planning and the supervision of the activities in which they are engaged, and they know a great deal about the things to be done. Thus, there are inherent advantages in delegating planning along with doing. The establishment of a separate staff assistant for planning adds to the executive payroll and necessitates the transfer of information from the operating people to the staff assistant. When setting up a staff position, one should always question whether this additional expense will be more than repaid.

Second, the establishment of staff adds to the complexity of organizational relationships. Not only are the number of relationships increased, but the particular position of the staff man is often hard to define, and more opportunity arises for misunderstanding. In addition, many people have a psychological resentment to receiving instructions and being checked up on, particularly by an individual whom they do not regard as their superior. This makes the effective functioning of the staff assistant an even more delicate matter. Therefore, valuable as staff may be, it should be used only when simple delegation does not fit the situation.

REQUISITES FOR SUCCESSFUL STAFF WORK

The use of staff is a relatively complex arrangement in administrative organization, and special care is required if it is to be fully effective. In addition to being sure that the concept itself is understood and that the proper people are selected for staff positions, a number of points deserve special consideration. Among these requisites for successful staff work are the following:

1. Provide the staff man ready access to necessary information through:
   a. Intimate and frequent contact with his boss.
   b. Easy communication with operating executives and other staff men.
2. Consult the staff man before taking any action in the area of his responsibility.
3. Expect staff man to take initiative in promoting needed action.
4. Insist that the staff man rely primarily on selling his ideas, rather than resorting to commands.

**Provide access to necessary information**

If the staff man is to serve as an extension of the boss's personality, as has been suggested, he must be intimately acquainted with that personality. Unless he is in frequent contact with the boss, he will have difficulty knowing what kinds of information the boss needs, and he certainly will be in a weak position to explain his senior's views on a given subject to other people in the enterprise. In fact, if he is out of touch with the top executive, his recommendations and representations may do more harm than good. Operating executives would be better off to receive no advice at all than to receive incorrect counsel from one who is presumed to be in a position to speak for the principal executive.

This need for close contact with the boss places an obligation on him to be available for discussion with his staff assistants and to share freely with them his information, his hopes, his prejudices, and his plans. Direct personal contact, conferences, and circulation of written material, letters, and reports are probably all necessary for this purpose.

The need for this kind of contact necessarily limits the number of staff assistants who can effectively serve a single executive. Of course, assistants who specialize in one area do not require as frequent contact as a general assistant, and to some extent contact with other staff assistants or with what the army calls a "chief of staff" can reduce the need for direct personal contact. Nevertheless, experience clearly demonstrates that the effectiveness of a staff man diminishes as his contact with his principal becomes more remote.

With respect to operating information, operating executives must also understand that the staff man is entitled to any information relating to his assignment and may, within reason, request reports on local situations. Fully as important are the informal channels of communication. The casual dropping in on another man's office, the brief telephone call to pass along news of current developments, comments made in the relaxed atmosphere of the lunch table or the hall, and the frank and unhurried discussions of men when they are traveling together away from the office, all these are important in keeping the staff man informed. Such flow of information depends more upon the social relations than upon organizational design. Still, by recognizing their importance, an executive can encourage and perhaps help provide occasions for such informal contacts. Successful staff assistance in both planning and control requires that the staff man really be in a position to serve as the eyes and ears of his principal.

### Consult staff before taking action

The effectiveness of a staff man can be either enhanced or undermined by the consistency with which his superior seeks his advice. For example, if the branch manager secures the approval of the sales vice-president for the appointment of a new sales supervisor while they are taking a five-minute rest at the end of the thirteenth hole in a golf game, and the personnel assistant to the vice-president learns of the appointment two weeks later, a precedent is set for further direct action. It is too late for the staff assistant to point out that the new appointee lacks certain important types of experience and that another man now in the headquarters office is well prepared for such an assignment. The next time the branch manager wants to make an important personnel shift he will try to arrange another golf game, and he will soon come to regard the personnel assistant's investigation of branch personnel as unnecessary meddling.

Quite a different situation would have been created if the vice-president had said at the thirteenth hole: "Sounds like a good idea. Let's talk it over tomorrow morning with Bob who follows such things for me." Not only might the particular appointment have been different, but the branch manager would have learned that the personnel assistant played an important role in the promotion of key personnel. The next time the branch manager wanted to make a personnel shift he would probably discuss the matter first with the personnel assistant; then the vice-president could quickly get the advice of both men and act with dispatch.

This practice of consulting a staff man before taking action in the area of his responsibility is not recommended primarily as a means of increasing his status; more important, it assures that the principal executive will receive the benefit of the counsel of the staff man, which is the chief reason for the existence of his position. It is also important if the staff man is to relieve the executive of personal attention to a lot of details of operation.

The importance of consulting staff before taking action has long been recognized in the Catholic Church. For centuries common practice has been to *require* an official to seek the counsel of his subordinates (sometimes including staff men independently appointed) even though he has an unquestionable right of command after such advice is received.

### Staff initiative

There are two views regarding the initiative the staff man should take. One holds that the staff should merely be on call for assistance and that the request for aid should be initiated by the principal executive or the operating division.

The second concept in no way bars request for aid from operating people, but it does presume that the staff itself will initiate considerable action. Under this view the staff is expected to do the boss's worrying about the assigned field of activity; he is expected to know if anything is wrong in his area and to feel responsible for promoting appropriate corrective action. While under special circumstances the first concept may be desirable, as a general rule the staff man should avoid acting like a doctor or a lawyer who hangs up his shingle and then hopes clients will seek his advice before they become incurably ill or involved.

This sense of responsibility, this acute dissatisfaction that a staff man should feel when all is not well in his field, does not mean that the staff man should necessarily attempt to secure perfect conditions within a short period of time. As an integral part of the boss's office, he must have a sense of relative importance, of strategic timing, of long-run versus short-run benefits, and similar considerations. If such

matters suggest delay or cautious action, this is a question of deliberate decision rather than lack of initiative. The staff man should
be ever watchful of ways to press forward and usually should keep
the principal executive fully informed of the reasons for postponing
action and the possible consequences that may arise from doing so.

### Voluntary acceptance of staff recommendation

The staff man makes recommendations both to his superior and to
operating executives working under the superior. To be most effective, these recommendations must be in a form that leads to action.
This means, among other things, that the staff man should not
swamp the executive with a large volume of data before it has been
analyzed and related to solutions of problems facing the executive.
Nor should he present proposals that are theoretically desirable but
clearly impractical in the particular situation.

Instead, the recommendations to the chief executive should be
prepared from his point of view; that is, expressed in language that
he and operating assistants will readily understand and integrated
with the total operating situation at the time they are made. As staff
becomes more highly specialized, this point of view becomes increasingly difficult to maintain, especially if frequent and close
contacts with the chief executive are not provided.

Recommendations made to operating personnel subordinate to the
principal executive likewise have to be couched in terms of the practical operating situation. In most cases, the proposals should be
"sold" to the operating executive; that is, they should win his voluntary acceptance. These proposals do not carry the weight of command, except when the staff man is speaking explicitly for the
principal executive or in those unusual situations where functional
authority is desirable. Since an appeal to authority should be used
only as a last resort, the staff man should rely primarily upon winning
voluntary acceptance of his ideas.

Even when a command is issued by the principal executive, ready
acceptance by the man who has to put the instructions into effect
will contribute much to their success. Consequently, the staff man
should be primarily concerned with achieving results, encouraging
the operating executives to take credit for new ideas, letting facts
speak for themselves, and holding himself always in the background
as one who is merely assisting other individuals to do a good job.

To win the full cooperation of operating people and at the same time to initiate changes in operating practice is not always easy. All too often the operating man wants to leave well enough alone. One device that may be helpful in this situation is to require the staff man to make a semiannual or annual report to the principal executive covering the present status and need of changes in the area of the staff man's responsibility. The staff man can then explain to operating executives that he cannot honestly and safely fail to report such conditions. This then removes from the staff man the onus of bringing the matter to the boss's attention. In addition, it provides an occasion for discussing changes that, if made, would permit turning in a satisfactory report.

From the preceding discussion we can see that not all people are qualified to undertake staff work. In this regard Leonard D. White has said:

> The qualities of a successful staff officer are negotiating ability rather than highly developed capacity to command; the possession of a broad range of practical knowledge rather than specialized expertness in one field; patience and persistence rather than a tendency toward quick and fixed decisions; a willingness to remain in the background, rather than a desire for personal prominence; loyalty towards the policies and views of superiors, rather than insistence on one's conclusions or recommendations. Such men can be found; and in the conduct of administration they are invaluable.[1]

## USE AND LIMITATIONS OF FUNCTIONAL AUTHORITY

Of all the concepts in the field of administrative organization, perhaps none is subject to as much misunderstanding and abuse as is functional authority. Since one of the simplest ways to regard this troublesome concept is as an extension of the staff idea, it will be considered here. The discussion will be centered around:

1. The meaning of functional authority
2. Limitations and dangers in its use
3. Conditions favoring its use

### Meaning of functional authority

*Definition.* We have noted that a staff man often investigates an operating problem and prepares a recommended course of action. If the recommendation is acceptable, his boss then issues it as an order

---

[1] *Introduction to the Study of Public Administration,* 3rd ed., The Macmillan Company, 1948, p. 59.

to subordinate operating executives and operating personnel. Often the staff man prepares the written statement regarding the new plan (order) and is expected to explain and interpret the meaning of the order to operating personnel.

An individual who has functional authority follows the same steps as those just described except that he issues the order in his own name instead of submitting it as a recommendation and having it go out over the name of the principal executive. Normally, an individual is granted such functional authority only over a limited type of activities. *Functional authority*, then, is permission to prepare and issue directions with respect to a specified group of activities, or aspects of certain activities; except for the source of issuance, such orders are to be treated as though they came from the principal executive himself.

Referring back to the discussion of delegation in the preceding chapter, we noted that often an executive delegates wide authority and responsibility for doing but reserves more or less of the planning. When functional authority is used, no change is made in the doing delegation. Certain limited parts of the planning, however, are turned over to a special assistant. Within the limits of his functional authority, this assistant decides the what, the when, and the how for those who actually perform the activity.

The reason for such an arrangement will be obvious to those who have had experience with the actual use of staff men. Often, the principal executive comes to place considerable reliance upon the recommendations of his staff, particularly on technical matters (for example, engineering, legal, medical, or accounting subjects). Everyone concerned, the staff man, the principal executive, and the operators, all recognize that his approval of the order is a perfunctory matter; consequently, administrative procedure is simplified by having the order go direct from the staff man to operating personnel.

*Effect of decisions.* Although the source of such a functional order may be different, it has the effect of any direction coming down the channels of command. The line supervisor is responsible for seeing that it is fulfilled, and his authority with respect to supervision and the exercise of sanctions is unchanged. Just as with any other direction, if he feels that execution of the order is unwise or impractical, he may go back to his senior executive and ask for a modification; although here it would be simpler to go first to the man who issued the instructions and try to get an adjustment before appealing up the line. Until the direction is rescinded or modified, he is expected to carry it out.

Functional authority is concerned only with the issuance of technical directions by one executive to people who are under someone else's line supervision; for example, when the chief accountant issues instructions to the warehouse foremen or the district sales manager. We do not say that a line executive has functional authority over his direct subordinates because the concept of line supervision includes authority to issue instructions.

Military administration employs essentially the same idea as functional authority. In this instance a staff man issues the direction "in the name of the commanding officer." For example, in defining the role of a control office, an Army manual states:

> The position of a control officer in regard to operating units of the organization is exactly the same as that of any other staff division. A control office is authorized to direct operating units, in the name of a commanding general, on matters which are the functional responsibility of the control office. . . .
>
> Despite existing ability to exercise directive authority in the name of the commanding general, this power should be used as infrequently as possible. Action should be obtained through informal agreement and through the wisdom of recommendation, rather than through the exercise of staff authority.[2]

By insisting that the directions be issued in the name of the commanding officer the Army maintains at least the fiction that all directions come down through a single channel of command, and at the same time it obtains almost as much flexibility as is secured through the use of functional authority.

*Transfer of planning authority.* In the discussion thus far considerable centralization of authority has been assumed. The only issue has been whether the central executive would himself issue all directions, or whether he would permit certain of his assistants to issue directions covering specified subjects in his behalf.

When, however, an enterprise or department has been operating with considerable decentralization of authority, the granting of functional authority is likely to meet with more resistance. For instance, when operating executives, who formerly have been free to discharge employees as they see fit, find that functional authority over such matters has now been granted to the personnel director, or when

---

[2] Army Service Forces, *Manual M703-1, Fundamentals of Control*, p. 6.

these operating executives find that changes in office procedure are being determined by a methods division, there are likely to be complaints regarding the loss of prerogatives. This is, indeed, just what has happened, for in effect the principal executive first centralized authority over such matters (thereby reducing the prerogatives of the operating executive) and then delegated functional authority to his specialized assistant.

An alternative arrangement is to give the personnel officer or the methods department *concurring* authority instead of functional authority. Under this set-up the operating executives would have to secure the concurrence or agreement of the specialized unit before taking action in the particular field, but they would not be under obligation to carry out the instructions of the specialized unit in the same way as if those instructions came from the principal executive himself.

*Channel of communication.* One further point about the application of functional authority may be helpful. To whom should the directions from a man exercising functional authority be directed— the executives immediately under the principal who granted the functional authority, operating supervisors, or individual operators?

The practical answer to this question appears to be that the instructions from the functional unit should flow directly to the level in each chain of command at which decisions on such matters are made. Thus, if authority is decentralized, several top layers of supervision may be by-passed in order to speed up matters. The man at the decision level should then keep his senior officers informed just as he would on matters that he decided for himself. The very existence of the decentralized authority may be taken as evidence that the top executives do not consider it wise to attempt to decide such matters personally, and only wish to become involved when operating results are in danger.

On the other hand, we may find a man in a functional unit issuing instructions to an executive who is clearly senior in status; for example, a man in charge of budgetary procedure may issue instructions to a vice-president. Where the granting of functional authority is well conceived in the first place and the man exercising it is technically competent, this sort of relationship is entirely workable—at least among civilians—and the military make it palatable by acting in the name of the commanding officer. Bear in mind here, as in all of the discussion of functional authority, that the device is fundamentally a shortcut designed to eliminate some organization formalities and red tape.

### Limitations on the use of functional authority

Understanding the nature of functional authority is one thing; knowing when to use it is quite another. In making practical applications of functional authority, one must be aware of its advantages and limitations. Since the illustrations given thus far have suggested the desirability of functional authority, let us look first at the principal dangers and disadvantages of its use.

The directions coming from several different functional executives may *overburden operating people*, and occasionally they may even conflict with each other. Consider, for example, the district sales supervisor who receives instructions for rather elaborate accounting records from the chief accountant, training directions along with requests for frequent individual ratings from the personnel director, elaborate and glowing instructions regarding the next sales campaign from the sales promotion director, and weighty instructions from the legal counsel, all in addition to what presumably are the major orders received from his line supervisor, the sales manager. Each of these executives in his zeal to fulfill his particular responsibility places heavy burden on the operating man.

The directions from the sales promotion manager and the chief counsel may also be somewhat *inconsistent* when applied to a particular operating situation, or the sales supervisor may receive an urgent request for revised budget data on the afternoon he is expected to have a training conference. Each of the executives with functional authority is empowered to go directly to operating supervisors, and only occasionally is provision made for some central clearance (like the chief of staff in army organization) to make sure that all the directions, when combined together, make a consistent, doable assignment.

Substantial use of functional authority tends to *weaken the influence of the line supervisor*. As more and more orders are received from the functional specialists, the operating man naturally tends to turn to them for interpretation, advice, and assistance in carrying out their particular instructions. This admittedly dilutes the authority of the line supervisor and can depreciate his status in the eyes of his subordinates. The reduction of the role of the foreman to little more than a stimulator to action in some of the highly "functionalized" shops has become a graphic example of this tendency. And yet the line supervisor is expected to see that the directions are carried out; he is the one who is supposed to get results.

The use of functional authority may further lead to *autocratic and inflexible administration.* Since the man with functional authority can speak with the authority of the principal executive, he is constantly tempted to rely upon official decree rather than voluntary agreement. This autocratic approach, as will be noted later in discussion of direction and control, loses the benefits of joint participation and, under some circumstances, results in indifferent work. Then, as operating conditions change and there really is need to modify the direction, the centralized executive may have lost intimate touch with the actual situation. Often a conference or two, perhaps with the principal executive, who is likely to be busy, will be necessary to achieve the merging of several compartmentalized viewpoints and the issuance of new directions. Where decision-making is kept within the jurisdiction of line supervisors, and particularly when such authority is decentralized, this source of inflexibility can be avoided.

### Conditions favoring the use of functional authority

Examination of the preceding limitations of the use of functional authority will show that much of the difficulty arises when functional authority is granted to several different executives and when it covers a substantial part of the total job of an operating person. Like many other refinements or short cuts, when used occasionally and in moderation, they work well, but when adopted as a primary basis of administration, they cause confusion. Functional authority works best under the following conditions:

1. *When only a minor aspect of a total operating job is covered.* This may be either a relatively unimportant phase, for instance, medical examination of plant workers, or accounting records in a district sales office. Or, it may be the detailed procedures to be followed in the execution of a plan already agreed upon by the line supervisor, as, for example, the particular steps to be followed in merit rating or in placing advertisements in local newspapers. Such activities should be performed properly, and when they constitute a relatively minor and somewhat alien part of the total

activity involved, it may be better to let some specialist stipulate how they should be done.

2. *When technical or specialized knowledge of a type not possessed by operating executives is needed.* For example, the typical operating executive in a manufacturing or distributing enterprise probably does not understand the intricacies of real estate, tax, or construction problems since he encounters these fairly technical problems infrequently. Also, these are the types of problems on which the principal executive would probably accept the advice of his assistant, so it may be simpler to authorize the specialized assistant to deal directly.

3. *When uniformity, or at least consistency, of action in several operating units is essential.* The need for a uniform basis for evaluating inventories located in several branches or the desirability of consistent extension of credit by two or more product divisions of a company illustrates this point.

If at least two of these conditions are present, the use of functional authority may be quite helpful. It provides an expeditious way of getting fairly technical direction to the operating people. On the other hand, its overuse can lead to considerable confusion; and if doubt exists regarding the desirability of the arrangement, it is probably wise to fall back onto the straight staff relationship. If the staff man has superior technical knowledge and also can get the backing of the principal executive when this is needed, he can accomplish almost the same results as when he has functional authority. When in doubt, be cautious about granting functional authority.

### Special Arrangements for Staff Work

Before leaving the general subject of staff, we should note some of the special ways staff may be related to other parts of the organization. Important in this connection are (1) the assignment of both staff and operating duties to a single individual or division, and (2) the duplication of staff units at several levels in a large enterprise.

#### Combination of staff and operating work

Small enterprises, particularly, may need to combine operating and staff duties. For example, a treasurer may be responsible for directing the financial activities and also serve as a general assistant to the president. In such a situation we say that a man has two hats, one to wear as an operating executive and the second as a staff assistant. Unfortunately, this is only a figure of speech, and all too often the employees contacted by such an executive are not sure whether he speaks in his capacity as treasurer or as an assistant to the president; in fact, he may not draw the distinction sharply himself.

If the concepts are clearly established, however, this confusion can be minimized, and a single man has often performed such a dual role effectively. In small units, where the expense of a full-time staff man may be prohibitive, this may be the only arrangement that is practical.

Service divisions may also be assigned a dual role. Again we are talking about the consolidation of two distinct organizational devices, an operating service and the extension of the abilities of an executive. The sales promotion department, for example, may perform a variety of services for salesmen, such as the preparation of samples and the mailing of letters to prospects designated by the salesmen, and at the same time it may act as an advisor to top executives and field supervisors on sales methods. Likewise, the engineering department may both perform engineering services and also be the chief source of technical advice throughout the company.

A similar arrangement is recognized in army organization where a single individual may both command an activity and also advise the commanding officer on, say, ordnance or artillery. Such a grouping is usually dictated by economy; it is less expensive to use the specialized ability of the executives of such divisions in both staff and operating capacities.

**Duplicate staff**

In large enterprises sometimes staff units are set up not only under the chief executive but also under the major departmental executives, and perhaps at a third level. Thus, there may be a legal assistant to the general manager, to the sales manager, and occasionally to the district manager. Such duplication of staff at two or more levels exists for cost control and budgeting, personnel, and other functions. The desirability of this arrangement depends upon (1) the volume of such work under each of the operating executives,

(2) the degree of decentralization of authority, and (3) the technical character of the staff advice, and, hence, the ease or difficulty of communicating it down the line of supervision.

Effective staff work requires that the information, the advice, and the supervisory assistance be readily available to the operating executive who is actually making the decision in the matter. Hence, if staff assistance is to be provided on specific operating issues, a large company has no alternative but to duplicate staff at the lower operating centers of administration.

If repetition of staff is needed, usually the staff man attached to the senior executive should concur in the appointment and assist in the training of staff men performing a similar function in subsidiary operating units. This practice, along with the parallel form of organization, which will be discussed in more detail under organization structure, promotes consistency and efficiency of administration, even when the staff advisors are nominally independent of one another and attached to separate operating executives.

## SUMMARY

The job of an administrator has been divided, in this book, into planning, organizing, assembling resources, supervising, and controlling. These tasks often are beyond the capacity of any single executive. The simplest, and therefore preferable, way to cope with this heavy load is to delegate part of the administrative tasks to subordinates who are also responsible for performance. Another possibility is the use of staff.

Staff assistants can help an executive in a variety of ways. Usually, their chief job is to assist with the planning. They may be asked to gather facts, analyze troubles, make recommendations, draft instructions, and secure suggestions and views of various people affected by a proposed order. Often, they assist the executive in directing by explaining and interpreting orders and by counseling with subordinates. Sometimes staff men are asked to keep track of what actually happens and to initiate corrective action when necessary; in this way they help in controlling.

In all these activities, the staff man is doing what the executive himself would do if he had the time and ability. The staff man always acts in behalf of the executive, and in this sense tries to function as an extension of the executive's personality.

Staff is likely to be useful when an overloaded executive cannot delegate down the line because (1) coordinated action of several operating units is particularly important, (2) expertness, adequate attention, and objectivity of a staff man will result in greater effectiveness, or (3) operating subordinates are already loaded to capacity. On the other hand, staff often increases administrative expense, and it inherently creates complex relationships. Consequently, it should be used with caution.

Even greater wariness is needed when functional authority is considered. Issuance of directions by one person for subordinates of someone else to carry out is likely to lead to confusion, unless the directions deal with a relatively minor and specialized phase of operations.

The needs of the particular executive should determine what, if any, staff help is desirable. Sometimes one or two assistants who cover a wide range of subjects are needed; occasionally a group of more specialized aides are advisable. In many situations no full-time staff is warranted, but certain operating or service executives devote part of their time to staff work. Whatever the scope and the time spent, staff work will be fully effective only if the staff man has ready access to information, is consulted regularly by the principal executive, takes initiative, and relies primarily on persuasion to get his idea accepted.

### SELECTED REFERENCES

Allen, L. A., *Improving Line-Staff Relationships*, National Industrial Conference Board, Studies in Personnel Policy, No. 153.

Dale, E., *Planning and Developing the Company Organization Structure*, American Management Association, Research Report No. 20, pp. 61-83.

Dalton, M., *Men Who Manage*, John Wiley & Sons, Inc., 1959.

Richards, M. D. and W. A. Nielander, *Readings in Management*, South-Western Publishing Co., 1958, Chap. 18.

Sampson, R. C., *The Staff Role in Management*, Harper & Row, Publishers, 1955.

Whisler, T. L., "The 'Assistant-to' in Four Administrative Settings," *Administrative Science Quarterly*, September 1960.

# *13*
# Decentralization

Few aspects of organization are more vital to effective administration than is decentralization. It is one means of dealing with rapid changes in our economy, and it is also a major aspect in modern leadership patterns.

## Meaning of decentralization

The central issue of decentralization, from an administrative point of view, is authority to plan—that is, *who in the organization hierarchy decides what is to be done?* Is a salesman, for example, free to decide what customers he will solicit, the type of sales promotion he will use, prices he will charge, credit terms he will offer, and when and how he will contact customers; or, is he given a prepared sales talk, an itinerary, and a list of conditions under which orders will be accepted? Viewing the problem from a higher echelon, are the executives expected to make detailed plans that are then carried out by their subordinates, or are executives primarily concerned with helping subordinates do their respective jobs well?

Decentralization also has an impact on the tightness or looseness of control, the extent of detailed planning, and the manner of supervision. But, typically, the dominant consideration is the organization level at which decisions are made, and other phases of administration are adjusted to fit the organization design.

This focus on the organization level of decision-making sets aside several other uses of the term *decentralization*. We are not

218

concerned here with physical location—the concentration or dispersion of plants and offices—nor with departmentation—the pulling together into a single unit or the dispersing of activities such as purchasing, training, or public relations.

Three broad questions that executives face time and again will be discussed:

1. What degree of decentralization is desirable in specific situations?
2. What are the obstacles to achieving effective decentralization, and how may they be overcome?
3. When is profit decentralization feasible and desirable?

The relation of decentralization to total organization structure and to other phases of administration will be considered in later chapters.

## How Much Decentralization Is Desirable?

**Degrees of decentralization**

Decentralization is an issue in each boss-subordinate relationship —between the president and vice-presidents, a vice-president and department managers, and so on down the organization hierarchy to first-level supervisors and operators. In each relationship a question always arises, "How much planning should the boss do, and how much should he delegate to his subordinates?"

When we look at the entire organization structure, the effect of these relationships at each level is cumulative. That is, the men close to operations have freedom to make decisions only if there has been a high degree of delegation at every supervisory level above them. Naturally, the planning is never completely centralized or completely decentralized. Instead, varying degrees of decentralization exist. A few illustrations will suggest the range of possibilities.

*Centralized administration.* In a very small enterprise where the chief executive has only a few unskilled people to assist him, this man will probably make detailed and comprehensive plans himself. He is thoroughly familiar with all phases of the operation, and the work typically is limited in volume and variety so that he can keep in close touch with all that goes on. Small divisions or sections in a larger company may be managed in a similar manner. In fact, larger companies that sell a limited range of products may operate in this manner even though much of their work is done in a series of branches. For instance, some automobile and equipment finance companies and dry cleaning chains have centralized administration.

Among the advantages of centralized administration are: the use of less-skilled personnel in subordinate positions and a resulting lower payroll expense; widespread application of unusual ability of the top executive; and close regulation over the quality of work and the risk incurred. The disadvantages include: the inability of any one man to keep track of varying local needs or a complex operation; and the effect on the sense of involvement and the development of subordinates.

*Limited decentralization.* Here the top echelons of a company, or a department, establish policies, programs, and major procedures; but the application of these plans to specific situations and the detailed day-to-day planning are delegated to first- or second-level supervisors. The Ford Motor Company, to cite a specific case, in its early years gave its assembly and sales branches only limited discretion in operations. Basic policies, production methods, and sales procedure, budgetary limits on expenses, major capital additions, and such matters were all decided in Detroit by top officials or their staff assistants. The branch manager, then, applied this basic plan to his particular assembly plant and sales district. Obviously, a great deal of detailed planning was necessary by the branch manager and his subordinates. But they operated within a clearly established pattern.

Proponents of limited decentralization feel that they get most of the benefits of centralized administration, notably the widespread use of good ideas of the top executives and centralized regulation of operations at least in those areas which they believe are important for purposes of consistency, efficiency, or control. On the other hand, limited decentralization does relieve the top executives of attention to a great deal of detail, and thereby frees their time for other matters. Also, more adaptation to local situations is possible than under centralized administration.

*Delegated authority.* Under this arrangement, operating decisions are pushed well down the line to superintendents, branch managers, and perhaps to first-line supervisors or even operators themselves. One large soap manufacturer, for example, gives its plant foremen discretion on selection of personnel, scheduling of output and shutdowns for maintenance, modification of production methods, and similar matters. In a very real sense, each foreman runs his own shop; but, he has been taught to seek assistance from staff experts on personnel, maintenance, and production methods. Before his appointment as foreman, he has been thoroughly indoctrinated with company traditions and customary practices. The authority is his, but higher management is reasonably sure he will follow the established pattern unless unusual operating conditions require special action.

Delegated authority provides even greater relief to senior executives, increases local flexibility, and generates more enthusiasm and personal pride in work among employees at lower levels. It does require a larger core of competent and well-trained supervisors, and often these supervisors are backed up by a group of central staff experts. And such human talent costs money.

*Bottom-up administration.* Under this plan, not only authority but also initiative is decentralized. Each plant, each unit, and perhaps each individual is made to feel a proprietary responsibility for his activities; he must figure out how they may be best performed, and then do the job in that manner. Centralized staff assistance is used only insofar as the operating people believe it will help them.

This extreme form of decentralization is often applied to foreign sales offices or manufacturing plants. The distance between headquarters and operating units makes communications slow and inaccurate, and the unfamiliarity of top executives with local operating conditions makes centralized planning of dubious value. Bottom-up administration is also well suited to a unique division of a company when the division is headed by a highly competent executive. It is used successfully by multi-product companies, such as Johnson & Johnson, that employ the profit decentralization concept.

Bottom-up administration stimulates employees to challenge, discover, create, decide, and initiate. This tends to enhance morale and provides excellent training for future executives. It relieves top executives of attention to details and provides flexibility through prompt action. On the other hand, careful selection and training of men in lower echelons is crucial since they are free to make wrong decisions as well as right ones. Mistakes will be made, but hopefully the cost of a few failures will be more than offset by the elimination of elaborate precautions devised to prevent any mistakes.

**No standard pattern**

The preceding examples should not be interpreted to mean that any one degree of decentralization is applied uniformly throughout a company. While some firms tend to employ more decentralization than others, considerable variation is necessary to fit the particular circumstances. (a) Departments vary. Some manufacturing concerns, for instance, have highly decentralized research departments but use only limited decentralization in their manufacturing plants. (b) Some subjects such as accounting are more likely to be closely planned centrally than are other activities like selling or training. (c) The form of centralized guidance also varies. Standard procedures are typically used for accounting, whereas specific decisions may be made centrally in collective bargaining with unions. A manufacturing plant may have great freedom of action except that rigid quality specifications and delivery schedules are determined centrally.

Decentralization has become fashionable—it is an "okay" word. So, executives often say they want decentralization but mean quite different things. We need, instead, to be aware of the possible variations and then determine what best suits each phase of our operations.

**Factors affecting appropriate degree**

Even if one is inclined to join in the modern emphasis on decentralization, there still remain the troublesome questions of what types of decisions should be retained for top management, just how far down the line the authority to make decisions should be delegated, and, in a given situation, whether limited decentralization should be employed instead of full delegation of authority? The answers to such questions appear to lie in a careful consideration of the following factors.

1. *Who knows the facts on which the decision will be based, or who can get them together most readily?*

Sometimes a single individual—salesman, machine operator, advertising manager, plant superintendent, purchasing agent—is in constant command, through the normal course of his work, of all the facts needed to make a given type of decision. Such a person is a natural point for decision-making on this issue. Many decisions, however, require information from several different sources—a decision whether to buy a new machine, for example, requires data on production methods, plant layout, future volume, availability of capital, workers' attitudes, and so forth. Channels of communication must be established to funnel all this information to a single point; the question, then, is whether it will be easier to pass general information down the line, or to pass specific information up the line. This raises considerations of the accuracy, time, and cost of such communication.

### 2. Who has the capacity to make sound decisions?

Clearly, if people at lower levels—salesmen, foremen, office supervisors, branch managers—lack the ability and experience needed to make a wise decision on a given question, there is a compelling reason to withhold decision-making authority from them. Such capacity, however, is usually a relative matter. Perhaps the president can make a very wise decision about window-washing, but the maintenance foreman can make one almost as good. Since we want to save the president's energies for more important matters, and the foreman's judgment on this subject is satisfactory, we should lodge the planning for window-washing with the maintenance foreman. On another matter, we may find that no one below a vice-president has the ability to make sound decisions.

### 3. Must speedy, on-the-spot decisions be made to meet local conditions?

The repair of railroad breakdowns, or the buying of fruit at wholesale auctions, obviously calls for someone with authority on the scene of action. A similar, though less dramatic, need for prompt action occurs in negotiating contracts, employing personnel to meet unexpected work loads, or adjusting the complaints of irate customers.

### 4. Must the local activity be carefully coordinated with other activities?

Sometimes *uniformity* of action is so important that all decisions on a given matter must be made centrally—for example, insuring that all customers in a given area are charged the same prices, or determining the length of vacation for all employees in a given plant. Other decisions, such as determining a weekly production schedule or laying out a national sales promotion program, require that activities in several areas be closely *synchronized;* here at least some central planning is required.

### 5. *How significant is the decision?*

A relatively minor decision—one that will increase or decrease profits only by a dollar or two, for example—clearly should be left to a junior executive or operator. The expense of communication up and down the channel of command, and of the time required for the senior executive to handle the problem, would be far greater than any savings that might result from his judgment. On the other hand, any decision that will have a major effect on the total operation, be it either a single transaction or a basic policy, should at least be approved by a senior executive.

### 6. *How busy are the executives who might be assigned planning tasks?*

In dividing up work among executives, overloads must be avoided. A top executive may already have so many duties that he will have to shirk additional responsibility for planning, or a plant superintendent may lack the time for careful analysis and thoughtful decision. If a busy executive has a distinctive contribution that only he can make, perhaps he can be brought in on one phase of the planning while the rest of the chore is assigned to someone else.

### 7. *Will initiative and morale be significantly improved by decentralization?*

Decentralization typically builds initiative and good morale in lower-level executives. We should be sure, however, that such feelings will be generated and that they are desirable in each specific situation. Companies that are faced with frequent shifts in consumer demand, in technology, or in the competitive situation must actively promote adaptability and initiative among their workers. In other enterprises, such as many public utilities, where the rate of change is slower, too much originality and initative among junior executives may actually create discontent and lower morale. Similar sharp differences in the need for initiative are also found in various departments of a single company. American tradition favors both the freedom of action and the dynamic individualism that are associated with a high degree of decentralization. But we do well to remember that there always have been limits in the proportion of the population that conforms to this tradition.

In using these factors as guides to the degree of decentralization that is appropriate in a specific situation, we have to determine how much weight to attach to each. Often the factors pull in opposite directions—the need for speed may suggest greater decentralization, while the desire for coordination may dictate greater centralization. Clearly, each factor must be carefully balanced against the others. Allowance must also be made both for traditional behavior and for growth in the abilities of individuals.

Two aspects of the planning process can be of great aid in decentralization. First is the concept of hierarchy of plans, and particularly hierarchy of goals. We have noted that these plans move from very broad and general objectives to successively more narrow and specific goals and standards. To a considerable extent, although not entirely, this narrowing of scope corresponds to the delegations and redelegations in the executive pyramid, so that even where the junior executive is assigned considerable authority, he operates as a part of a whole structure and accepts as his objective only a limited range of activity.

Second, standing plans—particularly broad policies, but also detailed procedures for those activities that permeate the entire enterprise, such as accounting methods—provide a pattern of behavior within which delegated authority is exercised. The indoctrination that a man receives through work, experience, and training functions in the same manner. These things contribute to unity of action even where a high degree of decentralization is employed.

### ACHIEVING DECENTRALIZATION

As with any plan, deciding what should be done and actually doing it are quite different matters. This is especially true of decentralization. All too often an executive sincerely agrees to delegate in a particular form, but for some reason the right to decide—with corresponding responsibility and initiative—does not pass down the line.

Effective delegation centers around a personal relationship between two individuals: the boss and his immediate subordinate. In practice, this is typically a growing and shifting relationship between the two men. Freedom and initiative which the subordinate is expected to exercise can rarely be spelled out in complete detail; the substance of the delegation takes on real meaning in the working habits which are developed from day to day. These habits and attitudes, in turn, are shaped by the subtle interplay of the two personalities involved.

A closer look at some of the tugs and pulls on the boss and subordinate involved in each delegation may reveal blocks to desired behavior. The following list suggests some of the common pitfalls. An executive who is plagued with a failure of real delegation to occur at a specific point in his organization may well find the root of the trouble among these stumbling blocks.

Let us first look at some of the reasons why executives are loath to delegate and then turn our attention to common reasons why subordinates hesitate to take responsibility.

**Reasons for reluctance to delegate**

1. Some executives get trapped in the *"I can do it better myself" fallacy*. A man who is both conscientious and has high standards of performance is naturally tempted to perform himself any activity that he can do better than his subordinates. This may be anything from writing advertising copy to directing repair work when a machine breaks down. Assuming that the executive really can do the job better (which is not true quite so often as he thinks it is), the executive must nevertheless reconcile himself to turning the job over to someone whose performance will be "good enough."

The choice the executive has to make is not between the quality of work he or his assistant will do on the specific task; instead, he should compare the improvement in performance resulting from doing the work himself against the benefits to the total operation which will arise from devoting his attention to planning and supervision, which only he is in a position to perform. Only after an executive accepts emotionally and intellectually the idea that his job requires getting most things done through other people will full use be made of decentralization.

2. *Lack of ability to direct* is another barrier to successful decentralization. The executive must be able to communicate to his subordinate, often far in advance, what is to be done. This means that the executive must (a) think ahead and visualize the work situation, (b) formulate objectives and general plans of action, and

then (c) communicate these to his subordinate. After the two men have worked together for a period of time, this process may be extremely informal, but the three key elements must still be present.

All too often executives have not cultivated this ability to direct. The author remembers well one of his first bosses, a very friendly individual with shrewd business judgment, who simply could not tell a man working for him what he wanted done more than a few hours ahead of time. Life for subordinates was a bit precarious because success depended upon guessing how the boss's mind would work before the boss himself had formulated his ideas. Here was a man who wanted desperately to delegate, but could do so only for repetitive situations because he was unable to identify and communicate the essential features of his long-range plans.

3. A third possible block to effective decentralization is *lack of confidence in subordinates*. Here, the executive hesitates to turn things over to his subordinate because:

"He'll take care of the details all right but miss the main point."
"I'm not sure of his judgment in a pinch."
"He has ideas but doesn't follow through."
"He's too young to command the respect of the other men."
—or some other doubt about the ability to get the job done.

When this kind of a situation is open and recognized, the remedy is clear. Either training should be started immediately or, if this is impractical, a new subordinate found. Often the situation is by no means so clear-cut, however. The lack of confidence may be subjective and almost unconscious. Where this is so, the executive is likely to give lip-service to decentralization but in the actual working relationship won't let go.

4. A related obstacle to decentralization is *absence of selective controls which give warning of impending difficulties*. Problems beyond those covered by the delegation may arise, and the executive naturally wants to avoid being caught with no warning. Consequently, the executive needs some feedback on what is going on. Such information is also useful for counseling and for appraising final results. While care must be taken that the control system does not undermine the very essence of decentralization, the executive cannot completely abdicate his responsibilities. Unless the executive has confidence in the adequacy of the controls set up, he probably will be very cautious about delegating.

5. Finally, the executive may be handicapped by a *tempera-*

*mental aversion to taking a chance.* Even with clear instructions, proper subordinates, and selective controls, the possibility still remains that something will go wrong. The greater the number of subordinates and the higher the degree of decentralization, the more likely that sooner or later there will be trouble. The executive who delegates takes a calculated risk. Over a period of time, he expects that the gains from delegation will far offset the troubles that arise. Until the executive sees this characteristic of his job, and adjusts to it emotionally as well as intellectually, he is likely to be reluctant to delegate.

These five obstacles to effective decentralization are all related to the attitudes of the boss—the man who is doing the delegating. Fortunately, the attitudes of most men can be modified, at least in intensity. So, when we are faced with a specific situation where authority is in fact not being delegated as planned, we should look first for reasons why the executive may be reluctant to turn over authority to someone else.

### Why subordinates avoid responsibility

Delegation, as noted above, is a two-sided relationship. Even when the boss is ready and able to turn over authority, the subordinate may shrink from accepting it. Something within the subordinate himself or in the relationship with his boss may become a block.

1. Often the subordinate finds it *easier to ask the boss* than decide for himself how to deal with a problem. Making a wise decision is usually hard mental work, and men are perpetually seeking formulas or short cuts to avoid this labor. If a man finds that he can take a half-baked idea or a problem to his supervisor and get an answer, naturally he will do so. In addition, making one's own decisions carries with it responsibility for the outcome. Asking the boss is a way of sharing, if not shifting, this burden. Over a period of time, asking the boss becomes a habit, and the man develops a dependence upon his boss rather than on himself.

A habit of taking all the nonroutine and tough decisions to the boss can best be broken by an agreement between the two men concerned to mend their ways. If the practice is of long standing, perhaps the boss will have to resort to refusal even to give advice. Then, after a period of letting the subordinate fend for himself, a more healthy coaching relationship can be established. The distinction between advice, decision, and orders will, however, remain blurred, and the executive must constantly be on his guard that his advice does not undercut the attitudes of initiative and responsibility he is striving to build.

2. A second factor which deters a man from embracing greater responsibility is the *fear of criticism* for mistakes. Much depends upon the nature of the criticism. Negative criticism is often resented where constructive review might be accepted. "The old man sure raised the roof, but I swear I don't know what I'd do differently if it happened again."

Unreasonable criticism is likely to evoke even sharper reaction. Unreasonableness, in this situation, must be defined in terms of the feeling of the subordinate. If he feels that unfavorable results were beyond his control, that his duties and authority were not clear, that his actions were wise in terms of the situation as he knew it at the time, or that he has not been given an opportunity to explain his side of the story, the criticism will have a cowing effect.

Negative or unreasonable criticism given publicly in a way which embarrasses a man before fellow workers adds salt to the wound. The impact of such criticism on a man's willingness to take on new responsibility is direct. He naturally will be inclined to be cautious and play it safe if he has learned from experience that taking on more risk may result in an embarrassing and unwarranted bawling out. The subordinate's feeling is, "Why should I stick my neck out for that guy?"

3. Most men hesitate to accept responsibility when they believe they *lack the necessary information and resources* to do a good job. The enthusiasm of a newly appointed training director in an industrial company, for example, was dampened when he found he had virtually no equipment and very poor secretarial help. Then, when top management officials not only were too busy to see him but also failed to keep him advised of changes in company planning which affected training needs, he lost most of his remaining initiative. Here again, much depends upon attitudes and expectations. A person reared in a restraining web of budgetary and personnel limitations can accept responsibility knowing full well he will have to battle for each step he takes. Generally, however, the frustra-

tions that go along with inadequate information and resources create in the man an attitude which rejects further assignments. Such a barrier makes effective decentralization difficult indeed.

4. A fourth obstacle to accepting responsibility is simply that the subordinate may already have *more work than he can do.* True, such an overload may be the man's own fault; for example, he may make poor use of his own time or fail to hire trained, competent assistants even though he has the authority to do so. But, from the point of view of his willingness to accept responsibility, the cause of the overwork is not the critical point. If he already feels overburdened, he will probably shy away from new assignments which call for thinking and initiative.

5. *Lack of self-confidence* stands in the way of some men's accepting responsibility. The executive believes the man can do the job and is willing to take the risk of the outcome, but the man is unsure of himself and does not like to take the plunge. Ordering the man to have self-confidence will have little effect. In many cases, however, self-confidence may be developed by carefully providing experience with increasingly difficult problems to help the man sense his own potentialities. To be sure, some men may not have the psychological make-up to carry heavy responsibilities —but general experience provides many examples of far greater latent ability than appeared on the surface.

6. Finally, *positive incentives may be inadequate.* As already noted, accepting additional responsibility usually involves more mental work and emotional pressure. The lower ranks of some companies place some social stigma on the "eager beaver" who is pushing to get ahead. Also, there is more or less risk of failure; failure is unpleasant and may result in embarrassing removal from the job. For these reasons, positive inducements for accepting delegated responsibility are needed. These inducements may take all sorts of forms, such as pay increases, better opportunity for promotion, fancier title, recognized status in the organization, more pleasant working conditions, additional power, personal recognition and approval by respected members of the enterprise, and other rewards both tangible and intangible. The important point is that the specific subordinate affected by delegation should be provided with a positive incentive which is important to him.

## Conclusions

Many delegations encounter none of these obstacles, and in other situations only one or two points interfere with effective delegation. In any case, the list of common reasons for reluctance on the part of the executive and of the subordinate suggests potential difficulties to look for, and provides a frame of analysis that should be useful even when the specific points do not happen to fit a given situation.

The main thing that all of us who are enthusiastic about decentralization have to remember is that the carrying out of such plans requires the adjustment of attitudes and behavior patterns of specific individuals and a workable adjustment in their relationships. Such adjustments are a normal occurrence in a dynamic society, but we must recognize that they take time and that some individuals are more adaptable than others. Our best plans will come to naught until these personal adjustments have been made.

### PROFIT DECENTRALIZATION

One form of decentralization—really a special combination of departmentation, delegation, supervision, and control—is highly important to larger enterprises: *profit decentralization*. Under this plan, a company is split up into product or regional divisions, each of which is responsible for its own profit or loss.

### Self-sufficient, semi-autonomous units

Two characteristics lie at the heart of the plan: (1) All the major operations necessary to make a profit are grouped under the manager of a *self-sufficient* unit. This, of course, is a matter of departmentation (discussed in Chapters 9 and 10). Typically, several such self-sufficient, self-contained units are established in a company. (2) The management of these units is so highly decentralized that each of them becomes *semi-autonomous*. In effect, we have a series of little businesses operating within the parent company. The manager of each unit virtually has both the resources and the freedom of action that he would enjoy if he were president of an independent company, and he is expected to take whatever steps are necessary to insure that his little business will make a profit.

Profit decentralization is the key concept in organizing large concerns such as General Motors Corporation—with its separate divisions for each automobile line and for Diesel engines, spark-plugs, and other products. The Du Pont Company has long used this type of organization, and the General Electric Company more recently divided its operations into approximately one hundred separate profit-making units. Profit decentralization is by no means confined to industrial giants, however. Small companies such as Johnson & Johnson and American Brake Shoe have found it admirably suited to their needs.

Ordinarily, the operating units are built around product lines, and the engineering, production, and sales of each line are placed within the decentralized division. The same idea, however, has been applied by department store chains, which place all their operations in each *city* on a profit-decentralization basis. In fact, this form of organization has become so successful and popular that most diversified companies use it in at least a modified form.

**Potential benefits**

A major advantage of profit decentralization is its stimulating effect on the *morale* of the key men in each of these self-sufficient, semi-autonomous divisions. Executives are able to see the results of their own methods, to take the action they believe best, and to feel that they are playing an important role. The resulting enthusiasm and devotion to the success of their particular division tend to be contagious to other people working in the division.

Since operating units established under profit decentralization are of a *manageable size,* fewer people have to exchange information, and they can communicate with one another swiftly and effectively. Executives can more easily comprehend the information that is funneled to them, for it is less diverse and more relevant to their immediate problem than in the complex and unwieldly operations of a large, highly centralized company. The decentralized unit is an operation that the executive can grasp.

Situations requiring administrative action are more likely to receive *adequate attention* under profit decentralization. In a large-scale enterprise, a product or an operation that contributes only a minor part to the total sales volume can easily be neglected; to put the operation on a more efficient footing may just seem more trouble than it is worth. In a smaller division, however, such problems become relatively more important, and executives are more likely to take necessary corrective action.

The smaller size of the operating units and the heightened ease of communication also lead to improved *coordination*, particularly in the critically important areas of servicing customers, matching production and sales, and keeping costs in line with income. Such integrated action is often hard to achieve in a large enterprise that has been organized functionally because bureaucratic attitudes are apt to interfere with voluntary cooperation and responsiveness to over-all needs.

By making both measurement and accountability more clear-cut, profit decentralization promotes more effective *control*. The profit-and-loss statement of each operating division provides a significant measure of results, for all the relevant activities are under the direction of a division manager. Top management need not make an arbitrary allocation of costs, or try to decide whether a poor showing was the fault of, say, poor selling or slow delivery. Moreover, since a self-sufficient division is also semiautonomous, its manager can be held accountable for resulting profit or loss. If the results are poor, he can be required to take corrective action; if they are good, he can be, and often is, generously rewarded.

**Limitations and difficulties**

If profit decentralization contributes all these impressive advantages, why are not all large enterprises organized in this fashion? Unfortunately, certain distinct limitations and problems are inherent in its use.

For one thing, not all companies can be *divided neatly* into self-contained operating divisions. Technology may prohibit a large operation from breaking up into several smaller ones. A steel mill, for example, cannot be split down the middle. General Motors can separate Chevrolets and Buicks; but if the Chevrolet division itself becomes unmanageably large, trying to divide it into two or more self-sufficient units would create serious technical difficulties. On the other hand, in operations such as wholesaling or retailing, which involve a large number of products, sales volume of any one product may be insufficient to support the expense of a separate management and staff of specialists. In still other companies, where a single sales organization is mandatory, it would be disastrous to split up this important activity and place it under the direction of several division managers. One of the limitations of profit decentralization, then, is that the operations of the company must lend themselves to being divided into self-sufficient units of manageable size.

A related problem springs from the auxiliary service activities that the company must perform for the operating divisions. Will a single central *service unit,* such as purchasing or plant engineering, be really *responsive* to the needs of each of several operating divisions? Will it be able to perform the work more cheaply than outside firms could? Will the operating divisions be required to use the service divisions? If so, what happens to their presumed autonomy and accountability for profits? These are not insurmountable problems, but they do emphasize that profit decentralization brings in its wake a series of potentially troublesome issues.

A great deal of double-talk about decentralization occurs these days. Some companies claim that their operating divisions are semiautonomous when, in fact, all major decisions and many minor ones are made by executives in the central office. Everyone agrees that top management should retain some influence over the operating divisions. In consultation with the division managers, top management should set long-range objectives and annual goals, establish the broad policies within which the divisions are to operate, approve the selection of key executives within the division, approve major capital expenditures (which, in effect, means approving any major expansion), and review any single transaction that might entail a major change in the profit or loss of the division. In addition, the headquarters office might want to establish certain procedures for accounting, personnel, or purchasing in order to assure consistent action throughout the entire company.

Clearly, in many areas the operating divisions are *not* autonomous. Furthermore, top management can interpret all these limitations so broadly that it may retain the right to interfere with the division operations almost anywhere it wants to. Objectives or policies may be made so specific that the division managers are left with little freedom of discretion, or the scrutiny of budgets may extend to such insignificant items that the hands of the local man are effectively tied. The point here is that the *manner* in which these particular processes are performed can either support or vitiate the underlying concept of profit decentralization. Therefore, if we organize along profit decentralization lines, we must also plan,

lead, and control in a manner compatible with profit decentralization.

Although we have referred to this type of organization as profit
decentralization, we must remember that profits, though important,
may be an *inadequate measure* of the performance of a division,
at least in the short-run. A given division may decide, with the full
approval of top management, to spend money on advertising, and
other activities, to improve its market position; for two or three
years it may spend large sums developing a new product. In other
words, the division may be achieving its objectives even though it
is showing a relatively small profit. Conversely, by keeping down
expenses for nonrecurring or deferable items, a division may make
a good profit showing even though it is slipping in, say, customer
good will or development of potential executives. This means that
the use of profit for purposes of control is valid only if it is interpreted with a full understanding of what is happening within the
division.

Perhaps the greatest difficulty in the use of profit decentralization
is to find executives with the *capacity and willingness* to work
effectively within the system. Unless administrators, both at headquarters and in the separate divisions, display certain work habits
and attitudes, profit decentralization will lead to chaos. The division
managers must be prepared to take the initiative on any matter
that affects the long-run success of their particular units. They must
be aware of the direct and indirect results of their own actions, instead of relying on someone in the home office to keep them out
of trouble. In other words, they must act as responsible stewards
of the resources put under their direction.

The top administrative officials in the company, in turn, must
accept their obligation to maintain a "hands-off" attitude toward
the decentralized divisions. As the president of a successfully decentralized company put it: "This calls for confidence in the capabilities of other people, a belief in teaching rather than telling, patience
while others are learning—perhaps through their own mistakes—and
a willingness to let others stand out in the public eye."

And yet we must remember that many executives of operating
divisions have been trained to concentrate on a particular specialty
rather than to take an over-all view of an integrated business unit,
and that the top executives of many corporations have achieved
their position through positive, aggressive action. We can easily

understand why the attitudes and behavior described in the two preceding paragraphs are difficult to achieve in practice. The key men in a company that adopts profit decentralization must have a realistic understanding of their new roles, and they must be flexible enough to adjust their behavior accordingly.

## Summary

How much authority to turn over to subordinates is a question faced by every executive and by senior administrators in designing an entire organization structure. At what level should the focus of decision-making lie?

Answers will vary by departments and by subjects. Nevertheless, in selecting an optimum degree of decentralization, the following factors should always be considered: Who knows the relevant facts or can get them easily? What is the ability of men at different levels? Are speedy, on-the-spot decisions necessary? What activities need to be closely coordinated? How significant is the decision? How busy are the executives concerned? Will morale be significantly improved by greater decentralization?

A second major problem is actually achieving the decentralization desired. Both the executive and his subordinate have to learn to work with the freedom upon which they agreed. In practice, the executive may hold back authority, or the subordinate may fail to accept the obligations thrust upon him. When decentralization fails to occur, the obstacles should be identified and steps taken to overcome them.

Profit decentralization is a special form of decentralization. It involves setting up self-sufficient, semiautonomous operating units. It enables large, diversified companies to break activities into more easily managed units. But to be effective, the separation of activities must be feasible, dependable measures of performance are needed, and most of all executives at both the corporate and the division levels must have a capacity and willingness to work in a federated system.

### SELECTED REFERENCES

Baker, H. and R. R. France, *Centralization and Decentralization in Industrial Relations,* Industrial Relations Section, Princeton University, 1954.

Dale, E., *Planning and Developing the Company Organization Structure,* American Management Association, Research Report No. 20, pp. 98-119, 188-195.

Dearden, J., "Mirage of Profit Decentralization," *Harvard Business Review,* November 1962.

Newman, W. H. and J. P. Logan, *Management of Expanding Enterprises,* Columbia University Press, 1955.

Simon, H. A., et al., *Centralization vs. Decentralization in Organizing the Controller's Department,* Controllership Foundation, 1954.

# 14
# Use of Committees

The use of committees, boards, councils, and similar groups as an administrative device may be traced back to Greek, Roman, and other ancient civilizations. It has been particularly popular in Anglo-Saxon countries where it has often been regarded as an aspect of democracy, and it is now found in all types of cooperative human endeavor—churches, schools (children are taught to form committees at about the same time they learn to write their names), unions, governments, and business enterprises. Yet, in spite of generations of diverse experience with the use of committees, probably no administrative device is more commonly abused than this one.

## Nature of a committee

A *committee* consists of a group of people specifically designated to perform some administrative act. It functions only as a group and requires the free interchange of ideas among its members. Membership on a committee typically is only a part-time assignment.

This definition includes both temporary committees, which are disbanded as soon as their particular missions are completed, and standing committees, which have continuing responsibilities. Moreover, it includes committees that perform auxiliary or staff duties, as well as those that make final decisions.

The definition is intended to exclude those impromptu conferences that frequently arise when an executive calls into his office

238

several of his assistants or a number of individuals from separate departments whose work is associated. Also excluded are those large conferences and meetings in which the interplay of ideas is limited to occasional questioning of the speaker. Such conferences can be important in training and directing, but their consideration here would tend to confuse the basic issues regarding the use of committees.

Committees are used for a wide variety of diverse purposes. Consider, for example, the following. A budget committee, usually composed of major operating executives, agrees upon over-all programs of operation. Then, if actual conditions do not permit the achievement of this program, it develops revisions necessary to keep the operation in balance. By contrast, the typical grievance committee consists of an equal number of representatives from the lower levels of management and the union, and is concerned with negotiating settlement of individual employee grievances.

A suggestion committee, on the other hand, should consist of individuals who are recognized for their fairness and objectivity, as well as their willingness to make changes; this group is charged with appraising the practicability of employees' suggestions and deciding upon awards that should be granted. A safety committe, to cite still another example, is made up of representatives from each important section or department (membership is considered an honor and is often rotated from year to year); while the group may develop new ways of securing safety, its primary purpose is to educate and generate enthusiasm of the members and their constituents for the program worked out by the safety director.

This variety of possible uses of committees means that the administrator should be careful to select those tasks where group action will be advantageous. Unfortunately, this is not always done. Some individuals regard committees as a sure-cure for all administrative difficulties. Whenever a difficult decision must be made or where action is not proceeding smoothly, the standard answer is "Let's appoint a committee." In many cases, group action is not called for, and often the duties of the committee are poorly defined. Such use of committees leads to habitual procrastination. It is an opiate taken in lieu of effective administrative action.

To know when to use a committee an executive should weigh (a) its advantages and (b) its limitations, and if a committee is desirable then he should (c) select the right members and make other arrangements so that it can operate effectively.

Important among the reasons for using committees are to:

1. Provide integrated group judgment
2. Promote coordination
3. Secure cooperation in execution of plans
4. Train members and obtain continuity of thinking

A single committee will rarely provide all these benefits, but often two or more can be secured, at least to some extent.

### Provide integrated group judgment

The old saying, "two heads are better than one," is a bit too simple for the administrator who is trying to decide where committees may be employed advantageously. He must look deeper to determine when group judgment will be a distinctly superior decision.

Group judgment is particularly valuable when a *wide range of experience* and knowledge must be brought to bear upon a particular question. Some management problems require consideration from a marketing, production, engineering, legal, and perhaps financial viewpoint. Others may not have as many different aspects, but call for intimate knowledge regarding different customers. By having several individuals meet together to discuss these problems, their combined backgrounds and abilities may be utilized.

An aspect of *safety* also occurs in group judgment. Group consideration tends to guard against personal bias and occasional mental oversight. Also, the diversity of backgrounds of the various members tends to make each of them view the problems from an over-all point of view, that is, they identify themselves with the general purpose rather than with their narrower departmental objective. Even if this matter of safety is viewed as an averaging process, the group decision will be better than the worst of the individual decisions might be, and it is likely to fall closer to the best of the individual decisions than the worst.

### Promote coordination

Committees promote coordination in several ways. Each member develops some *awareness* of the problems of other organizational units represented on the committee and of the effect of his own actions on these other units. Moreover, they provide for the *easy interchange* of current information among the members of the committee. Often, data presented in connection with one problem later proves to be helpful in dealing with other issues. And, committee meetings often provide the occasion when *coordinated plans may be agreed upon.* When no single member of the committee has authority over all of the operations involved, such a joint agreement on a course of action is vital to coordination. Even in those instances when a voluntary agreement cannot be worked out, the discrepancies can be recognized and referred to a higher executive for final decision.

Since coordination through a committee depends upon voluntary agreement of several individuals, to be most effective for this purpose the executives in charge of the activities to be coordinated should serve as members of the committee (with the possible substitution of over-all staff assistants, if such positions exist).

### Secure cooperation in execution of plans

Although group judgment is the reason usually stated for using a committee, research studies show that "selling" decisions more often is the real motive. And, in fact, committees may be very helpful in securing cooperation in the execution of plans.

Among the reasons why committees engender cooperation is the well-known psychological reaction to *participation.* When an individual has even a small part in formulating a plan, he is much more interested in seeing that it is properly executed.

Also, a plan approved by a committee typically carries more weight than one developed by a single member of the group. Subordinates, associates, and even seniors are more inclined to *accept decisions* resulting from careful group deliberation. A group decision is presumed to be a wise one, based on a full consideration of all the facts and free from prejudice, and the decision carries with it the combined social pressure and prestige of the entire committee membership.

Committee discussion of plans also helps in their execution by *clarifying instructions.* As a result of the discussion, the members know what is intended, and through their improved grasp of the total situation they are more likely to make consistent interpretation of the instructions issued.

### Train members and obtain continuity

Participation in committee discussion extends the contact each member has with the various activities of the enterprise and gives him some insight into the point of view and the problems of other divisions. Each member is likely to have to defend his own ideas, and consequently thinks them through more carefully. All this is good *executive training.* Sometimes the *continuity of thinking* that the multiple membership of committees makes possible is important. This continuity is formally provided in groups such as the United States Senate where only one third of the members are elected at any one time. Most committees have no set rules for filling vacancies, but rarely are all members replaced simultaneously. Consequently, some members always know the reasons for previous action, and this tends to promote a consistency and continuity of thinking that is difficult to achieve when an executive who has been making decisions by himself has to be replaced.

Rarely are committees used solely for the benefit of training the members or to secure continuity. In some circumstances, however, these can be real advantages, and, when added to one or more of the benefits already discussed, may swing the balance in favor of deciding to use a committee.

### LIMITATIONS OF COMMITTEES

The assignment of an administrative task to a group of people instead of an individual has a number of serious disadvantages. Before deciding to use a committee, an executive should weigh these disadvantages against benefits that may be secured from group action. The principal limitations of committees are:

1. Slow and expensive action
2. Divided responsibility
3. Danger of compromise decision

### Slow and expensive action

Getting a committee together for a meeting is often a difficult task, and the busier the individual members the more difficult this becomes. The treasurer may be out of town one day, the sales manager may have discussions scheduled with out-of-town salesmen on the following day, a board meeting may take up the time of two members on the following morning, and in the afternoon the controller leaves for a week's trip to branch offices, with a final result that the earliest time the full committee can meet is two weeks hence. If a meeting is called with one or two members absent, action on certain matters may have to be deferred until the absent members can be consulted.

For committees with recurring business this difficulty can be avoided in part by a regularly scheduled time for meeting. This usually means that any action of the committee must be postponed until the next regularly scheduled meeting. The result is that almost invariably action from a committee *takes longer* than from a single individual.

Committees are also *expensive* in terms of man-hours expended. An hour-long committee meeting of half a dozen executives will require a minimum of nine man-hours when preparation time is considered. The cost is the total value of the work these executives might do if they were not in committee. When committee meetings are frequent and are permitted to interfere with the performance of other work, this cost may be substantial.

The interchange of ideas, which is an essential aspect of committee work, increases time and expense involved. Each person is expected to state his views, to listen to the views of other members (however inconsequential), to comment on the differences, and to explain why he takes the position he does. Valuable as such discussion may be, it also extends the time needed to reach a conclusion.

### Divided responsibility

"That which is everybody's responsibility, is nobody's responsibility." Theoretically, this is not so, for each member of a committee should feel as much responsibility for seeing that the assignment is properly completed as he would if it were given to him alone. He may be restricted in the way he fulfills his obligation, and he may be outvoted in the committee meeting, but this in no way reduces his personal responsibility to do the best he can.

Unfortunately, the typical person does not live up to the theory. Most of us, when appointed to a committee, recognize some obligation to put in a physical appearance at the meeting when called; but we give little thought to the matter outside of the meeting and spend no restless nights if the deliberations bog down. If a reasonably satisfactory solution is suggested, we are quite willing to approve it, even though we might not do so if we had to make the decision alone. Then, if subsequent events prove the decision to be a bad one, we shrug our shoulders and say that it was not our idea anyway.

The *thinning out of responsibility* that tends to occur when a committee is appointed is most troublesome when the chief purpose of the committee is to secure group judgment, particularly if the judgment is a final decision rather than merely advice. It has been suggested that this difficulty be overcome by including in the minutes an account of the views and the votes of each member. Such a procedure is clumsy and interferes with arriving at good group judgment. Individual members sometimes become more concerned with the appearance of the record than with the final decision reached; they make speeches and take positions in an effort to impress their constituents or their senior executive. In most business enterprises, if committees are justified at all, they should not be hampered with the reporting of who said what, even though this may mean sacrificing some individual accountability.

The dilution of initiative among committee members can be partially overcome by assigning to the chairman of the committee responsibility for seeing that some type of action is taken. For this purpose, a chairman of sufficiently high stature relative to the other members is needed so that he can effectively prod them into action. This often works well when the primary purpose of the committee is to secure coordination or greater acceptance for a particular decision. Where the primary purpose is to secure integrated group thinking, however, care must be taken that the chairman does not so dominate the entire group that little is gained from holding committee meetings.

### Danger of compromise decision

When difference of opinion exists in a committee, a possibility always exists that some sort of average or compromise solution will be adopted. All too often some member says, "Let's agree on something; I have to get back to my desk." Witness the company that made such a drastic cut in expenses of a sales promotion campaign that the advertising effort was ineffective. Clearly, the decision should have been either to cut the expenditure entirely, or to give the campaign sufficient backing so that it would have a good chance of success. Committees do not necessarily lead to *undesirable compromises,* but there is an ever-present danger that they will.

Committee members may not approach problems with an objective and open-minded attitude. An unfortunate political atmosphere sometimes develops in which members support one another more as a favor than on the merits of the issue. Thus, if Mr. X knows he will be asking a favor of Mr. Y tomorrow, he may be very careful not to antagonize Mr. Y in the committee meeting this afternoon. It takes a careful selection of members and a skillful chairman to avoid this sort of difficulty.

*Voting is undesirable.* The danger of committee politics raises the question of when a majority vote should be used to reach a committee decision. When a committee is charged with making final decisions on operating matters, a vote may be necessary so that action can proceed. In most situations, however, counting the ayes and nays should be avoided, particularly in the early stages of discussion. Where the purpose of the committee is to promote cooperation or to bring about voluntary coordination among the members, a vote on a controversial issue is of no particular benefit. The fact that a single member is outvoted in a committee does not necessarily increase his willingness to cooperate in a particular activity.

A more effective technique in such circumstances is to be guided by the "sense of the meeting." Unless an individual feels very strongly on a particular point, he will probably join in the course of action suggested. Where a committee serves in an advisory role, a difference of opinion can be reported with the alternative proposal. This sort of a report is probably more useful to the man making the final decision than is a single recommendation adopted by a three to two majority. Such an informal committee procedure reduces the dangers of compromise and political action, but it will not entirely eliminate them.

## When to Use Committees

Categorical statements as to when committees should be used are as difficult to make as definite rules about when a child should be given a spanking. Each time the total situation should be appraised, and the remedies adapted to the particular conditions. Committees, like spanking, should be used sparingly, yet at times nothing else seems to be so clearly needed.

The most basic advice that can be given is never to establish a committee unless the advantages of group action appear clearly to outweigh those of assigning the task to a single individual. Contrariwise, be prompt and persistent in dissolving committees that have completed their mission or outlived their usefulness.

Recommending specific committees is hazardous. Nevertheless, the preceding analysis of advantages and limitations of committees does suggest some situations where group action is likely to be beneficial—and other circumstances when committees should be avoided.

**Conditions favoring the use of committees**

Committees are likely to be particularly useful:

1. *When a wide divergence of information is necessary to reach a sound conclusion.* A product research committee, a pricing committee, a budget committee, all deal with problems calling for information from several different departments, and often a committee composed of men who are intimately familiar with the details of these departments can provide good group advice and also assist in the coordination of action agreed upon.

2. *When the decision is of such importance that the judgment of several qualified individuals is desired.* The salary committee and an appropriations committee illustrate this point in internal operations; they protect against personal bias and their decisions are more readily accepted by all parties directly affected. Note in this connection that virtually all large enterprises—business, charitable, government, or religious—are headed up by a group, be it called board, council, assembly, or some other name. When discretion is wide, power is great, and vital issues are at stake, we believe that in numbers there is safety. The nine (not one) justices of the Supreme Court, to cite another instance, are provided to secure wise and acceptable decisions.

3. *When successful execution of decisions depends upon full understanding of their ramifications.* A committee to help plan the introduction of a new process, or the move to a new plant, for example, may be quite useful because considerable adaptation and implemen-

tation of the basic scheme is required of each member, and he must understand and be in full agreement with the procedure adopted.

4. *When activities of three or more divisions need to be adjusted frequently to secure coordination.* An advertising and sales promotion committee, a production scheduling committee, or an over-all management committee often serve as a vital link in the coordination of related operations.

Most of the committees mentioned above do not need to be given authority to make final decisions. Their over-all effectiveness will probably be enhanced if they are not concerned with political jockeying and counting of noses, but instead they rely upon giving advice to key executives or upon voluntary agreement among the members. The important exceptions are boards of directors, salary committees, and similar groups where a "safe" decision is reached; here the primary purpose is to secure group judgment, which becomes authoritative.

### Conditions unfavorable to the use of committees

Committees are usually not desirable:

1. *When speed is vital.* For instance, in the negotiations of a purchase or sale, or in dealing with emergencies, prompt action is usually more desirable than the slower action based upon deliberations of a committee.

2. *When the decision is not particularly important.* If the decision of a committee can affect expenditure of only a few dollars, if employees are glad to cooperate with any reasonable program, or if coordination can be achieved through established procedure and individual contacts, the expense of committee action will almost surely outweigh the benefits received.

3. *When qualified personnel are not available.* Even when a problem is suitable for committee action, a committee should not be established unless there are appropriately qualified individuals in the enterprise who can devote the required time to the committee. As will be emphasized later, the desired qualifications of members of a committee depend upon its purpose. If such individuals are not available in the company, or are so busy that they give the committee scant attention and send poorly qualified alternates who cannot speak for them, the committee is doomed from the start to be ineffective.

4. *When the problem is one of execution rather than decision.*

Committees function as a group, and it is costly if not impossible for several men jointly to explain and interpret directions, review actual performance, give praise or blame, and otherwise motivate the employees who are carrying out a plan. Supervision is a process that committees do poorly and expensively, if they do it at all.

### Execution of committee decisions

The preceding injunction against giving committees responsibility for execution naturally raises the question of who should be responsible for carrying out their decisions. Of course, in those situations where committees are advisory or depend upon voluntary agreement among the members (and this is true most of the time), responsibility for execution rests in the established channel of command. The creation of such a committee does not alter the authority nor the obligations of any of the operating executives. The committee functions in a purely *staff* capacity.

When committee decisions are authoritative, however, someone must be designated to see that their decisions are properly carried out; the committee itself is poorly suited to such a task. Two solutions work reasonably well. One is for the committee to have a *single operating executive,* such as is found in the relationship between the president and a board of directors of a business enterprise. Sometimes the chairman of the committee or its secretary acts in an executive capacity on behalf of the committee. This is a somewhat awkward arrangement since the operating deputy will have a whole group of bosses, but it is a far more workable arrangement than permitting each member of the committee to act in an executive capacity.

If a committee makes authoritative decisions on matters that clearly fall in the province of one or more divisions, the best solution is to have the existing operating executives carry out the committee decisions. The committee then has *functional authority* to specify what is to be done with respect to certain types of activities, and, as is always true for functional authority, relies upon the established channels of command for execution of its decisions.

### SUGGESTIONS FOR EFFECTIVE OPERATION OF COMMITTEES

Having decided to establish a committee, necessary provision to make it effective should then be made. Minimum steps toward this end are the following:

1. Define the duties and authority of the committee clearly.
2. Select members in view of the duties of the committee.
3. Support the committee with necessary staff assistance.
4. Design procedures to obtain prompt and effective action.
5. Appoint the right chairman.

## Define duties and authority clearly

A clear statement of the objectives, duties, and authority of a committee will contribute substantially to its success. The members themselves will then know what is expected of them and also what is outside of their assignment. All too often committees with fancy titles are simply appointed, and they flounder around because they do not know what they are supposed to do. Likewise, it should be made clear whether committees are to serve in an advisory, coordinative capacity, or whether their decisions are authoritative and, if so, upon whom.

Other executives will be concerned directly or indirectly with committee action, and they, as well as the members, should appreciate the role of the committee. They should know the kind of help that can be expected from the committee and also the problems that are outside its province and must be dealt with through other channels. If there is justification for appointing a committee at all, then its duties are important enough to warrant clear definition.

## Select members to assure objectives

There is no such thing as an ideal committee member—when speaking in general terms. The type and number of people needed on a specific committee depend upon its purpose. For instance, the key operating executives concerned should be on a coordinating committee. On the other hand, a committee primarily intended to win the cooperation of a large number of employees probably should be composed of a bigger group of individuals who are the natural leaders among their fellow workers. Members of a committee designed to bring together divergent information will be picked more for what they know than their relationship with other workers. Where wise, objective judgment is desired, as in the Supreme Court, the character of the individuals rather than representation should be the primary consideration.

Obviously then, the popular notion that all committees should be representative is a fallacy. Sometimes representation is highly important, but even here the particular divisions, factions, functions, or social groups that should be represented will be determined by the purpose of the particular committee. In other instances we are much more concerned with the ability of particular individuals, or perhaps with their authority to make commitments, to set up a revised sales program, for example. With committees, as in any instance of staffing, the job and the individuals must be fitted to each other.

As a general rule, the *number* of members on a committee should be kept as small as possible and still achieve the objective. The larger the committee, the more expensive and unwieldy it becomes. One means of keeping a committee small is to provide that certain individuals will meet with the committee when they can contribute to or benefit from the discussion, but not include them as regular members. When the desirability of adequate representation makes necessary a large membership, a practical solution is to divide the entire group into subcommittees, including an executive committee, and thereby substantially to reduce the frequency and length of the meetings of the full committee.

### Support the committee with staff assistance

A great deal of committee time can be saved by staff work prior to meetings. Sometimes the chairman does this work, or if he is too busy, it may be done by a part-time or a full-time secretary. Of course, if the duties of the committee fall within the province of a staff division, the chairman often gets assistance from this division.

The nature of such staff work is very similar to that already described in Chapter 12. The staff man prepares an agenda, assembles facts, perhaps draws up tentative recommendations, distributes the agenda and summaries of information prior to meetings to give members time to study the data and consult their own advisors before the committee session, prepares minutes, advises people of action taken, and follows up on unfinished business. When such staff assistance is provided, the members can come well prepared and concentrate during the meeting on interpretation and evaluation of the information presented.

### Design procedures for prompt and effective action

Standing committees, particularly, can often simplify and speed up their work by agreeing on procedures for the handling of certain types of problems. An appropriations committee, for example, may stipulate the supporting information for all requests and the summary of this information on specially prepared forms. Moreover, it may then provide that certain types of requests will automatically be approved unless some member wishes to raise a question about them. It can further simplify its work by insisting that related requests be considered at the same time.

Such committee procedures, along with the use of staff assistance, can go a long way toward overcoming the objection that committees often take up too much of the time of busy executives.

### Appoint the right chairman

The chairman is the key man in every committee operation. He guides the proceedings, sets the tone of the meetings, supervises and perhaps performs the staff work, and often consults informally with members between meeting sessions. He does not do all the work himself, but he sets in motion the mechanism whereby the group action becomes purposeful and efficient.

### SUMMARY

The primary justifications for the use of a committee instead of a single individual are to obtain the benefits of integrated group judgment, promote coordination, secure cooperation, or train the members. Committees can be particularly useful when a wide divergence of information is necessary to reach a sound conclusion, when the decision is of such importance that a "safe" judgment of several qualified individuals is desired, when successful execution of decisions depends upon a full understanding of their ramifications, and when activities of three or more divisions need to be adjusted frequently to secure coordination.

Committee action, however, is slow and expensive, responsibility is divided, and decisions may be a compromise. Consequently, prospects for outstanding benefits from group action should be present before a committee is appointed. Especially doubtful is the wisdom of committees when speed is vital, the decision is not particularly important, qualified personnel are unavailable, or the problem is primarily one of execution.

If we decide that a committee is warranted, then its effectiveness can be improved by carefully defining its functions, selecting members in light of the specific functions, providing staff assistance, adopting procedures that will expedite the work, and, last but not least, selecting the right chairman.

Committees are no panacea for management ills, but for proper purposes they can be extremely useful.

### SELECTED REFERENCES

Albers, H. H., *Organized Executive Action*, John Wiley & Sons, Inc., 1961, Chaps. 8 and 9.

"Committees: Their Role in Management Today," *Management Review*, October 1957.

Mylander, W. H., "Management by Executive Committee," *Harvard Business Review*, May 1955.

Richards, M. D. and W. A. Nielander, *Readings in Management*, South-Western Publishing Co., 1958, Chap. 19.

# 15

# Span of Supervision

As any enterprise increases in size, the question arises of how many employees can be adequately supervised by a single executive. This question of proper span of supervision presents itself time and again at all levels in the executive hierarchy; no administrative organization can be created without attention to it.

This is no new problem. The issue of a leader attempting to direct too many people was serious enough in the early history of the Israelites to be recorded in the Bible. In Exodus 18, 13-26 is the following account of how Moses set up an administrative organization:

> Moses sat to judge the people; and the people stood about Moses from the morning unto the evening. And when Moses' father-in-law saw all that he did . . . he said unto him: "The thing that thou doest is not good. Thou wilt surely wear away, both thou and this people with thee; for the thing is too heavy for thee—thou art not able to perform it thyself alone.
>
> "Hearken now unto my voice . . . Be thou for the people Godward, and bring thou the causes unto God. [Then] thou shalt teach [the people] the statutes and the laws, and shalt show them the way wherein they must walk, and the work that they must do.
>
> "Moreover thou shalt provide out of all the people able men, such as fear God, men of truth, hating unjust gain; and place such over them, to be rulers of thousands, rulers of hundreds, rulers of fifties, and rulers of tens; and let them judge the people at all seasons. And it shall be that every great matter they shall bring unto thee, but every small matter they shall judge themselves. So shall it be easier for thyself, and they shall bear the burden with thee. If thou shalt do this thing . . . then

thou shalt be able to endure, and all this people shall go to their place in peace."

So . . . Moses chose able men out of all Israel, and made them heads over the people, rulers of thousands, rulers of hundreds, rulers of fifties, and rulers of tens. And they judged the people at all seasons; the hard causes they brought unto Moses, but every small matter they judged themselves.

Whenever there are expansions to the plant, new sales territories opened up, increases in company-provided services, or other changes leading to the addition of employees, the question arises of whether some present executive can take on the supervision of the new employees and still perform his present duties satisfactorily. If it is decided that a new supervisor should be added, then what executive has the time and capacity to direct his activities?

The issue of span of supervision poses a dilemma. If a small span of supervision is desirable, then the number of executives and probably the number of levels of supervision between the senior executive and the operating employee will have to be increased. On the other hand, if management desires to keep the number of strata of executives small, there will have to be an offsetting increase somewhere in the number of individuals reporting to a supervisor.

This dilemma is illustrated in Figure 19, which shows eighty-one employees along each base line. Theoretically, one executive can supervise all these workers, but the average time he can spend with each would be so small that he obviously could not give effective direction or keep track of what each was doing. If the chief executive decided that he could keep track of nine assistants, and that each of these could supervise nine workers, then we would have the situation shown in the middle of the diagram, with a total of ten executives and two supervisory levels. Perhaps nine would be found to be too wide a span, and the number of immediate subordinates to each executive would be reduced to three. This narrow span would require four supervisory levels, with a total of forty executives. Clearly, the optimum span lies somewhere between eighty-one and three. In making the choice we should always remember that as the span of supervision is reduced the number of executives and, frequently, the levels of supervision are correspondingly increased.

Of course, in practice a constant span for all executives is not necessary. Some executives may be able to direct the work of only three or four immediate subordinates, whereas others can take care

(A) Span of 81 per executive:  I supervisory level, I executive.

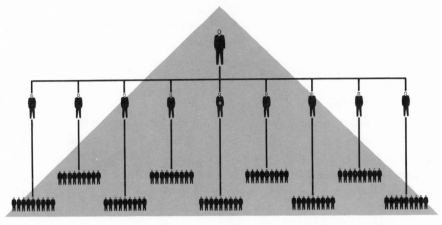

(B) Span of 9 per executive:  2 supervisory levels, 10 executives.

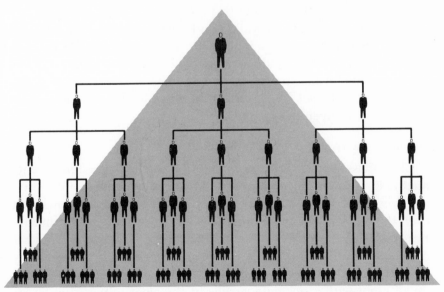

(C) Span of 3 per executive:  4 supervisory levels, 40 executives.

FIGURE 19. *Diagram of Different Spans of Supervision.*

of ten or twelve. Nevertheless, the underlying dilemma between the span and supervisory overhead will always be present.

In dealing with the dilemma presented by span of supervision, the administrator should consider the following:

1. Factors limiting the effective span of supervision
2. Objections to increasing the number of executives and levels of supervision
3. Guides for selecting the optimum span for each executive
4. Methods for relieving an overburdened executive when delegation to intermediate subordinates is impractical.

## FACTORS LIMITING THE EFFECTIVE SPAN OF SUPERVISION

### Time and energy

The limits on the number of people a man can effectively supervise arise fundamentally from the physiological and mental capacity of individuals. The number of hours a man can work per day or per week are circumscribed. What constitutes a full day's work is, to be sure, strongly influenced by habit and attitude; but even under the stimulus of war conditions it was found that the typical worker did not increase his total output by working for sustained periods of over sixty hours per week, and in some occupations maximum output is reached in a shorter period.

Even if the executive is willing and able to devote long hours to his job, his nervous energy is limited. After a number of hours of concentrated effort, his judgment is not so sharp, his patience gives out sooner, he evades tough issues, and accepts sloppy work in the hope that it will "get by." Clearly, the total work any man can do well within a given period is limited.

### Mental capacity and personal adaptability

Closely associated with the confines on a man's time and energy are the limits on his mental capacity and personal adaptability. Anyone who has tried to supervise twenty or thirty people knows that even the routine, day-to-day relationships raise a variety of difficulties. Joe likes lots of fresh air, the bookkeeper wants the windows closed; Sally turns up with a new engagement ring, and the efficiency of the female employees falls about 10 per cent; Pete, who has been up all night with a sick wife, arrives at the office with a chip on his shoulder, and when Bob accidentally knocks his papers off the desk,

Pete tells him what he thinks of him in picturesque language; a rush order arrives and three or four people have to be temporarily withdrawn from their regular duties, and this upsets the flow of work to other people; and so it goes.

The ability of a supervisor to view such things in an understanding fashion diminishes as the number of problems increases. With only a half a dozen subordinates, he can be firm with one subordinate, encouraging to another, and give a pep talk to a third, depending upon the individual and a variety of environmental factors. But with twenty or thirty subordinates, most supervisors are forced to adopt a limited supervisory procedure and hope that it is effective in all cases.

Individual executives vary, of course, in the amount of time and energy they can and will devote to their jobs. They also differ in their capacity to adapt to a variety of situations. For some, supervisory responsibility imposes strong moral obligations and creates considerable nervous strain when all is not going well; others shoulder such responsibilities and are content to rely upon intuition and good luck to get over the rough spots. Because of these individual differences in the basic limits on span of supervision, we cannot expect to find a fixed formula that will apply in all situations.

## Complex supervisory situation

Good supervision requires current information, thought, and personal attention to the subordinates and activities being directed. Such knowledge and attention is restricted not only by the factors already discussed, but also by the supervisory situation itself. For example, if the people and activities being directed are widely spread over a large territory, the task of getting information regarding local conditions will be correspondingly increased. Likewise, if the *variety* of activities becomes greater, the time and energy needed to keep informed about what is going on will consume a higher proportion of the executive's time.

As the supervisory situation becomes more complex, an executive reaches the physical limits on his time and energy, and he extends his mental capacity and personal adaptability to their limits. These are compelling reasons why an executive cannot give adequate attention to a larger and larger number of immediate subordinates.

### OBJECTIONS TO INCREASING THE NUMBER OF EXECUTIVES AND LEVELS OF SUPERVISION

The factors just discussed indicate the desirability of keeping spans of supervision small. Why not, then, give each executive only a few immediate subordinates? The difficulty in doing so is that it increases the number of executives and, more serious, it often increases supervisory levels in the organization. This, too, has its disadvantages.

**Inaccuracy of communication**

One of the objections to increasing the levels of supervision is that communication up and down the executive pyramid becomes more difficult and less accurate.

This was illustrated by the experience of a utility company that had just adopted a new form to record information from people who wished to buy appliances on the time-payment plan. During the first few weeks credit interviewers, who, incidentally, had not participated in the preparation of the form, had difficulty in using it. They frequently asked their supervisor where to put down certain types of information and complained that other questions were hard to get answered without irritating the customer. The supervisor explained the use of the form and helped the men devise questions to bring out obscure information.

Later, when his manager asked how the new form was going, the supervisor replied: "The boys are having a little difficulty getting used to it, but it is going to give us some excellent information. I think it will be a great improvement." A short time afterward the vice-president asked this manager how the new form was working out, and he replied: "Just fine. It's really a big improvement." Thus, with only two intermediaries the vice-president received a report which was almost diametrically opposed to the views of the people who were using the new form.

Let anyone who thinks that human beings are good conductors of ideas consider the difficulty of getting an accurate report of an accident. Even the eyewitnesses do not agree; by the time each of them has told somebody, who has told somebody else, the facts of the case are obscure indeed. The same difficulty is present in business. An executive may have three or four men in his office to discuss a particular plan; but by the time each of them tells his subordinates and they tell their subordinates, there is likely to be a substantial difference in the instructions received by the men on the firing line. The more people through whom the ideas must pass, the greater danger of serious distortion.

Of course, some methods exist for improving this communication. Reports containing objective data may be prepared and circulated; an executive may issue written instructions that are passed down through several strata of the organization so that all the people concerned at least see the same words; staff men may be used to obtain information and to interpret instructions of the chief executive. These devices are cumbersome and, at best, only supplement the information that should flow up and down the channel of command.

On the other hand, some intentional twisting of ideas will probably occur. An executive may fail to report trouble if he wants to create a good impression of his administration, or he may magnify difficulties if he is seeking new equipment or some other change. Similarly, in passing information down the line, he will hold, interpret, or amplify ideas in a way that he believes will secure the results he desires. Usually there are no clear falsehoods, and the executive probably believes he is acting in the best interest of the enterprise; but as was seen in the case of the new form used by the utility company, a shift in emphasis by two or three successive individuals can seriously modify the accuracy of communication.

### Inflexibility

Communication through several layers of supervision is not only inaccurate, it also takes time. When a change in operations is under consideration, executives at all levels should, if possible, contribute information and advice in the diagnosis of difficulties and the development of the new plan. When several layers of supervision are involved, this may require some little time. For instance, the production vice-president may be tied up for several days in the negotiation of a new labor contract. When he is free, the production manager may be away for two days inspecting some new equipment. By the time he gets back and does see the production vice-president, the plant superintendent is busy each afternoon with a supervisory training program. All of which means that it may be two or three weeks before the desired information is assembled.

Similarly, delays may be encountered in explaining and selling the decision once it has been made. If a problem has top priority, it will, of course, be handled with much more dispatch; but this solution is not available for all problems because it causes too much disruption to other activities. The more levels of supervision involved, the slower is likely to be the action.

In contrast, the company with, say, only two levels of supervision can move much more quickly. The senior executive, in one or two conferences with his supervisors, has most of the information available, and the organization structure permits action to be taken quickly. Of course, insofar as authority to make decisions is decentralized, fewer supervisory levels will be involved in any particular operating problem. Even a large company may approach the flexibility of a small enterprise. However, where decentralization is not practical, additional strata of executives tend to slow up decision-making and add to the inflexibility of a large concern.

### Danger of layering

Another communication difficulty that is accentuated by added levels of supervision is layering. In its narrow sense, *layering* refers to an insistence that communication flow exclusively up and down the channels of command. This going through the proper channels often results in a communication passing through several layers of supervision in order to get from one part of the enterprise to another. The difficulty is illustrated in Figure 20 where a request by worker *D* for information from worker *G* would have to flow through three supervisory levels and five supervisors, and the reply would follow a similar circuitous path.

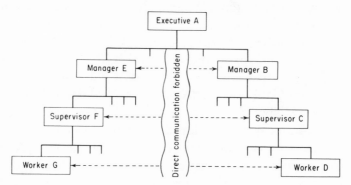

FIGURE 20. *Diagram Illustrating "Layering."*

Undesirable though it usually is, layering must not be condemned too quickly. The executive who is embarrassed to find that some of his colleagues have received information from one of his subordinates before he himself finds it out or, more serious, that subordinate employees have proceeded to take action on the basis of facts the executive knew nothing about, is likely to insist on layering in order to keep things under control.

A more practical solution is that adopted by R.C.A. As indicated in Figure 21, R.C.A. decided that contacts between units should be carried out in the most direct way, but at the same time specified that each member of the organization should keep his supervisor fully informed regarding any problems arising out of such contacts.

The danger of layering enters into a consideration of the span of control because layering is more likely to be serious when there are narrow spans and many levels of supervision.

---

### Radio Corporation of America

*Channels of Contact*

The organization structure and the organization chart define lines of responsibility and authority; but do not indicate channels of contact.

    ✿    ✿    ✿    ✿

The Radio Corporation of America Organization permits and requires the exercise of common sense and good judgment, at all organizational levels, in determining the best channels of contact necessary for the expeditious handling of the work.

    ✿    ✿    ✿    ✿

Contacts between units of the organization should be carried out in the most direct way.

    ✿    ✿    ✿    ✿

In making such contacts, however, it is the duty of each member of the organization to keep his senior informed on:

1. Any matters on which his senior may be held accountable by those senior to him.

2. Any matters in disagreement or likely to cause controversy within or between any units of the Company.

3. Matters requiring advice by the senior or his coordination with other divisional units.

4. Any matters involving recommendations for changes in, or variance from, established Company policies.

---

FIGURE 21. *One Way of Avoiding Layering.*

### Expense of supervision

An increase in the number of executives, which inevitably results from reducing the span of supervision, is expensive. Figure 19, on page 255, shows how the number of executives and levels of supervision increases as the span of supervision is lowered, and, of course, each time an executive is added there is a corresponding addition for his salary and often for office space and secretarial and other assistants. Supervisory expense, like any other expense, may be fully justified in terms of the results achieved. Nevertheless, when contemplating a reduction in the span of control, the additional expense is certainly one of the items to include in the reckoning.

### Effect on morale

Additional levels of supervision generally have a bad effect on executive morale. The most immediate effect of interposing a supervisory level is a reduction in the direct personal influence of the senior executive. When working through intermediaries, a man cannot make his ideas, aspirations, and determination as vivid as is possible in face-to-face contacts. Executives and operators who are denied this direct contact with the personality of the "big boss" inevitably feel a remoteness and a lowering in the value attached to their efforts.

Closely associated with the loss of personal contact is what Gen. Otto Nelson has aptly called "pride of place." In his study of military organization he states:

> Both senior and junior officers are generally impatient at delays incident to going through channels. Juniors whenever possible like to deal directly with the highest authority. Officers heading organizational entities resent being placed far down the chain of command. In all sorts of ways "pride of place" exerts a dynamic force and it is a rare organizational entity in the War Department and the Army, the chief of which if given any opportunity, does not try to climb higher on the organizational ladder. . . .[1]

[1] *National Security and the General Staff*, Infantry Journal Press, 1946, p. 579. General Nelson goes on to point out the dangers of conceding too much to personal desires for status: " 'Pride of place' has usually won out in time of peace, resulting in far more individuals reporting to one man than he could control. Where there are ambitious subordinates, soft-hearted commanders, and the compliance characteristic of peacetime, 'pride of place' flourishes. The awakening always comes but usually not until war or other emergency threatens. The serious incidents in the form of grave errors, neglects, or delays forcibly remind the commanders of the limitations imposed upon them by 'span of control.' "

Moreover, a narrow span of supervision and the resulting increase in levels of supervision permit, perhaps encourage, centralization of decision-making. This centralization, the sociologists and social psychologists insist, leads to poor morale. J. C. Worthy, reporting on twelve years' study of several hundred organizational units, states: "In organizations characterized by many levels of supervision and elaborate systems of control, the individual has little opportunity to develop the capacities of self-reliance and initiative. . . ." [2]

These influences of a narrow span of supervision on morale should be regarded as a tendency, an ever-present danger, but not as a fixed relationship. For example, narrow span of supervision does not always mean a high degree of centralization and functionalization. Employees who report to an executive so overburdened that they get scant advice and assistance from him may welcome an intermediary who has a regular place at the council table and can secure the attention of the senior executive when it is necessary. Key executives can and should meet with employees several layers below them for discussion, even though official instructions come down the channel of command; in fact, one of the chief reasons why the Army insists that high commanding officers have only a few operating units below them is to make time for field trips and personal observation of operating conditions. Nevertheless, an adverse reaction to additional levels of supervision is common enough to warrant careful attention when dealing with the span of supervision issue.

## Guides for Selecting the Optimum Span for Each Executive

The preceding discussion of the pros and cons of a narrow or wide span of supervision develops the nature of the problem but unfortunately gives no single answer or formula. In fact, the analysis indicates clearly that what may be an effective span for one executive may be either too large or too small for another.

Empirical studies suggest that executives in higher echelons should have a span of three to seven operating subordinates, whereas the optimum range for first-line supervisors of routine activities is usually from fifteen to twenty employees. Even these limits permit a variation of as much as 100 per cent in the number of executives required, and many successful administrators have had a span of

[2] See Worthy's *Big Business and Free Men*, Harper & Row, Publishers, 1959, chap. vii for amplification of his views.

supervision outside these rule-of-thumb limits. Consequently, choice of a practical span of supervision, like most other aspects of organization, requires personal judgment.

Several points, however, so often influence the wise choice of the number of immediate subordinates that the skillful organizer will consider them each time he makes a decision on this issue. These guides to the optimum span for each executive are:

1. Variety and importance of activities supervised
2. Other duties of the executive
3. Stability of operations
4. Capacity of subordinates and degree of delegation
5. Relative importance of supervisory payroll
6. Practicality of relieving an extended span of supervision.

### Variety and importance of activities supervised

The number of people an executive should try to supervise is strongly influenced by the activities they perform. Consider, for example, the contrast in supervisory work in the following two situations. In the first example, thirty-five clerks are employed by a department store to verify and sort the sales slips for charge account customers. Thousands of slips pass through this section daily, and all that is required is to check the multiplication, addition, and computation of sales tax, and then to sort the slips into batches for entry into the accounting records. Employees must understand quite a variety of transactions, but fundamentally the work is highly routine. There is a supervisor and an assistant supervisor, and these two men are able to do a satisfactory job of supervising the section.

The second example is that of a general manager who arrived at his office to find the personnel director waiting for him. A jurisdictional issue had arisen between the electricians union and the carpenters union over who should do certain work on a new elevator. Both unions insisted that the company take a position in the matter; to do so might result in a strike of maintenance men, which would necessitate shutting down the entire plant. Before this discussion was completed, the sales promotion manager came bursting in, bubbling with enthusiasm for a new plan he had developed when he lay awake the night before. It involved special packaging and a tie-in with radio advertising. It was a wow! (Just like the plan he had two weeks before.)

In the meantime the controller was waiting to discuss a possible change in account classification. A recent tax ruling indicated that the company might reduce its tax liability by a change in inventory valuation procedure. The saving was not certain, however, and the change in procedure would upset comparisons with results of previous years. Consideration of this subject had to be cut off because the general manager had an appointment with an important customer; and so the day went.

Clearly, if the general manager in the preceding case attempted to supervise seventeen or eighteen subordinates, as do the men in charge of verifying sales slips, his supervision would be quite inadequate, and he would probably develop stomach ulcers in the process. The variety and the importance of the activities he supervises demand much more time and energy than does the routine work in the accounting section. In applying this concept generally, variety may refer to differences in location or any other aspect of the activity that calls for the expenditure of additional time and effort in supervision.

### Other duties of the executive

Executives have several duties in addition to supervising their immediate subordinates, and the amount of time they are expected to spend on these other duties will affect the number of people they can supervise.

The nature of this problem is indicated in Figure 22. Here we note that a president who is expected to spend at least a third of his time on top administrative planning, another third on more specific planning and control, and at least 10 per cent representing the company at Congressional hearings, public gatherings, and other places, has only 20 per cent of his time left for the immediate supervision of key operating executives. A foreman, by way of contrast, may spend approximately a quarter of his time making up special orders, filling in reports, and doing other activities that he might delegate, but the remaining 75 per cent is available for directing his immediate subordinates. This immediately suggests one of the reasons why the foreman probably can supervise more men than the top executive.

The diagram is merely illustrative, and the time available for supervision must be investigated in each instance. For example, if a sales vice-president is expected to spend half of his time selling goods to large customers, obviously his span of supervision should be reduced. Similarly, the industrial relations man may be expected

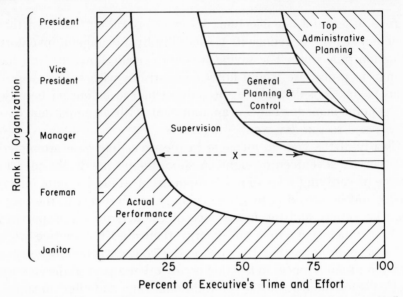

FIGURE 22. *Diagram Illustrating Varying Proportions of Time Spent on Different Executive Duties.* The optimum number of immediate subordinates depends partly on the time devoted to supervision—represented on the diagram by horizontal distance X.

to spend a large part of his time negotiating with unions, or the production manager working on product development; such duties as these will affect the number of people they can effectively supervise. These two points, the other duties of an executive and the variety and importance of activities supervised, account in large measure for the empirical rule that the number of immediate subordinates should become fewer in successively higher positions in the administrative hierarchy. They certainly are more important than the often-quoted point by Graicunas regarding the geometric increase in the number of relationships possible among subordinates.

### Stability of operations

Every experienced administrator knows the difficulties in tackling a new job, in changing the methods of performing an old one, in making drastic expansions or contractions in the volume of work, in adjusting to other changes in operations. He thinks longingly of the time when things will be running on an even keel, when methods (determined centrally or by the workers themselves) will have become habit, when each person in the group knows what normally may be expected of the others, when his section, department, or company really has *going-concern value*. Clearly, the stability of operations, or lack of it, makes a lot of difference in the supervisory work required.

If stability can be forecast over a long enough period to warrant an adjustment in supervisory load, it certainly should be one of the considerations in deciding how many subordinates to assign to a particular executive.

### Capacity of subordinates and degree of decentralization

Capable and experienced subordinates are relatively easy to supervise. They understand directions quickly, ask fewer questions, require less checking, make fewer errors, and usually are more easily motivated to do a good day's work.

Such a reduction in need for supervision occurs in the plant, the office, and the field. A sales manager, for instance, with experienced, self-reliant salesmen already well established in their respective territories has a lighter supervisory task than does the sales executive of a new company who must build a sales force from newly recruited men.

Also important, especially in the higher echelons, is the effect that capacity of subordinates has on the amount of decentralization that is practical. When an executive finds he can decentralize authority to make decisions, he eases his supervisory burdens substantially. Of course, as noted in Chapter 11, delegation does not mean abdication. The executive must still spend some time indicating objectives, checking results, and, above all, counseling or otherwise assisting his subordinate. Nevertheless, the total time and effort required should be considerably less than when he attempts to plan and control operations in detail.

This factor of capable subordinates and a high degree of delegation permits the presidents of some of our largest corporations to have a wide span of supervision.

### Relative importance of supervisory payroll

Span of supervision has a significant influence on the size of the executive payroll, as has already been noted. In highly competitive industries, if payroll is a large part of costs, this expense aspect of span of supervision should be given particularly careful consideration. In industries where quality of products or service is more important than price, and in those industries, such as chemical processing, where labor is only a relatively small part of the total cost, the choice of span will probably be determined more by other factors than by an increase or decrease in executive payroll.

**Practicability of relieving an extended span of supervision**

Span of supervision is but one aspect of administrative organization, and a change in the span for a particular executive should be made only after considering its effect on the entire structure. For instance, careful consideration of departmentation may show that the activities under an executive should be divided into seven divisions; to then say that this man's span should be nine or five may well require impractical departmentation. Similarly, a change in span will have to be reconciled with the basic scheme of centralization or decentralization.

If these other compelling reasons result in an executive's having a somewhat light supervisory load, this can usually be adjusted by giving him additional duties or using him for special assignments. On the other hand, if circumstances appear to require a man to overextend his span of supervision, then the various means of partial relief should be carefully studied. The more important of these devices are discussed in the next section of this chapter. Somehow, someway, the overextended span should be corrected.

## METHODS OF RELIEVING AN OVERBURDENED EXECUTIVE

Executives may become overburdened for a variety of reasons. Combining two or more divisions may not be practical, the need for unity of action may prevent a high degree of decentralization, or other considerations already suggested may result in the concentration in a single administrative post of more duties than a single man can effectively perform. What then may be done to provide at least partial relief to the executive in such a position?

Probably the most common way of relieving an extended span is to give the executive an assistant, an *alter ego*, who shares with him the duties of the position. For instance, there may be a plant superintendent and an assistant plant superintendent, or a president and vice-president, who work together so closely that from an organization point of view they constitute a single administrative office. An inevitable problem in such an arrangement is how to divide the work load and still maintain unity of action. Sometimes there is a division by subjects, and subordinates know, for example, that technical matters should be discussed with Mr. X while labor problems go to Mr. Y. Occasionally the division will be in the nature of contacts, with one man concentrating on external relations while the other spends most of his time on internal contacts.[3]

More likely, there is no clear-cut division of duties between the executive and his assistant, the allocation of work depending upon what problems are pressing at the moment, the particular experience of the individuals with those problems, and the preferences and natural abilities of the men involved.

The executive and his assistant must form a close partnership if this arrangement is to work. It will break down if each does not keep the other fully informed of his actions, and inconsistent directions will be given; for if subordinates discover that one man is more lenient on, say, price concessions than the other, they will adjust their requests and advice to whoever happens to be in the office. Difficulties of dual subordination are likely to arise because one partner does not know just what the other has said to an employee.

In other words, this partnership or alter-ego concept may work, but it is inherently difficult. To be effective there must be a proper blending of personalities and experience in working together. The senior man must have complete confidence in his associate since, as in a legal partnership, typically either of the men can speak officially for the office. The relationship is so highly personal that if either of the two men is replaced, the scheme may break down. The arrangement is often a useful one, but because of its inherent weaknesses, it should be avoided if some other provision is practical.

A second and closely related measure for relieving an extended span of supervision is the use of *staff* assistants. These men play quite a different role from that of the type of assistant just discussed. The assistant, or alter ego, is clearly in the No. 2 spot, and makes decisions and initiates actions just as the senior executive does. The staff assistant, or the assistant *to* the executive, is, at least theoretically, a nonentity; he does his work on behalf of and in the name

---

[3] If the assistant makes all contacts with subordinates, then we might say that the senior man had only one subordinate, whereas the assistant had the wide span of supervision (made practical because he was relieved of so many other duties). Usually, however, the senior man feels free to give directions to subordinates, and actually both the supervisory and other duties are shared by both men.

of the senior executive. Since the nature and the pros and cons of staff have already been discussed in Chapter 12, we need only point out here that if the staff concept is properly understood, it does provide a very helpful means for relieving an overburdened executive.

One other rather simple arrangement should at least be mentioned. Occasionally one can appoint an intermediary executive to supervise some but not all of the subordinates of the overburdened executive. Thus, a sales vice-president with ten branch managers reporting to him may turn over five of them to a western zone supervisor, while the other five continue to report directly to him. As will be explained more fully in Chapter 17, *uneven strata* have drawbacks. The morale of the western managers may be hurt because they do not report directly to the vice-president, and the problems of the eastern branches are likely to receive preferred treatment. While the arrangement has earmarks of expediency, it may, nevertheless, be the most practical in some circumstances.

### SUMMARY

In administrative organization the dilemma of extended spans of supervision versus additional executives and management levels presents itself time and again.

The limits on the time, energy, mental capacity, and personal adaptability of every executive must be recognized. On the other hand, increased supervisory overhead usually makes internal communication less accurate, diminishes flexibility, adds expense, and may lower morale. There is no simple formula for balancing these pulls in opposite directions; individual ability and the total supervisory situation need to be considered in a decision for each executive.

The skillful organizer will analyze at least the following points in arriving at an optimum span for an individual: variety and importance of activities supervised, other duties the executive is expected to perform, stability of operations, capacity of subordinates and the degree of delegation, relative importance of supervisory payroll, and practicality of relieving the executive if overburdened.

When there are compelling reasons for giving an executive more subordinates than appears wise, provision of an alter ego, use of staff assistants, or creation of uneven strata may provide a practical solution.

## SELECTED REFERENCES

Haimann, T., *Professional Management,* Houghton Mifflin Company, 1962, Chap. 16.

Healey, J. H., *Executive Coordination and Control,* Bureau of Business Research, Ohio State University Press, 1956.

Koontz, H. and C. O'Donnell, *Readings in Management,* McGraw-Hill Book Co., Inc., 1959, pp. 40-59.

Stieglitz, H., "Optimizing Span of Control," *Management Record,* September 1962; see also "Analyzing the Manager's Span of Control," *Management Record,* July 1960.

Worthy, J. C., *Big Business and Free Men,* Harper & Row, Publishers, 1959, Chap. 7.

# 16

# Organization Structure

Organization structure deals with the over-all organizational arrangements in an enterprise. While often an administrator can deal with an organization problem in a narrow focus of, say, departmentation or delegation, from time to time he must sit back and look at his organization as a whole, and consider whether basic alterations might produce more effective results.

*Significance of organization structure.* A clear grasp of organization structure is helpful in making the more frequent detailed adjustments in organizational arrangements. These changes should be made in a way that is consistent with the basic pattern. If an exception is necessary, it should be recognized as such and not treated as a general precedent. For example, a company with a structure calling for decentralized operations may decide to centralize negotiations of union contracts because of union insistence on a company-wide contract. But if this exception paves the way for the centralization of a large variety of other personal activities, a serious rift will result in the whole decentralized structure, and a potential source of friction and delay will have been created. Just as policies provide the framework within which procedures and programs are developed, so too will the organization structure provide the pattern around which the detailed administrative relationships should be woven.

Organization structure is like the architectural plan of a building, and the larger and more complicated the building, the more important a central architectural plan becomes. Many a New England farmhouse just grew without any general plan; the first two or three rooms were constructed when the family was small and time and materials were scarce. As the family grew, a wing with one or two more bedrooms was added; then perhaps a larger kitchen was placed on the back; and when Aunt Nellie came to live with the family, still another wing with its own sitting room was built.

The materials and quality of workmanship in these sundry additions varied with conditions at the time they were erected. Some had deep foundations, others were built on the surface of the ground. Often the floor levels didn't match, particularly on the second story. Such structures serve their purpose reasonably well, but they would have been more efficient had there been a central plan around which each of the major additions was made. Certainly a modern plant or office building cannot be constructed in such a haphazard manner; nor should organizing a business enterprise be approached in such a haphazard way.

The function of the architect is to consider the purposes of the building, the types of space and special features needed, the relative cost of alternative means of construction, and similar considerations; then he must develop a single, optimum arrangement that recognizes each of the considerations. The pleasing exterior lines, for instance, must be consistent with the size of office space and elevators needed for operational purposes within; the plan for a large assembly room must not create structural weaknesses; and provision must be made for heat, light, safety, and the like. Before this modern building is erected, engineering plans and specifications covering structural steel, electric wiring, plumbing, and the like are needed; but vital as these engineering specifications may be, they do not provide the over-all design. A good architect is one who is familiar with the possibilities and limitations of various materials, processes, and equipment; thus, his final plan is not only a creative adaptation to broad objectives, but also a practical program for detailed execution.

Similarly, the administrator when designing an organization structure must take into account the benefits of specialization, the limitations on functional authority, problems of communication, and a variety of other specialized aspects of organization. He is considering them here, however, as individual parts that need to be fitted together into an integrated structure. The resulting whole is greater than the sum of its parts.

*An approach to organization structure.* In designing an organization structure, one starts with the objectives and the activities of the enterprise. These should have been established by previous planning, and, with minor modifications, are accepted as fixed in the organizational planning stage. With this background information, organization structure can usually be developed by considering:

1. *Primary departmentation;* that is, the major operating divisions into which the work may be best divided,
2. *Focus of operating authority;* that is, the units and particularly the levels at which most of the operating decisions will be made,
3. *Facilitating units* that are needed to guide and assist those charged with primary operating duties,
4. Adequate provision for *top-management functions,*
5. *Structural arrangements* that will add simplicity, consistency, and otherwise contribute to the smooth working of the organization.

Several of these points have already been considered in previous chapters, and consequently only brief treatment will be necessary here. In dealing with organization structure we shall assume familiarity with the more detailed questions and will consider departmentation, delegation, staff, and similar issues merely as part of a general whole. In other words, we are treating them here from quite a different point of view than was taken in Chapters 9 to 15.

Before exploring each of these five aspects of organization structure, we should note that a department manager or division director may have problems of organization structure within his particular sphere of activity, just as the top executive of an enterprise is concerned with the entire organization structure. The departmental executive must, of course, arrange his activities in a manner consistent with the over-all structure, but this often leaves him considerable latitude.

The departmental manager, like the president, should from time to time consider the primary departmentation of activities under his direction, the focus of operating decision-making, the special units necessary to facilitate activities, and the general structural arrangements. Questions of organization structure arise even within small units although, as the number of people and variety of activities are reduced and the companywide or departmental pattern limits the alternatives, organization structuring of subsidiary units becomes more simple. Nevertheless, at any executive level, an ability to think of organization as an integrated whole instead of a series of semi-independent problems is a distinct asset.

## PRIMARY DEPARTMENTATION

### Designating major departments

Grouping activities into major operating departments is the most obvious and usually the first thing to consider in establishing an organization structure. In some enterprises this primary division is inherent in the nature of activities, as for example in a small manufacturing concern where selling, manufacturing, and office work are clearly separated activities.

In many enterprises, however, the best primary departmentation is by no means so evident. For example, life insurance companies typically have major operating units for sales, investments, and central office work on issuing policies, collecting premiums, paying claims, and the like. Such an organization, shown in Figure 23, is used by the Equitable Life company. The Prudential Life Insurance Company, on the other hand, divides operations among eight regional, home offices, each of which performs virtually all of these operating activities for policy holders in its area. Top executives at Prudential contend that splitting operations on a regional basis has fostered rapid growth, though admittedly when a home office is first opened expense ratios temporarily rise.

Primary departmentation should be re-examined periodically because changes in company policies or in external conditions may modify the organization that is most effective. A magazine publisher, for instance, for many years permitted the editor of each of its five magazines to handle his own layout, art work, proofreading, and the like in addition to editorial work. In effect each magazine was a center of operations, with the distribution, advertising, and financial departments acting as service units. Owing to rising costs and competition, however, all activities except editorial work were transferred to centralized operating departments. This permitted editors to concentrate on magazine content—which had always been their primary interest—and other specialists to concentrate on processing activities. The shift resulted in much needed economies.

Another example of a change in primary departmentation is re-

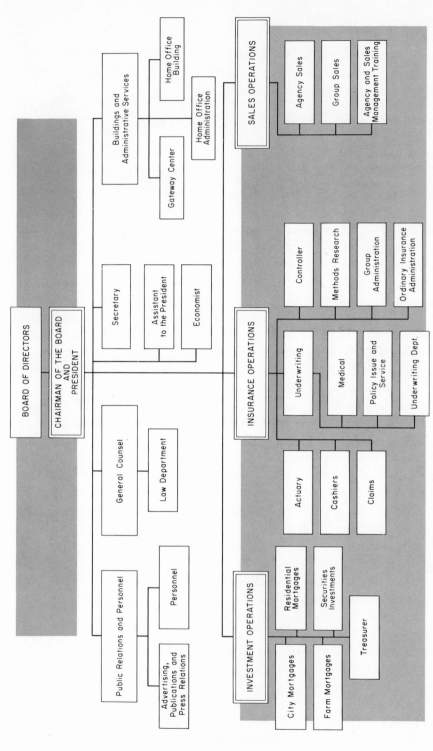

FIGURE 23. *Basic Organization Structure of the Equitable Life Assurance Society of the United States.*

flected in the two charts of an electronics company shown in Figure 24. This company manufactures radios, television receivers, sound systems, telephones, switchboards, and completely automatic switchboard systems, and it also operates radio and television broadcasting stations. The former organization was primarily functional, with each department (except broadcasting) dealing with all products. In the new organization separate divisions have been created for the different types of products, and the manufacturing, engineering, and sales activities have been allocated to these divisions. Differences in the manufacture of telephone equipment and that for radio and television, and a desire to improve control over expenses were the primary reasons for this shift.

Guides to effective departmentation have already been discussed in Chapter 9. Fundamentally, the administrator must seek a division of activities that provides the greatest advantages of specialization, facilitates control, aids in coordination, secures adequate attention to important activities, recognizes local conditions, develops people, and keeps expenses low. These considerations are applicable to primary departmentation as well as to refinements in departmentation, which were discussed in the earlier chapter.

**Follow a consistent basis**

An additional point that should be given careful consideration in establishing an organization structure is the desirability of creating primary departments on a consistent basis. Thus, if most operating activities are divided among territorial divisions, a distinct advantage occurs in having all operating activities classified territorially. Or, if the primary departments are functional in character, then the consistent use of a functional departmentation is likely to result in a simpler organization structure.

The first chart in Figure 24, for example, shows divisions for engineering, manufacturing, quality control, and sales—each functional in nature—and also a sound-equipment division. This naturally led to some confusion as to who was responsible for the engineering, the manufacturing, and the sales of sound equipment. A university runs into a similar difficulty when it sets up major departments by subjects, and then establishes a school for adults or for teachers which is really a "customer" department whose interests cut across those of several of the older departments.

Following one basis of departmentation through all operating

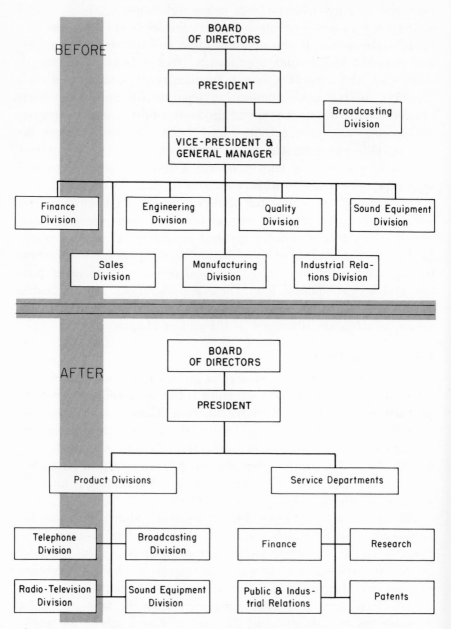

FIGURE 24. *Chart Showing Revision of Electronics Company Organization.*

activities is not always practical. Many manufacturing companies, for example, have a West Coast branch that combines manufacturing, selling, and financial operations, whereas the rest of their company is divided along functional lines. In situations such as these, the need for local knowledge, adequate attention, and coordination on a geographic basis outweighs the advantages of the single, consistent basis of departmentation.

Nevertheless, each time two or more different bases are used for major operating divisions, the organization structure is made more complex. It is often harder to establish clear lines of responsibility and, consequently, control is more difficult; frequently special provisions for coordination are required. For these reasons a consistent basis for departmentation of operating activities is desirable, though it is not essential.

## Focus of Operating Responsibility

The second vital characteristic of organization structure is the level at which operating decisions will be made. In the discussion of decentralization in Chapter 13, we noted that the number and quality of employees, the procedural flow of information, and the need for elaborate planning and control measures all are affected by the extent to which authority is decentralized. Therefore, along with the plans for primary departmentation must go a concept of centralization or decentralization. In the more picturesque language of L. S. Fish, "Where are you going to put the real horsepower?"

To cite a well-known contrast, for many years the Ford Motor Company used a highly centralized organization in which a great many of the policies, methods, procedures, and programs were decided in the headquarters office. In contrast, the General Motors Corporation has emphasized decentralized authority, at least to the heads of the various major divisions; the chief executives of Chevrolet, Fisher Body, Frigidaire, and other similar units have been granted wide discretion in guiding the activities of their particular divisions. No executive has really thought through his organization structure until he has conceived of the general pattern of decentralization he expects to employ.

Complex operations require a decision as to which units should have a staff role and which should be centers of operating responsibility. The United States State Department with its divisions for various geographical areas of the world, and also its divisions for international trade, cultural relations, diplomatic relations, and petroleum, wheat, and other products, faces such a dilemma. As long as State Department activities continue to be concentrated on policy-making and planning, this dual organization can be made to work reasonably well; but if the Department takes on operating functions, it will be necessary to distinguish sharply between units that carry the operating responsibilities and those which are primarily intended to perform planning and coordinating staff work.

This type of problem is by no means confined to governmental operations. A large meat-packing company with plants located from the Atlantic to the Pacific, for example, has a group of regional executives and also a set of executives for beef, pork, produce, and other major products it handles. This particular company places primary responsibility on its several regional executives, but the structure is by no means as clear as it should be, and some confusion is the inevitable result.

Frequently, consideration of primary departmentation and the focus of operating responsibility go hand in hand, and from this should come a clear concept of the major blocks in the organization structure.

## FACILITATING UNITS

Once the major operating units have been tentatively decided upon, as suggested in the preceding paragraphs, the need for facilitating units should be considered. Such units often constitute vital refinements in the organization structure.

The nature and the typical relationships of facilitating units have already been discussed in the chapters on service divisions, staff, and committees (see Chapters 10, 12, and 14). A thorough grasp of these concepts is essential background for an administrator who is thinking of placing facilitating units in an organization structure. The basic problem at this stage of organization planning is to decide what additional divisions, sections, committees, or other organizational units are needed to assure that the operating departments function effectively and efficiently. The more important points that should be considered in this connection are discussed below.

### Coordination of operating units

The fact that operating departments need to be coordinated does not necessarily mean that special organization units should be created. In a great majority of situations such coordination can be obtained through voluntary cooperation of the executives concerned and supervision by the senior executive, as will be explained in Chapter 23. Nevertheless, in some situations the problems of coordination may be so numerous and complex that a special unit or standing committee is desirable.

Companies manufacturing highly styled or other fast-moving products sometimes find a special division charged with coordination of purchasing, production, inventories, pricing, and sales promotion contributes substantially to profitable operations. Food companies, such as coffee roasters, which deal with a perishable and fluctuating-price article, often have a similar need. The experts in buying, processing, and selling may not have a thorough knowledge of the other functions. Even if they do, they often are too busy concentrating on their major responsibility to anticipate all the detailed adjustments necessary to fine coordination.

When considering organization within a large department, a similar need may be found. For example, many manufacturing departments have a production-planning and control unit that coordinates the flow of goods from one shop to another. Coordinating committees are, of course, even more common than full-time units.

Such coordinating units are almost always organized on a different basis than the major operating departments. Thus, if the operating departments are grouped along functional or territorial lines, the coordinating units are likely to deal with products. On the other hand, if the major operating divisions are based on products, the over-all coordination may be in terms of purchasing or advertising. The coordinating units or committees are intentionally designed to crisscross between several operating departments. As activities of an enterprise become larger and more complex, the need for such facilitating units increases.

### Consistent action throughout the enterprise

Activities such as record-keeping or storage of supplies are typically found in most operating departments, and occasionally there may be compelling reasons why these activities should be performed in a consistent, if not uniform, manner. The growing recognition of the advantages of decentralizing is reducing the emphasis on uniformity of action. Nevertheless, in some cases the need for consistent action may be sufficiently important to justify a staff unit that follows an activity throughout the enterprise.

The increased emphasis on fair treatment of employees, for instance, and the rise of labor unions, which are quick to call attention to personnel action in one department that is not as favorable as that of another department, make reconcilable personnel practice within an enterprise highly desirable. One of the reasons for establishing a separate personnel division is to secure this consistent action.

Consistency of accounting practice is essential to sound, consolidated financial statements, and for this purpose almost every enterprise has some form of central accounting unit. To cite still another illustration, occasionally the maintenance of consistent selling prices is so complex that a central unit is established for this purpose.

### Assure adequate attention

Operating executives, naturally and appropriately, concentrate on their major responsibilities. In so doing they may neglect activities that are important to over-all results. This type of situation may call for placing the secondary activity in a separate division. For instance, one of the reasons why quality control may be specifically separated from production operations is to be sure it receives adequate attention; the more important the quality is to successful operation, the higher in the structure is the separation likely to be carried.

Likewise, public relations is such an elusive and yet important aspect of total operations that its guidance is frequently placed in a separate division. Of course, if the need for adequate attention is combined with advantages of specialized skill or the need for independent control, then the pressure for a separate auxiliary division is even more compelling.

### Provide control arms

In every large-scale enterprise, special methods for assuring that activities conform to plan are necessary. Auditing of records, inspection of finished goods, and similar devices are often used. These mechanisms of control, sometimes called control arms, are usually separated from the operating departments to secure objectivity and independence of judgment.

Keeping the control arm fully separated from operations at all echelons is not always practical, however. If a department manager as well as the senior executive wish to use budgets as a control device, for example, it may be desirable to have the senior budget officer rely upon a budget section within the department for detailed information, rather than attempt to secure all necessary information through a separate organization. This arrangement has the advantage not only of economy, but also of encouraging control close to the scene of action. As long as the senior executive receives full and objective reports, such an arrangement is generally desirable.

### Common use of specialized skills or facilities

Frequently, facilitating units are added to an organization structure in order to utilize fully special skills or facilities. Printing, traffic, legal, IBM tabulating, technical or economic research, and industrial engineering divisions are examples of this type of auxiliary unit. It is too expensive for each of the operating units to have its own specialists, and so a single division is established to serve all departments of the company.

Separate service divisions, as contrasted with self-contained operating departments, add to the complexity of an organization structure, and should be established only when it is clearly evident that significant economy will be obtained.

### Relieve overextended spans of supervision

When a key executive has more people reporting to him than he can adequately supervise, and consolidation of subordinate divisions is impractical, the addition of staff assistants may provide a practical remedy. These assistants serve as eyes, ears, and idea men for the hard-pressed executive, and thereby shorten the time the executive must devote to a particular problem. Here again, complexity in organization relationship is increased, and staff assistants should be added only when their use strengthens or simplifies other parts of the organization structure.

### Location of facilitating units

The facilitating units must be placed in the organization structure where they will be effective and at the same time not unduly interfere with the main stream of operations. Generally, service units are best placed in the department that makes the most use of them, unless they are important enough to warrant immediate supervision by a top executive. (See Chapter 10.)

Control, coordinating, and long-range planning units normally report to the senior executive, inasmuch as they perform functions that he might himself perform if he had the time and specialized ability. Having a control or a coordinating unit subordinate to an operating executive whose activities are being regulated is clearly undesirable; to do so weakens the guidance over that executive and places him in an anomalous position vis-à-vis other department executives.

Unfortunately, this may place a large number of division executives under the immediate supervision of the senior executive, and even with staff assistance the senior executive may not be able to handle the load. The Army overcomes this difficulty by providing a chief of staff who supervises all staff divisions, and otherwise acts as the alter ego of the senior executive. The chief of staff coordinates and sifts staff recommendations before submitting them to the top executive. This permits the commanding officer to spend more time on urgent matters. True, the staff units are somewhat subordinated, but this is partially offset by the greater prestige and influence of the chief of staff, who must be a member of the "inner circle." Another arrangement, more common in business, is the grouping of several, though not all, of the auxiliary units under a service director or a vice-president.

Note that a major difference exists between the role of such a director and that of an operating manager. The manager typically assumes a proprietary interest in his department and operates in a semi-independent sphere of administration. The chief of staff or service director, on the other hand, must work intimately with the senior executive to assure unity in administration.

*Summary.* The foregoing suggestions of possible facilitating units is certainly not intended as a recommendation that all such units are needed in every organization structure. Quite the contrary.

Such units should be established only when the need for them is clear. The list is intended merely as review of possibilities.

In contemplating the total organization structure, the administrator should at least check the need for separate units to coordinate operating divisions, secure consistent action throughout the enterprise, assure adequate attention to significant functions, make general use of specialized skills or facilities, relieve overextended spans of supervision, and provide control. Such units can, when properly employed, fill in the gaps and otherwise facilitate the smooth operation of the organization.

(A concluding summary and references will be found at the end of the next chapter.)

# 17

# Organization Structure (*Continued*)

## TOP-MANAGEMENT ORGANIZATION

For every enterprise someone must establish basic objectives and policies, select the top executives, and provide broad, over-all guidance to the affairs of the firm. In sole proprietorships and partnerships these top administrative functions are performed by the owners, inasmuch as such firms do not have an existence separate from the people who own them. Corporations, and almost every medium and large scale enterprise is a corporation, pose a different sort of problem because they are independent social institutions, separate and apart from the owners or any particular set of officers. As Chief Justice Marshall said many years ago:

> A corporation is an artificial being, invisible, intangible, and existing only in contemplation of the law. Being a mere creature of the law, it possesses only those properties which the charter of its creation confers upon it, either expressly or as incidental to its very existence. . . . Among the most important are immortality, and, if the expression may be allowed, individuality; properties by which a perpetual succession of many persons are considered the same, and may act as a single individual.[1]

If the corporation is an artificial being, who, then, is to decide the types of products or services it will sell, whether facilities will be expanded and if so at what location, its basic attitude towards

[1] *Dartmouth College Case*, 4 Wheaton 636, (1819).

organized labor and government regulations, whether new capital is to be secured by additional stock or bonds, the desirability of a merger with a competing firm, whether the chief executive should be discharged because the firm is losing position in its industry, and other such issues?

### Indifference and impotence of stockholders

The stockholders or owners are in a weak position to exercise any real leadership in the affairs of corporations, at least of large corporations. Aside from the right to vote on changes in the charter or the financial structure, and a few relatively insignificant rights, a stockholder's power to influence the affairs of the corporation is confined to his voting for directors. Of course, if an individual owns a large proportion of the shares of stock outstanding, his influence on the administration of the corporation via the election of directors may be substantial. If such an individual wishes to influence administration, however, he almost always is a director or an executive of the company because he can then deal more directly with administrative matters.

In fact, the great majority of stockholders show considerable apathy toward the administrating of affairs of the company they own. Typically, if they do not like the way the company is being administered, they simply sell their stock.

The influence of stockholders is further reduced by two common practices. First, in most corporations, the holders of the majority of the stock represented at an annual meeting can elect *all* the directors. Consequently, a stockholder with even a 25 per cent interest can secure representation on the board of directors only if those with majority control so desire. Second, most stockholders do not attend meetings personally, but authorize someone to act for them by proxy. Since the existing management of a corporation is in a favorable position to secure such proxies, it usually controls the votes of a majority of the stock represented at the meeting. This impotence of stockholders adds to their indifference.

To be sure, a growing practice is to submit proposed actions such as new pension plans, managerial bonuses, new plants, or similar changes to stockholders for their approval. Here again proxies are used; the stockholder, lacking adequate information to decide otherwise, almost always votes as recommended by the company management. Only in rare instances does a dissatisfied group of stockholders go to the trouble and expense of trying to reverse recommendations of the board of directors.

Clearly, then, stockholders of most corporations cannot and will not provide the dynamic leadership needed in the performance of top administrative functions.

### Role of the board of directors

If the basic direction of a corporation does not come from the stockholders, as such, what then of the board of directors?

Legal theory and a considerable body of the older management literature give support to the concept that the board of directors is the real central point of direction and control of corporate activity. Unquestionably, the legal power to appoint officers, expend funds, and otherwise direct the management of a company is vested in the board of directors. But, in practice, real question exists of just what a board should do with respect to objectives, policies, organization, and executive personnel.

Should the board of directors be depended upon to originate and initiate action on such matters? Should it serve primarily as a counsel to company executives? Should it decide the specific path to follow? Should it confirm decisions of executives before they are put into effect? Should it give executives considerable freedom of action, and then concentrate on a review of the effectiveness of the executives' operations? For any major change in company operations, each of these steps—initiate, counsel, decide, confirm, review—should be taken, and the crucial issue is which should be done by the board.

*Composition of a useful board.* The effectiveness of any committee depends in a large measure upon the qualifications of its members, and the board of directors is no exception.

Many companies have boards of directors composed mostly, if not entirely, of *company executives.* Such men have intimate knowledge of internal problems of the company, and they have a strong incentive to make the company a success. However, their daily contact with specific company problems and their concentration on achieving short-run goals is very likely to interfere with their perspective and objectivity regarding over-all company operations. It is a rare individual who can be a hard-driving executive one hour, and a sagacious, dispassionate viewer of the company's chances of success the next hour. Also unrealistic is to assume that a vice-president or department manager will take a critical view of the general competence of the chief executive during the few hours he is acting as a director when during the rest of the working relationship, he is clearly subordinate to the chief executive, and, in fact, is dependent upon the latter for his job.

Moreover, company executives are in daily contact with one another and will normally work out their problems as they arise. At best, a board of company executives serves only as a top-management committee. At worst, it merely gives perfunctory approval of decisions already made, and perhaps serves as a status symbol.

An alternative is to have a board composed predominantly of *outside directors*—lawyers, bankers, other businessmen, large stockholders (or their representatives), or retired executives. Such a board has greater objectivity and more diversified perspective. Unfortunately, such men rarely have an intimate knowledge of company problems and, more serious, lack time to acquire such knowledge. Men with the maturity, experience, and judgment desired in directors are, by that very fact, likely to be heavily involved in other activities. All too often, these men are forced to give virtually no thought to company problems except during the hour or two each month they are actually at the meeting of the board. The combined effect of lack of company knowledge plus lack of time means that these men cannot be expected to initiate action and really guide the destinies of the company.[2] Consequently, their primary function is one of advice.

Since both outside and inside directors have their advantages, the strongest board of directors usually can be formed by combining men of each type. In order not to be dependent upon a single point of view regarding company activities, more than one executive should serve on the board. On the other hand, if the board is made too large, over, say, seven or eight individuals, a free interchange of ideas becomes difficult, and consequently some committees may be necessary.

Of more importance than any particular balance between inside and outside directors is the competence and attitude of the individuals involved. Insofar as practical, the board should be made

[2] Danger also exists that those individuals who are providing services or have other business relationships with the company will be confronted with occasional problems of divided loyalty.

up of men of varied experience and talents. They should not be
rubber stamps, figureheads, or watchdogs, and all should have a
genuine concern for the over-all success of the company.[3]

*Realistic functions for the board of directors.* From what has been
said, we see that we cannot look to the board of directors as such
to provide the dynamic, creative element in the administration of
an enterprise. In fact, most companies will have difficulty enough
in assembling a board of men reasonably well informed on company
affairs, unquestionably loyal to the over-all interests of the company, objective and independent in their personal judgment, and
possessing sufficient time and interest to understand the problems
the company is facing. The full-time executive must carry the
responsibility for the basic exploration and analysis of present and
future problems, for well-considered and integrated plans of dealing with these problems, and for the spark and push that will give
the corporation the perpetual life that is supposed to distinguish
it from an individual. Nevertheless, a board of directors can and
should render valuable assistance to executives in the performance
of these tasks, in the following ways:

1. Boards of directors should normally be asked to *confirm management decisions on major changes* in objectives, policies, organization, and single transactions that will have a substantial effect on
the stability and success of the company. In the vast majority of
cases, the board will probably approve the proposals of management without even minor changes. Nevertheless, the necessity of
getting such decisions confirmed by a sympathetic, but semi-independent body will have a salutary effect upon the executives. The
possibility that the board may challenge or think of some additional
aspects will lead executives to a thoroughness and caution that
otherwise might be omitted.

2. The board should be a source of *constructive counsel* to the
company executives. In this capacity the board does not formally
approve or direct executive action. Instead, views are exchanged
as to the business outlook, the possibilities of new governmental

---

[3] A few very large companies, notably Standard Oil Company (New Jersey)
and the Du Pont company, employ full-time directors. These are men who
have been executives but are freed of operating duties so that they can devote
all their attention to board problems. While highly effective for these firms,
few corporations can afford the expense of this arrangement. Some smaller
companies hire "professional" directors on a part-time basis, but the scarcity
of good men limits the use of this arrangement.

legislation, customers' and competitors' reaction to a contemplated new product, general wage policy to be followed, the desirability of pressing a tax suit, the prospects for refinancing a bond issue at a lower interest rate, and a variety of such questions. These discussions take place while the plans are still in a formative stage, and through them the executives get the benefit of the diverse experiences of their directors.

3. The board should *select the chief executives and determine their compensation* and should confirm the selection and compensation of other key executives in the company. This is a very important and delicate matter, and the objectivity of the board can be particularly helpful in this connection.

4. The board should regularly review the results of current operation. This serves two purposes. It helps keep outside board members informed about company operations; it also provides board members with an opportunity to *ask* what Professors Copeland and Towl call *discerning questions.* The discerning question is one that deals with some fundamental aspect of the company's operations; often the director asking the question does not have any factual basis for believing something is wrong, but he is uncertain in his own mind that the best action is being taken. Perhaps a majority of such questions can be answered satisfactorily by the company executives, but some of them will lead to investigations and perhaps significant changes in operating plans.

5. Executives can often get considerable help from their directors through *informal counsel of individual directors.* A discussion at lunch or even an occasional telephone call on a matter on which the director is well informed may be very useful. In one company, for example, the treasurer was approaching retirement age, and because he and some other company executives were also on the board, it was not propitious to discuss his replacement at a formal board meeting. The president and two of the directors talked over the problem at lunch twice, and reluctantly agreed that the replacement would have to be a man from outside the firm. These two directors helped the president select the new man, who was then rotated around in several positions in the company. Several years later, formal action by the board led to the retirement of the treasurer and the appointment of the new man in his place. But, the really constructive work had been done informally several years earlier.

### Effective organization for top administrative duties

Throughout this discussion a recurring theme has been the need for long-range, broad-gauge guidance of corporate affairs. We quickly concluded that stockholders, as such, could not provide such direction, and now we find that the board of directors may be helpful but usually cannot be assigned full responsibility for this type of planning. Primary reliance then must be placed upon full-time company executives. We cannot just leave the topic at this point because some thought must be given to who among the full-time executives will perform this function.

A danger exists that busy operating executives of companies will not provide the broad perspective that is needed. Since very few companies can afford a board of full-time directors, some other provision should be made. Among the possibilities are the following:

1. The company may have two top executives, a chairman of the board and a president, or a president and a general manager. The particular title is not important, as long as one of the men is sufficiently free from operating responsibilities to do the type of thinking just discussed and has the interest and ability. Incidentally, the chief executive who has reached retirement age may or may not qualify for this second position. We must distinguish here between a graceful device for shelving a grand old man and the provision for broad-gauge, top-management thinking.

2. A small company may be able to afford only part of the time of one of its executives for such work. For example, in one firm the vice-president carried a light load of operating duties so that he would have enough time to consider proposals for new products, effects of new government legislation on company activities, the use of a combined sales force with another company, and similar problems. Such an arrangement calls for a very versatile executive, but at least the importance of this type of work is recognized and some provision made for it in the allocation of total duties among the executives.

3. The chief executive may retain responsibility for long-range planning, but rely heavily on a staff assistant to assemble and analyze information. Such a team arrangement combines the full time of a lower-paid staff man with the experience and prestige of the chief executive. As with any team, its effectiveness depends

upon the combined qualities of the men involved and how well they work together.

Still other arrangements may be better suited to the particular situation in a given company. But, somehow, someway, provision should be made for the long-range, broad-gauge planning that is essential to the continued success of every company.

## STRUCTURAL ARRANGEMENTS

Setting up primary departments, determining the centers of operating responsibility, adding facilitating units where needed, and providing for top management are vital aspects of organization structure. In addition, organization structure deals with the *arrangement* of the operating departments and facilitating divisions that have been decided upon. Important in this regard are:

1. Span of supervision
2. Even strata
3. Parallel departmentation.

As we shall see, these considerations deal with much more fundamental issues than merely providing a symmetrical and well-proportioned organization chart. Span of supervision has been discussed in Chapter 15; the nature and significance of even strata and parallel departmentation will be considered here.

### Even strata

*Reasons for seeking even strata.* As a general rule all individuals reporting directly to a single executive should be of about the same status or rank. Under this concept only shop superintendents and top-production staff men would report to the production manager; and, the president will have reporting directly to him only the top operating men and perhaps a vice-president in charge of service divisions. By this rule, the department store organization, indicated in Figure 25, which has both division merchandise managers and individual buyers reporting directly to the general merchandise manager, would be considered an undesirable structure.

The advantage of even strata is partly a matter of attitude and morale among the junior executives. If, say, two or three foremen report directly to the production manager, whereas all other foremen report to shop superintendents, bad feeling may be created

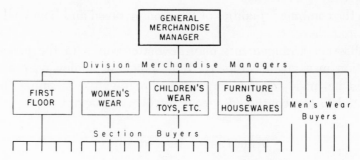

FIGURE 25. *Organization with Uneven Strata.*

among foremen who deal with the production manager only indirectly and receive instructions from men of lesser stature. Moreover, a shop superintendent may feel some loss of prestige when the "big boss" gives as much attention to foremen as to him. Even when titles clearly distinguish between the two levels of junior executives, this attitude toward relative status is likely to occur.

More serious is the danger that the senior executive will attach unwarranted significance to those activities that he supervises more closely. For any of us, the difficulties we know best are apt to seem the most serious; the problems we ourselves have to solve are likely to appear the most difficult and the most urgent. Consequently, the executive who has subordinates on different levels has difficulty maintaining a properly balanced perspective on all the operations. Because of his higher position, his views and his requests are apt to be given priority; and if his perspective becomes warped, he is likely to condone or even demand favored treatment for "his" divisions.

*Strata may not be clear-cut.* In actual practice, however, this concept of even strata is often difficult to follow. In the first place, which executives should be considered on the same level is not always clear. Does the manager of a department processing and selling a by-product rank along with the sales manager for the major product? Should advertising be separated from sales, purchasing from production, accounting from finance, and should the heads of each of these activities report directly to the chief operating executive? Certainly the number of employees in a department or division is an inadequate criterion; for example, in a commercial bank a supervisor of routine transit operations or bookkeeping may have ten times as many employees as the executive responsible for the bank's investment, though clearly the latter is the more important position.

Perhaps the best guide in deciding which departments, divisions, or sections should report directly to any key executive is the extent to which the activity must be considered by that executive in formulating his over-all policies and programs. In addition, where several units perform similar activities, as when there are a number of branch offices or manufacturing plants, the executives in charge of them usually should be considered to be on the same organizational level, even though admittedly a substantial difference in size or importance exists among the branches or among the plants. These guides will help to establish strata among the executives, but the status of a few borderline cases will always be determined by executive personality or by the span of supervision of the senior executive.

*Even strata and span of supervision.* Another problem with uniform strata is that the number of subordinate units do not always constitute a reasonable span of supervision. For example, twelve branch managers may be more than a sales manager can adequately supervise and also perform his other duties. Then, just because an assistant sales manager is appointed to take over the supervision of seven of these branches is scarcely reason enough to insist that a second assistant sales manager be appointed to supervise the remaining branches. Or, turning back to the department store merchandise manager shown in Figure 25, if we assume the merchandise manager has ample time to supervise the four division merchandise managers and the five buyers of men's wear, it could well be argued that niceties of organization structure do not justify the expense of an additional division merchandise manager for men's wear.

In other words, having all people reporting to a given executive on the same organizational level may be desirable, but in particular circumstances the cost may outweigh the benefits. When faced with a situation of this sort, careful attention should be given to the possibility of using staff assistants (typically of lower rank), which will permit the executive in question to supervise a greater number of subordinates. Reallocating duties or modifying the extent of decentralization is another way to provide full-time jobs while maintaining even strata.

*Titles can show difference in status.* If after exploring these possibilities, a decision is reached that junior executives of different levels should report to a senior man, then the difference in status should be indicated by title. For example, staff assistants or directors of service divisions should have titles that clearly distinguish them from executives responsible for major operating divisions. At the higher echelons the more important executives can be named vice-president while other executives reporting to the president carry the title of manager or director. Titles may also be helpful in such situations as that of the department store merchandise manager already discussed. Here it might be desirable to indicate that a single individual is actually filling two separate jobs, those of general merchandise manager and division merchandise manager for men's wear. In other words, we should recognize that the executive has "two hats." The use of titles in the ways suggested reduces to some extent the disadvantages of uneven strata, but should be regarded as only a partial remedy.

**Parallel departmentation**

Larger enterprises having several branches, plants, or field offices performing similar activities may find parallel departmentation useful. Under this scheme, the sections and divisions in each of the operating units are established on the same basis.

Figure 26 shows how IBM World Trade Corporation uses this principle. The organization in each country is set up on a similar basis, and the various operating divisions have their counterparts at regional and world headquarters. There are variations, of course. For instance, not all countries have engineering laboratories which report to the Director of Development Engineering; some look to their local General Manager for services and immediate supervision. In some places selling of electric typewriters and time systems has been separated from marketing of the major line—data processing equipment. Nevertheless, the same basic pattern is used in all parts of the world.[4]

Further examples of this same pattern may be found in equipment finance companies, railroads, chain stores, government bureaus, and military establishments.

*Advantages.* The chief advantage of parallel departmentation is

[4] The IBM World Trade Corporation also illustrates the *skip-level* concept. Regional Managers supervise most (though not all) of the Country General Managers, but these Regional Managers do not have staff of their own. They take over supervisory tasks of the Area General Manager and rely on his staff organization for any specialized help they may need.

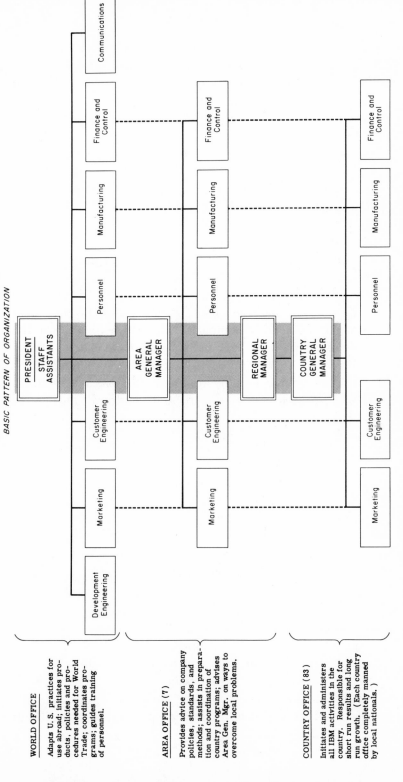

IBM WORLD TRADE CORPORATION
*BASIC PATTERN OF ORGANIZATION*

WORLD OFFICE

Adapts U.S. practices for use abroad; initiates products, policies and procedures needed for World Trade; coordinates programs; guides training of personnel.

AREA OFFICE (7)

Provides advice on company policies, standards, and methods; assists in preparation and coordination of country programs; advises Area Gen. Mgr. on ways to overcome local problems.

COUNTRY OFFICE (83)

Initiates and administers all IBM activities in the country. Responsible for short run results and long run growth. (Each country office completely manned by local nationals.)

FIGURE 26. *Parallel Structure in the IBM World Trade Corporation.*

the ease with which executives in the headquarters office and the subsidiary units may work with each other. A branch sales executive, for instance, needs to go only to one man in the headquarters office for assistance and guidance. On the other hand, a traffic executive with a counterpart in each of the operating subsidiaries knows just where to turn if new freight regulations call for adjustment in company procedures.

Parallel departmentation also makes the transfer of personnel easier. The finance manager of a small branch can be transferred to a similar position in a large branch without spending a lot of time learning a new pattern of organizational relationships. A man may be given training and experience that will fit him for any of several positions. Of course, many informal relationships must be learned in each new situation, but a similar grouping of duties substantially reduces the difficulties of transition.

Also, when several departments or divisions are set up in the same manner, control over them is made easier because results of one unit can be readily compared with those of other units. This principle of *deadly parallel* has already been discussed in Chapter 9.

Parallel departmentation, then, has distinct advantages over and above the somewhat dubious argument that the best setup in one situation is *ipso facto* good for all units performing similar operations.

*Disadvantages.* The chief difficulty with parallel departmentation is its lack of adaptability to local conditions. Warehousing, for example, may be a major problem in one branch but only a minor one in another. A personnel officer may be an extremely valuable part of the executive group in one branch, whereas personnel transactions in a small branch are so infrequent that its personnel officer finds trouble keeping busy. In a railroad one division may be the source of bulk carload traffic (for example, coal), while another division is primarily busy with the delivery of L.C.L. freight. Of course, almost every local manager will say, "My problem is different," and keen judgment is often required in deciding when this is mostly personal whim and when local conditions are sufficiently different to justify deviation from the established pattern.

Another danger of parallel departmentation is that the executive payroll will be somewhat higher than necessary. Separate operating executives and staff officers may be included in the local organization because it conforms to the general pattern; whereas if activities were grouped purely on the basis of local considerations, fewer positions would be created. The most common way of overcoming this difficulty is to go ahead with the more elaborate organization, and then have one executive serve in two positions. In small Army commands, for example, often the same officer serves in both a staff and a line capacity. Even with this modification, however, full-time assignments are not always possible for executives who are appointed because of the general pattern.

Finally, we should note that the benefits of parallel departmentation vary at least in part with the frequency and importance of the contacts between the executives concerned. Thus, if competitive conditions and adjustment of product design require that the national sales manager keep in close touch with each district operation, parallel departmentation is much more beneficial than when district sales managers have a considerable freedom in conducting their business. Where a high degree of decentralization exists and only occasional contact is made with the headquarters office, for example in a foreign subsidiary, little is gained by insisting on parallel departmentation.

Parallel departmentation, then, like even strata, may add strength to the organization structure. Considerable judgment is necessary in its application, however, because variation in local needs, additional executive expense, and infrequency of contacts with other offices may make it more troublesome than helpful.

## NEED FOR BALANCE

Organization structure is concerned with the total configuration of duties and relationships within an enterprise. The discussion in this and the preceding chapter has called attention to a number of aspects or fundamental characteristics of organization structure, but each of these points must be considered in relation to the whole.

Basic departmentation, focus of operating responsibility, facilitating units, and structural arrangements provide a logical way to think about organization structure; but fixed conclusions can rarely be reached on any one aspect until the others have been carefully considered. The study of facilitating units may well lead to a modification of tentative conclusions regarding primary departmentation. Considerations of structural arrangement will be modified, or modify, plans for decentralizing operating responsibility. Frequently, a compromise has to be made on one point to secure what appear to be greater benefits in another direction. This usually requires much mental effort, discussion, and give and take of ideas; but out of this effort should come a balanced, workable structure.

The final structure inevitably will give *relative* emphasis to particular functions, locations, or services. This emphasis should reflect the key factors for success of the company. And the key success factors will vary from company to company. Thus, research and development is of crucial importance to pharmaceutical and chemical firms, and should be so treated in the organization structure. On the other hand, advertising takes on relatively more importance in a mail-order company than in a chemical company. Similarly, maintenance—a relatively minor function in department stores—is a key activity for an airline. The identification of key success factors requires insight into industry trends and company strategy for taking advantage of those trends. In other words, the relative emphasis—or balance—in organization structure should be closely related to the unique nature and objectives of each specific company.

And finally, serious error will result if the organization is regarded as a fixed, static thing. To be sure, major changes in structure cannot be made every week since these usually involve modifications in attitudes, expected roles, procedures, and work habits. On the other hand, organization structure is merely a social device to help accomplish certain objectives. If a coal mining company decides to diversify, for example, its organization clearly will need revamping. Or, if a local bakery wants to sell its products through grocery stores as well as its own shop, the role of sales promotion becomes very critical. Any of a variety of internal or external forces may make such a realignment in organization desirable.

Preferably, the administrator keeps in the back of his mind an evolving concept of the structure best suited to his enterprise; and then seizes upon opportunities, such as changes in the executive personnel, changes in physical processes, or expansion of new lines, to introduce new relationships in keeping with the general structure he has conceived.

## Use of Organization Charts and Manuals

Organization charts and manuals are useful tools for presenting information regarding the administrative organization. They should not be regarded as essential, however; being mere tools of communication, they are available for the executive to use or not as he sees fit. In other words, they are in a very different category from departmentation, authority relationships, or organization structure, for these are inevitable and vital to any cooperative action. It will be sufficient for purposes of this discussion to note briefly the nature and the advantages and limitations of these tools.

### Ways of describing organization

*Organization charts.* An organization chart is a graphic portrayal of certain aspects of the organization. Usually such charts show only the principal divisions or positions and the lines of formal authority. This is true, for example, of most of the organization charts in this book.

Charts are often limited to certain departments or relationships that it is desired to emphasize. So-called *functional* charts list the principal duties of each division or position within the appropriate box; *manning* charts list within the respective boxes the number and title of all positions in that unit, and sometimes list the names of present incumbents. Thus the content of any particular chart should be determined by the purpose for which it is designed.

The design of an organization chart can range from a mechanical drawing to an artistic creation. Mechanical charts consist of little more than lines drawn between standard-size boxes in which are written the appropriate titles. In the more artistic charts, attention is paid to balance, spacing, style of printing, and perhaps to the use of colors and the general impression created regarding dominant and subordinate departments and divisions. Such charts are more like advertising copy than an engineering blueprint.

Considerable precedent exists for showing the senior executive at the top with subordinate levels below in pyramid fashion; sometimes the same arrangement is used going from left to right instead of from top down. Often when portraying organization structure, comparable units are placed on the same line, and the size and weight of the boxes and of the printing suggest relative status. However, there are no fixed rules, and the chart maker is still free to invent new ways of showing relationships.

Generally speaking, then, organization charts should be thought of as a form of graphic presentation. Their use and their form should be determined by what is effective in getting ideas across to their audience. Since one of the basic principles of graphics is simplicity, rarely should several different and complex relationships be shown on a single chart. If such a role for charts appears to be a humble one, it can nevertheless be highly potent.

*Titles.* When designing an organization structure, the administrator often faces a question of what titles to use for the positions created. Certainly in business, and to a lesser extent in government and military organization, the use of titles varies so greatly that insisting on fixed meanings is almost impossible.

In a single company, however, titles may take on distinctive meanings, and they should be used consistently, particularly when it is wished to identify comparable types of units or levels of status. If, in a given company, titles already have accepted meanings that fit into the contemplated organization structure, they certainly should be used; however, if the meanings of the words are vague or it is desired to indicate a change of concept, then some new title should be created. The list given in Figure 27 will suggest many possibilities for new titles.

*Position descriptions.* As a part of organization analysis and clarification, written descriptions of executive positions are often useful. Sometimes such position descriptions are quite brief, indicating little more than the channel of line authority and the principal duties of the position, as is true of the description of a district sales manager in Figure 28. At other times much more detailed descriptions are desired. These often include a brief statement of objectives or functions, followed by clearly phrased lists of duties, relationships, and authority. In the position description for a controller, shown in Figure 29, qualifications required of a man filling the job are added to the statement of duties.

The choice of amount of detail to be included in position descriptions is determined, again, by the purpose they are to serve. Primary considerations will be stability of operations and relationships, the freedom which is delegated down the line to change organizational arrangements, the effect detailed planning may have on flexibility, the need for clarifying the organization in the minds of a number of different individuals, and the additional trouble of preparing more-detailed statements.

*Organization manuals.* Organization manuals are typically made up of organization charts and executive position descriptions for all or a large part of an enterprise. These documents are put together

## Titles for Executives and Technical Men

Titles frequently consist of two or three parts, and all sorts of permutations and combinations can be made as occasion warrants.

### A. Basic Titles

| | | |
|---|---|---|
| Director | Chief | Technologist |
| Administrator | Leader | Technician |
| Manager | Commissioner | Assistant |
| Executive | Chairman | Aide |
| President | Secretary | Associate |
| Officer | Specialist | (Specific function or occupation) accountant, engineer, chemist, expediter, treasurer, controller, statistician, and the like |
| Superintendent | Consultant | |
| Supervisor | Expert | |

### B. Adjectives Denoting Rank

| | |
|---|---|
| Deputy | General |
| Assistant | Chief |
| Associate | Principal |
| Vice | Special |
| Executive | Administrative |
| Staff | |

### C. Descriptive Adjectives

| (Function) | (Product) | (Organization Unit) |
|---|---|---|
| Sales | Fuel Oil | Division |
| Production | Wax | Department |
| Control | Baked Bean | Bureau |
| | | Section |
| (Geographic area) | (Subject matter) | Unit |
| Denver | Refining Cost | Group |
| East Coast | Tariff | Office |
| City | Catalytic Cracking | Project |
| Plant X | | Service |
| | | Branch |
| | | Region |
| | | District |
| | | Zone |
| | | Territory |

FIGURE 27. *Roster of Executive Titles.*

---

*District Sales Manager*

Responsible to the Sales Vice-President, the District Sales Manager:

1. Prepares semiannual sales programs and budgets for his district, utilizing information provided by the Sales Promotion and Finance Divisions.
2. Reviews and recommends changes in sales policies and procedures relating to pricing, delivery, credit terms, advertising tie-ins, and product line.
3. Supervises, through Area Supervisors, all sales efforts in his District—to fulfill approved sales programs, meet budgets, and carry out policies.
4. Selects, trains, and compensates all sales personnel in his District, in cooperation with the Personnel Division.
5. Directs the operations of his District Sales Office, maintaining sales records for each customer and supplying reports and market analyses as requested by other company executives.
6. Personally contacts a sample of customers to retain a first-hand feel of the market; assists salesmen on their request in dealing with key customers.

Reporting directly to the District Sales Manager are Area Supervisors and the District Office Manager.

---

FIGURE 28. *Illustration of a Brief Position Description.*

so that a single source of information regarding the organization may be readily available. Often the manual is in loose-leaf form so that individual pages may be easily revised and inserted.

### Advantages and limitations of organization charts and manuals

*Advantages.* Often, the greatest benefits from organization documents come during their preparation. The executives themselves should, and usually do, participate in the process of drawing up the charts and writing the position descriptions; and this provides an *occasion to think objectively and critically about existing organizational arrangements.* Fuzzy authority lines are clarified, overlapping interests are recognized and some sort of *modus operandi* is agreed upon, major duties and responsibilities are re-emphasized, the occasion for needed changes in organization is provided, and clarification is provided for all the key people as to how the organization is expected to function. Note that these benefits consist primarily of the attitudes and understandings of those who participate in the work; they exist in the minds of the men, and once the manual is finished, it is of help to them largely as a check on their memories.

The organization manual with its charts and descriptions may be useful as a *training device*. When new employees, and particularly new executives, are brought into an organizational unit, the manual provides a compact guide to who does what. For most training purposes, a manual that is stated in broad terms is the more useful; one that contains a lot of detailed qualifications may well confuse the basic structure. In fact, if the manual is quite detailed, it may be necessary to prepare a simplified version for training purposes.

Organization manuals sometimes serve as the *official and latest word* on all organizational issues. In such cases they are used primarily by executives as a reference to justify doing what they want to do. Clearly, if the manuals are to serve as the official dictum, they need to be detailed and specific, and, of course, they must be revised each time there is any change.

*Limitations.* One of the chief disadvantages of written organizational documents applies particularly to this last statement. They almost always are *hard to revise*. An unwarranted sanctity exists about the printed word and the printed chart, and the burden of proof is clearly upon him who would make a change. Even with mutual understanding as to needed modifications, much time is required to revise wording, obtain the necessary signatures, and get the new document issued. When people are busy on other matters, temptation is strong to leave the document as it stands rather than negotiate a revision. The more detailed the document, the more frequently changes are likely to be needed. And if organizational change can be made only via revisions in the manual, delay is almost certain.

Actually, the organization is a group of understandings and behavior patterns among the executives and other employees; it is a living, changing thing. Unless these official organization documents are flexible and adaptable, they become at once a throttling influence and a source of confusion to those who are inclined to take extralegal action to get the job done. Therefore, in most situations it is preferable to think of position descriptions and charts as a picture of the organization at the time they were issued, and to expect that they will get out of date. They must be revised from

# AMERICAN - Standard

TITLE: Comptroller                          DIVISION: Control and Finance

REPORTS TO: Vice President, Finance          DEPARTMENT: Control

I. BASIC FUNCTION

The Comptroller is responsible for development, installation, and management of a coordinated activity of accounting, budgeting, and reporting systems which will provide for optimum management control of operations and opportunity for decision-making; he ensures that the President and other members of corporate management are fully and promptly informed concerning areas and circumstances in which variances from plans and budgets occur and makes recommendations for action. He is accountable to the Vice President, Finance, for his results and advises and makes recommendations to him wherever accounting, budgeting, or management control reporting considerations are involved in the determination of over-all Corporation objectives, policies, and plans.

II. PRINCIPAL ACTIVITIES

1. Sees to the development, installation, and operation of an effective system for accounting for and reporting results of operations.

2. Sees to the establishment and operation of budgetary, forecasting, and reporting systems which contribute to effective and timely control of operations and which set forth the financial implications of plans, proposed actions, and actual performance.

3. Makes sure that corporate management is fully and promptly informed concerning areas and circumstances in which variances from plans, budgets, and authorized policies or procedures occur.

4. Ensures that plant controller and other operating division control positions are staffed with competent personnel; personally authorizes appointment of division controllers with the concurrence of operating division heads.

5. Sees to the preparation and review of Corporation-wide budgets and financial forecasts and sees that operating division and subsidiary company managements are properly advised and assisted in preparation and presentation of their budgets and forecasts.

6. Sees to the timely preparation and submission of reports necessary to meet corporate management, legal, and other external requirements.

FIGURE 29. *Job Description for Corporate Controller*

7. Sees that the corporate books of legal requirements are safeguarded and that these books and records are properly kept and that all financial statements issued for the Corporation are consistent with good accounting practices.

8. Ensures that all activities in the Corporation for which he is functionally responsible are reviewed periodically and that they conform to authorized policies and procedures, furnishing assistance where improvement or correction is required; reviews all audit reports relative to his assigned functions and follows up to see that corrections or improvements are made.

9. Makes recommendations to the Vice President, Finance, with respect to the establishment of policies, procedures, programs, and practices necessary to the execution of his function.

III. SCOPE AND ACCOUNTABILITY

1. The incumbent is accountable for directing the control function of all foreign & U.S. Operating Divisions. Also directs corporate budgeting, forecasting, profit planning, general manufacturing accounting and accounting services.

2. The department includes _____ salaried employees with total annual payroll of over $_____.

3. The incumbent is responsible for administering the annual department budget of approximately $_____.

IV. POSITION QUALIFICATIONS

1. Bachelors Degree in accounting plus C.P.A. certificate and/or graduate degree in accounting.

2. Very broad knowledge of the Control function of a large multi-plant manufacturing corporation with subsidiaries including budgeting, manufacturing accounting, general accounting, profit planning, and the principles and techniques of these and related control functions.

3. Thorough knowledge of corporate objectives and policies relating to the control function and over-all management of the corporation.

4. Demonstrated ability to administer a large organization through subordinate managers.

5. Must be effective in contacts with top management of the divisions and the corporation.

*of American Radiator & Standard Sanitary Corporation.*

time to time if they are to continue to serve a useful purpose, but organizational change need not await such revision, and frequent minor revisions can be avoided.

The preparation of charts and manuals sometimes creates friction and bickering. Often, workable arrangements are accepted as long as they remain implicit, whereas spelling them out may involve loss of prestige. Unless there is real need for clarifying duties and relationships, then drawing up and circulating a document that causes heartaches or jealousies can have a negative rather than positive influence on the effectiveness of an organization. Consequently, the timing and the detail in which an organization is described should be decided in terms of the net effect it will have on the individuals concerned.

Organization manuals are *limited* in the picture they can give of the way operations are actually conducted. This is particularly true of organization charts, which are two-dimensional and, as suggested earlier, should attempt to portray only certain aspects of the organization. Some experienced administrators believe charts do more harm than they do good because they oversimplify really complex relationships. For example, charts give very little information about the degree of decentralization, and they are oblivious to informal channels of communication. Even the more detailed position descriptions leave much unsaid.

These limitations should be acknowledged, and even emphasized, to the people that use the organization documents; but this is scarcely reason for discarding the tools entirely. A clear understanding of the organization is highly important; the lack of it may lead to a sense of confusion, frustration, or even injustice. Organization charts and position descriptions can contribute to this understanding, particularly as training devices. As we shall see in the chapters on executive personnel, position descriptions are also useful in connection with selection, development, and compensation.

In general, then, if organization charts and position descriptions are regarded as tools, and limited ones at that, they can be put to effective use. They should not, however, be permitted to become an end in themselves; and except as a deliberately created device for centralized control over organization, they should not become a source of inflexibility.

## Conclusion of Part II

The administrator's task of *organizing* has now been considered from several angles. In the earlier chapters of this part of the book, key organization issues were analyzed as somewhat separate problems. Departmentation, service divisions, authority delegation, staff, committees, and decentralization are all features of organization that often demand concentrated attention by themselves. On the other hand, the administrative organization should also be viewed as an integrated whole. Such a view has been taken in the last two chapters on organization structure, where the emphasis has been on making all the parts fit together into a balanced whole.

With plans laid, as indicated in Part I, and organization established, as indicated in Part II, the manager must turn his attention to the remaining phases of administrative work—securing executive personnel and other resources, supervising, and, finally, controlling. These are the subjects of the remaining parts of the book.

While these major phases of management provide a practical framework for thinking about principles of administration, we will do well to remind ourselves that in practice they are not so neatly divided. The executive, of necessity, moves back and forth from one phase to another in performing his daily tasks. Nevertheless, interrelated though administrative work may be in actual operation, it will be better understood by developing a clear picture of each phase. In line with this analytical approach, Part III concentrates on executive personnel and building effective relationships with outside interest groups.

### Selected References for Chapters 16 and 17

Bennet, C. L., *Defining the Manager's Job*, American Management Association, 1958.

Blau, P. M. and W. R. Scott, *Formal Organizations, A Comparative Approach*, Chandler Publishing Co., 1962.

Brown, C. C. and E. E. Smith, *The Director Looks at His Job*, Columbia University Press, 1957.

Chandler, A. D., *Strategy and Structure*, The M. I. T. Press, 1962.

Pfiffner, J. M. and F. P. Sherwood, *Administrative Organization*, Prentice-Hall, Inc., 1960.

Stieglitz, H., *Corporate Organization Structures*, National Industrial Conference Board, Studies in Personnel Policy, No. 183.

White, K. K., *Charting the Company Organization Structure*, American Management Association, 1963.

# III

# Assembling Resources

# 18

# Building External Relationships

## Universal problems of obtaining resources

Assembling resources is one of the major divisions of administrative work, as are planning, organizing, directing, and controlling. People to man the positions of the organization, funds to purchase the necessary materials and to provide working capital, physical facilities with which to work, all must be brought together for the use of the enterprise if it is to function.

In a broader sense, the enterprise is also dependent on a favorable legal, economic, and social environment. Laws that enable a company to operate must be enforced; business institutions such as wholesalers or transportation firms must be ready to serve the company, and key political groups must at least tolerate company activities. Such resources are not brought into a plant, as are materials, but their support is nevertheless essential.

Common to the task of assembling both tangible and intangible resources is a question of the type of relationship—or alliance—the administrator should establish with each outside group. Analysis of

313

detailed provisions for raising capital, assuring a water supply, buying real estate, and the like would carry us far beyond the scope of this book. But, the central issue of relationships with outsiders is so pervasive we should at least suggest an approach for resolving it. The present chapter outlines such an approach.

Another area of importance—to which every executive should give personal attention—is the effective selection and development of his immediate subordinates and other key men under his general direction. This is a universal problem of high significance to the enterprise, and to society generally. Chapters 19 and 20 are devoted to its consideration.

### Interdependence of the enterprise and its resource groups

No enterprise operates in isolation. Even a so-called "integrated" company obtains at least some raw materials and supplies from outsiders, and sells goods and services of some sort to outsiders. Normally, a whole array of dealings occurs with people who are not employees of the company; stockholders provide capital and bankers make loans, equipment manufacturers supply repair parts, fire departments rush to put out fires, government may give subsidies and tamper with wages, retailers serve as a distribution channel to consumers—to mention only a few of the possibilities.

Continuing support from such outside groups is crucial to the achievement of company objectives, if not to its very survival. Here is a simple example. After driving through a heavy Oregon fog, much past lunchtime, the author arrived at the village of Government Station at the base of Mount Hood. And then a most welcome sign loomed up—"Fresh huckleberry pie—Huckleberry cobbler." We could hardly wait to get into the small restaurant only to be told, "Sorry, the Indians just aren't bringing in the berries this year." The specialty of the house was nonexistent because of a breakdown in supply.

Sears, Roebuck and Company ran into similar difficulty on a more sophisticated level, when it opened several of its Latin American stores. Local manufacturers were not accustomed to providing a continuing flow of standard products—which Sears merchandising requires. For some products, it took several years for Sears to find, or train, dependable suppliers; often adjustments in production technology, financing, and executive attitudes were necessary. In this instance, Sears did not adopt a defeatist view just because "the Indians were not bringing in the berries."

A manufacturer of greeting cards, to cite a different example, found that its sales were sharply restricted because retailers had difficulty maintaining an attractive assortment of cards—cards became soiled or mislaid, and popular designs were frequently out of stock. In this case, the manufacturer developed a display rack, inventory system, and reorder plan that helped the retailer and—in turn—the manufacturer.

We should note in these examples, and others that will readily come to mind, that often satisfactory relations with outsiders create *mutual reliance*. The Latin American manufacturers became dependent on Sears, just as Sears had to rely on them; retail stores found the greeting card stock plan feasible only if the manufacturer provided a good assortment and could fill reorders promptly. In both cases desired results were achieved only as plans for mutual assistance were put into effect.

In fact, most parts of our economic system have become highly interdependent. For example, a strike of a few construction electricians in New York City can upset production schedules in a plant in Indianapolis; and on the other hand, slow deliveries from Indianapolis can cause temporary layoffs of construction workers in New York City, as well as dislocations in other places. Consequently, if an administrator is to achieve his objectives, he must give some attention to "managing" his outside relationships as well as managing activities within his company (or department).

### Alternative types of alliances

The administrator faces a whole range of possible ways of dealing with outside groups. These vary in terms of scope, specificity of understanding, length of agreement, degree of involvement, and other aspects. The variety of alternatives are suggested in the following illustrations.

*Informal agreements.* The most common and simplest way of dealing with outsiders is a mere informal agreement to work together in some particular fashion. For example, a manufacturer of air-conditioning equipment may work closely with building contractors. He provides them with technical information about his product and furnishes assistance with difficult installation problems. In return, he hopes the contractors will recommend his equipment to their customers and that the contractors will do a good job of installation so that the equipment actually performs at its best. The manufacturer may also work closely with architects and engineers, exchanging technical information and perhaps redesigning equipment to meet new requirements. Normally, such relationships have no formal commitment of one party to support the other, but there is a *tacit understanding*—often based on years of working together —that mutual assistance will be provided.

The relationship of a company with its commercial bank is often of a similar nature—even though the banking service is vital for continued operations. The company deposits money in the bank, and the bank in turn provides a variety of services such as checking accounts, collections, foreign exchange, credit information, and general financial advice. In addition, the bank may "open a line of credit"—an advance understanding that the company may borrow up to a stipulated limit for short-term needs. Sometimes the agreement between the company and the bank is set forth in an exchange of correspondence, but these are rarely enforceable legal contracts. Predominantly, the understanding is based on a long association, and the correspondence simply confirms an oral discussion of changes in, say, the size of balances to be maintained or the conditions under which the credit line will be enlarged.

While many aspects of such informal agreements are explicitly discussed, crucial parts of the agreement may be merely implied from business custom or from what is regarded as fair. For instance, a company that regularly buys most of its requirements for, say, steel plates from a single supplier expects to be "taken care of" during periods of shortage—at least for its most urgent needs. And in some realms, such as relations with legislators, the understandings may be almost wholly implicit.

*Formal contracts.* When the dealings between two parties become of vital interest to at least one of them, a legal contract covering the major points of understanding (or potential disagreement) may be wise. Exclusive sales agents, for instance, may reasonably ask for written assurance that the territory will be theirs at least for a period of years if sales performance meets minimum standards. Similarly, if a company enters into a long-term purchasing agreement with a key supplier, both the company and the supplier will probably want a written contract which records the agreement regarding amounts, price, and other conditions of sale. Written contracts, however, rarely cover the full range of relationships between two parties; they are supplemented by custom and subsequent informal agreements as to interpretation. Long-term contracts, like treaties between nations, rarely anticipate all of the problems which will arise, and they need even greater provision for renegotiation.

*Partial ownership.* Another means of tying down a desired long-run relationship and obtaining more flexibility than the typical long-range contract is partial ownership. It is common practice, for example, for steel companies to have at least a partial ownership in ore properties and mining companies. Similarly, large oil companies often invest in crude oil production enterprises. When such investments represent only a minority interest, they are usually accompanied by a formal agreement that the investor will be entitled to his proportionate share of the output.

The partial ownership approach has been followed to a lesser extent in *forward integration,* that is, buying an interest in wholesalers or retailers. Companies such as Firestone and Singer have established retail outlets, and many manufacturers have established their own distributors to replace wholesalers. More often, however, manufacturers have provided financial assistance by granting leases on outlets they own, guaranteeing—directly or indirectly—the payment of rent on properties financed by other interests, or by financing fixtures and equipment. Here again, the purpose is to attract and retain the close cooperation of a vital outside group.

*Representation on board of directors.* In the past, membership on the board of a bank, a key supplier, or an important customer was used to maintain a close alliance between the two corporations. As more and more companies are becoming publicly owned this practice is being discontinued. Two disadvantages are (a) the board member may find himself in an embarrassing conflict of interest situation when either of the two companies wishes to modify the previous relationship, and (b) a board composed of *watchdogs—*men primarily concerned with protecting their own interest group, be it a bank, raw material supplier, or labor union—is rarely qualified to provide the long-run, objective point of view that should characterize a board of directors (see Chapter 17). Where partial ownership exists, representation on the board makes more sense; but to the extent that board members have their respective axes to grind, top-management functions will probably be performed by executives of the company outside of board meetings.

*Agreements on specific projects.* Some undertakings, such as the building of a huge plant or a large shopping center or the drilling of a wildcat oil well, may lead to a temporary partnership. An engineer, several different equipment manufacturers, one or more financial institutions, a potential customer or raw material supplier, may form what the British call a *consortium.* Each party has a particular contribution to make to the project. When the project is completed, the formal relationship is dissolved. Of course, informal relationships may have been developed on such a project which lay the basis for additional joint undertakings.

In all of the preceding examples, the relationships have been significant enough to each party to open the possibility of considerable give-and-take in arriving at a basis for cooperative action. Obviously, every company will have many minor dealings with outsiders that do not warrant such special attention. Examples include the purchase of miscellaneous supplies that are readily available, the normal use of the telephone and the post office, the typical purchase of insurance, and the like. In these situations, *and* when the company is too small to make any dent on the external environment, the administrator merely accepts conditions as he finds them. He forecasts the conditions under which such resources will be available to him, and then simply treats these as premises or limits in his own internal planning. The major outside relationships, however, need to be *managed* in the sense that desirable alliances have to be selected and nurtured.

This brief review of possible types of alliances with outside groups is only suggestive. Even though it is incomplete, it does indicate that careful attention to building sound external relations is often very important. How should an executive go about building such relationships? Three basic steps are almost always involved:

1. Designing desired relationships.
2. Negotiating mutual agreements.
3. Maintaining workable relationships.

**Designing desired relationships**

*Where are strategic improvements possible?* In the time he devotes to external relationships, the administrator naturally wants to focus on the areas that are crucial to the long-run success of his company. So the first question he should ask himself is which sets of relationships are most likely to have a strong influence on the growth or decline of his company? And a related question, "Are the conditions under which the resource is provided likely to be satisfactory for our purposes?" If his answer to this last question is "Yes," then he has no design problem; he can move on to negotiation with one or more satisfactory suppliers of the particular resource.

Perhaps the answer will not be so simple. For example, when frozen foods were first brought on the market, the manufacturer, General Foods Corporation, could not rely on regular grocery wholesalers because they lacked refrigeration facilities. Moreover, transportation was inadequate, and there was even question about the type of retailer best suited to handle the product. Consequently, considerable effort was required to *design* a distribution system suitable for the new products. Adjustment also had to be made on the supply end to get farmers to raise the particular types of fruits and vegetables that were best suited to the freezing process. Or, to cite a more recent example, manufacturers of prefabricated houses faced a whole host of external relationship problems—local building codes, union restrictions, local builders with enough capital and sales promotion ability to promote local sales, fire underwriters' approval, and the like. Here again a need arose to think through the kind of external relationships which would be most effective.

A useful approach to such design problems is to (a) list all the necessary functions that must be performed by somebody, (b) combine these activities into groups that can be readily performed by existing institutions (dealers, finance companies, truckers, brokers, and the like) or, if necessary, new institutions, and (c) think through the relationships between these institutions—services rendered, types of control, and the sources of remuneration. In other words, the design is a plan of organization. Special recognition must be given to the fact that the various divisions will be independent enterprises instead of parts of a single administrative unit.

*Factors influencing choice of design.* Considerable ingenuity and judgment is necessary in conceiving of a new type of relationship that will accomplish the aims and at the same time be attractive to other parties whose cooperation is sought. Among the factors that frequently require careful attention are these:

1. *Reducing uncertainty.* A prime motive in many alliances is the reduction of a serious risk. Thus, a lumber company may seek a tie-in with timberlands so that it can be sure of an adequate supply of lumber at a

reasonable price. Or, a company may decide to sell only through
franchised dealers to secure greater influence over the sales promotion
and repair service related to its products.

2. *Costs.* Every relationship requires some *quid pro quo*. Banks expect
minimum balances, dealers receive commissions, a close relationship with
one contractor may mean loss of patronage by others, steady customers
expect more service, direct or three-cornered reciprocity may rear its ugly
head, and so forth.

3. *Flexibility.* Usually the stronger the alliance, the more difficult it is to
form a new one. For instance, a carefully cultivated and close relation
with retail drugstores restrains a shift of sales promotion effort to selling
through supermarkets; close alliance with the medical profession has
made several pharmaceutical companies hesitant to enter the proprietary
field.

4. *Competitive strategy.* The desirability of a given alliance depends in
part upon what competitors are doing. Rather than compete with major
companies on their own ground, a small oil refinery appealed to independent filling station operators on the basis that independents must
stick together. A U.S. watch company that was late in adding Swiss
movements to its line, as its major competitors had done, has made an
agreement with a Japanese manufacturer. An airline, foreseeing large
capital requirements for new planes, started before its competitors to
make its securities attractive to institutional lenders.

On the basis of these and related factors, the executive should
try to conceive of a division of labor in each area of external relationships that will put his company in a sound long-run position.
Unless he fully understands the design he would like to achieve, he
is poorly equipped for the next stage—negotiation.

### Negotiating mutual agreements

Deciding what you want and getting others to agree to it are,
of course, quite different matters—especially when the others probably pride themselves on being independent businessmen. More
than skill in presentation and persuasion is needed. Unless the arrangement as a whole is considered desirable by the outside party,
it is unlikely that a sound, continuing relationship will develop.
Mutual trust and a willingness to cooperate in overcoming unforeseen obstacles are not built on a slick sales talk.

As background for each negotiation the administrator should
learn as much as he can about the other party—his present activities,
aspirations, strengths, and needs. Often the desired relationship involves only a portion of the total operations of the other party.
Consequently, he must recognize how the new proposal will fit in
with these other activities. The other person will have his own set

of objectives, which will not coincide fully with those of the man proposing a change.

Recognizing that at least two, and perhaps more, different sets of objectives are involved, the aim is to identify a working arrangement which is *mutually* advantageous. The trick is to (a) find areas where joint effort will be beneficial, (b) explore the manner in which such joint effort might be carried out so that each party can test the feasibility of the proposed cooperative effort, and (c) agree upon a division of the benefits that will accrue to one or both parties. Incidentally, the inevitable bargaining that occurs in point (c) has been overemphasized by economic and labor theory; creative economic acts take place in stages (a) and (b).

Now, the advantage of having done the design-building, suggested in the preceding section, is that the negotiator will have a much clearer idea of the essential features he wishes to obtain and where concessions may be made with little or no harm. Some give-and-take is often necessary, but the good bargain is one in which each party will gain far more than he sacrifices.

Negotiation with outsiders may require use of one or more of the strategies discussed in Chapter 6. Especially if several different parties have to agree on an alliance, a choice may have to be made between, say, mass concentrated offensive or avoiding a decisive showdown. At times united action will be called for, whereas a lone hand is most appropriate in other circumstances. Strategy will, of course, also be involved in the design stage. In military terms, perhaps the design stage incorporates basic strategy, whereas negotiation is more a matter of tactics. But in both stages winning true acceptance is important since good continuing relations with outsiders rely so heavily upon voluntary cooperation.

### Maintaining workable relationships

*Being alert to actual and potential deterioration.* All social relationships are likely to vary over time. Just as supervision and control are necessary within an enterprise, they are likewise needed in external relationships. Normal control systems will usually flag minor deviations from the plan—a late shipment, poor service to an important consumer, and the like. And, where the performance of the outside party is especially important, we are developing ways to make checks in the other man's establishment. For example, aircraft manufacturers may make or observe quality inspections in subcontractor's plants, and automobile companies receive frequent reports on car sales from their independent dealers.

More difficult to keep track of is the impact of economic, political, and social changes upon those with whom we do business. What was a sound relationship five years ago may no longer be so today. Routine control reports rarely reflect these kinds of changes directly. And, the physical and legal separation of business associates may permit trouble to grow unnoticed. For example, one company found that being the major supplier of paperbags to independent grocery stores was of little value in face of trends to packaged merchandise and supermarket selling. A fruit packing company had relied for years on two employment offices to supply it with seasonal labor, but with mechanization and alternative employment opportunities, one office has closed its doors and the other shifted to other kinds of labor; now the packing company is having difficulty in getting even the substantially smaller number of seasonal hands it wants.

If sound relations are to be maintained with outsiders over a period of time, some executive in the company should keep in touch with each outside firm and group whose activities are vital to the company. Then if changes occur in the economic position or even in executive personnel, the possible impact of these shifts on continuing good relations with the company should be weighed. Keeping track of, say, a jute merchant in the Philippines, or the Sheik of Kuwait, may not be easy, but for some companies this is an important part of maintaining workable relations with raw material suppliers.

Then, if trouble is brewing, there may be time to ward it off or at least prepare an alternative.

*Frank consultation about desired changes.* The concept that relationships with outsiders will be conducted on the basis of understanding and confidence also imposes burdens on the company itself. In the usual continuing relationships, the outsider should be consulted about contemplated company changes that will affect him. Since he will be vitally affected, he would like at least the opportunity to consider the proposal and suggest modifications. Also such consultation opens the way for modifying the working relationship.

Advance consultation may not be feasible, however, when a new product or some other competitive move is being considered. Nor is consultation feasible when the outsider might do considerable damage before a change detrimental to him is put into effect—the purchase of a raw material supplier or a change in distributorship are cases in point. These examples of when a company may justly be reluctant to show its hand early and fully reemphasize the need to keep a watchful eye on the other man. He, too, may be reluctant to reveal his plans. Consequently, the need arises to understand the total pressures and opportunities he faces.

## SUMMARY

Every administrator has to maintain continuing cooperation of various firms or groups outside his enterprise—distributors, suppliers, bankers, regulatory agencies, unions, and the like—as well as to guide the cooperative efforts of his own employees. These outsiders provide a flow of goods and services that are essential to the life of the company. At the same time, the company is more or less important to each outsider. Consequently, a whole series of alliances are developed which provide the ground rules for the way these various independent parties will work with each other.

One way of thinking about an administrator is as a manager of social relationships. He has to run his own shop *and* maintain outside relationships in a way that accomplishes two ends at the same time: (a) Each necessary outsider must find it advantageous to deal with the company, and (b) the inducements offered to get this cooperation must be feasible. That is, the goods, money, satisfactions, and other outputs generated by the company must at least equal the combined demands of the outsiders. If some outsider places too high a price on his continued cooperation (this might be money *or* restriction on how the company operates), there may not be enough in the central "kitty" to go all around—and the company fails. The administrator, thus, has the dual role of trying to increase the size of the "kitty" by devising ingenious ways of running his business, and of negotiating alliances with outsiders that will permit the operation of the business in this fashion.

Clearly, the managing of external relationships is crucial to maintaining a favorable balance between inputs and outputs. The administrator should take three basic steps in this process: (1) carefully plan the form and content of each desired relationship in terms of the objectives and strategies of his company; (2) negotiate agreements with outsiders that are mutually acceptable and as near his plans as possible; and (3) exercise continuing surveillance of established relationships to ward off deterioration and/or to anticipate future changes. To some extent, this managing of external relationships is divided among various executives in a company, but the senior executive often takes part in the process and at a minimum must be sure that the work is done and done well.

Finally, while the discussion of external relationships in this chapter has been in terms of a business enterprise, the function is present in all types of administration. A hospital manager, for example, must maintain good relations with the medical profession, financial supporters, local government, patients, and similar groups. Also, a subordinate executive within a company has a series of "publics"—budget officer, personnel man, purchasing agent, departments sending work, departments receiving work, and the like; many of his contacts may be prescribed by S.O.P., but much room always remains for redesigning, negotiating, and maintaining effective relationships with persons outside his unit.

### SELECTED REFERENCES

Berg, T. L., "Designing the Distribution System," in W. D. Stevens, ed., *The Social Responsibilities of Marketing*, American Marketing Association, 1962.

Clee, G. H., "The Appointment Book of J. Edward Ellis," *Harvard Business Review*, November 1962.

Leiserson, A., "Interest Groups in Administration," in F. M. Marx, ed., *Elements of Public Administration* (2nd ed.) Prentice-Hall, Inc., 1959, Chap. 14.

Ridgeway, V. F., "Administration of Manufacturer-Dealer Systems," *Administrative Science Quarterly*, March 1957.

Thompson, J. D. and W. J. McEwen, "Organization Goals and Environment," *American Sociological Review*, February, 1958.

# *19*

# Executive Selection

The vital need for capable executives if an enterprise is to be successful needs little emphasis. It is they who engage in the continuing process of planning, who mobilize and allocate resources, and who carry out the day-by-day direction and control of activities toward the company's objectives.

Moreover, the task of executives is becoming more difficult. The increasing size of administrative units in business, government, Army, and elsewhere has added to the complexity of administration. Also, the impact of world events and governmental action penetrates to almost every department and division. Employees are becoming less tractable, that is, their zone of acceptance has narrowed. All these things call for executives with great capacity and skill.

## Distinctive aspects of executive personnel problems

The development of executive personnel cannot be tackled in the same way as replacing a machine that is broken down or handling a rush order from an important customer. Executive personnel problems are distinctive in the following respects.

A relatively *small number* of people are involved. Only in the larger companies is an executive directly concerned with the selection and development of as many as one hundred people, and often the number of present and potential executives will be more nearly a dozen. This means that individual personalities play a dominant part in the action that can be taken.

There are *close personal contacts* among the executives and the potential executives being considered. These men not only work together and go through trying experiences together, but often have social relationships outside of business. It would be dreary employment indeed if a man could not find among his business associates some of his best friends. These business and social relationships are often of some years' standing, and the men themselves expect them to continue. All this has a bearing on the objectivity and positiveness of action that should be expected.

The development of executive personnel is primarily a *long-run* problem. Unless it is so regarded, constructive action will be difficult. It is possible to anticipate vacancies some time ahead, to appraise individuals before the day for appointing a new officer, and to map out individual development programs. The fact that this development is long-run in nature has its disadvantages, however; it permits procrastination, and this is particularly likely to occur when something unpleasant needs to be said to an associate. Also, quick results of effort are difficult to see. This may lead to discouragement or unwise curtailment of expenses during slack time.

To a considerable extent, both the costs and the results of executive personnel work are *intangible*. Even though a company's executives may be its most valuable asset, they cannot be recognized on its balance sheet because there is no clear way of measuring that value. As a result, the effort that is sometimes devoted to saving a few dollars that can be measured would often yield far greater returns if directed toward developing executive personnel.

While these distinctive aspects make executive personnel problems difficult to handle, and many unknowns remain, measures exist that will substantially improve the selection and aid in the development of an outstanding corps of executives. The discussion in this book will focus on basic steps that can be used in small as well as large companies, or even by the manager of a single department.

A sound executive personnel program should accomplish the following:

1. Determine what executives are needed;
2. Appraise present performance and select for promotion;
3. Assist in the development of men to fill needs effectively;
4. Compensate executives wisely.

Practical steps for accomplishing these ends are discussed in this and the following chapter.

## Determining Executive Needs

Three basic steps are involved in determining executive personnel requirements. These should be taken, regardless of how small the enterprise or informal the action may be.

1. Determine the duties of each position from a study of the desired organization structure.
2. Develop "man specifications" of the qualities and other characteristics needed by an executive to fill each position satisfactorily.
3. Analyze the age and ability of existing executives and, by comparison with requirements found in steps 1 and 2, develop plans for filling gaps and providing necessary replacements.

The promotion program indicated in this last step cannot be completed until the selection and development processes have also received attention. Nevertheless, in any study of the need for executives, we must recognize that a vacancy anticipated some years hence may require the immediate selection of one or more candidates so that they may acquire the necessary experience and training before the actual appointment must be made.

### Organization analysis

Organization analysis provides the basis for intelligent steps toward the improvement of executive personnel. This is the simple matter of knowing what your objective is before you start trying to achieve it. Inasmuch as administrative organization has already been explored in the preceding section of this book, we need do little more here than note that a clear concept of organization structure, including some kind of descriptions of the duties of key positions, is assumed as an essential background for the measures discussed in this section.[1]

For purposes of executive personnel planning we should think in terms of the "ideal" organization structure—or, at least, of the structure as it will be several years hence—rather than of the present structure. The existing organization may be outmoded, and at least some of the positions will have been adapted more to individual personalities than to organization principles. Moreover, during the next

[1] Chapters 16 and 17, *Organization Structure*, summarize the steps necessary in organization analysis and also give samples of position descriptions, which are the connecting links between organization analysis and executive personnel programs. If the position descriptions reflect existing organization, some adjustment may be needed to tie in with the *future* organization pattern.

few years the volume and nature of company activities may change, and personnel requirements should be adjusted to these changes insofar as they can be forecast with reasonable accuracy. In other words, continuing by means of replacements the existing corps of executives is not necessarily the most desirable thing. Rather, sights should be set on a group of men that will be best qualified to direct the activities of the company in the future.

Position descriptions, we may note in passing, are not always well adapted for the preparation of man specifications. They may be either long or very terse, as the illustrations in Chapter 17 show; or they may not be written at all, and exist only in the minds of the executives themselves. Also, the purpose for which a position description has been written will affect its contents. For example, a description may emphasize the functions and relationships of the unit as a whole rather than the particular part of the work done by its director. On the other hand, a position description for use in recruiting and placement may well include aspects common to many jobs in the company, whereas a description prepared for job evaluation is more concerned with points that distinguish one job from another.

If proper allowance is made for these differences, however, any reasonably complete description can serve as the basis of the next step, man specifications.

## Man specifications

The kind of an individual who can satisfactorily fill position X is indicated by what may be called *man specifications*. Broadly considered, such specifications are of two types; they may be performance requirements, in that they stipulate what a man must be able to do, or they may be more indirect, in that they stipulate the qualities, experience, and other characteristics an individual should possess.

*Use performance requirements.* Performance requirements, such as ability to supervise and inspire salesmen, ability to devise sales promotion campaigns, ability to budget expense and then live within the budget, and the like have the advantage of being simply and clearly related to the duties involved. If a man can meet these standards, he is qualified for the position; if a man fails to come up at least to the minimum standard on essential requirements, he is not satisfactory. Consequently, they should be used wherever practical.

The difficulty is, of course, in finding out whether a man has such abilities, particularly when he is being considered for promotion or is being recruited from a different operation. He often has had no opportunity to demonstrate his ability to perform certain tasks essential in the new position. Also, abilities change and often grow, and it is only fair to a man to recognize that what he did tolerably well five years ago, he may be able to do creditably now. So, while performance requirements can be very useful, often we must supplement these with a list of personal qualities that can be more readily observed.

*Supplement with personal qualities.* When we start to list the qualities a man must possess to fill adequately an executive position, we move into a foggy area. Although there has been considerable discussion and some investigation of the subject, as yet no agreement exists on what makes a good executive—except that such things as a wart on the side of the nose or ears located far up on the head are *not* important.

Chester I. Barnard has this to say about the active qualities of leaders:

> I shall list and discuss briefly five fundamental qualities, or characteristics of those who are leaders, in their order of importance as regarded for very *general* purposes . . .
>
> A. Vitality and endurance. We should not confuse these qualities with good health. There are many people of good health who have little or moderate vitality—energy, alertness, spring, vigilance, dynamic qualities—or endurance. . . .
>
> B. Decisiveness. . . . It depends upon a propensity or willingness to decide and a capacity to do so. . . .
>
> C. Persuasiveness. . . . The ability in an individual to persuade and a propensity to do so. Just what these qualities are defies description . . . but at least we may say that persuasiveness involves a *sense* or understanding of the point of view, the interest, and the conditions of those to be persuaded.
>
> D. Responsibility. I shall define responsibility as an emotional condition that gives an individual a sense of acute dissatisfaction because of failure to do what he feels he is morally bound to do, or because of doing what he thinks he is morally not bound to do, in particular concrete situations. . . .
>
> E. Intellectual capacity. I have intentionally relegated "brains" to fifth place. I thereby still make it important, but nevertheless subsidiary to physical capacity, decisiveness, persuasiveness, and responsibility.[2]

[2] "The Nature of Leadership," *Human Factors in Management*, S. D. Hoslett, ed., Harper & Brothers, 1946, pp. 23-26.

QUALIFICATIONS CHECKLIST

1. Experience in terms of level, type, breadth, and type of organization
2. Technical and professional ability
3. General mental ability
4. Verbal ability
5. Quantitative reasoning
6. Abstract reasoning
7. Judgment on problems of organization
8. Policy judgment
9. People judgment
10. Skill in negotiation
11. Flexibility
12. Physical vitality and endurance
13. Self-confidence and emotional maturity
14. Capacity for being the No. 1 man vs. need for close supervision
15. Level of aspiration (and reasons for this aspiration)
16. Interest in broad theoretical matters
17. Interest in and liking for dealing with people
18. Interest in administrative work
19. Tempo
20. Social and ethical standards and philosophy (including dependability and sense of responsibility)
21. Work habits
22. Interest in the particular type of organization
23. Staff or line interests
24. Courage
25. Decisiveness
26. Ability to gain the confidence of others
27. Marital adjustment
28. Standing in own field

FIGURE 30. *Personal Qualities That May Suggest Man Specifications*
(Milton M. Mandell, cited below).

The *specific* qualities needed by specific executives, however, vary with the needs of each job. A list of qualities that were significant in a wide range of positions studied by Milton M. Mandell [3] is given in Figure 30. Using this list as a guide, an administrator—or preferably a group of executives—can develop a set of characteristics the

[3] For a full discussion see Milton M. Mandell, "The Selection of Executives," in M. J. Dooher and E. Marting, eds., *Selection of Management Personnel*, American Management Association, 1957, pp. 187-320.

man appointed to position $X$ should possess. The specifications should concentrate on the important qualities (that is, not everything in the list), fill in more detail where appropriate, and give some guidance as to relative weight. Since the preparation of such specifications rests heavily on subjective judgment, some difference of opinion may arise about details. But with agreement about the duties, usually the differences on needed qualifications can be resolved.

Such a list is of real practical value in selecting men for promotion or transfer. It serves as a guide in making what is inevitably a complex judgment. Without it an intuitive decision in which personal likes and dislikes play a large part is apt to be used. Even a more rational decision may be guided by only one or two factors unless care is taken to build a balanced specification list.

*Distinguish between innate and acquirable characteristics.* One further useful step can be taken in preparing a list of qualities an executive should have for a given position. It pays to distinguish between those qualities that an executive must bring with him to the job and those that he can develop after he gets on the job. For our purposes the former may be called *innate* and the latter *acquired*.[4]

Richard Weil, Jr., former president of Macy's, New York, emphasizes this distinction in his executive appraisal chart, shown in Figure 31. Of the six qualities to be considered in selecting an executive, three appear on the left half of the chart under the heading "Realm of no compromise"; these are character, intelligence, and intuition. The other three, experience, adaptability, and special skills, are shown on the right side under "Proper realm of compromise."

Mr. Weil recognizes that an individual will possess each of the factors to a greater or lesser degree and that no single individual can be expected to have the maximum degree of all qualities. Consequently, he urges that a minimum degree of each of the innate factors be established as qualifications on which there is to be no compromise. There will be minimum satisfactory levels for each of the other qualities also, but if a candidate cannot be found who

[4] It does not matter here whether the innate qualities are inborn or developed during childhood. As long as they are characteristics that cannot be developed by an individual after he has been selected, they belong in the no-compromise category.

# EXECUTIVE APPRAISAL CHART

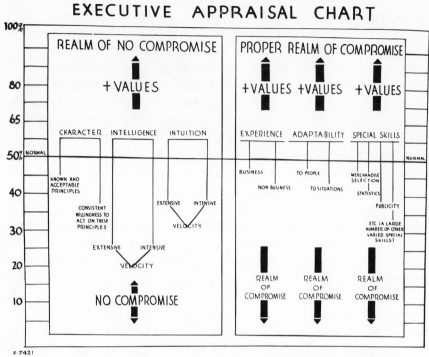

F 7421

FIGURE 31. *Chart Showing a Logical Approach to Executive Selection.*
Chart prepared and reproduced by the courtesy of Richard Weil, Jr.

comes up to the minimum for all factors, clearly the compromise should be made on a factor that can be developed after the job has been filled.

The significance of the distinction between innate and acquired qualities is brought out in the following example. The senior credit man of a commercial bank, whose duties included investigating loan applications, investigating the quality of commercial paper, acting as an intermediary between the loaning officer and borrowing customer, maintaining a current check on the credit status of borrowing customers, and answering inquiries from customers and correspondent banks, was considered to need the following qualities:

 Ability to make decisions
 Alertness
 Analytical ability
 Initiative
 Accuracy

Five to ten years' experience in statement analysis, investigation, and contact
  work
Complete knowledge of credit procedures of the bank
Ability to meet and deal with people
Oral and written expression.

In making a selection for this job, the bank's officers considered
the first five qualities in the noncompromise group, whereas, if
necessary, they would compromise on the other qualities. Without
the kind of analysis here suggested, a temptation would arise to
promote a man who had his full quota of experience and knowledge
of bank procedure and got along well with people, even though he
was deficient in ability to make decisions or in analytical ability.
Such an action would live to haunt the bank officers because the
man probably never would develop the desired mental qualities;
whereas had they compromised on the experience or diplomacy, the
man might have been weak during the first few years on the job,
but in the course of time could have overcome these handicaps.

## Promotion programs

Organization analysis and man specifications indicate the quality
of executive personnel needed in an enterprise, but they do not tell
*how much* or *when*. To be effective, executive personnel planning
must proceed into this quantitative phase.

Here again, precise planning is difficult because the life span of
individual executives is unknown, the chances of voluntary resig-
nation are hard to estimate, the speed with which young executives
will develop is problematical, and expansion or contraction in the
total number of executives required is subject to all the hazards of
general business forecasting. Nevertheless, as with any long-run
investment, we must make the best plans possible and then modify
and shift these in light of current developments. In this connection
a company should try to provide for the following:

1. Replacements for positions that are likely to be vacated within the next
   few years,
2. *Runners-up* for each key position; that is, some place in the organization
   should be an individual who could step into an unexpected vacancy without too much disruption in operations,
3. *Comers*, or likely candidates for vacancies several years hence.

*Replacements for anticipated vacancies.* Some vacancies can be
anticipated with a reasonable degree of accuracy. Companies with

a fixed retirement age know that certain positions will be vacated when the present incumbent reaches that age, if not before. Even without formal retirement arrangements, the age of an executive provides some guide as to when a replacement may be needed.

On this basis alone some companies have been able to anticipate an acute executive turnover five to ten years hence. One concern that had expanded rapidly and then remained stable in size found that not only would all its senior executives drop out within the next ten years, but also most of its junior executives and many of its department heads. This posed a serious problem of how younger men could be moved up through the ranks of department manager and be adequately prepared for the senior positions when the vacancies occurred.

Vacancies in executive positions arising from other causes can sometimes be predicted. Expansion of a new plant or a sales territory may be planned well in advance, and the need for additional executives can be recognized in this early planning stage. Occasionally the performance of some present executive is so unsatisfactory that plans must be made to transfer him to other work, and this, again, will indicate the need of a replacement.

Vacancies created by retirement, expansion, or transfer normally will be filled by promotion. Then, the present positions of the men to be promoted will have to be filled, and, if these vacancies in turn are filled by still other promotions, a third set of vacancies occurs, and so on down the line. Thus, a vacancy near the top may create the need for replacing a whole series of executives.[5]

Definite advantages accrue from preparing *tentative* plans for filling these vacancies. The gaps in the experience and training of the men selected can be filled in, and time remains for further observation to confirm the tentative selection.

[5] If careful review of men within the company does not disclose satisfactory candidates for the anticipated vacancies, a search for good men outside the firm should be started. Promotion from within helps morale, simplifies transitions, and involves less risk in making the selection. It can lead to trouble, however, if unqualified men are promoted. Not only will the specific positions they take be inadequately filled, but other executives may relax in their efforts to prepare themselves for future promotion. The recommendations in Chapter 20 indicate how a company can help prepare a man for promotion, but this desire to help should in no way mean a willingness to promote unqualified men. Once a man is appointed to a position a variety of pressures are created not to remove him, so the right initial choice must be made, even if this means bringing in a man from outside the company.

The tentative aspect of such plans deserves emphasis. Retirement of an executive may not come as soon as anticipated, economic conditions may postpone an expansion, careful observation may disclose that some individual in the chain is not prepared for promotion, thereby postponing the anticipated shift to fill his position. The need for men may come much sooner than expected, necessitating the transfer of experienced men into positions expected to have been filled by younger men, and so forth. Not infrequently, it is desirable to think of alternatives and to plan on an either-or basis.

Because of these necessarily tentative aspects of planning for executive personnel, as a general rule to tell a man that he is slated for promotion is unwise. The move may not work out, through no fault of his own, and explaining such situations without causing bitter disappointment is difficult. Tentative though the plans must be, they are a marked improvement over evading the issue and trusting that luck will provide the right men at the right time.

Because the common tendency is to procrastinate on executive personnel matters, the anticipated vacancies and the tentative plan to meet them should be put down in black and white. This may be done in the form of replacement tables listing a contemplated chain of promotion when a withdrawal occurs, or it may be done more dramatically on an organization chart showing in color anticipated retirements and other shifts within a five-year or even a ten-year period.

Such a chart, or even the tables, are almost sure to cause a stir among those who see them. Older executives sometimes dislike thinking of another person in their place. Other executives, perhaps unconsciously, will be thinking of modifications in the social structure that the contemplated shift will create. Thus, this interest created by the tables or charts should be channeled into constructive actions toward the development of executives in keeping with the whole personnel program.

*Runner-up for each position.* Not all vacancies in executive positions can be anticipated, as is necessary for the promotion schedule just described. Premature death takes its toll; actuarial figures show that out of a typical group of men forty-five years of age, approximately one-third will not live to see retirement at age sixty-five. An additional number will withdraw from active duty because of poor health. Then, some other executives will voluntarily resign to accept other business positions, to live in different locations, or to carry out a variety of other personal aims.

Highly desirable is to have in the enterprise a man qualified to step into an unexpected vacancy in any key post. These runners-up need not necessarily be an immediate assistant to the executive for whom they are considered a potential replacement. They may, for example, be managing a smaller though similar department, or be holding a staff position in the headquarters office. Moreover, the same man might be considered runner-up for two positions, neither of which was expected to be vacated in the near future. On the other hand, if the company is expanding and executive transfers are frequent, preparation of a table showing both a first and a second replacement for each key executive position may be advantageous.

The preparation of such a list of possible replacements serves several purposes in addition to that of a handy reference in the event an unexpected vacancy occurs. It provides a partial inventory of executive talent within the company, and the ease or difficulty of finding men to put on such a list will point to weak spots in the whole executive development program. Also, an examination of the adequacy of the preparation of runners-up for their respective posts will show the need for certain types of experience or other forms of individual development.

Any attempt to list runners-up for each of the key positions in a company is almost sure to raise the question of whether to try to have fully competent and trained men backing up each position. If executive turnover in the company is low and the present incumbent is relatively young, it may be hard to find a post where a fully qualified runner-up can have stimulating work that keeps him on his toes and also enables him to earn enough money to be glad to stay with the company.

Large concerns that have a number of positions calling for similar talent are more likely to be able to find suitable work for runners-up; in fact, in the alternative job the man may advance clear beyond the position for which he was once listed as a runner-up. A program for developing runners-up is not always practical, however, especially in small companies. Sometimes it is decided to run the risk of an unexpected loss and hope that a satisfactory replacement can be found outside the company in case one is needed. Occasionally companies hire and train competent young men, and then help them find good positions in other firms if suitable openings do not develop within the company.

*Comers.* A third step should be taken in determining the need for executive development. Each enterprise should have enough young men with potential executive ability to fill the ranks of junior executives five to ten years hence and to be the senior executives of the next generation.

The number of such comers, from all sources, deserves careful consideration. If they are too few in relation to the openings that develop, the latter will be filled inadequately unless qualified persons are introduced from the outside, which tends to undermine morale. On the other hand, an oversupply of individuals with exceptional talent is both costly and undesirable. These men will become impatient waiting for an opening that really challenges them, and some will seek more rapid advancement elsewhere. The study of anticipated vacancies and experience with unexpected executive turnover, already discussed, should provide the basis for at least an informed guess on future needs for new executives. In addition, allowance should be made for some comers that do not develop as hoped and for resignations for any of a variety of reasons.

Experience of many companies shows that out of a group of men regarded as comers, less than 50 per cent may be available for appointment to executive positions five years later. Other companies which take greater pains with their selection and with providing openings as rapidly as the men develop have been able to reduce this turnover significantly. A practice found in a few companies, and more commonly in a single branch or department within a company, is aggressive action to find positions outside the department for comers, junior executives, or even senior executives who cannot be used effectively within the unit. Through this graduation process the intake of comers can be stepped up; it provides a continuing supply of potential executives and a lot of new ideas; but it is likely to be expensive unless the organization can be geared to make full use of its transient members and their fresh ideas.

*Summary.* Organization analysis, accompanied by specifications for men needed to fill the positions in the planned organization, provides a total picture of the quality of the executives needed. An examination of the adequacy of promotion plans, runners-up, and comers, together with the individual executive appraisal described in the next section, will indicate the number, type, and time of additional talent needed. In this way, a sound guide to executive requirements will be provided. While particular forms and written documents may be helpful, the general method of analysis reflected in the steps outlined is much more important and can be adapted to a wider range of enterprises.

## Executive Appraisal and Selection

The appraisal of executives serves several purposes in administration. It provides a guide for the improvement of the work of the executive in his present position, it serves as a basis of promotion, and it is closely linked to incentives. These different purposes should be kept in mind, for they affect to some extent the process of appraisal that should be used.

If the man is being considered for promotion, then the requirements of the new position are pertinent. On the other hand, if the purpose of the appraisal is to help decide what can be done to make the man more effective in his present job, or if it is to be used as a guide to "in-grade" salary increases, then the present job should set the standard.

The principal tools to use in sizing up the work and potential abilities of an executive are:

1. Group judgment
2. Periodic appraisals of performance of present duties
3. Evaluation of qualities for promotion
4. Trial on a series of jobs
5. Psychological tests.

**Group judgment**

One of the simplest but most important principles to follow in appraising an executive is to obtain the opinion of several individuals before arriving at a final conclusion. The opinion of the man who is his supervisor will, of course, carry great weight because he has been in a position to observe closely the executive and his work. All of us, however, have likes and dislikes that often unconsciously influence our judgment. We may value a particular trait or action so highly that we overlook some significant weakness.

Consequently, the opinion of the supervisor should be substantiated by that of others who have also had the opportunity to observe the man. The executive second above the one being rated, the manager of another department, or a senior staff man who has had frequent contact with him may be asked to join the immediate supervisor in the appraisal. Generally, it is desirable to secure their independent opinions first and then have a conference to iron out any differences; but this particular procedure is not nearly so important as the basic idea of obtaining group, rather than individual, judgment.

This group judgment should be used when the really controlling decisions are made. For instance, if an executive is allowed to pick personally his immediate assistant and this assistant is the only one who receives the necessary training to take over the executive's position, probably the use of group judgment when the executive vacates the position will come too late to be of value. As already noted, replacement tables and runner-up lists help to bring decisions such as this out into the open at a date when constructive action is still possible. It is then that group judgment should be insisted upon. Decisions regarding executive personnel are too vital to the success of an enterprise to be left entirely to a single individual.

### Judging performance on present job

The performance of any executive can be appraised directly in terms of the objectives and the standards set for his division and department. These standards should have grown out of the organization analysis and company planning already discussed.[6]

The performance standards for each position should be as objective as possible since this simplifies the appraisal process and makes the results more readily acceptable to the executive himself. Even more important, however, is the comprehensive view of the total job of the executive. In this connection the outline of management objectives shown in Figure 32 may be useful. Specific standards for each position will have to be filled in, but the outline serves as a reminder of the variety of the responsibilities of an executive.

The use of performance standards instead of executive qualities or characteristics for judging the current work of an executive is recommended for two reasons. First, there is no advantage in taking a roundabout and uncertain path when a direct one is readily available. For example, there is little point in discussing a man's enthusiasm, initiative, or dependence upon his mother if in fact he is

[6] See especially Chapters 2, 16, and 17.

getting good results. To the extent that performance leaves something to be desired, then the pertinent question is what can be done to improve it—not whether the man's score on some rating scale is 74 or 68.[7] Likewise, an appraisal of a man's performance relative to other executives is not particularly useful here since he is already on the job and will remain there unless his performance is very unsatisfactory. Second, appraisal in terms of performance standards is useful year after year. After the executive and his supervisor have gone over a list of generalized executive qualities three or four times, the annual review loses its punch, whereas there is a recurring need for assessing the past year's results.

Frequently during the year occasions will arise to compare particular results against the program. The type of review urged here emphasizes over-all performance and is definitely personal in nature. It seeks to answer a question of vital interest to every executive, "how am I doing," and then uses the reply to help lay a constructive plan of individual improvement.

### Evaluating qualities for promotion

Appraising executives for promotions differs from judging performance on present jobs. For instance, the appraisal must focus on personal qualities since in this preliminary selection process demonstrated ability to perform duties of the higher position usually is lacking. Emphasis is shifted to innate qualities, and acceptable minimums may be set because there normally are several candidates, at least when men outside the company are included. Also, with several possibilities for each vacancy, a need arises to compare one individual with another.

*Assemble information on outstanding qualities and deficiencies.* Judging a man's capacity to serve in a position he has never filled is always difficult. One of the simplest steps in this direction is to ask several individuals to list *both* the most outstanding and the weakest characteristics of the men being appraised. Although not comprehensive in coverage, this procedure often throws considerable light on the qualities of an individual.

As a *minimum* there should be an annual appraisal consisting of (1) a discussion between the executive and his supervisor of the

[7] Perhaps the corrective action will include psychological diagnosis of the difficulty, but this calls for a more clinical approach than is possible with an over-all rating.

---

### General Objectives of Management

#### I. PLANNING

Formulate well-considered objectives and plans—covering all operations, activities, and expenditures for each year, or longer, ahead —as a basis for authorization, a guide to achievement, and a measure of performance.

#### II. ORGANIZATION

Develop and maintain a sound and clear-cut plan of organization through which the executives can most easily and effectively direct and control activities.

#### III. EXECUTIVE PERSONNEL

Develop and administer a constructive personnel development program that will gradually ensure that all positions in the organization are filled by individuals fully qualified to meet the requirements of their respective positions.

#### IV. OUTPUT

Accomplish all duties and responsibilities fully, effectively, and harmoniously.

#### V. COSTS

Keep all costs and manpower at an economic minimum, consistent with essential purposes.

#### VI. BETTERMENT

Plan, stimulate, and develop improvement in methods, products, facilities, and other fields as applicable, keeping abreast of the best thought and practice throughout the industry; and ensure that outmoded procedures and uneconomical facilities are abandoned.

#### VII. EMPLOYEE RELATIONS

Make sure that all employees are accorded fair and equitable treatment, and that they are inspired to their best efforts.

---

FIGURE 32. *Executive Performance Guide.* Adapted from a table prepared by Standard Oil Company of California.

strong and weak points of the executive's performance during the past year, and a consideration of what should be done to overcome deficiencies and to prepare for more responsible positions to which the executive can reasonably aspire; and (2) the writing of memoranda to be placed in the personnel files by the man's supervisor, and perhaps by someone else familiar with his work, giving the type of information indicated by the following key questions:

1. What is the most outstanding thing the executive has done in the past year?
2. List, in order, his three strongest abilities or characteristics.
3. List, in order, his three greatest weaknesses or deficiencies.
4. What should be done to correct these weaknesses?
5. Does he want a transfer or promotion? To what position? Do you think he has potentialities for promotion? To what position?
6. Is he doing anything to qualify for such a promotion—or to improve his present performance?

This simple procedure, which is applicable to even the smallest enterprises, will encourage among all executives an analytical and constructive view toward personnel development. Over a period of time it will build a record regarding executives far superior to the opinions that can be assembled when the need arises to fill an actual vacancy.

*Compare candidates by ranking.* When several individuals are being appraised at the same time, the use of a ranking process for each quality considered by the company to be important is most advantageous.

In ranking, the proficiency of the several candidates is compared, and the candidates then listed from highest to lowest—or at least in percentile or quartile brackets. This avoids the confusion of one rater using the word good to mean the same thing that another rater does by excellent. It also catches the rater who wants to put everybody in the same grade; possibly all employees of his division are excellent, but they cannot all be in the top percentages. Moreover, it stresses the difference between individuals, which is usually the significant thing in making selection for promotion.

The nature of such appraisal by ranking is indicated in the accompanying form used by the Navy for all officers (Figure 33). This form has been designed with great care since these fitness reports play a critical part in determining whether the officer will be promoted or retired. The general ideas can be readily adopted by any enterprise having several potential candidates of approximately the same rank or grade. Once a number of qualities considered important in several likely jobs have been defined, then those making the appraisal can be asked to rank the men they know, either by comparing each man with the others or, at least, by ranking him in the upper, lower, or middle groups.

7. For each factor observed check the appropriate box to indicate how the officer compares with all others of the same rank whose professional abilities are known to you . . .

| Rating Factors | Not observed | Bottom 10% | Next 20% | Middle 40% | Next Top 20% | Top 10% |
|---|---|---|---|---|---|---|

**A. SEA OR ADVANCE BASE DUTY**

*How does this officer compare in:*
1. Standing deck watches underway?
2. Ability to command?
3. Performance in present duties?
4. Reactions during emergencies?
5. Performance at battle station?

**B. INITIATIVE AND RESPONSIBILITY**

*How well does this officer:*
1. Assume responsibility when specific instructions are lacking?
2. Give frank opinions when asked or volunteer them when necessary?
3. Follow through despite obstacles?

**C. UNDERSTANDING AND SKILL**

*How well does this officer:*
1. Grasp instructions given to him?
2. Use ideas and suggestions of others?
3. Rate in technical competence in his specialty?

**D. LEADERSHIP**

*How well does this officer:*
1. Inspire subordinates to work to the maximum of their capacity?
2. Effectively delegate responsibility?
3. Transmit orders, instructions, and plans?
4. Organize his work and that of those under his command?
5. Maintain discipline among those under his command?

**E. CONDUCT AND WORK HABITS**

*How does this officer compare in:*
1. Ability to work with others?
2. Ability to adapt to changing needs?
3. Military conduct—bearing, dress, etc.?

8. Indicate your attitude toward having this officer under your command. Would you: ☐ Definitely not want him?  ☐ Prefer not to have him?  ☐ Be satisfied to have him? ☐ Be pleased to have him?  ☐ Particularly desire him?

9. Considering all officers of the same rank whose professional abilities are known to you personally, would you promote him if ☐ 90% ☐ 70% ☐ 30% ☐ 10%—were to be promoted?

10, 11 and 12 (These questions call for any commendable or adverse reports, comment on mental or moral weakness, clear and concise appraisal of officer.)

FIGURE 33. *Excerpt from U.S. Navy Officer's Fitness Report.*

*Apply information to specific requirements.* The ranking and reports on outstanding characteristics just described provide appraisal information of a general nature. When a man is being selected for a specific position, of course, one must concentrate on the particular qualities required. The general information already assembled should be useful, but additional evaluation of particular points will probably be needed.

### Trial on a series of jobs

Executive appraisals used in selection for promotion are by their nature indirect, and a large element of personal judgment is involved. One should, therefore, supplement this approach whenever practical. Actual trial on a series of jobs is the most reliable means for checking tentative selections based on appraisal.

*Job rotation.* Trial on a series of jobs can be illustrated by the experience of a manufacturing company that recognized that its president would have to be replaced in about five years. A careful appraisal of all candidates within the company indicated that the Director of Engineering would probably be the best man to move up into the top position. While the man appeared to have all the desirable qualities, most of his experience had been in the design and creative end of the business, and the directors of the company were not certain how effective he would be in getting out production on time at economical cost or whether he would give balanced treatment to all departments.

Consequently, they arranged to put him in charge of production for two years. After he had proved himself there, he was made general manager of a subsidiary company, which had all types of activities from product assembly to sales and customer service. Here again his performance was quite satisfactory, and although the president's illness precluded still a third assignment that had been planned, the directors of the company were able to make the appointment with considerable assurance that they had the right man. Had the man proven to be inept and unhappy in either of these posts, probably both he and the directors would have agreed that he would be most successful back in the engineering department where there was no question as to his competence.

Trial on a series of jobs may be difficult to arrange. The vacancy to be filled must be anticipated long enough in advance to permit testing candidates in other jobs. Often more troublesome, positions in which the candidates can demonstrate desired ability must exist within the company and also be open for a short-run appointment. This raises the question of what will be done with men currently in the positions and who will fill them after the men being tested are again transferred. Fortunately, this trial on a series of jobs can also be closely linked with the training of the executive, and if job rotation and horizontal promotions are customarily used for training purposes, it will be much easier to find suitable posts in which a man's performance under fire can be watched.

*Special assignments.* A much more limited form of on-the-job trial can be obtained through temporary assignments. The candidate may be asked to fill a position during the vacation of the regular incumbent, but this has restricted value for selection purposes; the department or division will probably continue to operate on momentum, and the candidate will not be expected to introduce major changes while he is serving in a pinch-hitting capacity.

Special assignments, such as planning the introduction of a new product, negotiating the lease of a warehouse, or membership on an important trade-association committee, place the candidate in different working conditions and often throw some light on his strength and weakness. Sometimes a practical solution is to give a candidate greater freedom of action in his regular job and then observe how he handles himself and the results achieved when the initiative and authority are his. These more limited assignments are particularly valuable when it is not practical to transfer the candidate to a series of positions where he can assume full responsibility for a considerable period of time.

To secure the full benefit of trial on a series of jobs, this device should be combined with periodic appraisal and group judgment. In other words, the performance of a candidate in these different situations should be observed by several individuals, who then join together in a reappraisal of the potentialities and development needs of the particular individual. A wide area of personal judgment still remains because the circumstances existing at the time the man is working in a particular position make a marked difference on the ease or difficulty of success. Furthermore, this method is only a forecast of how the man will behave in a new position on the basis of his behavior in the past. Nevertheless, this very complexity of the selection, along with its vital significance, makes the more analytical measures that have been described essential to sound administration.

**Psychological tests**

Psychological tests are being used in a variety of ways in the selection and placement of employees. Unfortunately, only a limited amount of work has been done in the selection of men for higher executive posts.

A variety of psychological tests are available to measure such things as interest, intelligence, personality or social intelligence, achievement in special fields of learning, and a number of physical skills. The application of these tests to executive personnel problems, however, encounters several difficulties. As we have already seen, no general agreement exists as to the qualities that are essential to executive success. In fact, these qualities vary from one situation to another. This makes it difficult for the psychologists to develop tests which have usefulness in a variety of companies and other enterprises. On the other hand, single companies may agree upon desired qualities and characteristics, but the number of successful and unsuccessful executives is usually too small a sample to validate a test.

The selection of executives is something like picking a college football team. It is possible to develop a set of tests that could be given to every member of the squad. They would seek to measure such characteristics as weight, physical strength, endurance, reaction time, bodily coordination, pugnaciousness, emotional stability under pressure, competitive spirit, cooperativeness, intelligence, and perhaps others. In actual practice, aside from a physical check-up, which is used for negative rather than positive selection, such tests are not given. Instead, the coach simply sends men out on the field and watches them closely to see how each one plays. Now, if men for the football squad had to be selected the first day the freshmen arrived on the campus, a variety of tests might be extremely useful since they would reveal much more than a brief interview. Fortunately for the coach, he doesn't have to make the decision until he has had considerable opportunity for on-the-job trial.

Executive selection, like that of a football team, can usually be based on observation of the candidates in actual performance. In those situations, such as recruitment of potential executives from colleges, where a considerable number of men are being considered and little opportunity occurs to observe them at work before the selection is made, properly designed and administered psychological tests can be of help. In a vast majority of cases, however, one need not resort to this indirect method.

## SUMMARY

Executive personnel planning requires that the duties set forth on a position description be translated into the specifications of a man needed to fill that position. Performance requirements are a direct and simple way to state such specifications, but since these may be impractical to apply, often a list of personal qualities believed to be essential is developed for each position.

The number and timing of executive shifts is difficult to predict accurately, but this aspect of personnel needs can be *tentatively* laid out in promotion tables.

The actual selection of executives normally takes place in successive stages. Younger men, or comers, are first identified as potential material. Then from this group one or more candidates for specific positions are chosen. Finally, when a vacancy does occur, some one individual is moved into it. The better the job selection at the earlier stages, the easier it is to find satisfactory people later. The comers and candidates for expected vacancies are, of course, being observed all the time; and since a large part of the executive force will be regarded as candidates for still higher positions, selection should be a continuous process throughout the executive pyramid.

A number of basic procedures, if conscientiously followed, will be of considerable help in making these selections. When selecting a man for a particular position, distinguish between the innate qualities and those that can be acquired after a man gets on the job. Then, to the extent that compromise on desirable characteristics in the candidate is necessary, the concessions may be concentrated on qualities or characteristics that can be developed.

Group judgment should be made on all critical decisions. As background for specific selection, appraisals should be made periodically and a summary record sent to the personnel files along with other evidence of the man's performance. Finally, whenever possible, a man should be placed in a number of different positions where he may demonstrate abilities needed in some higher post.

Significant here is that numerous forms, complicated ratings, and specialized tests are not necessarily part of the steps suggested.

These devices may be useful in certain situations, but danger exists that some complex rating scheme will be given unwarranted emphasis. Instead, a few simple measures carefully and regularly followed are more likely to produce satisfactory results. These will require some hard work and unemotional thinking by almost all of the executives, but they are well worth the price.

(References will be found at the end of Chapter 20.)

# 20

# Executive Development and Compensation

## DEVELOPING EXECUTIVE PERSONNEL

The two phases of an executive personnel program already discussed clear the way for well-directed attention to development of individual executives. The analysis of need for executive talent will indicate the positions that are to be filled by promotion, and the appraisal of individual executives, which is a necessary step in selection, will also show the type of development each man requires in order to be adequately prepared for his next position.

Some of the qualities needed must, of course, be regarded as innate, but another large group of desired characteristics can be developed under favorable circumstances. Development activities should be directed to the creation of the needed reservoir of executive talent, as well as to the improvement of the performance of men in their present jobs.

The most useful methods of executive development are:

1. Learning on the job
2. Rotation among jobs
3. Use of committees, conferences, and courses
4. Assistance in individual development

### Learning on the job

Learning on the job always has been, and will continue to be, the chief means of developing executives in an enterprise. This is because the experience of doing a thing is real, complete; it becomes im-bedded in the emotional, mental, and unconscious reactions.

Some experiences, however, are more valuable than others, and the speed at which learning takes place on the job varies signifi-cantly. Consequently, if primary reliance is to be placed on learning on-the-job, it must be done effectively. The hard-boiled realist who insists that one learns best by doing is actually practical only when he assures that conditions surrounding the job are conducive to such learning.

*Enthusiasm for learning on the job is vital.* The speed and the nature of learning on the job depend largely upon the attitude of two individuals, the trainee and his boss, and the relationship be-tween them. Unless the supervisor wants his subordinate to develop and has some appreciation of how to go about this, and the sub-ordinate desires to learn and recognizes the kind of help he should try to get from his boss, the learning process is likely to be slow.

We must, therefore, create among the executives of the company the belief that training subordinates is an important part of their job. This belief can be cultivated by the example set by top execu-tives themselves, clear-cut statements of the importance to be at-tached to executive development, recognition in periodic appraisals of executives of their success or failure in training young men, and some judicious missionary work on the part of the staff man guiding the executive-personnel program.

Given this belief in the desirability of learning on the job, those involved should discuss the ways and means of expediting the learn-ing process. The training will deal primarily with two positions, the trainee's own job and that of his boss. What can be done to speed up and round out his learning of the duties and relationships of these two positions?

*Need for delegation plus coaching.* The executive or potential ex-ecutive will learn most from his present job through a wise com-bination of delegation and coaching. One veteran executive states the idea briefly as "turn the man loose and then help him out of his difficulty." It is necessary, of course, to tell the man what results are wanted and perhaps show him one way of achieving them, but executive development will not be aided by insisting that he come to his supervisor for detailed instruction.

Instead, by putting the man on his own, he will have to think through the action to be taken and will be much more sensitive to the reasons for success or failure. He will also be developing self-confidence and a capacity for carrying responsibility. Since this is a specific application of decentralization, several of the limitations already described in Chapter 13 may apply here. Nevertheless, almost every situation may have more or less decentralization, and for executive development the more decentralization the better.

The decentralization just recommended should not be accompanied by the withdrawal of the supervisor from the activity. Instead, he should assume the role of a coach who observes closely what is going on and makes suggestions of how performance may be improved. A climate of confidence is necessary if this coaching is to be most effective. The man should feel free to ask for help and admit difficulties without a fear of being severely censured. The supervisor, just as are the truly great athletic coaches, should be a readily available source of friendly, constructive criticism.

The periodic appraisals of individual performance, already described, provide an occasion for an over-all review of performance, but the counseling on specific actions should be much more frequent and directly related to current problems. Also, the coach should take time to explain why he gives the advice he does so that the trainee may apply the same ideas to a variety of situations. Coaching, such as has been suggested, can greatly enrich the experience an executive gets while performing decentralized tasks.

*Shadowbox the boss's job.* The developing executive should also learn a lot about his supervisor's job. This can be done best by having the employee figure out what he would do if he were in his chief's shoes. Initially, the executive should share with the trainee facts regarding the problems he faces, the variety of angles that must be considered, and the reasons for the decision he makes. Later, the subordinate should be asked, "How would you handle this question if you were in my position?" "What would you do if you owned the business?" The supervisor can then explain why he does or does not follow the recommended course. Finally, it may be practical from time to time actually to delegate part of the work in the form of special assignments.

As the younger man learns at least to shadowbox the senior position, he broadens his perspective, and he comes to his chief with reasonable recommendations instead of problems or unworkable ideas. While this type of training is particularly important for a man who is slated to replace his chief, it will contribute to the development of almost any executive.

### Rotation among jobs

Most executive positions call for a broader view and more varied experience than can be provided in any single job down the line. Consequently, learning on the job should be coupled with a scheme for rotation among different jobs. This rotation for training purposes should, of course, be incorporated into the plans for replacements as reflected in promotion tables.

*Cook's Tours are not enough.* The job progression being discussed here is quite different from the Cook's Tours often provided for college men just entering a company. These brief tours, where a man spends only a few weeks in each department, have considerable value as a means of orientation and perspective of the entire operation. Job rotation in the executive ranks is a different matter. Here a man often stays on a job for several years, and he must earn his salt, and his spurs, as he goes along.

*Job progression that rounds out experience.* Executive development through job rotation may be illustrated by the experience of an executive in a company operating a chain of dry goods stores. Phil Simon was spotted as a comer while still in his twenties; his outstanding performance, first as a salesman and then as a section manager, marked him as a potential store executive. He was first transferred to a fairly small store, the manager of which was a demon on watching expenses. After three years under this man, Phil knew how to balance work loads, get the lights turned out, save wastage of boxes and other wrapping materials, and keep repair costs under control.

He was then made promotion and display manager under a man who had a real flair for catching the public's interests. No holiday, Boy Scout Week, or public event went unnoticed in that store's promotion. This involved many intangibles, but by the end of two years Phil was coming up with ideas as often as his chief.

Phil's next assignment was as assistant merchandise manager in one of the largest outlets of the company. This required learning the quality characteristics, customer preference, cost, and pricing of a large variety of goods. At the end of five years he was still learning, but he was then transferred to be assistant general manager of a medium-sized store where he gained experience in coordination of all the activities of the store.

Two years later he was made manager of one of the company's smaller outlets. During his four years here he demonstrated clearly that he had been learning in each of the jobs he had held and was competent to give over-all direction to an entire store. At the age of 44 he was again promoted, this time to be general manager of one of the largest stores in the chain.

*Select good training spots.* Some jobs are better training posts than others, and job rotation works best when men can be moved in and out of the positions that provide good experience. One of the key factors in a good training spot is the attitude and the knack of the supervisor. Also, positions where a man carries full operating responsibility are good training posts, particularly if a variety of activities are involved; such positions are likely to be found in operating branches or subsidiary plants.

If a young man cannot be put in a key operating post, either because there are few such positions within the company or because they are already filled by competent individuals, then a position as general assistant to the key operating man may be used for training purposes. Staff positions often provide excellent training spots because a man has opportunity to come in contact with many operating departments; he also gets experience in developing new plans and in securing voluntary acceptance of such plans.

After these good training spots have been located, care should be taken that they are not filled with people who, for one reason or another, are not promotable material.

*Compensate for lack of experience.* Job rotation often involves putting a man in a position for which he has had comparatively little previous experience. In fact, this may be the very reason why the man has been transferred to that position. This means that an initial loss of efficiency may occur at the time the transfer is made. To keep this loss at a minimum, the positions above and below the one just being filled should be occupied by experienced individuals. Many a technical sergeant in the Army has had to bolster a second lieutenant while the latter was still learning what made things tick.

This lack of background is likely to be more serious when the man is transferred from one major function to another, for example, from production to sales or finance, because such a wide divergence of skills will be needed. To attempt to provide interdepartmental experience while a man is still young and need not occupy key positions is only a partial answer; if done while he can perform only routine work, the trainee may fail to have an opportunity to gain knowledge of broad issues, and often he becomes familiar only with one section of a large department. Another way to provide breadth of experience is to assign a man to a staff position that requires close contact or actual work in other departments but does not call for technical knowledge.

The movement of men in and out of jobs is not all a net loss, however. The men being rotated are competent individuals and will bring a fresh viewpoint to each job. They will have new ideas and will be anxious to make improvements, whereas an executive who has been in a position for some period of time is likely to find himself defending the changes he has already made, and hence he is less progressive. Here again a balance is needed between the experienced hand and the new blood that has been introduced into a section or a department.

*Need for tradition of horizontal promotion.* The effect on the morale of the other executives of rotating men among different jobs should also be carefully watched. One of the most likely sources of bad feeling will be among the junior executives who aspired to move up into their boss's position and then find someone from another department has moved into the coveted spot.

Where horizontal promotions are rare, this feeling may be strong, but once job rotation has been well established as a company practice, it need cause no serious difficulty. The executives will then realize that the chances of vertical promotion are small, and that the real opportunity lies in moving about and extending one's general knowledge and background. Such a system actually increases the opportunities for the capable men to get ahead because they do not have to wait until the one job immediately ahead of them is vacated.

### Committees, conferences, and company courses

Although the learning that occurs in a series of jobs is most important in executive development, occasionally committees, conferences, or company courses can be used to supplement these primary measures.

*Committees.* Committees often provide an executive an opportunity to learn something of the problems and the point of view of men in other departments. Committee recommendations should reflect broader considerations than are likely to come from any one of its members; men have to explain and defend their own ideas. All this is good training for the growing executive.

For reasons pointed out in Chapter 14, committees are rarely established for training purposes alone, but, given a sound operating reason for establishing a committee, its training possibilities should not be overlooked. Members of the committee can be appointed with an eye to executive development as well as to the direct results of the committee's deliberations.

*Conferences.* Special conferences on particular subjects, such as auditing, collective bargaining, sales training, cost accounting, and the like may be held by larger companies having a number of professional or technical men working in the same area. Typically, the conferences last for two or three days and provide an opportunity for stimulating discussion on technical problems and for the exchange of ideas and experience. Here we have a device intended to improve competence in a specialty, whereas other measures are often intended to broaden the executive's viewpoint.

*Company courses.* Courses, on any of a wide variety of subjects, deserve consideration in building an executive personnel program. Such courses may deal with general administration, control and motivation, economics of the industry, or with specific techniques. A course in job-instructor training is an example of the last type of course.

The use of company courses has two serious limitations. One is the purely mechanical problem of finding a subject and a time when enough executives can meet together to make the course worth while. The second is concerned with the way the course is conducted. Experience demonstrates that a series of lectures makes so little dent in executives' behavior that it is rarely worth while. Active mental participation and the relating of the subject matter to one's own personal experience and problems are necessary if the course is to influence behavior rather than merely impart information. This means that the number taking the course must be kept small, and a discussion or conference method employed.

For particular purposes, under favorable circumstances, courses may be very useful. In general, however, company courses are one of the few tools of executive department that have probably been used too much rather than too little.

### Assistance in individual development

In the earlier discussion of appraisal of an executive's performance, the need for following through with a constructive program for individual improvement was stressed. This is an essential and crucial aspect of executive development.

*Constructive advice.* In addition to the training a man can receive within the company, his development can often be assisted by outside activities. For example, one man whose primary background has been engineering may be advised to join in church, school, or other community affairs in order to develop leadership experience; another man, weak in the use of financial figures, needs an evening accounting course; still another executive finds difficulty in expressing himself before a group of people, and he needs special work in public speaking. Perhaps another individual is having difficulty with his personal finance problems, and he needs advice and help in that regard; often the suggestion of the right book to read is a real help.

Advice on the correction or development of certain personal traits, if given wisely, may make a marked difference in a man's effectiveness. The use of psychiatrists to overcome certain personal quirks, which almost all of us have, is becoming more common among businessmen. Sometimes a plan for improvement of personal health is needed. This list can be continued indefinitely because these are individual development needs and vary from person to person. The responsibility for their correction must rest largely with the individuals themselves, but a man's supervisor, a senior officer, or personnel counsellor can often help with suggestions and with direct assistance in certain areas.

*Use of universities and professional societies.* Probably the most common form of assistance in individual development is in the support of formal educational activities. Some companies will pay the tuition for any evening school course related to a man's work. Others map out a specific educational program and then enable him to attend the necessary classes. An increasing number of executives are attending seminars and university-sponsored conferences. Less frequently, companies relieve executives for several weeks and pay the expense of executive development programs now being offered by several universities.

Also of growing importance is the participation of company executives in professional societies and trade association work. One of the outstanding characteristics of American business practice is the freedom with which executives discuss their problems with each other and exchange know-how. This contact with executives in other companies is particularly important for the company that seeks to be abreast of the latest developments and also follows a policy of promotion from within.

*Summary: executive development.* Executive development should be done on an individual basis and adapted to the need of the particular person. Periodic appraisals of performance and of qualifications for promotion will indicate the areas in which each executive needs improvement. This should be used in planning with the man his own personal development efforts.

Primary reliance should be placed on on-the-job learning—through coaching and shadowboxing the boss. Closely related to this is rotation among a series of jobs and special assignments that provide diversified experience. A third supplementing source of help is provided off the job—in company courses and conferences, and in professional societies or university programs. Still other means of development may be identified in counseling sessions. Essential throughout all such activities is an eagerness on the part of executives to create opportunities for learning and growing—for themselves and for others.

### EXECUTIVE COMPENSATION

The setting of executive compensation is always a ticklish problem. It inevitably depends largely upon personal judgment, and it is charged with a lot of emotional reactions. Although financial remuneration is only one of the incentives to which executives respond, its proper handling is vital to good executive morale.

Many technical points are connected with executive compensation, and personal factors often complicate the picture. However, these should not be permitted to obscure a basically sound and reasonable approach to the salary structure for the entire enterprise. The following paragraphs consider first the underlying salary structure and then give brief attention to bonuses, stock options, and other special arrangements for compensation.

**Building a sound salary structure**

A basic salary structure should provide (1) good internal alignment, that is, a reasonable relationship among the salaries of the executives within the enterprise; and (2) practical external alignment, that is, a relationship of company salaries to those paid by other firms that enables the company to attract and retain capable executives and at the same time keeps its total salary expense at competitive levels. Moreover, the design and administration of the structure must be sufficiently flexible to recognize differences in the contributions of individual executives. These general requirements might well be applied to the compensation of all employees although special considerations enter into the payment of unionized craftsmen as contrasted with executives.

In setting salaries that conform to these requirements, we should distinguish between a reasonable salary for a given position and variations above or below this amount that reflect how well the man in that position performs the various duties. By first concentrating on the *value of a position,* regardless of the incumbent, the problem can be reduced to more manageable terms. After this is done, adjustment can be made for the quality of individual performance.

Approximate salaries for each position in the organization can be established through the following steps:

1. Decide upon the relative importance and difficulty of the executive positions.
2. Decide how the general salary level of the company should compare with outside salaries.
3. Provide a salary range for each position to allow for differences in individual performance.

*Alignment of positions.* The relative status of executive positions within an enterprise can be decided upon in several ways. The nature of each position will presumably have already been defined in the organization analysis. The top executives, perhaps including some members of the board of directors, will have a general sense of the relative importance of the positions and will, after some discussion, be able to rank the jobs and then decide the spread between those in adjacent places.

A more systematic procedure is to make a separate analysis and ranking for each of several factors that are considered important by the management in the operation of the enterprise. Such *compensa-*

*ble characteristics* might well include minimum experience necessary for a position, mental and educational requirements, ability to contact and influence people, imagination and creativeness needed, responsibility for people and their work, and responsibility for financial decisions. The separate ranking for such factors can then be added together to obtain a composite score for each position. If a large number of positions are involved, some of the more refined techniques used in job evaluation can be applied here. If only relatively few positions are being studied, a consensus can usually be reached on their relative status along some numerical scale without resorting to an elaborate rating technique. Whatever the procedure followed, the judgment cannot be precise because of the many intangibles that enter into executive work.

*Relating salary level to rates paid outside.* Comparing company salaries to those paid by other firms again presents some difficulties inherent in administration of executive compensation. Differences in the size and nature of company activities and in the administrative organization make it difficult to measure "average market price" or typical salary paid for a given type of work.

Usually, however, approximate figures can be established for some positions at the lower end of the scale, such as auditors, chief accountants, branch managers, and other jobs where considerable similarity of duties exists in several companies in the same industry. And, at the other end of the scale, some similarity exists between the duties of the chief executive of comparable sized firms in the same industry. Care is necessary in interpreting data for the top company executive, but as a rule some central tendency will be found in the statistics on this point. Possibly, comparable data for other positions will be available, and if so it should be used; however, if values can be established for both ends of the scale, the others can be slotted by interpolation. The available salary information can be clearly summarized on a graph by using company evaluations of the positions along the horizontal scale, as is done in Figure 34.

After the data on outside salaries are assembled, the company must decide whether it wishes to pay more, the same, or less than the typical salaries of other firms. This decision will depend upon a variety of factors, such as the profitability of the company, its financial structure and the attitude of its owners, cost of living in the locations and social strata where the executives live, supplementary benefits offered, and nonfinancial incentives provided by the company. Once this decision is made, the approximate salary for the top officer and for several of the lower officers can be set, and a salary curve drawn for the company officers. Such a salary curve is shown in Figure 34.[1]

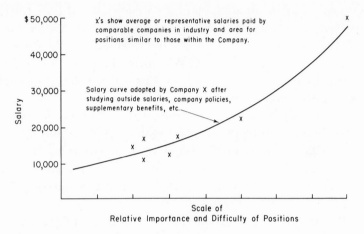

FIGURE 34. *Relation of Salary Curve to Outside Salaries.*

*Providing for differences in performance.* Setting one salary for each position is a mistake because this fails to provide for differences in individual performance. As an individual gains experience in a position, the quality of his work typically improves, and there should be some recognition of this fact in his salary. Also, as a result of promotion and transfer, a given position will be filled by several different individuals, and the work of one executive may be either better or worse than that of the others. Consequently, a salary range for each position is desirable in order to provide for this difference of individual performance.

The starting rate will normally be significantly below the company salary curve, whereas the rate for exceptional performance will be correspondingly above the salary curve. This range should be wider than that typically provided for nonexecutive positions be-

[1] In this connection remember that salaries normally step up by a percentage, rather than by constant amounts. Sometimes the alignment scale provides for this percentage increase in pay, in which case the company salary curve should theoretically be a straight line.

cause of the wide difference in the quality of individual performance. Usually the top of the range should be 35 per cent to 50 per
cent above the bottom.

*Example of salary structure.* A salary structure, including the features just described, is shown in Figure 35. First, the various executive positions were compared one with the other and placed along
the lower scale, and then the general level of salaries was established
by top management after available evidence had been obtained
on salaries obtained outside for comparable positions. Finally, mini-

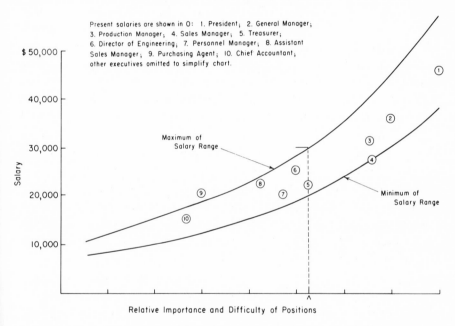

FIGURE 35. *Illustration of Salary Structure of a Manufacturing Company.*

mum and maximum curves were set, with the maximum 50 per cent
above the minimum. Once an executive position has been evaluated
and placed along the bottom scale, the minimum and maximum
salary can be quickly and easily determined.

The chart also shows the present salaries of ten of the company
executives. Note that, whereas the positions of production manager
and sales manager were evaluated at the same point, there is a
$4,000 difference in their salaries; this reflects the fact that the
present sales manager has just been promoted to that position. The
wide salary range permits the outstanding director of engineering to

receive more than the treasurer, even though his position is not considered quite as important. The purchasing agent, who is above the maximum for his position, was given that salary before systematic study had been made of the total structure; and, while his pay will not be reduced, he cannot expect a raise as long as he remains in his present position.

This guide for establishment of salaries provides considerable flexibility. In addition to a wide range to allow for differences in individual performance, it is simple to adjust the range either upward or downward as duties in the position change. For some positions, where the duties are partly built around the man rather than the job, it may be hard to decide whether the man's performance in his original job is unusual or the job itself has changed. This will not make much difference in the pay check whichever way it is done, as long as care is exercised not to give credit twice.

*Need for flexibility.* The salary structure proposed should be regarded as a guide rather than as an inflexible standard. Particular reasons may exist as to why a man's pay does not fall exactly where the quality of his performance would indicate. For example, an executive placed in a position primarily for training purposes in connection with a job rotation plan may be receiving a higher salary than the quality of his performance on that particular job warrants. Young men who have risen rapidly in the executive ranks are likely to be paid in the lower part of the range for their positions; it is considered psychologically desirable not to increase a man's salary too rapidly and to leave some room for future increases. In a sense, the man is not being paid as much as he is worth, but this is offset by the customary practice of not reducing salaries when a man's effectiveness begins to taper off. The special incentives discussed in the next section may also influence the base salary.

Such reasons as these may well justify a salary that is "out of line." Nevertheless, a concept of what the normal range for the position should be is essential so that the magnitude of the exception will be recognized. Without a basic salary structure, the exceptions may be perpetuated and still other inequities added.

### Bonuses, stock options

*Financial incentives for executives.* The use of direct financial incentives for executives is complicated by the fact that results of the efforts of a particular executive are often difficult to measure and are likely to be strongly influenced by economic conditions, action of competitors, and other factors clearly outside the influence of the executive. Consequently, having a large proportion of executive compensation consist of incentive pay is usually unwise. In most circumstances, if financial incentives are to be used at all, it is preferable to treat them as extra payments beyond a reasonably adequate base salary.

The use of limited financial incentives has a number of advantages for private-profit enterprises. The executives are given a positive financial spur toward greater effort; generally recognized as fair is to allow the executives to have a share in the improved returns accruing to the enterprise at least in part because of their efforts; some flexibility is introduced into executive payroll expense since incentive compensation is likely to be low when the company's earnings are low; and, recognition for outstanding performance in one year is not permanently incorporated into the payrolls. A firm with a financial incentive plan may reasonably keep its base salaries at or below the general market average, thereby reducing the *net* cost of the incentive; in actual practice, however, this is not always done.

The basis upon which the incentive compensation is paid should be tied as closely as practicable to the work of the individual executive. The sales manager, for example, often receives a bonus on sales volume. However, this illustrates one of the hazards of an incentive plan. An incentive based on one aspect of a job may lead the executive to slight other parts; for example, the sales manager may become more interested in sales volume than gross margins received or developing good will of customers. Companies with reliable output standards and budgets may tie incentives to expense ratios, savings under budgets, and similar figures. In general, however, such standards should be used as only one of the measures and incentives for executives should be tied to over-all performance, even though this may be more difficult to measure.

*Executive bonus funds.* A relatively simple and flexible plan that can be adapted to many enterprises is an executive bonus fund. Typically, a fixed percentage of the net profits of the company is set aside for the executives. Part of this fund is divided among the executives according to percentages or shares established along with the base salary. The balance of the fund is allotted to executives by top management or a committee of the board of directors for unusual performance during the past year. This gives all executives who participate in the fund a fixed interest in the net profits, and also creates a "kitty" from which an executive may get much or little depending upon his individual performance.

*Stock purchase plans.* Another type of financial incentive is an arrangement for executives to acquire common stock of the company at a favorable price. Having become stockholders the executives then have a continuing interest in the prosperity of the concern. Such arrangements are much less common today than they were in the past. As corporations become larger and pass from the hands of one or a few stockholders, special opportunities to purchase stock are harder to arrange. More stringent legal regulations covering the issuance of additional stock have further complicated the picture. Income tax regulations, which, in general, treat any difference between current market price and the purchase price paid by the executive as personal income and which take about half of all corporate income before it becomes available for dividends, have made stock purchases less attractive than high annual salaries, both to the executives and to the company. The sad experience of executives who purchased company stock and then watched its value decline drastically in depression has led to the conclusion that junior executives with limited resources should not risk their savings in the stock of the company from which they draw their monthly pay check.

*Stock options.* In one situation, however, opportunity for stock purchases may be very helpful. A company badly in need of new top management may be unable to pay high enough salaries to attract the kind of new leadership that is needed, and a liberal arrangement to buy stock may be the most practical alternative. Usually the new executives are given an option to buy a stipulated amount of stock at a fixed price. They will not exercise this option, of course, unless the value of the stock rises above the price they have to pay. But if they succeed in making marked improvements in company earnings, they stand to profit handsomely.

The arrangement is attractive to stockholders because the company gets new management without incurring high overhead, and any reduction of the share of total dividends going to old stockholders will be more than offset by the larger dividends that can be paid. The use of stock options, however, is obviously suited only to special circumstances and should not be regarded as a common basis of executive compensation.

*Pension plans.* High personal income taxes have become a significant factor in the compensation of executives in the top echelons. Some of the large corporations have explained substantial salary increases for their top executives by pointing out the relatively small portion of the increase that the executives were able to keep for their own use.

Probably a more significant result of high income taxes is the interest of the executives in pension plans, which have the effect of spreading income over a larger number of years and, consequently, of reducing the average tax rate. The Internal Revenue Service is, of course, suspicious of any plans that look like deliberate attempts to evade taxes, and insists that any recognized plan cover a substantial number of the employees. The Service also watches closely any bonus plan that pays money not directly to the officers but into a pension fund.

These are only some of the ways executive compensation may be adapted to the tax structure. The issue is quite intricate, and any company giving its executives an annual compensation of over $25,000 each should obtain specialized and technical advice on how tax regulations affect its particular situation.

*Conclusion regarding compensation.* This discussion of executive compensation should not be interpreted to mean that financial remuneration is the only incentive for executive effort. As will be pointed out in the discussion of motivation, a variety of nonfinancial incentives may influence behavior to a greater extent than financial reward. Especially after an executive reaches a high income tax bracket do nonfinancial factors increase in relative influence. Nevertheless, in modern society financial remuneration is essential. Poorly handled, it can cause poor morale, internal bickering, and a failure to attract and retain competent executives. Properly handled, it can contribute to a feeling of fair treatment and security that nurtures the constructive effort of the executives, and within limits it can serve as a positive incentive to more effective effort.

## ORGANIZATION FOR EXECUTIVE PERSONNEL PROGRAM

*Key role of supervising executives.* Primary responsibility for executive personnel must rest with the line executive supervising the man concerned. Time and again in the discussion of company needs, selection, development, and compensation, the vital significance of the supervisor has been emphasized. Consequently, responsibility for executive personnel starts with the top executive and extends throughout the administrative pyramid. Developing subordinates should be regarded as one of the inherent duties in every executive post.

*Staff assistance.* This basic responsibility should be supplemented with a staff man or agency. A variety of technical questions arise in connection with selection, appraisal, development, and compensation upon which expert advice can be very helpful. Moreover, coordinated action is needed in connection with the analysis of company needs, preparation of promotion tables, planning job rotation, deciding on company-sponsored development programs, building a salary structure, and similar matters. Finally, the proper handling of executive personnel is so crucial to effective operations that the chief executive may want someone to follow this matter closely, suggest and stimulate action where it is needed, and report from time to time on current progress and efficiency. It would be a grave error to assume that a staff unit charged with these duties relieves the line executives of their basic responsibility, but we can hope that the staff unit will be of considerable assistance on executive personnel matters.

The staff work just described should be headed up by someone who is considered a part of the top-management group of the enterprise. The numerous decisions affecting the personal welfare of a large number of executives cannot be delegated to someone who is out of touch with the needs, the successes and failures, and the feelings of the key officials. In a small company with only fifteen or twenty executives involved, this staff work will probably be a part-time assignment of one of the senior officials who has the interest, ability, and objectivity required. In large companies it can well be a full-time assignment in itself, or combined with some closely related staff duties, such as organization planning.

The company personnel officer may be asked to perform the executive personnel staff work, but this is not always desirable. The personnel officer may be too busy with problems of rank-and-file workers; he may not be of the necessary stature in company operations; he may be primarily concerned with collective bargaining, and not qualified for executive personnel work. In other instances the personnel officer is ideally suited for the assignment. Because of the nature of the duties, this is one of those assignments that should be made primarily on the basis of personality, rather than organization logic.

*Executive personnel committee.* A third desirable feature is an executive personnel committee. The intangible nature of the problem and the importance of the decisions make group judgment desirable on executive personnel matters. Usually the committee should be small and include, in addition to the top staff man on executive personnel, one or two other men whose fairness, wide knowledge of the company activities, and human understanding make them highly respected by all executives in the enterprise.

Duties of this committee should probably include review of promotion schedules and rotation plans, of final selections to fill vacancies, and of proposed salary changes. The authority of the committee must be adjusted to the circumstances. For example, the committee approval of recommendations received from operating people regarding junior executives might be final, whereas for senior executives the committee's views might be considered recommendations to the chief executive, or perhaps to the board of directors.

## Summary: Executive Personnel

The selection, development, and compensation of key subordinates is an omnipresent and crucial duty of every executive. He will also have to spend some time on assembling other resources, but none poses as universal a problem as obtaining good executives.

Determining the number and qualities of executives needed and selecting men for these positions were discussed in the preceding chapter. The dynamic aspect of an executive personnel program comes in the third phase, executive development. Men grow in perspective and understanding, and they develop distinctive skills. A company can aid in this development by stressing the value and techniques of learning on-the-job, by rotating men through a succession of jobs that will provide training for future responsibilities, by wise use of committees and conferences, and by assisting in the personal adjustments of each individual. This is a continuing activity that should be an integral part of current operations.

The program should also give attention to the ticklish question of executive compensation. Generally, this can be handled best by setting up a sound salary structure and by wise use of bonuses and other forms of supplementary pay. The plan must be equitable and at the same time flexible enough to fit the highly individualistic nature of a cadre of executives.

### SELECTED REFERENCES FOR CHAPTERS 19 AND 20

Bellows, R. M., T. Q. Gilson, and G. S. Odiorne, *Executive Skills: Their Dynamics and Development*, Prentice-Hall, Inc., 1962.

Dooher, M. J. and E. Marting, eds., *Selection of Management Personnel*, American Management Association, 1957.

Houston, G. C., *Manager Development*, Richard D. Irwin, Inc., 1961.

Merrill, H. F. and E. Marting, eds., *Developing Executive Skills*, American Management Association, 1958.

Patton, A., *Men, Money and Motivation*, McGraw-Hill Book Co., Inc., 1961.

Warner, W. L. and J. Abegglin, *Big Business Leaders in America*, Harper & Row, Publishers, 1955.

# IV

# Supervising

# 21

# Direction

With plans drawn up, the organization designed, positions filled by competent people, and other resources at hand, the enterprise is ready to go. Directions are now needed to start the action. This process of *direction* is concerned with the way an executive issues instructions to his subordinates and otherwise indicates what should be done.

Direction is an essential step in administration; without it virtually nothing would happen. After all, the people in the lowest level of the administrative hierarchy carry the real burden of actual performance, and, aside from nondelegated duties, the only excuse for having executives is their influence over the behavior of the doers. The direction process is such an elementary part of administration that it is likely to be taken for granted. Men who have held supervisory positions for several years simply assume that anybody can give instructions and that they have nothing to learn about the process. As H. A. Simon has observed:

371

No step in the administrative process is more generally ignored, more
poorly performed, than the task of communicating decisions. All too often,
plans are "ordered" into effect without any consideration of the manner
in which they can be brought to influence the behavior of the individual
members of the group.[1]

As with other phases of administration, there are better ways and
poorer ways of giving directions; and since planning becomes effective only through this step, it clearly warrants careful attention.

Direction is a part of supervision. *Supervision* refers to the day-to-
day relationship between an executive and his immediate assistant;
and it is commonly used to cover the training, direction, motivation, coordination, maintenance of discipline, and minor adjustment
of plans to meet immediate situations that take place in the executive-subordinate relationship.

These various parts of supervision are, of course, closely interrelated, and a discussion of any one part, such as direction, inevitably touches upon some of the other phases. For example,
training and direction are almost inseparable, and the manner of
directing is closely associated with problems of motivation. Since
motivation is considered in the next chapter and the training of
executives has already been discussed, attention in this chapter will
be focused on the following points:

1. Characteristics of a good instruction
2. Follow through or countermand of an instruction
3. Standard practice and indoctrination
4. Explanations
5. Consultative direction

### Characteristics of a good instruction

Every instruction should have certain characteristics. As a minimum, an instruction should be reasonable, complete, and clear;
often it should also be in writing. Unfortunately, meeting these
standards is not quite so simple as it sounds.

*Compliance should be reasonable.* Asking a man to do something
he considers unreasonable has a bad effect on morale. The reaction
of the man upon receiving such instruction is likely to be, "Who's
he think I am anyway? Superman?" Moreover, the unreasonable
request undermines control, inasmuch as it is not practical to hold
the subordinate responsible for its fulfillment. In thinking about

[1] *Administrative Behavior,* The Macmillan Company, 1957, p. 108.

whether an instruction is reasonable, an executive should consider whether the man who will receive it has the necessary experience and ability to perform it satisfactorily. Also, he should consider whether materials, equipment, external conditions, company rules, and other aspects of a total operating situation will permit the man to comply if he uses a reasonable amount of effort and ability.

*The instruction should be complete.* Merely to say to the controller, "Set up a cost accounting system for the branch offices" is certainly vague. Not even the purposes of the system and the use to which it will be put are indicated. A complete order should leave no question in the mind of the man receiving it as to what is to be done. The quality and quantity of performance that will be considered satisfactory should also be understood. If the man is not given a free rein to carry out the assignment, then the method also should be specified. And, the time factor should be indicated; to request an analysis of shipping expense within two hours is quite a different order from requesting an analysis that may extend over two weeks or two months. The quality and quantity standards combined with the time allowed for performance will, of course, have a marked effect upon whether compliance is reasonable.

*The instruction should be clear.* The important thing is that it should be clear *to the person receiving the order.* Too often the executive giving an instruction thinks the order is clear because he has a definite picture in his own mind as to what is to be done. This is not enough. He should try to place himself in the position of the subordinate and then consider what the subordinate needs to be told. Also, the language used should be readily understood by the subordinate. This matter of clarity is particularly important in written instructions to branch offices where subordinates do not have opportunity to ask questions as to the meaning, and the executive is not in a position to observe frequently how the order is being carried out.

*Written instructions.* In theory, then, if not in practice, orders should be reasonable, complete, and clear. The matter of putting instructions in writing is a more debatable point. Those who advocate the use of written plans will point to a number of benefits. The planning itself is often improved because the very process of writing instructions forces the executive to think things through more carefully and be more specific. Written instructions can improve communication partly because those who receive them have time to study the content of the order. Also, they assure that uniform directions will be received by all the people directly affected, inasmuch as duplicate copies can easily be distributed.

These improvements in communication are particularly important when training new personnel or when issuing complex instructions that are hard to grasp from a single oral statement. Perhaps most important, written instructions provide a more reliable memory than the human brain. If it is down in black and white, there need be no debate what the boss said to Jim two weeks ago. Written procedures and manuals provide sustained instructions even to the old hands who may wish a reference guide for exceptional problems and a reminder of standard methods.

This improvement in planning, communication, and memory is not all net gain. The preparation of written instructions involves expense, particularly the time of key men who must at least participate in the preparation. Also, expressing standing plans in writing adds an element of inflexibility. Even minor changes require the sometimes painful process of formal revision, and the tendency is either to continue to use instructions when they have been outmoded or to disregard them, both of which are undesirable. And finally, the quantity of written material an individual will actually read and use approaches a limit. If an executive writes only occasional two- or three-paragraph memoranda, they will probably carry considerable weight; whereas if two or three pages of detailed instructions come to the subordinates twice a week, these are likely to receive only a scanning and be filed away in a bulging file of instructions for emergency use only.

These pros and cons on the desirability of putting instructions in writing suggest that this may be desirable when (1) several individuals are subject to or directly affected by the instructions, (2) execution of the instruction will extend over a considerate period of time, (3) the instructions are so complex and detailed that an individual cannot carry them all in his mind, or (4) the matter is of such importance that special steps to avoid the possibility of misunderstanding are needed. Chances are that one or some combination of these conditions will be present so that any executive giving directions should ask himself the question, "Should this instruction be in writing?" A practical procedure in many situations is to put the main features of the instruction in writing, but to cover the background and the interpretation orally.

**Always follow up an instruction**

Another well-recognized principle of direction is that once orders are issued, they should be followed up to see that they are executed, or the instructions should be countermanded.

*Effect of indifferent follow-up.* If an executive gives directions and then permits subordinates to decide if and when they will carry them out, the entire administration becomes lax. Time schedules lose their significance, additional inspections are necessary to discover what has and has not taken place, and the success of a subordinate depends in no small part upon his ability to guess when to take the boss seriously.

Disregard for instructions and even laws can become a common practice. For example, a surprising laxness of enforcement is reflected in the following notice that was posted one winter by a New York bus company:

> *A Request*
>
> Smoking on Buses not only is Unlawful,
> it is objectionable to many riders
> who do not smoke on buses.
> Now, during the winter season when
> windows are closed, and out of consideration
> for others, we especially request the
> cooperation of all patrons in observing
> the "No Smoking" law.

Carelessness in following up instructions is sure to result in inefficiency.

*Instructions that were not forgotten.* Mr. R. K. Davies followed a procedure while he was operating head of the Petroleum Administration for War that made an indelible impression upon those who operated under him. On each communication he sent to his subordinates, he attached a little green slip, carrying a notation such as, "Please prepare reply," "Please take care of and report action on," or some similar instruction, plus a due date. Even oral instructions were usually confirmed by a brief note and the omnipresent little green slip with its due date. Mr. Davies' assistant then maintained a tickler file with a record of each of these instructions.

As sure as the sun rose on the day a reply was due, a call would come from Mr. Davies' office if the matter had not already been attended to. An extension of time might be obtained for good reasons, but the matter was never forgotten. The result was that these instructions got worked on in the evening instead of being placed in a desk drawer; the tempo of work in the entire agency was speeded up. The green slips and tickler file were, of course, merely mechanisms that happened to fit in this situation. The general principle, however, can be used by any executive from the president to the first-line supervisor.

*Careful direction required.* Insistence on execution of instructions carries with it some burdens on the executive. He must be very careful about the instructions issued. If he asks that a particular task be performed with unnecessary speed, it may not be done as well as it might otherwise be, or expenses may be increased through extra overtime or interruption of other work already in progress. For similar reasons he must be careful to distinguish between results that will be satisfactory and those that are desirable but should not be considered as essential.

Moreover, the executive must be prepared to countermand instructions when their fulfillment is no longer necessary. This sounds simple, but for some executives it is embarrassing and apparently involves some loss of face; so the temptation is to let the instructions remain in force, without insisting on their execution. Actually, the respect for the executive who is cautious about the orders he permits to remain extant, and then maintains a firm surveillance to see that they are carried out, is usually much greater than the respect for an executive who never admits making mistakes even though the facts in the situation indicate the contrary.

### Standard practice and indoctrination

*Standard practice simplifies instruction.* The purchasing agent of a textile mill interrupted a conference with a salesman long enough to ring for his secretary, and when she appeared at the door, he held up two fingers. In a few minutes the secretary reappeared with two glasses of ice-cold Coca-Cola. Except for a thank you at the end, not a word was spoken, and yet an instruction had been given and promptly carried out. The explanation lies, of course, in the standard practices that had previously been set up. The meaning of the sign, the place to get the Coca-Cola, an envelope containing petty cash to pay for it, and the way it was to be served, all had become an established pattern. The instruction necessary to initiate action had been reduced to a minimum.

The use of standing operating procedures and of customary ways of doing things is a very important part of direction. For example, a naval commander can issue a terse order that may move an entire navy across an ocean, primarily because volumes of standing operating procedure have been issued and practiced many months and even years before. Standard practice greatly simplifies the instructions that are necessary to tell the accountant to prepare a monthly balance sheet, the branch manager to add two new salesmen, the credit manager to investigate the financial standing of a potential customer, and in like manner a large number of operations in any enterprise.

Without these customary ways of doing things, the executive issuing the instruction would at least have to specify in considerably more detail the quality of performance he desires; and, except in highly decentralized operations, he would also have to deal with how the work was to be done.

Reliance upon standard practice does not modify the characteristics of a good order. The order must still be complete, in the sense that the person receiving it should understand what is wanted, the quality and quantity standards expected, and the method to be followed. To the extent that these have already been covered by standard-practice instructions or customary behavior they need not be repeated. If, however, the executive wishes any deviation from the customary behavior, obviously he must include this in his instructions.

In actual operations, a large part of inadequate direction can be traced to misunderstandings about standard practice. The executive sometimes assumes a pattern of behavior quite different from that which the subordinates consider to be proper. This can lead to serious results, particularly when the executive does not make frequent observations of how the work is progressing. Primary responsibility for avoiding this kind of trouble must rest with the executive, for his job is to issue instructions that are reasonable, complete, and clear. He should know how his subordinates will interpret a given set of instructions. If there is doubt, he should either make the individual instruction more explicit or give his subordinates further training in what he regards as standard methods.

*Indoctrination.* Another aspect of direction, related to the use of standard practice, is that of indoctrination. In this connection indoctrination means instilling in subordinates a set of beliefs and attitudes so that the men will look upon an operating situation in a desired way.

The significance of indoctrination in the process of direction is illustrated by the experience of a large company that had just signed its first agreement with a companywide union. For many years this company had paid high wages, but expected in return unquestioned loyalty to the company. The management had taken the position that the unions magnified and even created friction between workers and their supervisors and tried to get the workers to look to the union, rather than to company management, for aid in overcoming their personal troubles. Consistent with this attitude, management had done everything it could to discredit the union.

Then, with changes in legislation and public attitude toward unions, the majority of the company employees joined a union, and the management had to engage in collective bargaining. Top executives of the company felt they should make the best of the situation and work closely with the union. Accordingly, procedures for the handling of grievances and other matters were prepared.

In spite of announced policy of cooperation with the union and the various procedures implementing that policy, friction continued between the union and many foremen and superintendents. The company found that no amount of formal instruction could cover the many relationships with the union, and that many of the "old guard" supervisors, who continued to have a belligerent attitude toward the union, rarely missed an opportunity "to put the union boys in their place." Only as the company has been successful in changing this attitude and in indoctrinating the executives with a belief that union-company relationships should be conducted on a harmonious basis has this friction been removed.

The way department stores treat customers provides quite a different illustration of the significance of indoctrination. Almost all stores give lip service to the slogan, "The customer is always right." In actual practice this may mean (1) if the customer can prove the store made an error, the salesperson should gracefully make an adjustment; (2) if it is not clear just what happened, the customer should be given the benefit of the doubt; or (3) even though there is good reason to believe the customer is taking unfair advantage of some store service, such as the exchange of merchandise, the service should be rendered rather than antagonize the customer. The instructions given salespeople can indicate to some extent the store view of this matter, but here again the interpretation of the instructions, and the spirit in which they are executed, depend upon the beliefs and attitudes of the salespeople themselves. They must be indoctrinated with the traditions of the store if they are to carry out the instructions as desired.

Indoctrination, then, is more general and usually more pervasive than standard-practice instruction. Often it is not clearly defined, and an employee has to absorb the feel, or the philosophy, with which activities are conducted. Indefinite though these attitudes may be, they do make a marked difference in the way instructions are understood and carried out. The wise executive will deliberately try to create a set of attitudes among his subordinates that will lead them to performance of activities in the manner he desires. Indoctrination is a significant supplement to formal instruction, and it is even more important when authority has been decentralized to a high degree.

*Relation to training.* Both standard practices and indoctrinated attitudes should be developed through training. Of course, subordinates will develop customary patterns of behavior, or habits, and will possess certain attitudes and beliefs even though the executive takes no initiative in the matter. In view of their importance to effective direction, however, an executive should try to mold these habits and attitudes so that they will be useful to him.

Careful and advanced development of standing plans will make the training job easier, and the better the training is done the simpler will be the process of direction. Instilling beliefs and attitudes is a more elusive process, and is probably done more by setting an example, sharing experiences, and appealing to emotions than it is by written pronouncements and logical arguments. Whatever the techniques employed, such training is a preliminary and significant part of giving directions.

### Explaining why

Generally, when issuing instructions one should explain why the order is being given. Instructions always leave more or less of the detailed planning to the person receiving them, and often unanticipated conditions arise that call for interpretation of the instructions. The person understanding why the order was originally given is in a much better position to adapt his actions and interpretations to the over-all purpose.

For instance, the accountant who is asked to compute sales commissions for the first six months will have some basis for deciding what to do with adjusting entries if he knows the use to which the final figure will be put. Explaining why also contributes to morale, because the person sees the relation of what he is doing to the wider activity, and has a little more sense of personal importance.

> It is recorded of Napoleon, the most autocratic of men, that he never gave an order without explaining its purpose, and making sure that this purpose was understood. He knew that blind obedience could never ensure the intelligent execution of any order. Marshal Foch, in his *Principles of War,* makes the same point in his distinction between *passive* and *active* obedience. "Command," he says, "never yet meant obscurity." Active obedience implies initiative, and intelligence in the exercise of this initiative requires a knowledge of how the specific objective fits into the general plan.[2]

Care must be taken that the explanation does not result in confusion of the instructions actually issued. One employee was heard to remark after he emerged from a lengthy session with his chief, who had gone to great pains in explaining the total over-all problem they were working on: "It sounds awfully important, but I'm not sure just what he wants me to do. There was no need of all that talk if he only wants a little information from two suppliers."

The desirability of explaining why an order is issued will depend primarily upon: (1) the extent to which the subordinate must exercise his own initiative and judgment in carrying out the instruction; (2) the capacity of the subordinate to comprehend the total situation; (3) the importance of training the subordinate; (4) the time available for discussion when the order is issued; (5) the likelihood that the instruction will be unpopular with the subordinate; and (6) the extent to which the subordinate already understands the reasons as a result of his previous training.

[2] J. D. Mooney, *Principles of Organization* (rev. ed.), Harper & Brothers, 1947, p. 131.

## Consultative direction

*The principle involved.* Consultative direction carries the idea of explaining why an instruction is issued one major step further. Before an order is issued, the people responsible for executing it are consulted about its workability and better ways of accomplishing the same results.

If several subordinates are affected by a single instruction, they will typically meet together with the executive to discuss the most practical course to follow; if only one subordinate is involved, then there need be a meeting only between that man and the executive. To be effective the executive must not so dominate the situation that his request for suggestions is merely perfunctory. Instead, he must share with those being consulted information regarding the total situation, and suggestions advanced should receive objective consideration even though they differ from what the executive had in mind at the beginning of the discussion.

The manager of a sales branch who uses consultative direction will not merely call his salesmen together and tell them of a new product that is to be added to the company line, explain what they are to do in helping to promote it, and perhaps close by giving the salesmen an opportunity to ask questions. Rather, he will tell the men all he knows about the new product and the advertising and other sales promotion that is to be undertaken by the headquarters office, and then ask for suggestions on how the product can be introduced in their districts so as to get the greatest volume of orders without seriously undercutting the sales of the existing line.

No doubt some of the ideas suggested by the salesmen will be rejected by the men themselves, others may be impractical for reasons that the manager can explain, and still others will be similar to ideas the manager himself had already considered. Psychologically it is desirable to treat the latter suggestions as originating with the men, rather than to say, "I've already thought of that." Of course, the manager may introduce ideas into the discussion, provided they are subjected to the same critical review that is given other suggestions. Out of this discussion, perhaps extending over several meetings between which additional facts can be assembled, will come a program for promoting the new product that is different and better than any one of the men, including the executive, would have thought of by himself.

Consultative direction modifies the autocratic character of centralized planning. Instead of an instruction being regarded as the personal whim of an executive, it becomes what Mary Parker Follett has called "the law of the situation." This difference can be illustrated by the way instruction was given in a controller's office just after they learned that a special report would have to be finished two days ahead of schedule. The report was to be sent to the board of directors in advance of its next meeting, and a change in the date of the meeting led the president to ask that the report be finished up early. The controller might have said to the men working on the report: "Sorry, boys, call up your wives and tell them you won't be home for dinner tonight. We all have to stay late so that that report can be finished up by tomorrow afternoon." The typical reaction to such an instruction would have been some grousing about the need for planning, the timing of the announcement, broken dinner dates, and so forth.

Instead, the controller called the men concerned into his office and told them of the change in the date of the directors' meeting. He pointed out that if the report was to serve any useful purpose it would have to be completed earlier, and then asked each man to tell how far along he was and what would be necessary to complete his part by the next afternoon. Before the discussion was over, it was perfectly clear that some, though not all, of the men would have to work late that night. It was the situation, however, that dictated this late work, and not the cantankerous notion of an individual. Such depersonalizing of instructions can be secured to some extent without consultative direction, but it is particularly effective when the people themselves participate in the preparation of the instruction.

*Benefits of consultative direction.* The participation provided by consultative direction leads to greater *cooperation and enthusiasm* for one's work. Studies of human behavior show over and over again that active participation in the preparation of plans and a feeling of having contributed to those plans significantly increases the energy that is put into their execution; a man will work a lot harder for an idea if he has some feeling of authorship.

Consultative direction *improves the plans* that are finally adopted; at a minimum, the plans are likely to be more workable because those who have to put them in effect have had a chance to point out practical difficulties and suggest alterations. Not infrequently a creative or basic suggestion will be made that will make a program much more efficient or effective.

More harmonious personal relationships between an executive and his subordinates usually result. *Bossing is minimized,* and the executive becomes more a coordinator of ideas.

*Personal development* is encouraged. Subordinates have an opportunity to think beyond their immediate job, to test out new ideas, to secure a sense of creative workmanship. This type of supervision, of course, fits in neatly with the techniques of executive development discussed in the preceding chapter.

Finally, the subordinates will have a full understanding of why a plan is adopted, and they will appreciate how the various steps are expected to fit together to accomplish a given purpose. This greatly *simplifies* the task of issuing and interpreting *instructions.*

*Dangers connected with consultative direction.* If consultative direction is to be used as an administrative tool, the executive should recognize that some risks are involved. Fortunately, these dangers can be avoided or minimized, provided the executive operates with care.

The possibility is ever-present that the *instructions* issued under consultative direction will *not be complete and clear.* All too often some extended discussion of an operating problem breaks up when one member of the group has to meet another engagement, and no clear-cut agreement as to the action to be taken has been reached. In other instances the discussion may lead the executive to see a number of steps that need to be taken, but these are never stated in a succinct fashion. The discussion of a problem leads some executives to assume that complete instructions and follow-up are unnecessary.

What should be done is this: someone, usually the executive, should summarize the plan agreed upon. This then becomes the order from the executive. Like any other order, some or all of it should be reduced to writing if a large number of people are affected, if execution will extend over a long period of time, if it deals with a highly important operation, or if it is detailed and complicated. The risk is that after a full discussion this crispness of instruction will be lacking.

A second danger is that *insubordination may develop.* Some individuals think that the privilege of participating in the drawing up of a plan gives them license to change it later. Particularly if a man suggested the idea in the first place and then discovers that a small modification will work better, he is likely to feel free to make this change without consulting his superior.

Another source of insubordination is the feeling that being consulted has become a right and that instructions need not be carried out unless a prior opportunity to discuss them is afforded. The employee may take an attitude that, "The boss didn't ask me for my ideas, so I don't see why I should follow his." To avoid this, subordinates must understand clearly that conditions do arise that make consultation impractical and that the executive may, at his own discretion, issue instructions that have the full weight of administrative authority behind them.

A third danger is that consultative direction may become a fetish and be used for little things or in situations when the *time and expense* of consultation are definitely greater than any benefit that may be expected. The factors to be considered in deciding when to use consultative direction are like those for explaining the why of an instruction: extent of delegation, capacity of subordinates, importance of training subordinates, time available, importance, and popularity of the subject.

Consultative direction, like many good things, should be used with a sense of moderation and appropriateness.

### Summary

Direction is that vital step between preparation and actual operation; it is the issuing of instructions and otherwise indicating to subordinates what should be done.

Every instruction should possess three basic features: (1) compliance should be reasonable; (2) the instruction should be complete as to what is to be done, and when; and (3) it should be clear to the person receiving it. Moreover, at least the main points of an instruction should be written when several individuals are involved, execution extends over a long period of time, the subject matter is complex and detailed, or action of major importance is involved. Once an instruction is issued, care should be taken to see that it is carried out, or it should be countermanded.

The process of direction can be greatly simplified by establishing standard practices, for then an instruction need cover only new parts of the plan, such as when or how much. Indoctrination also contributes to clear understanding of instructions and is especially significant if authority has been decentralized. Consequently, direction should start with the development of desirable work habits and attitudes.

Explaining why an instruction is being issued is generally desirable. This leads to better understanding and contributes to morale. Consultative direction goes even further and lets the subordinate participate in the planning and formulation of the instruction itself. Such consultation usually improves cooperation, aids in planning, minimizes bossing, and helps in executive development. However, if consultative direction is used, care must be taken that it does not result in fuzzy directions or insubordination. Neither explanations of "why" nor consultative direction should be carried to the extreme; they involve time and expense, and on minor matters or when subordinates lack interest, this more elaborate direction is unwarranted.

### SELECTED REFERENCES

Dimock, M. E., A *Philosophy of Administration*, Harper & Row, Publishers, 1958, Chap. 12.

Haimann, T., *Professional Management*, Houghton Mifflin Company, 1962, Part V.

Marx, F. M. and W. S. Sayre, "Morale and Discipline," in F. M. Marx, ed., *Elements of Public Administration*, Prentice-Hall, Inc., 1959.

Pfiffner, J. M., *Supervision of Personnel* (2nd ed.), Prentice-Hall, Inc., 1958.

Strauss, G. and L. R. Sayles, *Personnel: The Human Problems of Management*, Prentice-Hall, Inc., 1960, Parts II and III.

# 22
# Motivation

## Role of motivation

All administrative action is of no avail unless members of the enterprise are willing to contribute effort toward the fulfillment of their assigned tasks. Somehow, some way, each individual must desire to execute his duties effectively. The role of motivation is to intensify this desire.

The issuance of directions, however well conceived and phrased, does not mean that they will be followed. We have already noted in the discussion of authority that employees have a zone of acceptance. Instructions falling within this zone will be carried out; those outside will be disregarded or sabotaged. Fortunately, through the appropriate use of motivation, this zone of acceptance may be enlarged.

Even more important in day-to-day operations is the *degree of acceptance*. There is a marked variation between the results of grudging acquiescence and enthusiastic, intelligent cooperation. Effective motivation succeeds not only in having an order accepted, but in gaining a determination to see that it is fulfilled efficiently and well.

An administrator needs keen appreciation of human behavior if he is to provide the maximum motivation among his associates. Helpful for this purpose are recent concepts developed by behavioral scientists. We learn from them (1) a general frame of reference about behavior, and (2) guides to more specific incentives that an executive can use to induce desired performance.

## DETERMINANTS OF BEHAVIOR

**Individual response to the total environment**

An individual takes an action when the satisfactions he derives from doing so outweigh the discomforts and sacrifices that are involved. This does not necessarily mean that people behave in a rational manner based on logical analysis; far from it. Motives that are strong today may be weak tomorrow. Habits and inertia play a large part. Expectations and fears may be ungrounded. One or two factors are likely to influence the decision, rather than a careful appraisal of all that is involved. Nevertheless, to the individual the tugs and pulls are real, and he responds to them.

A consulting firm specializing in salesmanship has frequently been employed by large companies to give their executives training in human relations. At first thought this sounds like a superficial approach to a fundamental problem. But closer investigation shows that the technique proposed rests on sound ground. An executive is told to think about the reaction of the people who are to receive an instruction from him, and to separate those reactions that will make the subordinate want to follow the instructions from those which will deter him. These are called plus and minus factors. Then, when giving the instruction, the executive is expected to emphasize the plus factors, and if he cannot actually remove the minus factors, he should at least have thought of a way to respond if some one mentions them.

This particular procedure is, of course, merely good salesmanship, but it also happens to be useful in the supervisor-subordinate relationship because it leads the executive to take the point of view of his subordinate and to try to appreciate the diverse pulls that will determine that man's behavior. Fundamentally, it is similar to the approach of the social psychologist, stripped of its sophisticated language. The technique still leaves unanswered, of course, just what the reactions will be (a supervisor close to his men may be in a better position to forecast this than a dozen social scientists), and it smacks too much of a top-down approach. Nevertheless, it illustrates that the analytical approach to motivation can be stated simply and put to practical use.

The task of management, then, is to create a situation in which the actions that the employees choose because of the net personal satisfactions they will derive therefrom, are also actions that produce desirable results for the enterprise as a whole.

### Factors guiding individual reactions

*Individual needs and characteristics.* The way an individual will react to particular instructions and measures intended to motivate him is often hard to predict and even more difficult to explain. Human attitudes and behavior are very complex and as yet inadequately understood, even by the scientists who devote their lifetime to studying them.

The reactions of a person are determined in part by his individual needs and characteristics. His biological needs for such things as food and shelter influence his reactions, but the income of most workers carries them far beyond the minimum requirements of this sort into desire for safety, sociability, and self-actualization.

Two general points are significant when we think of needs of individuals. (1) As our hopes and expectations with respect to a particular need come closer and closer to being fulfilled, the need becomes less of a driving force. The *marginal* value of, say, more food or air tends to go down as we get more of it. In fact, a satisfied need is not a motivator of behavior [1] (although fear of being deprived of such satisfaction may cause strong protective action). (2) Most individuals have a hierarchy of needs, and as one need is more or less satisfied, another rises in importance. Man is never fully satisfied; he generates new wants, or raises his expectations regarding old wants, as fast as previous desires are met. This restlessness is indeed fortunate from a managerial viewpoint, because the desire for more satisfaction of some sort is the source of individual motivation.

The aspirations of specific individuals will be set partly by social custom and attitude; they will also be influenced by a person's emotional and temperamental make-up. In the present discussion it matters little whether these psychological reactions are based upon physical strength, health, or glandular balance. It is important to recognize that man does not live by bread alone and that there are significant differences among individuals in their emotional make-up.

[1] See D. McGregor, *The Human Side of Enterprise*, McGraw-Hill Book Company, 1960, pp. 36 ff.

*Patterns of belief.* Individual behavior is also conditioned by the beliefs of the person.

> . . . Man acts in terms of what he perceives, and what he perceives must pass not only through his eyes, ears and other special senses to reach his consciousness, but also through the dark and irridescent waters of his belief.[2]

These beliefs will exist for every field the individual comprehends. For example, they may include ideas such as the following: committees are good; people who don't speak English are dumb; rattlesnake meat is poisonous; adding machines are always right; breaking a mirror will bring bad luck; God is a loving and omniscient person; one's fellow worker is generally trustworthy; Wall Street tycoons fleece the poor man; the white race is superior; monopolies are evil; and innumerable other accepted ideas.

These beliefs may be right, partly right, or dead wrong. They range from deeply ingrained convictions to notions readily abandoned. Some are based on personal experience while many others are picked up from parents, playmates, movies, business associates, and other persons. An executive should realize that any instruction of his will be interpreted in terms of these beliefs and that his attempt at motivation will be made easier or harder because of them.

*Social organization.* The beliefs and reactions of an individual are strongly influenced by the social organizations of which he is a part. These informal groups will always be found when men are associated together. They are formed spontaneously around a neighborhood, church, classroom, work place, interest in baseball, former experience in military service, or other unifying factor that provides a common interest and sense of belonging together. A single individual often belongs to several such groups, although there may be considerable overlapping, especially in a small community.

Many attitudes and beliefs will be acquired from these informal groups. In fact, considerable social pressure is exerted upon the individual to conform to group norms. This is clearly evident in the reception a new method is likely to receive from a group of plant employees. When the proposed change threatens to upset the existing group relationship, and particularly if the effects of the change are unknown, there is likely to be strong group resistance

[2] A. H. Leighton, *The Governing of Men,* Princeton University Press, 1946, p. 288.

against it, and each individual is under pressure to join in the group reaction. Continuance as an acceptable member of the group is often more important than holding the job itself, and consequently the individual tends to accept the ideas of the group.

*Summarizing:* Motivation should be undertaken with a full appreciation of these influences on behavior. Individual needs and characteristics, patterns of belief, and informal social organization guide the way an individual reacts to a request or suggestion. We must understand them, for they determine what shall be plus factors and minus factors in a given situation.

PRIMARY INCENTIVES

The administrator's job of motivation has been described as that of creating a situation in which actions that provide net satisfaction to individual members of the enterprise are at the same time actions that make appropriate contributions toward the objectives of the enterprise. The brief comments on what influences employees' attitudes, and hence what gives them satisfaction or dissatisfaction, indicate the nature of the motivation problem, but provide little positive guidance to the executive who faces a practical problem of trying to get people to carry out a set of plans. He wants to know whether out of all this study of systems of beliefs, individual needs, and social organization, he can do anything to increase individual satisfaction or reduce dissatisfaction. He wants a utilitarian and pragmatic twist to the findings of the psychologist and the sociologist.

Principles of motivation are difficult to establish because human behavior is extremely complex and not easily understood; individual differences in human beings are substantial; and people are continuously learning and changing. Not surprising, then, is that the experimental data provide no clear-cut guides for executive behavior.

Nevertheless, agreement is widespread on a number of factors to which most men respond. The relative importance of these factors will vary with the individual and the particular situation, but they carry weight often enough to warrant serious consideration by every administrator. He will usually get his plans carried out more effectively to the extent he can provide:

1. Higher financial income
2. Social status and respect
3. Security
4. Attractive work
5. Opportunity for development
6. Worth-while activity
7. Personal power and influence
8. Treatment of each subordinate as an individual person
9. Voice in his own affairs for each man
10. Just and diligent supervision

### Higher financial income

Several studies of human motivation have shown that the use of financial income as an incentive has been overrated; other considerations may be more important in some circumstances. It does not follow that financial income is unimportant. For the vast majority of people the possibility of higher financial income is a spur (though not the only one) to cooperation and effort.

Some jobs can tie financial income directly to one or more aspects of the results achieved. Sales commissions and piece rates are among the most common examples of this arrangement. Direct financial incentives, however, are generally useful only when the results reflect the man's own efforts rather than extraneous factors, and when results not included in the incentive can be prevented from deteriorating. Another arrangement is the granting of bonuses on the basis of personal appraisal, rather than according to an automatic standard. Aside from those paid to top executives, such bonuses are usually a relatively small part of the total compensation.

By far the most common financial incentive is the possibility of a permanent increase in pay while remaining in the same position, or an increase in pay that accompanies promotion. This type of incentive fits in with the United States tradition that each person has the opportunity to advance to positions of ever-increasing responsibility and compensation. It has been and should continue to be used as a motivating force.

The threat of lower financial income can also be used as an incentive in a limited way. Disciplinary layoffs, demotions, or discharges occasionally have to be used for employees whose conduct is unsatisfactory. Modern personnel practice and union pressure both frown upon use of these devices, except as a last resort for an irresponsible employee. They should be resorted to only for the violation of a well-recognized and important rule, or after there have been at least two warnings and conscientious effort to help correct unsatisfactory performance.

Even when used in this restricted manner, however, the possibility of reduced income does serve as incentive to a large number of employees who might be more lackadaisical if the *possibility* of such action did not exist. Witness the deterioration in effort that sometimes occurs among Civil Service employees, where efforts to avoid the political spoils system have almost eliminated the possibility of disciplinary layoffs or discharges. The possibility of layoff, demotion, or discharge, of course, becomes much more realistic when a company is cutting back on the number of its employees or when such cuts are not governed by seniority rules. In all these situations the threat of a cut in financial income is a negative incentive. Under a negative incentive an employee is concerned with whether he can "get by." His enthusiastic cooperation must be won by other means.

### Social status and respect

Most men will put forth a considerable amount of effort in order to win the respect of their associates, that is, to maintain and improve their social status. In fact, the desire for higher compensation is in no small measure due to the prevailing attitude that the amount of money a man earns, or spends, is a measure of his success.

To be held in high regard by one's fellow workers is a real incentive. The salesman who can get an order from the tough customer, the moving man who can handle a loaded wardrobe trunk by himself, the accountant who really knows all the angles on income tax, and the weaver who can keep his looms running most of the time are all respected citizens. Recognition as a first-class workman, whatever the position held, provides deep satisfaction to almost every person. Moreover, an individual likes to feel that he is important to his department or group; while he may not be indispensable, he likes to feel that his contribution is important enough so that group action will not be the same without him.

Most men are also responsive to the attitude of their neighbors and other acquaintances who are not employed by the same establishment. Working for a well-regarded company and having a title that sounds impressive contribute to one's social status. This is particularly important for charitable and government enterprises, or professions like the ministry, where financial remuneration is relatively low, and a man must derive some of his compensation from the respectability of his calling.

The attitude of the boss is also important. Of all individuals, certainly here is one who should give recognition to a job well done. Especially when there is a personal loyalty between a man and his supervisor, the man will often go a long way in order to maintain the respect of his chief.

Social status and respect is not an incentive that an executive can pass out as he sees fit. The attitudes of fellow-workers and neighbors are not necessarily more favorable just because a man carries out his instructions conscientiously. Nevertheless, an executive can do things that contribute to the stature of an individual in the eyes of his associates.

Recognition given publicly, explanations of the importance of a man's job to other people, identifying the individual as having contributed to the over-all success of the enterprise, all contribute to a man's social status. Medals and ceremonies have a more limited place in business than in military operations, but the public recognition they convey is similar to the recognition an executive should try to cultivate for those of his men who perform effectively.

**Security**

Security, at least economic security, has become a well-recognized goal for individual action. Old age pensions, unemployment insurance, life insurance, accident and sickness benefits, and other forms of economic protection have grown by leaps and bounds during the last generation. While much of this protection is provided or sponsored by governmental action, there remain a variety of formal and informal arrangements that independent enterprises make for their own employees. These measures contribute to the satisfaction of an employee with his job. The critical question is, "How much?" since the expense of many of the plans is quite high and relatively inflexible.

A sense of security, however, embraces much more than economic matters. It also includes a self-confidence that comes with a personal adaptation to a given environment. Self-confidence with respect to a job stems from a number of things, not the least of which is knowing what to do, how to do it, and how well one is doing it. These are factors in self-confidence that every executive should provide to his subordinates. The feeling of security of the man who knows his job and knows that he is doing it well differs sharply from that of the individual who is still bewildered and not sure of his ability to measure up to the job ahead of him.

Uncertainty breeds a feeling of insecurity. While there are some Micawbers, most of us have a penchant for imaging all manner of trouble when we do not know what is going to happen. Grapevine information regarding a possible change in executives, in methods, or in other features of a work situation often gives rise to all sorts of rumors and uneasiness.

Executives at all levels can do much to remove this source of insecurity by sharing information with their subordinates. In particular, subordinates should know as far in advance as possible about changes which will affect them. One of the best ways to remove fear of such changes is to have those involved participate in the discussions and planning of the change. Often the subordinates will bring forth suggestions that will be useful, but the important point here is that if they have an opportunity to understand the reason for the shift and to know that serious consideration is being given to things that affect them, much mental anxiety can be avoided.

These measures for increasing an individual's sense of security cannot, of course, be provided piecemeal as a direct reward for increases in efficiency. They are incentives only in a general and perhaps negative sense. The effort, the enthusiasm, the drive of a person is undermined if he feels insecure. On the other hand, when he is free from this worry, he is in a position to devote his energies to constructive work. The executive who can make his workers feel secure significantly increases the chances of successful execution of his plans.

**Attractive work**

The work a man does on his particular job, and especially his attitude toward it, has a significant bearing on the enthusiasm with which he carries out plans. When a man has a feeling of craftsmanship, when he takes real pride in the accomplishment of a job well done, his work can provide him basic satisfaction. Milling an edge to a fine tolerance, producing an intricate drawing, hiring a group of salesmen, writing a clear job description, and innumerable other tasks all take skill. Most men take pleasure in doing well those things that call for their particular skill.

Closely related to craftsmanship is creativeness. Both the capacity and the opportunity for creativeness are less common, but when it is present in a job, it can be a challenge and a source of deep satisfaction. Creativeness is not confined to artists and inventors; the engineer, the advertising copywriter, any top executive, and many others have an opportunity to exercise originality.

Still another source of satisfaction from many jobs is that of adventure. Executives, salesmen, production workers trying to set a better record than another department, and many others get a thrill out of meeting competition and unforeseen hazards. Jobs vary in the opportunity they provide for craftsmanship, creativeness and adventure; nevertheless, at least some of these satisfactions can be derived from almost every job since they arise in part from the attitude of the worker himself and the way the work is directed. The supervisor can do much to build up these sources of satisfaction.

The work will be more attractive and challenging if it makes the best use of a man's ability. One company transferred a salesman with only a fair record to a temporary assignment in the office. His ability to deal with people plus a willingness to attend to detail was better suited to supervisory than to selling work, and he is now an outstanding success at his new job. Experienced executives can provide many similar illustrations of the marked effect on performance of "putting a square peg in a square hole." This best use of a man's ability is primarily a matter of personnel placement; it can be achieved to some extent by reallocation of duties.

Of course, at any given time there are limitations of what work needs doing, and the employee may have misconceptions of his own ability. These difficulties in application should not be permitted to overshadow the stimulating effect of making the best use of a man's ability insofar as it can be arranged.

Working conditions, such as adequate light, comfortable temperatures, attractive surroundings, good eating and toilet facilities, protection against accident, and so forth do make a difference in the attractiveness of a job. Their contribution to greater employee satisfaction depends to a large degree upon the attitudes and the beliefs of the workers. What were regarded as attractive hours and working conditions in 1900 would cause discontent today. Beyond basic minimums it is more the improving of conditions that is important. The new lunchroom or the five-day week boost morale when first installed, but within a few years they become an accepted thing and lose their motivating effect (except that they must be continued to avoid a negative reaction). Most companies, therefore, attempt only to keep up with the cultural pattern in the industry and the community, perhaps occasionally leading but not relying upon arrangements for work to provide a large, positive stimulus to greater effort. Social recognition, treatment as an individual, and opportunity to participate have been demonstrated to be better stimuli to action than even the most generous paternalistic action.

### Opportunity for development

In addition to attractive work in their present jobs, most individuals are concerned about opportunities for development. People grow and change, and they like to feel that as they gain experience, they will have a chance to move into positions of greater responsibility and respect.

This is especially true in the United States where our traditions and heritage emphasize development. The hard-working pioneer opened up a territory where his children often became leading citizens in a thriving community. Immigrants have passed through apprenticeship to become supervisors or business enterprisers, and they or their children have become our leading statesmen.

The nature of our frontier has changed, and our social and economic structures are less fluid, but the desire to advance continues to be a strong current in our aspirations. The executive who provides his subordinates with an opportunity for development has a forceful means of winning support for the execution of his program. Measures for executive development described in Chapter 20 serve this purpose well, and similar techniques can be used for nonsupervisory personnel.

Some executives or entire companies take the view that desire for personal development is such a good incentive that they should assist employees to find suitable employment for their new talents, even though this means that some of them will have to transfer to other departments or companies.

### Worth-while activity

Men will work harder when they feel they are performing some really worth-while service. This is eloquently demonstrated in the time and effort devoted by volunteers to the Community Chest, Boy Scouts, church activities, political reforms, and many other service activities. Just as dominating objectives provide a unifying force for coordination, so do they stimulate effort to fulfill individual missions.

The spur of a worth-while activity is by no means confined to charitable causes. The man who is being paid for his services by a private-profit enterprise still likes to feel that his activities are worth while. If he can see that people are happier, toil and drudgery is being reduced, suffering relieved, physical and social strength improved, or in some other way the world is a somewhat better place to live because of his efforts, he is much more likely to work with enthusiasm and zeal. In other words, he should believe the objectives of the enterprise are socially desirable.

The administrator should seek to harness the enthusiasm that comes with believing in a cause. Two steps are necessary. The employee should be made to believe as deeply as possible in the desirability of the concern's objectives. Secondly, individual employees must see how their activities make a significant contribution to the success of the enterprise in achieving these objectives.

### Personal power and influence

Unquestionably, many people get satisfaction from the exercise of personal power and influence. This does not necessarily mean that they resort to unethical means to obtain power, or that they are careless or arrogant in its use. It is simply the exhilaration they get from being able to commit the company for large sums, from feeling that their influence was important in the passage of a new piece of legislation, from pulling open the throttle of a large locomotive.

An executive can add or take away from the power of his subordinates by a change in delegation. He may give the man additional duties, perhaps including the supervision of more people, or he may increase or decrease the authority of the man to make binding decisions. Even though the power that can be conveyed by administrative delegations is limited, it still may be significant. A man who desires such delegation will try to prove himself worthy by cooperating with his supervisor and by effectively carrying out his duties.

### Treatment as an individual person

Danger always exists that employees will be thought of merely as persons who perform certain duties for the enterprise. Although his work may absorb a considerable part of the efforts of an individual, he has many other interests. Family relationships, living arrangements, personal health, hobbies, religious and social life, aspirations, obligations, all are important to the individual.

A reasonably satisfactory adjustment and integration of these outside interests must be made if the person is to perform most effectively on his job. The employer should not attempt to direct the personal affairs of his employees, but there is need for a sympathetic recognition of these problems and a willingness to help in meeting them. This treatment of subordinates as individual persons can go a long way in winning their loyal support and cooperation.

The personal relationship between an employee and his supervisor should be at least agreeable. Often it is possible to develop a friendliness and loyalty that is a strong influence in carrying out instructions enthusiastically. At the other extreme, personal friction may become so strong that the subordinate prefers not to carry out instructions merely because he has been asked to do so by his supervisor. Personal likes and dislikes cannot be molded at will, but every supervisor should try to keep his relationships with subordinates as pleasant as possible, so that personal loyalty will be at his disposal as an incentive.

One fairly simple though important way of giving recognition to subordinates as individuals is to share with them information about current problems and future plans. The man who is "in the know" feels complimented by the confidence and is more likely to identify his interests with those of the enterprise.

### Voice in own affairs

One of the more difficult things for well-meaning executives to remember is that people like to participate in forming decisions that will affect them. Even a plan that is quite beneficial to employees may receive a cool reception if it is prepared and announced in a haughty or condescending manner.

This desire for a voice in the planning that bears upon a man's own work has several sources. The man on the firing line feels that he has intimate knowledge that should be brought to bear on the decision. Since the decision will affect his work significantly, it is a sign of respect to be consulted in the matter. Many people do not like to feel beholden to others. A person is more likely to understand and support an action that he has helped plan. Whatever the explanation, this desire for participation is prevalent, and becomes increasingly strong among competent and self-reliant persons. It is particularly significant to motivation because it affects the attitude of an individual toward his assignment.

The executive should recognize and take advantage of this desire for a voice in one's own affairs. As a minimum, he should be sure to advise each person in advance of changes which will affect the latter's work situation. Even if the change is relatively insignificant, such as electricians putting in some new wiring, the man should be accorded the courtesy of knowing what it is about. On the positive side, the process of consultative direction discussed in Chapter 21 can often be used to gain ideas and win support of subordinates for a program. It creates an attitude of working together rather than working for, and the resulting "we" feeling often is a strong incentive.

### Just and diligent supervision

The attention given to a man's grievances and needs, the manner of commendation, and the fairness of disciplinary action can add much to the spirit that a subordinate applies to his job.

Grievances should be settled promptly. The way should be open for a man to register complaints about his treatment, and if he feels his immediate supervisor has been unfair, channels of appeal should be provided. These grievances, petty though they may appear to be to the supervisor, should be examined promptly and the man informed either of corrective action being taken or of the reasons why the situation cannot be adjusted. Unless these annoyances and feelings of mistreatment can be aired and adjusted, the employee will carry with him a gnawing discontent that may seriously detract from his enthusiasm for his job.

On the positive side, each executive should take the initiative in seeing that his subordinates are well serviced. He should represent their interests to other departments and higher echelons in administration. This representation may relate to compensation, working conditions, flow and quality of work, opportunities for advancement, and other points of concern to his men. Diligent attention to such matters will avoid many grievances before they develop, and will build loyalty on the part of the men.

The executive should also use commendation to build cooperation among his subordinates. Outstanding performance should not be left unnoticed. Generally desirable is to recognize and praise the performance in the presence of others, for this not only tells the man of his chief's opinion, but also adds to the prestige of the man in the eyes of his associates. In giving commendation take care to do it fairly; if only one man is singled out when others are equally deserving, or the achievement really represents group effort, then those who have been overlooked may feel disgruntled.

The praise should be sincere and deserved. If a man needs encouragement, it is better to pick out some part of his performance that is worthy of commendation than to give broad and unwarranted compliments; otherwise, the commendations may soon come to be regarded as "hot air," and may even be a source of embarrassment at subsequent salary reviews or when the need for improved performance is being discussed.

Reprimands also serve an important role in motivation. While they should be given promptly, the supervisor should take time to get and weigh the relevant facts, and he certainly should not be angry. Generally the reprimand should be given in private, and the offender should have an opportunity to tell his own story.

When disciplinary action is necessary, it should not be given in a spirit of retribution, or for the prime purpose of humiliating the offender. The purpose of discipline is to bring about improved conduct in the future; hence one must consider the circumstances and provocation, and the attitude, previous conduct, and personality of the individual. Also consider the effect of the disciplinary action on the attitude of other workers; too harsh a punishment may make the man a martyr, whereas too lenient treatment may be interpreted as meaning that the executive considers the matter lightly.

The matter of equity is likewise important. Rules of desirable conduct should be generally known. Where penalties for violation are severe, this fact should be announced in advance. In most situations warning of penalties if the act is repeated is all that is necessary. Particularly important is to be sure that disciplinary action be equitable as between individuals. Unless consistency and fairness characterize the action, its constructive influence on future behavior is likely to be lost.

In all this range of supervisory activities opportunities arise either to create discontent or to build a cooperative spirit. Consequently, the executive should never forget that just and diligent supervision will contribute greatly to his success in getting plans carried out.

### Summary

The effective execution of plans requires a desire to see them succeed on the part of those who have to do the work. Therefore, an executive must understand what motivates the actions of people working for him.

Each individual has a variety of desires and beliefs that shape his reactions to any particular instruction. It is the task of the executive to arrange the total work situation, or perhaps modify individual and group attitudes, so that each of his subordinates finds greater satisfaction in carrying out instructions than in following any of a number of alternatives open to him. In fact, he needs not merely passive acceptance, but a positive desire to do the work effectively and efficiently.

In building such an attitude in his subordinates, an executive should consider a variety of measures. Important in this connection are higher financial income, social status and respect, security, attractive work, opportunity for development, worth-while activity, personal power and influence, treatment as an individual person, voice in own affairs, and just and diligent supervision. Some of these measures provide a general background of cooperative effort; others can be related directly to performance of particular instructions. They, of course, should be used in varying combinations to meet specific situations, for an individual reacts to the total situation.

In reviewing this general approach to motivation two final points deserve emphasis. One is the tremendous importance of little things in building the enthusiastic support of subordinates. The other is the need for economy in the use of specific incentives. Stronger motivation than is necessary not only wastes the executive's time, but may lessen the effectiveness of these incentives when they are used

later. Much need remains for a sensitive and sympathetic understanding of human behavior in the motivation phase of administration.

### SELECTED REFERENCES

Argyris, C., *Interpersonal Competence and Organizational Effectiveness,*
Richard D. Irwin, Inc., 1962.

Davis, K., *Human Relations at Work,* McGraw-Hill Book Co., Inc., 1962.

Leavitt, H. J., *Managerial Psychology,* University of Chicago Press, 1958.

McGregor, D., *The Human Side of Enterprise,* McGraw-Hill Book Co., Inc.,
1960, Part I.

Selznick, P., *Leadership in Administration: A Sociological Interpretation,*
Harper & Row, Publishers, 1957.

Whyte, W. F., et al., *Money and Motivation,* Harper & Row, Publishers,
1955.

# 23

# Coordination

## Significance of coordination

In administration, coordination deals with synchronizing and unifying the actions of a group of people. A coordinated operation is one in which the activities of the employees are harmonious, dovetailed, and integrated toward a common objective.

Coordination is one of the primary goals of every manager. However, the good manager spends only a small part of his time specifically engaged in coordinating. Instead, he achieves integrated action largely through skillful use of *all* phases of administration—planning, organizing, assembling resources, supervising, and controlling. Ideally, coordination permeates all activities; it is not an appendage tacked on like chrome trimming on an automobile. Nevertheless, an essential aspect of supervision is to make sure that, in fact, activities are proceeding in a coordinated manner.

The need for coordination is not new:

As long ago as the 18th century, James Watt's production men were sending memos to his designers: "We beg that you pay more particular attention to the manner of the flanges on the castings. We have had much reason to complain of this part hitherto, and we have been obliged to chisel out the irons to the proper cone. This expense may well be saved by some attention paid by you." The sales agent was complaining: "The wheels of the implanted motion are so bad they must be replaced with new ones. The connection rod top has broken. The connection rod gudgeons have a slot the full thickness of a worn shilling. The racks and sectors are badly fitted and many other matters." And the engineers were

retorting: "Why does thou not send a list of particulars instead of saying simply and in general that things do not fit?" [1]

Many executives today face increasingly complex tasks of coordination. As an enterprise grows in size the task of synchronizing its
many activities becomes more difficult. A high degree of specialization in departments and in jobs necessitates a neat dovetailing of
effort in order to secure unified results. Then, new techniques,
changes in competitive conditions and in volume of business, added
governmental regulations, and other forces introducing change in
customary methods of work add to the task of coordination. Fortunately, our knowledge of how to obtain coordination is also increasing, so an executive with a modern kit of managerial tools should
be able to cope with these added complexities.

When faced with a need for securing better coordination, the
administrator should consider:

1. Simplified organization
2. Harmonized programs and policies
3. Well-designed methods of communication
4. Aids to voluntary coordination
5. Coordination through personal guidance

We have already examined two of these topics—organization and
planning; all that need be done here is to show how they can contribute to unified action. Then measures more specifically pointed
at coordination will be discussed.

### SIMPLIFIED ORGANIZATION

**Departmentation that aids in coordination**

In every enterprise certain activities need to be closely synchronized with others. These may be purchasing and sales in a retail store, maintenance and operations in an airline company, parts
fabrication and assembly in an automobile plant, or adjusting claims
and legal work in an insurance company. If such related activities
are placed in the same administrative unit, coordination is made
easier. More informal contacts are likely between the people whose
work is closely related, and a single executive is charged with seeing
that the activities are dovetailed.

Functional specialization, which is so characteristic of modern

---

[1] Quoted in *Management News*, April, 1950.

enterprise, leads to an organization that is divided into a whole series of units, each of which is concentrating on only one phase of the total operation. Then, for any goods to be produced or services rendered, contributions from each of these specialized units must be drawn together. This creates a major problem of coordination. As the enterprise grows, each unit becomes larger and more bureaucratic. A time comes when some of the benefits of specialization must be sacrificed and closely related operations placed under a single chief in order to coordinate them more easily. Along with this creation of product or territorial divisions often goes the decentralization of authority; thus, the man on the spot can make what adjustments are necessary to secure unified action.

The important point here is that when an executive faces lack of coordination, he should at least consider some rearrangement of departments so that the activities that have been out of step are organizationally closer together. Luther Gulick has remarked, "Whenever an organization needs continual resort to special coordinating devices in the discharge of its regular work, this is proof that the organization is bad."

**Clear-cut organization and procedures**

The lack of a clear understanding of exactly who does what often leads to poor coordination. One company had to delay the introduction of a new product for a month because neither the advertising division nor the product development division had taken the legal steps necessary to establish and protect the trade name. Each assumed the other was taking care of the matter, and the slip-up was discovered so late that magazine advertising had to be postponed for a month and other sales promotion delayed. Another company found that discrepancies in its year-end inventory value arose primarily from a misunderstanding as to who was to enter return goods into the inventory account.

In still another firm, rush orders had a habit of sitting around the shipping room for hours because the regular delivery man knew he was not supposed to take the orders, and no one person was charged with responsibility for finding someone else to make the special delivery. This particular situation came to a head when the production manager found an order he had gotten out quickly at considerable interference with the flow of work still in the shipping room two days later. These are all examples of twilight zones where no one feels responsible. They, of course, are more likely to occur when some new or unusual activity is being undertaken or after a shift in personnel.

Trouble can also arise when two executives both feel they are responsible for the same activity. On more than one occasion both the purchasing department and the maintenance division have thought they were the ones to buy repair parts and minor pieces of new equipment, which results in difficulties with the suppliers and sometimes overpurchasing. Occasionally when such fuzzy organization leaves overlapping responsibility, the confusion is confounded by jurisdictional jealousy, and these jealousies in turn seriously interfere with voluntary coordination.

Clear-cut organization and procedures that are well known to all persons concerned will enable an executive to avoid the kinds of difficulties just described. For this particular purpose it is not so important that the organizational procedures be the most efficient ones conceivable as it is that all activities are covered and that each person knows what he is responsible for and how his work relates to that of other individuals. Of course, the simpler the organization, the easier it is to establish such a clear understanding.

## HARMONIZED PROGRAMS AND POLICIES

### Consistency among plans

The ideal time to bring about coordination is, of course, at the planning stage. In fact, one of the chief reasons for developing plans some time ahead and in some detail is the opportunity this provides for re-examining and checking one plan against the other to be sure that they all do fit together into an integrated, balanced whole. Two aspects of planning are particularly important in achieving coordination in such a review: consistency among the plans, and timing of the activities.

Especially the plans developed by different individuals or divisions should be checked for consistency. For instance, one company found that its personnel director was planning to hire several college graduates with the idea that they would be moved quickly from one position to another so that they could step into junior executive posts within three to five years. Several of the operating executives in whose departments these young men would have to work planned no such rapid promotion; they doubted that anybody could be prepared for a junior executive position with less than ten years of experience. Clearly, the planning for executive development in this company was not synchronized.

A similar type of difficulty in quite another field is illustrated by the United States' avowed policy of stimulating international trade and stabilizing currency values through a balanced flow of foreign exchange, while at the same time continuing to maintain import restrictions designed to reduce the flow of specific commodities into the United States.

The president of a soap company found that his executives at the main plant were making shifts in equipment that would permit an expansion in capacity to take care of the rising demand, whereas a number of other executives were assuming that a branch plant would be constructed within two or three years that would take such a load off the main plant that its total volume would probably be lower than at present.

To secure consistency among plans, an administrator should first check one against the other to see whether they all add up to a unified program. When discrepancies are discovered, it is not always easy to correct them because there may be good reasons for moving in each of the proposed directions. Sometimes the difficulty is corrected by choosing one or the other of the alternatives, but at other times a *new* course of action is necessary in order to achieve proper balance along with coordination.

**Proper timing**

Coordinated activities must not only be consistent with each other, but also be performed at the proper time. For example, in one of the classic illustrations of coordination, an assembly line in an automobile plant, timing is one of the cardinal features. The numerous parts, many of which are carried on overhead conveyors, must arrive at the assembly line at just the right moment. It will not do to put the wheels for a yellow convertible onto a blue sedan. Also, the speed of the assembly line itself and the assignment of work must be adjusted so that one group of employees is not idle for lack of something to do while others are finding it difficult to finish one job before the next job rolls along.

Proper timing is vital, though perhaps not so conspicuous, in many other operations. A premium promotion campaign of a breakfast cereal company, for example, calls for synchronization of a whole series of activities. The procurement of the premium itself, printing of the package announcing its offer, the shipment of such packages to wholesalers and their subsequent release to retailers, the reservation of time on a radio network for advertising, the employment of talent and the preparation of script for TV programs, the design of newspaper advertising copy, the placing of newspaper advertising in numerous local papers, sales meetings describing the campaign to salesmen, salesmen's promotional work among retailers and wholesalers, arrangement of physical facilities, and special employees to send out premiums when requested, all must be performed at the proper time if the campaign is to achieve its maximum effectiveness. In fact, premature advertising, delay in sending out premiums, and similar slips might cause such confusion and ill will that the campaign would have a negative rather than a positive result.

Even operations that involve only a relatively few steps need to be properly timed. A minor change in a company pension plan requires work with actuaries, lawyers, union leaders, and others and the preparation of new forms, instructions to payroll clerks, and announcements to employees. These steps can and should be synchronized through proper programming.

## WELL-DESIGNED METHODS OF COMMUNICATION

Good communication aids in coordinating activities. For instance, one must know promptly whether operations are proceeding in accordance with plan so that adjustments can be made when necessary. Moreover, a wide variety of activities, particularly those of a detailed nature, are impractical to plan far in advance. Coordination of these is achieved only as the people directing and performing them have current information regarding related work.

Communication of information on operating conditions and anticipated changes is also vital in preparing programs for the future. So often when something goes wrong we hear the comments: "Why didn't somebody tell me?" "How was I to know?" Communication systems should provide, as a normal matter of business, for the flow of the bulk of this information needed for coordination.

Much of the detailed information needed for coordination can be provided by *working papers* that follow an established path from one department to another. When Mr. Smith buys a necktie at a department store and asks that it be sent to his home and the cost charged to his account, for example, coordinated action of several departments is needed. Out of the thousands of packages sent to the delivery department, the right one must be selected and left at the correct address. Also, someone must locate Mr. Smith's account among the thousands of charge customers and make an entry for the exact amount of the transaction. Other accounting entries are needed too for computing sales compensation, inventory on hand, and gross profit of the haberdashery section. Actually, all of this is done in a routine manner because the salesperson makes out a slip with several duplicate copies containing the necessary information, and these are routed to the departments concerned.

In a similar manner the specifications, route sheet, and similar papers permit the easy flow of work through a large factory. An established flow of working papers is needed for premiums and dividends on policies in a life insurance company. In virtually every enterprise some activities can be coordinated primarily through the proper flow of well-designed working papers.

A similar communication device that contributes to coordination is the *written report*. In the coordination of production and sales, for example, regular reports of inventory on hand and orders in production will be of considerable aid in planning sales activities and making delivery promises. Likewise, a report from the sales department of orders received and in prospect, classified by types of products, will be of great assistance to the production department in scheduling its work.

A great diversity of such reports is possible, of course, many of which will be useful for control as well as for coordination. The distinctive thing about an established report system is that it specifies who is to make out the report, what information is to be included, when it should be prepared, and to whom it should be sent. This is important because it relieves the employee of the important and difficult task of continually deciding what part of the information he possesses should be passed on to others, and in what form.[2]

Other means of communication should be incorporated into the total system. Regular oral reports are more time-consuming but provide opportunity for explanation and interpretation, which is often highly important in coordination. Where personal contact is

[2] See H. A. Simon, *Administrative Behavior*, The Macmillan Company, 1957, p. 159.

not practical, letters, memos, and special reports should be used to supplement information on the regular reports and working papers.

In connection with all of these means of communication, attention should be given to mechanical devices such as teletypes, telautographs, electronic computers, intercommunication systems, mimeographs, and hectographs, which can be used to speed up the dissemination of accurate information to the various people that need it.

*Summarizing:* Since coordination is concerned with the interrelationships of separate activities, it can be no better than the transfer of information about those activities to some common point or points, where the dovetailing takes place. Part of this transfer can come through informal contacts, as will be pointed out in the later paragraphs; but the big bulk of it should come through formal means of communication. Hence, the executive who is seeking to improve coordination should make sure that a free and prompt flow of pertinent operating data occurs throughout the enterprise. Care should be taken in designing the various forms and reports used. An over-elaborate system will not only add to expense, but may defeat the very purpose of providing the right data to the right man at the right time.

### AIDS TO VOLUNTARY COORDINATION

In any enterprise, most of the coordination should take place through voluntary cooperation of the members. The billing clerk and the delivery man, the employment officer and the chief accountant, the advertising copywriter and the purchasing agent, and numerous other combinations of employees must adapt their work to secure unified action. These are not cases where one man has authority over the other, and it would create an impossible organizational arrangement if this were attempted. Instead, when the work of two individuals is related, each is expected to tell the other enough about his needs and operating difficulties so that they can agree upon a coordinated course of action.

Of course, they may not always agree, and then the problem must be carried on up the administrative hierarchy until a satisfactory solution is developed by the senior executives or is finally resolved by the single executive who directs the actions of both groups. But these should be exceptional cases, for if the precise nature of all relationships had to be specified by a superior executive, it would create an intolerable burden. Consequently, the wise executive will do what he can to promote voluntary coordination.

Voluntary coordination will be made easier by clear-cut organization, harmonized plans, and well-designed systems of formal communication, which have already been discussed. It may be encouraged in several other ways that are important enough to deserve careful consideration by an administrator seeking unified action.

**Instill dominant objectives**

A dominant objective that is accepted by people whose activities need to be coordinated has a potent influence on voluntary cooperation. This is, perhaps, most apparent during time of war, when customers and suppliers, competitors, labor unions and management, and numerous departments and individuals within an enterprise will put themselves to considerable trouble in helping the other person if by doing so there is a greater contribution toward winning the war. Once this single overpowering objective is removed, petty bickering, jockeying for position, and general indifference to the problems of the other person become much more common.

The value of a dominant objective is also apparent in the playing of a football team. A spirit of teamwork prevails as long as winning the game is the primary purpose of all the members, but when some of the players seek personal glory and recognition from the grandstand, the task of getting coordinated action is much more difficult.

These dramatic examples of dominant objectives may seem far removed from anything that is possible for a division or departmental executive. Nevertheless, the basic idea can be applied to a variety of situations. In many companies, such as a telephone company, the concept of customer service is sufficiently strong to act as the catalytic agent for coordinated action. Achieving departmental production or sales goals, extending a no-accident record, beating the budget, getting the jump on a competitor, having the best guard force in town, getting the mail delivered on time, and other such objectives often can be made sufficiently strong in the feelings of a majority of the members of the enterprise to assist significantly in the coordination process.

The existence of such objectives spells the difference between a live and enthusiastic team and an assembly of individuals who find little sense of achievement in helping to make the organization tick. Every executive should seek to imbue his subordinates with such objectives as a vehicle for voluntary coordination.

**Develop generally accepted customs and terms**

Voluntary coordination is more likely to occur when people work easily with one another. This can be brought about, in part, by fostering the development of widely accepted customs of work and terminology. Each company has a certain lingo of its own, a typical formality or informality among employees, customs such as the use of written memoranda, and many other folkways. To a large extent these just grow, although they may be encouraged or discouraged by executive action. The executive should be aware that these customs affect the ease with which people work with one another. Together with social compatibility, they determine whether a given individual fits readily within a group. If he does, coordination takes place more easily.

**Encourage informal contacts**

Informal contacts are essential in supplementing formal communications. Many explanations, questions, and ideas are too intangible or tentative to be included in formal reports and written documents, and yet they are important to a complete understanding of a situation.

When talking informally over a cup of coffee, one executive can point out ways that inefficiencies in the other man's department are causing him difficulty, without registering a formal complaint that appears in the record; one man can tell another how annoyed the chief executive was when delivery to an important customer was delayed; possible changes in organization or procedures can be discussed without upsetting morale; background data on labor negotiations or an important sales contract can be exchanged. This information that is communicated through informal contacts provides an essential background and understanding needed in voluntary coordination.

In any enterprise the executives and other employees will naturally form social groups, or what the sociologists call informal organization. It is largely through these relationships that the communication just described takes place; they are the stems and the branches of the proverbial "grapevine." An acquaintanceship with these informal groups is valuable to the executive who seeks coordination because they indicate where voluntary adjustments will be easy and where they may be difficult. Moreover, week-end conferences, company dining rooms, joint projects, and similar means promote friendly relations among the men whose work should be coordinated. Such attention to informal relationships, then, should be regarded as one of the important aids to voluntary coordination.

The effectiveness of personal contacts in producing voluntary coordination will be substantially increased by following four principles that Mary Parker Follett has recommended:

1. Coordination by direct contact of the responsible people concerned,
2. Coordination in the early stages,
3. Coordination as the reciprocal relating of all the factors in a situation,
4. Coordination as a continuing process.[3]

These principles contain much sound advice. It is easier to resolve difficulties when talking with Joe on a friendly basis than when writing a memorandum to a so-and-so in the headquarters office. Also, adjustments are easier while plans are still in the formative stages and before the work is actually started. There is considerable inertia in human conduct, and what may be a matter of relative indifference before action is started becomes a real hardship if the change has to be made in midstream. Then there is need for a willingness to give and take, to recognize the operating problems of the other fellow and together work out a solution that takes into account all the factors in a situation. Finally, a single contact is rarely enough. As operations proceed, the executive should check with others affected by them to make sure that harmonious results are being achieved. These simple guides will help develop coordination at all levels of administration.

**Provide liaison men where needed**

In special situations the direct personal contact of key executives is not frequent enough to provide all the informal exchange of information that is desirable. To overcome this difficulty, men known in the Army as *liaison officers* may be appointed. The liaison man is familiar with operating conditions and needs of his own unit and

[3] See H. C. Metcalf and L. Urwick, eds., *Dynamic Administration, the Collected Papers of Mary Parker Follett*, Harper & Brothers, 1942, pp. 297-303.

explains these to other divisions with whom he maintains close contact. At the same time he observes the operating needs of the latter group and reports these back to his own unit. The desirability of such liaison between the artillery and the infantry needs little explanation, particularly to an infantryman.

In large business concerns, liaison men are sometimes very useful working between the headquarters office and branches scattered over a wide geographical area, or between the production and sales departments. These men do not have authority to make binding commitments; their primary function is to provide an easy exchange of information and to suggest voluntary means of coordination.

The use of liaison men is not a complete substitute for direct personal contact. Nevertheless, where these men have the knowledge and capacity to understand fully operating problems in all of the units they work with (and if they don't, it is better not to have them at all), they can provide some of the personal explanation and interpretation that is so conducive to voluntary coordination.

**Use committees**

Committees provide an opportunity for direct personal contact and informal exchange of ideas and views. Often they are created for the explicit purpose of bringing together the men whose activities need to be coordinated and providing the setting in which voluntary coordination can take place readily. Even when the committee has other duties, the personal relationships established facilitate cooperation at other times.

Committees are not without their limitations, and are better adapted to some situations than to others. For a discussion of these points and suggestions for improving committee effectiveness, see Chapter 14.

COORDINATION THROUGH PERSONAL GUIDANCE

Simplified organization, harmonized programs and policies, well-designed methods of communication, and aids to voluntary coordination will go a long way toward securing unity of action. There will always remain, however, a residual group of coordination problems that must be handled by supervising executives. The more effective are these other devices, the less will remain for the executive, but he can never completely relieve himself of the task of watching the progress of the various activities under his direction to be sure they are proceeding harmoniously. He will need to prod here, restrain there, provide supplementary help in another quarter, revise schedules to meet emergencies, arbitrate sincere differences of opinion among his subordinates, all to maintain a balance and unity in the total results.

When the work load assigned to an executive is so heavy that he is unable to perform these coordinating duties effectively, he may rely upon one or more *staff* assistants. These men, acting on behalf of their chief, follow operations closely, encourage voluntary coordination, and when necessary recommend to the senior official action he should take. In some circumstances, particularly in the Army where the staff concept is well understood, these staff assistants perform a major service in securing coordinated action. In smaller enterprises, however, this more complex means of coordination is less likely to be necessary. If staff is to be used, the nature of the job, as discussed in Chapter 12, should be clearly understood.

SUMMARY

Coordination is concerned with harmonious and unified action directed toward a common objective. It is not a separate activity, but a condition that should permeate all phases of administration.

An executive faced with the need for improving coordination should consider a number of approaches. Sometimes changes should be made in the structural or built-in provisions for coordination. Important here are: (1) creating divisions and departments in which the most frequent coordination problems can be resolved within an organization unit itself; (2) clarifying the organization and procedures so that no doubt exists as to who does what; (3) designing flow of working papers, reports, and other methods of communication so that information needed for coordination advances promptly to the right persons as a normal procedure.

In some situations there is need to harmonize programs and policies. Plans, especially those developed by separate individuals or divisions, should be checked for consistency. Also, the scheduling and other timing arrangements should be reviewed.

Still another approach is to promote voluntary coordination among subordinates. This can be done by instilling dominant objectives, developing generally accepted customs and terms, encouraging informal contacts, providing liaison men where needed, and using committees.

Finally, some coordination problems remain that can be resolved best by the personal attention of the supervising executive. He will observe the flow of work and expedite lagging activities, interpret instructions, referee minor disputes, adjust plans to meet emergencies, and take other steps to maintain smooth, harmonious action.

Generally, coordination will be achieved only through a well-balanced combination of several of these approaches.

### SELECTED REFERENCES

Guest, R. H., *Organizational Change: The Effect of Successful Leadership*, Richard D. Irwin, Inc., 1962.

McGregor, D., *The Human Side of Enterprise*, McGraw-Hill Book Co., Inc., 1960, Chap. 5.

Simon, H. A., *Administrative Behavior* (2nd ed.), The Macmillan Company, 1957, Chap. 8.

# *V*
# Controlling

# 24

# Essential Steps in Control

Administration has been described as a continuing cycle of planning, organizing, assembling resources, supervising, and controlling. The next three chapters of this book will deal with the final phase of this cycle, control; that is, assuring that the performance conforms to plan.

*Control relies on other phases of administration.* An executive cannot expect to have good control over his company or department unless he also follows sound administrative principles in his other duties. A well-conceived program, workable policies and procedures, assembly of the necessary resources, training personnel, clear instructions—all contribute to the results desired. The better these things are done, the easier will be control.

In a comprehensive study of administration, however, planning, organizing, assembling resources, and supervising are themselves major phases. Consequently, we shall assume here that the preparatory steps have already been taken. The administrator has given his instructions and is now concerned with seeing that they are well executed.

Even when control is used in this more specific sense, the line between it and other phases of administration is not sharp. For example, the development of goals is an essential part of planning, yet many of these same goals may be used as standards in the process of control. Also, corrective action often includes a refinement or revision of plans. Like all the other phases of administration, control is closely interwoven into a complicated matrix. For practical analysis it must be treated separately, and yet in doing so the risk is that someone will forget it is really only a part of the total process.

*Steps in control process.* The administrator is interested in control of a large diversity of things. He wants to be sure that individual and departmental output is of satisfactory quality and volume and is completed when needed. He wants to keep all sorts of costs in line: payroll, materials, supplies, financial, services, and a wide range of intangible costs not directly reflected in the financial records. He wants to be sure that resources—people, buildings and equipment, inventories, accounts receivable, and the like—are carefully acquired, properly protected, and effectively used. If he is responsible for several separate activities, the areas needing control are, of course, multiplied.

A discussion here of specific controls for such a diversity of things is impractical. The basic steps in any control situation, however, can be set forth, and suggestions made that will be useful in handling a great many individual problems. Here again we are primarily concerned with the underlying process of administration.

Any control process has three basic steps:

1. Setting standards at strategic points.
2. Checking and reporting on performance.
3. Taking corrective action.

### SETTING STANDARDS AT STRATEGIC POINTS

The setting of standards for use in controlling operations is theoretically a simple task. Planning requires objectives and goals; these are the results one hopes to achieve. There will be an entire hierarchy of such goals in any enterprise, as was pointed out in Chapter 2. The general objectives of the company are broken down into objectives for individual departments and sections. From these we develop goals for quality, cost, and output. Supporting these figures should be production-time standards, sales quotas, cash-disbursements plans, schedules, budgets, and even more specific standards for detailed operations.

These goals become the standards for purposes of control. Without an idea of targets and aims, control makes no sense. And, once planning has established these goals, it might appear that control could begin with the process of checking actual results against them.

In actual operations, however, at least two important steps should be taken before attempting to compare actual operations with standards. (1) If the control is to have an effective influence on performance, the administrator should make sure that the goals are properly identified with individual responsibility. (2) Also, the administrator cannot review *all* aspects of performance; consequently, he must select certain points that will give him an adequate indication of what is going on with only a limited expenditure of his time. These steps lie at the heart of good control systems.

### Tie control standards to individual responsibility

The control of expenses, of governmental relations, of recruitment of high quality salesmen, or of any other activity becomes potent only when somebody does something about it. For example, knowing that telephone expenses are running above the budget or last year's figures does not do much good as long as the item is treated as a general over-all expense. As soon as responsibility for the increase can be assigned to specific individuals, however, the chances that corrective action will be taken increase.

Clear-cut organization will, of course, aid in locating the individual or individuals responsible for meeting a specific objective or standard. If duties have been clearly defined, the people who are concerned with the activity that is to be controlled are easily identified. The degree of decentralization may be somewhat more difficult to discover, and yet this, too, is significant for control purposes. It will be unfair and ineffective, for example, to criticize a branch warehouseman for making a lot of long distance telephone calls if his supervisor has instructed him to place all requests for additional shipments by phone instead of by mail.

Similarly, little is gained by asking a department store buyer to help control advertising expense if decisions regarding amount of space and its use for different products are made by the merchandise manager. Recognition of such partial decentralization has led some department stores to allocate to the various commodity sections only those expenses that are authorized by the section manager. These are known as his controllable expenses, and the difference between sales and controllable expenses for the section is called *contribution* to overhead and profit. Standards are then set for the monthly and annual contributions of the section and for the principal items of controllable expenses, whereas the standards and the responsibility for overhead expenses are related to the store executives who make the storewide decisions concerning them.

Some objectives, particularly those of an intangible nature, such as employee morale or customer good will, are hard to pin down to individual executives. Perhaps the most that is feasible will be to see that certain measures are taken that contribute toward these objectives. The fact that in some situations tying control standards to individual responsibility may be difficult in no way reduces its significance as a principle for effective control. Instead, we may have to admit that in these situations there are practical limits to which we should try to carry control.

**Concentrate on strategic control points**

*Need for control points.* In a department or enterprise the total number of objectives and standards involved in the work of all the individuals is very large. B. E. Goetz points out:

> Quality control involves an almost unbelievable number of standards. Consider dimensions alone. A power shovel or an adding machine contains approximately a thousand parts. Every hole in each part has depth, diameter, angle of axis with respect to each of two surfaces, and has distance of center from each of two edges. If the hole is tapped, further dimensional standards fix size, shape, and pitch of threads. Every flat surface requires three dimensions to locate a single point, two angles to give the position of the surface, and various dimensions to prescribe its perimeter. Curved surfaces are more involved. Finally, all dimensional standards are double: an upper and a lower limit within which the dimensions must fall or the part be rejected. All these dimensions are usually given on drawings but must be further implemented with fixtures, tools, gauges, and directions with respect to machine settings. To these dimensions must be added specifications as to composition, again fortified by tolerances to accompany each standard. There yet remain standards of finish and of performance: colors, smoothness, grain, hardness, toughness, and strength.[1]

[1] *Management Planning and Control*, McGraw-Hill Book Co., 1949, pp. 99-100. See also Chapter 5 and pp. 233-235 in the same book.

In addition to quality standards, standards are set up for the quantity of goods to be produced in various periods, a variety of cost standards expressed both in physical and dollar units, and standards covering the maintenance and use of various kinds of assets necessary for the production of the item.

While the individual performance standards in office and sales work may not be quite as detailed or precise, they are still numerous and diversified. Every activity will have standards, in somebody's mind if not actually written out, for *achievement, cost,* and *investment.* For instance, a cashier's office will have standards of achievement in terms of service and accuracy; standards for payroll, supplies, and other expenses; and standards for inventory, fixtures, and other investments.

No executive can attempt to check the performance of activities under his direction against all these numerous goals. The time and effort required to do so would be staggering. Especially as an executive moves up in the administrative hierarchy and has a correspondingly wider range of activities under his direction, such minute control becomes an impossibility. Consequently, the executive must concentrate on certain points in the operation, or on composite figures, which he hopes will indicate how well a considerable number of standards are being observed. Even at this limited number of control points, sampling and other devices may be necessary to keep the burden of control within reasonable bounds.

The particular points in a flow of operations that are used for control should fit that specific situation, as the following examples will show.

*Quality control points.* The nature of control points is well illustrated in quality control. A small baking-powder company, for example, tests the quality of its products by taking a sample from each batch of powder that is mixed and using it to bake biscuits; if the biscuits rise satisfactorily and the production manager does not have a stomach-ache after his lunch at the plant, it is assumed that the standard mixing formula has been followed. A single inspection of the finished product is also used by a radio manufacturing company (really an assembly operation). The finished chassis is tested after all the parts are put on and the wiring is completed. If it works, it is placed in a cabinet and shipped to the customer; if it doesn't, it is sent to a special department where the various parts and circuits are tested and the difficulty corrected.

Automobiles are also tested at the end of the assembly line to make sure that the engine, brakes, lights, and other features work properly. Yet, few of us would want to buy a car if this was the only inspection point, for defects might exist that would cause trouble only after several thousand miles of driving. Partly for the reason that *defects may be covered up*, there are frequent inspections in the manufacture of airplanes, bombsights, and other delicate instruments.

Another consideration in establishing inspection points is the possibility of *catching defects early* before expenses are incurred on a product that will have to be scrapped later. Thus, if it costs twenty dollars of direct labor to fabricate a part, and during the course of a week a raw-material inspector could catch faulty material for, say, ten parts that would later have to be discarded, his work each week would save $200 in direct labor. Even if it cost $150 a week to maintain the inspector, there would still be a net gain of $50. Of course, any change in salvage value or possibility of reworking the material would modify the gain attributable to the early inspection.

In elaborate manufacturing operations the setting of inspection points becomes a very tricky problem. Machine operators and foremen will catch many errors themselves. Inspection at some points is simple and quick while at others it may seriously interfere with production operations. Sampling may be adequate at one stage, whereas 100 per cent inspection is needed at another. There are all manner of testing machines and automatic controls, from crude scales to electric eyes. This poses a nice question of what combination of inspection and other controls at various points will provide the desired quality at a minimum cost.

*Control through approval of payroll changes.* Quite a different example of the use of control points is found in the practice of some executives' insistence upon personal approval of all payroll additions or changes. Often in units of several hundred people all changes in pay rate, if not the actual pay checks themselves, must carry the written signature of the chief executive.

Probably one of the most extensive uses of this device was made by Harold L. Ickes when he was Secretary of the Interior and administrator of half a dozen government agencies. Over most of this widespread domain—involving thousands of additions, promotions, in-grade pay increases, and separations from the payroll—Mr. Ickes exercised personal control. At first glance this appeared to be an extreme example of governmental red tape.

In actual operation the practice was not unduly burdensome because the daily order on which such changes were listed received prompt attention, and questions were raised only for good cause. Mr. Ickes used the device as a means to keep in touch with what was going on. A number of payroll additions in a division, the work of which was presumably contracting, naturally required an explanation. High turnover in another division might be a sign of poor morale, and so forth. Few major changes in operations can be made without shifting people about, and hence the payroll may serve as a strategic control point.

*Control of correspondence.* Another governmental practice, and an irritating one to businessmen who take on special assignments in Washington, is the control over outgoing correspondence. In addition to limited delegations on permission to sign outgoing mail, so that most governmental executives find themselves drafting letters for someone else's signature, it is not uncommon to encounter a central legal review. There is little that is more annoying to an operating executive, the traditional man of action, than to have a bright young law school graduate from the central legal staff turn up with a letter that should have been delivered two or three days before and say that there are some possible legal implications in the document that he would like to explore. In some agencies these so-called legal implications actually include operations questions, and thus there is very broad central staff control on outgoing correspondence.

We can understand why such a control point is used. Special care is needed with public statements of governmental officials because these statements carry with them much of the prestige and authority of the government itself. Moreover, the government must be careful to be consistent in its actions in dealing with different people, and a "man of action," who has not had experience with the ramifications of apparently simple governmental decisions, needs some control on his decisions. We see, then, why the top administrator, who is responsible for the agency's activities, may decide that a second look at outgoing documents is a good way to keep a check on what is happening.

A somewhat unusual practice that illustrates the use of critical control points is that of the president of a small and highly profitable company, who regularly opens and distributes the morning mail. He started this custom years ago when he and his partner were the only employees of the company, and he continued it even after the company's sales covered the entire country. He comes to the office half an hour before the normal opening time and goes through all incoming correspondence, often reading those letters that are not of purely routine nature. When he goes on a vacation or on an extended business trip, he insists that one of the other executives take over this duty. His explanation for performing what in many companies is considered to be one of the most elementary duties is that it enables him to keep in close touch with what is happening in all departments. Customer complaints, questions by suppliers on the payment of bills, important proposals that he has not yet heard of, and many other points are likely to become evident in this correspondence. Actually, he peruses the content of only a sample of the total incoming correspondence, but he happens to like this way of keeping in touch with what is going on.

These examples serve to illustrate the nature of strategic control points. The particular points mentioned in the examples have no outstanding merit; in fact, they will be desirable in only a few types of situations. The idea of picking strategic points at which to exercise control, however, is highly important to effective administration.

*Guides for selecting strategic control points.* The literature on applied management abounds with descriptions of control schemes that have been found effective in certain situations. The fundamental steps in control are almost always the same, and a large part of the difference in these schemes is in the particular strategic points found useful and in the nature of the reports prepared. Unfortunately, there appears to be no simple rule for identifying good control points. The most that can be said is that those that have proved of real value often exhibit one or more of the following characteristics. Strategic control points should be (1) timely, (2) economical, (3) comprehensive, and (4) balanced.

Control points should be *timely* in that they help spot significant deviations when control needs to be exercised. The example of an early quality inspection before additional processing costs are incurred represents a whole class of control points. Department stores often set up "open to buy" limits designed to regulate buyers' activities before firm commitments to purchase merchandise are made. Similarly, many companies require the approval of a construction or research project before detailed plans or commitments can be made.

Very similar are those controls designed to stop action before serious damage is done. Thus, the time to check the hiring of wrong people or the placing them in the wrong positions is when the initial selection is made, rather than after they have been put on the job. Standards of preventive maintenance are designed to avoid machine breakdowns when the whole flow of work through the department will be disrupted, other schedules thrown out of joint, and man-hours lost waiting for repairs to be made.

The possibility of covering up defects if occasional checks are not made while the job is being done has already been illustrated in quality control. This has a parallel in other operations where brief delays and other sources of inefficiency may accumulate if a check is not made often enough to pick up the small errors that in total loom large but are hard to identify later. Clearly then, timeliness is one aspect of a strategic control point.

Control points should also permit *economical* observation and report. For example, sales data must be reported for accounting purposes, and it is quite simple also to classify them by salesmen for control purposes. In many other instances, however, the control data are not ready-made; then the expense of special inspection and reports must be considered.

In some situations measurement of results is so difficult or expensive that the control is placed on the process instead. For instance, it is difficult to measure the wisdom of a particular decision by the purchasing agent; so, often emphasis is placed on making sure the agent went through certain steps, such as developing clear specifications, securing a required number of bids, and the like. Similarly, in controlling the quality of some products and services it may be more economical to establish controls over the process than to attempt to test the final product.

Still another consideration relating to economy is whether the control will seriously retard the operations. A major objection to the review of outgoing correspondence mentioned in connection with government operations is the delay that often results. For this reason most businesses permit people to go ahead and send out their letters, but may provide for reviews of carbon copies. Similarly, the investigation of the credit standing of a customer after an order is received may seriously interfere with delivery service; hence credit limits should be established before the order is received; and these limits once established may guide the extending of credit for a whole succession of orders over a period of a year or more. So, a second consideration in picking strategic control points is the direct and indirect expense involved.

Especially for executives in higher-level positions, at least some of the control points should provide *comprehensive coverage*. Control points that summarize or consolidate several operations are useful for this purpose. Over-all expense figures are of this nature, and these may be expressed as a ratio to volume. Such ratios need not be only in dollar terms; often man-hours per ton of output, or pounds of cotton per dozen sheets will provide the really significant operating data, unadulterated by price changes. If some general norm is applicable to various operations, results may be expressed in relation to this; for example, modern salary administration often provides a range of salary for each job, and it is fairly easy to show how all salaries in a division or department compare with this range or its midpoint.

Some of the comprehensive controls deliberately attempt to check activities at a bottleneck through which everything must pass. Mr. Ickes' control of payroll changes was of this nature. In a small business often one or two executives sign all checks, and in larger businesses sometimes the department head approves all expense vouchers.

For large enterprises, however, top executives must rely primarily on summarized data. For example, the type of comprehensive financial figures watched closely by the executive committee of the du Pont company for each of its operating subsidiaries is indicated in Figure 36. Such comprehensive control points tend to cover up significant operating detail, and there may be some delay in assembling the information; but for general control of decentralized operations, these limitations usually are not too serious. In any event, the possibility of establishing some sort of comprehensive controls should be explored when picking strategic control points.

Control points should be selected to promote *balanced* performance. Anyone who has dealt with piece rates knows that a strong incentive on volume of output is likely to have an adverse effect on quality of production and care of equipment. The same tendency is found in many areas. If close controls are established over expenses, attention to the quality of the service or product is likely to be neglected; contrariwise, if an executive is being pressed for high-quality service his expenses are likely to rise. In the sales field, if the controls all center on the orders actually received, some sales-men will neglect the cultivation of new prospects and push for an immediate order even though it jeopardizes customer good will.

KEY OPERATING FACTORS WATCHED IN EACH DEPARTMENT
BY DUPONT EXECUTIVE COMMITTEE

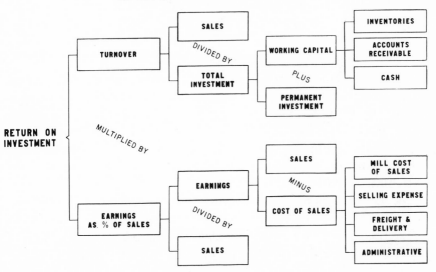

FIGURE 36. *Comprehensive Financial Control Points Used by du Pont Company.* See "How the du Pont Organization Appraises Its Performance," *Financial Management Series, No. 94,* American Management Association. A series of charts is prepared for each product department, showing the above data for the preceding ten years, monthly data for the current year, and a forecast for the balance of the year.

Controls over only part of the total duties of an individual often emphasize the tangible results that are relatively easy to measure and neglect the intangible achievements. For example, accounting figures of expenses and income may receive considerable attention, whereas executive development, which is very difficult to measure, is glossed over. To guard against such imbalance controls should be established over the intangible and other aspects of performance that are not covered at other control points. Perhaps the intangible items can be covered only in periodic appraisal of the executive's performance (see Chapter 19) or through personal supervision. Whatever the method of observation, no system of strategic control points is complete without adequate provision for balance.

*Summary.* The first step in administrative control is setting standards at strategic points. These standards come directly from the objectives, deadlines, specifications, and other goals established as an integral part of the planning process. For practical purposes, however, the administrator usually must (1) make sure that the standards are stated in terms of individual responsibility so that the administrator will know whom to praise or blame for deviation of actual results from the standard; (2) pick out strategic points in the whole flow of operations that will enable the administrator to keep track of what's going on without having to take time to check on all phases of all activities.

Considerable judgment is necessary to figure out the best control points in a particular operation. Important considerations in picking these strategic points are: (1) catching important deviations in time to take constructive action, (2) practicability and economy in making observations, (3) providing at least some comprehensive controls that consolidate and summarize large blocks of detailed activities, and (4) securing a balance in the control so that some aspects of the work, such as building long-run good-will or developing executives, will not be slighted because of close controls on other phases. Setting standards at the right points is the foundation of simple and effective control.

## CHECKING AND REPORTING ON PERFORMANCE

The second basic step in the process of control is to compare actual performance with the standards and goals already established. There are questions here of when the checking should take place, by whom it should be done, and how it should be reported so as to facilitate corrective action.

### Use required confirmation sparingly

Most executives keep the control over certain matters in their own hands; that is, they insist on checking personally before the work is permitted to proceed. For example, before credit is granted to a customer, the treasurer may insist on examining the credit file to make sure that the various credit standards are being observed. In many companies price changes can be made only with the approval of the top executive. Even more common is insistence that expenditures above the budget, transfers and promotion of personnel receiving a salary above, say, $10,000 per year, or exceptions to established methods and procedures be approved by the executive who is exercising the control. The executive feels confident that the work is done right because he has checked it before it moves on to the next step.

Under some circumstances the duty of checking and giving prior approval may be delegated to men who have special control responsibilities. The use of inspectors in a plant who must approve raw material or parts before they are used in processing is quite common. Occasionally a controller may be empowered to authorize exceptions to the budget. Similarly, the personnel officer frequently checks personnel actions for conformity with standards and policies before they become official. Such men are said to have concurring authority. As pointed out in Chapter 12, this arrangement is likely to lead to serious difficulty unless the basis upon which the control agent withholds approval is clearly defined.

The chief reason for using required confirmation, instead of a subsequent check, is the added assurance that standards will be maintained. On the other hand, it is a cumbersome arrangement that may delay action, and when concurring authority is used, this may be a source of internal friction. For these latter reasons such prior review should be used sparingly.

Not infrequently what appears to be an insistence on confirmation is really a reluctance of the executive to delegate authority because he is unable to state clearly the standards of performance desired. He is not sure just what he does want his subordinates to do; consequently, he has them move only a step at a time and come back for further directions before carrying the project to completion. In other words, some of the planning still remains to be done, and the executive feels that it is unwise to turn this planning over to subordinates. When working through a new and important problem, this may be a very practical procedure. For more repetitive or less important problems, however, it suggests an inability to plan and a lack of confidence in subordinates.

### Concentrate on exceptions

A large part of the activities of any enterprise must proceed without waiting for the confirmation of some higher executive. Control here is concerned primarily with appraising current and completed action as a basis for regulating future activities.

This appraisal can be simplified by concentrating on unexpected or unusual results. As long as operations take place according to plans and operating conditions are as forecast, there is no need for corrective action. It is the exceptions—for example, low output, high expense, large sales orders, delayed raw materials, jump in labor turnover, and the like—that call for special attention.

Consequently, the busy executive often asks for reports on only the exceptional matters. He then assumes activities are proceeding normally (as planned) unless a report to the contrary is received.

Such a reporting scheme will work well only if plans are clear to both the executive and his subordinates and if there is a definite understanding as to responsibility for reporting exceptions. Rarely is it wise to place complete reliance on this arrangement; some comprehensive data or personal observation should be used to keep tab on results. But this "exception" reporting may be applied to a large array of standing plans and detailed activities.

**Observe personally for thorough understanding**

*Use of direct contacts.* Personal observation should always play a part in checking on results. Military men have long recognized the value of having commanding officers either locate close to the scene of action or at least make frequent visits so that they can see for themselves. One very able president of a manufacturing company insists on spending two weeks every year traveling with salesmen and calling on customers himself. Even though this causes inconvenience in the head office, the president believes he can get information regarding the acceptability of the company products, effectiveness of advertising, salesmen's reactions to training schemes, and other facts not adequately revealed in written reports.

The general manager of a leading department store feels much the same way. Every morning he takes a walk through the store observing the number of customers, display of merchandise, and behavior of salespeople; he also chats informally with employees at all levels in the organization. To reduce the interference with his other work he will take occasional telephone calls, or he may talk with some visitor as he makes his tour, but at least for one hour his office is wherever you find him. There is no doubt that this man knows what is going on, and his informal visits also have a good effect upon employee morale.

*Benefits of personal observation.* Just what an executive learns from direct observation and personal contact is sometimes difficult to define. A realistic mental picture of the operating situation, an acquaintanceship with the people involved, the tone of voice and confidence with which statements are made, the reaction of people to suggestions, the ease and informality of asking questions and giving information, all add up to an understanding of what is happening that is impossible to get through written reports.

Oral reports provide some, though by no means all, of the advantages of direct observation. They provide an opportunity to observe personal reactions and answer questions on points that are not made clear. If an informal atmosphere is maintained, one can draw out more about the feelings and motivations of people than one can from the typical written document.

Unfortunately, this method of checking on performance is time-consuming. It is a physical impossibility for an executive directing the work of a large number of people to inspect personally the operations or even the results at strategic control points. Consequently, except for first-line supervisors, personal observation must be used primarily on a sampling basis, or for information on certain types of performance only. And being a limited sample, the executive must be careful to supplement his own observations with more comprehensive data.

Nevertheless, the executive who has been in the shop this morning, or talked personally with customers last week, is in a much better position to understand and appraise other reports on performance that he receives. Moreover, his personal contact with people on the firing line usually helps in motivation.

### Design reports for action

*Promptness.* The promptness of reports can add significantly to the effectiveness of control. This is clear when some undesirable practice is going on. For instance, if the spoilage rate is high or if one section in the office is working overtime because of a failure to transfer workers from other sections, the sooner this is discovered and corrected the greater will be the saving.

Prompt reports also help in diagnosing the difficulty. A report showing high delivery expenses for the month of January that is not received until the last week in February has lost some of its usefulness. When the executive talks to the delivery foreman about the cause of the high expense, the chances are that the foreman will cast about in his own mind for possible excuses such as snowstorms and breakdowns. Whereupon the executive tries to remember what happened. He may be able to reply that the snowstorm hit on Saturday and was cleared up by the first of the week, or that the breakdown occurred in December. This give and take is likely to continue for a time until the executive finally says, "Well, keep your eye on it, John, and see if we can't do better in the future."

In contrast, when the report is received two days after the completion of the period, the foreman probably really does remember what caused the difficulty, and he and his supervisor can discuss constructive plans for avoiding it in the future. The longer the lag between the time events take place and the time the report is made, the more difficult it is to get at the real source of the trouble.

Prompt reports often contain some inaccuracies. The people preparing the reports may not have time to reconcile figures from two different sources, to make special adjustments, to go back and look for possible errors. Generally this type of error is not large enough to cover up the salient features, and for control purposes preliminary figures quickly supplied are the most useful. The revised figures can be prepared later as they are needed for accounting purposes or detailed analysis.

The executive who wants the prompt reports should recognize that they are necessarily preliminary in nature and not heap unreasonable criticism on the head of the report clerk who would probably prefer to take two weeks longer and make a report that needs no revision. Happily, modern communication devices and office machinery are making it easier to prepare reports that are both prompt and reasonably accurate.

*Content of report.* A temptation exists to think that the more information a report contains the more useful it is for control purposes. This is not necessarily so, and certainly the detailed reports are burdensome to prepare. The salesmen, the foremen, and most other people primarily concerned with getting results find the preparation of reports a distraction, particularly if they are complex or detailed.

This is no new problem. We find the Duke of Wellington writing from Spain about 1810 to the British Secretary of War, Lord Bradford, as follows:

My Lord,

If I attempted to answer the mass of futile correspondence that surrounds me, I should be debarred from all serious business of campaigning.

I must remind your Lordship—for the last time—that so long as I retain an independent position, I shall see that no officer under my command is debarred by attending to the futile drivelling of mere quill driving in your Lordship's Office—from attending to his first duty—which is, and always has been, so to train the private men under his command that they may, without question, beat any force opposed to them in the field.

I am,

My Lord,

Your obedient Servant

(WELLINGTON)

The selection of strategic control points reduces the need for voluminous reports. The report should, of course, contain a *comparison* of actual performance with the standards set at these points. In addition, the report will be more useful if it contains an *explanation* of any wide deviation from the standard. Finally, the report should as a rule contain *proposals* for corrective action, if any such action is called for. However, such recommendations may be omitted if they seriously interfere with the promptness of the report or if correction of a difficulty is clearly outside the scope of responsibility of the person preparing the report.

*Method of presentation.* Reports should emphasize the outstanding features of the performance being reviewed and the spots where corrective action is needed. All too often the man preparing the report prefaces it with a technical explanation of a statistical computation or a series of qualifications because these are uppermost in his mind at the time the report is put together. Instead, the report should be prepared from the point of view of the man who is to receive it. If explanations or qualifications are included at all, they should not be permitted to interfere with the principal message conveyed.

Statistical or financial information can often be presented forcefully in graphic form. Some companies use large wall charts; a few have large chartrooms where executives may find the latest information portrayed on a whole series of charts. Such special facilities are not necessary for the use of graphic presentation, however; an ordinary hectograph or ruler and a few colored pencils is all the equipment that is needed to give a clear visual presentation. A series of perhaps a dozen charts showing current performance as against past trends at strategic control points will become one of the most valued tools of almost any executive.

Explanatory material and supporting statistical data usually should be brief and clearly related to any charts that are used. When only qualitative data are being presented, it is usually wise to present a summary of highlights before the detail is given. This is but another way of helping the executive who received the report to grasp quickly the important facts. Then, if he wishes, he can proceed to examine the supporting information, and perhaps ask for even more detail; but he is relieved of the burden of sifting through a large mass of information to discover the crucial features of past performance.

*Summary.* Most executives use a combination of methods for checking on performance. At a few very important points they require their own confirmation, or that of an independent expert, before action proceeds. For most of the activity, however, they rely upon a series of prompt and well-designed reports that enable them to see quickly a summary of recent operations and the exceptions that call for their further attention. To understand really what lies back of these reports and to appraise the more intangible aspects of operations, they make occasional visits to the scene of action and personally confer with many individuals regarding current methods and results. These methods of checking performance against standards at strategic control points enable executives to keep their fingers on the pulse of operations.

## CORRECTIVE ACTION

The first two basic steps of control—setting standards at strategic points and checking actual performance against these standards—are really preliminary. They may be done to perfection and yet no control results unless all this checking has some influence on the behavior of people performing the actual operation. In other words, the third step, corrective action, is necessary before any real control occurs.

Comparison of actual results with the established objectives and standards will almost always reveal some places where the results have not come up to expectations. As soon as such deviations are known, the person performing the operation will often initiate corrective action himself. In addition the supervisory executive should check to see that the trouble is being corrected. If it is not, the executive should take steps either (a) to correct the past action, or more likely, (b) to bring similar action in the future closer to the desired goal. Broadly speaking, this corrective action will be brought about by some combination of the following steps:

1. Adjust physical and external situations
2. Review the direction, training, and selection of subordinates
3. Improve motivation
4. Modify plans where necessary

**Adjust physical and external situations**

Differences between achievement and plans often result from shifts and unexpected obstacles in the work situation. The operating plans and goals are, of course, based on forecasts covering conditions under which the work is to be performed, and every executive must spend a significant part of his time working with these environmental conditions. He will attempt to make the conditions conform to these forecasts, or be even more favorable for achieving the goals.

The action of an executive to maintain these working conditions takes many forms. He tries to see that the work arrives from other departments, or perhaps from material suppliers or customers, in the form and at the time anticipated. If breakdowns occur in physical equipment—typewriters, automobiles, computers, processing equipment, and the like—he sees that repairs or replacements are made with the least interruption to operations. He is concerned with the maintenance of satisfactory working conditions; he expedites various supporting activities, such as direct-mail advertising for salesmen or ready availability of parts for repairmen. In a variety of other ways he seeks to create the setting in which achievement of goals is unobstructed.

**Review the direction, training, and selection of subordinates**

A second broad area of corrective action is making sure that the individuals assigned to the work are properly qualified and directed. All too often failure to meet standards can be traced to inadequate direction. Hence the executive needs to review again with his subordinates just what is wanted and how they should go about accomplishing it. There should be no second time for "Oh, I didn't understand."

The difficulty may run deeper than a misunderstanding of instructions. Perhaps the man whose performance needs to be improved lacks the necessary training and experience for his assignment. The corrective action should then consist of providing this training as rapidly as possible, perhaps giving the man temporary assistance in the interim. Generally, if the man can learn to handle the assignment within a reasonable period of time, he should be left on that job. It was management's mistake in assigning him the work for which he was not yet prepared, and in the interests of good morale the man should be given an opportunity to show what he can do when properly trained.

Nevertheless, occasionally experience shows that a man lacks some of the basic abilities needed to perform a job or it is impractical to keep the man in a position while he is growing up to it. A transfer of the man to work for which he is qualified and his replacement by a more capable individual is the positive action required, provided such transfers can be made without serious disruption in morale.

**Improve motivation**

Operating achievements may not have come up to standard partly, at least, because the people doing the work did not put forth enough effort. If lack of motivation occurs, the executive must probe deeper to uncover personal barriers to energetic action.

Possibly some aspect of the work situation or the job itself is a source of irritation. Correction of such annoyance will permit greater effort. Positive incentives directly tied to the desired goal may also be necessary. These range from intangible rewards of status to increases in pay, as was pointed out in Chapter 22.

Imposing penalties or other disciplinary action rarely generates more than a bare minimum of effort on the part of the person disciplined. However, occasional disciplinary action for infraction of rules may be necessary to establish a normal pattern of behavior among all employees. Consistent discipline coupled with consistent rewards enable members of the organization to *anticipate* the personal results of their efforts; in this way, desired behavior is encouraged in the future before corrective action is necessary.

**Modify plans where necessary**

Corrective action usually includes at least some revision of plans. Many external forces cannot be adjusted by executive action, notably sales orders, competitive prices, availability of labor and materials, and similar factors influenced by general business conditions. Consequently, there is need for continuing appraisal of results in terms of these changing conditions and for adjusting plans accordingly.

Similarly, breakdowns or other interruptions to operations may call for a revision of schedule and perhaps different methods and reassignment of the work. When one discovers that a particular individual is not able to carry out his assignment, the lack of a satisfactory substitute or the upsetting effect of his transfer may make an adjustment in the work assigned to him more practical than a transfer to a different position.

Moreover, a careful review of operating experience may suggest ways that standing plans may be improved. Standards may be too high, policies need qualification so as to avoid frequent exceptions, or methods should be adjusted to make better use of existing facilities and personnel. If operating results are much better than the established standards, perhaps the reasons for the achievement can be discovered and introduced as a standard practice. For special projects and other nonrecurring activity, experience may show which mistakes to avoid and which measures proved to be particularly effective. These should be noted as guides to planning of similar projects in the future.

Such revision of plans is an essential part of corrective action. At the same time it starts anew the administrative cycle of planning, direction, and control. The revised plans must be communicated to those who are responsible for executing them, and provision made for checking actual performance. Any dynamic enterprise should anticipate that control will bring with it revision and adaptation to meet changing conditions.

## SUMMARY

Once plans are laid, necessary resources assembled, and directions issued, the executive must take action to assure that performance conforms to plans. Three steps are involved in this control process: (1) setting standards at strategic points, (2) checking and reporting on performance, and (3) taking corrective action.

Control standards come directly from the objectives, specifications, and other goals developed in the planning process. To be most useful in control, however, these goals should be tied to individual responsibilities. Moreover, control should be simplified by concentrating on strategic points. Selecting these strategic points is the crux of simple and effective control; they should provide timely, economical, comprehensive, and balanced checks.

Comparison at the strategic points of actual performance with the control standards should be done through a combination of methods. Prompt and well-designed reports should cover the bulk of operations. These should be supplemented by personal observation to secure thorough understanding. For some crucial operations, a separate review and confirmation may be required before action is allowed to proceed.

When this comparison of performance with the strategically selected standards shows significant deviations, corrective action is necessary if the control is to have any real influence on results. Corrective action normally consists of adjusting the physical and external situation to permit the desired action; reviewing the supervision, training, and selection of those doing the work; improving motivation; and modifying plans where necessary.

The control process either completes the task of the executive or, more likely, shows the need for further action and thus starts another administrative cycle of planning, supervision, and control.

### SELECTED REFERENCES

E. I. du Pont de Nemours and Company, Treasurer's Department, *Executive Committee Control Charts*, American Management Association, 1960.

Lemke, B. C. and J. D. Edwards, eds., *Administrative Control and Executive Action*, Charles E. Merrill Books, Inc., 1961.

Richards, M. D. and W. A. Nielander, eds., *Readings in Management*, South-Western Publishing Co., 1958, Chaps. 13 and 14.

Sherwin, D. S., "The Meaning of Control," *Dun's Review and Modern Industry*, January 1956.

Terry, G. R., *Principles of Management* (3rd ed.), Richard D. Irwin, Inc., 1960, Part V.

# 25
# Budgetary Control

Budgetary control can be one of the most effective tools of administration. When properly used, it aids in planning and coordination, as well as in control.

The procedural aspects of budgeting have been ably covered in books on the subject and need not be discussed here. Since our interest is in the basic processes of administration, this chapter more appropriately concentrates on (1) the way budgeting assists in planning, coordination, and control; and (2) the conditions that are necessary to obtain these benefits of budgetary control.

*Fundamental steps in budgetary control.* There are three essential steps in every application of budgetary control:

1. *Statement of plans for a future period, expressed in specific numerical terms.* More precisely, the budget consists of a statement of the anticipated *results* of operating plans, rather than a description of the activity. These results are expressed in some common denominator, usually dollars, although occasionally in man-hours, pounds of material, or other physical units.

2. *Consolidation of these estimates into a well-balanced program.* The figures for the various activities and divisions covered by the budget must be added together, checked for consistency and workability, and reviewed in terms of over-all objectives.

3. *Comparison of actual results with the budget and adjustment of plans when necessary.* As in any control technique, a report showing deviations of actual operations from standards is significant only insofar as it provides a basis for corrective action.

441

A great danger exists that the mechanics of budgetary control will receive so much attention that one or more of these three fundamental steps will be pushed into the background.

*Variety of situations to which budgetary control may be applied.* The budget idea has numerous applications. One large utility company, for example, has detailed coal budgets showing in tons the purchase, storage, transfer, and consumption for each of its power plants and for the system as a whole. Somewhat simpler purchase and production budgets for individual commodities are prepared by many companies. In times of labor shortage or rapidly changing volume of activity, some firms prepare manpower budgets expressed in terms of different types of labor.

The chief reasons for preparing such budgets in units other than dollars are: (1) the dollar figure is too general and may cover up significant differences in size or quality, and (2) price changes are confusing when plans really call for physical levels of activity. To tie into over-all budgeting, however, it may be necessary to prepare figures in dollars, as well as physical units.

The most common type of budget used in business deals with capital expenditures. Large sums are often involved, and the board of directors may insist upon approving budgets before commitments are made. When *capital expenditure budgets* are used, all the anticipated projects for a period are summarized and presented at one time. This gives the board a better idea of the total sum involved and also avoids the necessity for separate consideration of each small project. Under typical procedures, the board relies upon the treasurer or controller to see that actual expenditures do not exceed the approved budget. Unexpected needs may, of course, lead to a revision of the budget.

*Cash budgets,* covering all receipts and disbursements, are more inclusive. They differ significantly from profit-and-loss budgets because of changes in the size of inventories, accounts receivable and other assets, and in liabilities. They are almost indispensable to a company that has to operate on a narrow margin of cash without upsetting the efficient flow of work.

The most useful type of budget from the point of view of general administration is the *profit-and-loss budget.* Since it normally covers all the profit-and-loss accounts, all of the major activities of the enterprise are included.

These different examples of the use of budgetary control indicate how the basic idea may be applied to different phases of a company operation. Since the profit-and-loss budget is the most inclusive and the most valuable for purposes of general administration, it will be the subject of more detailed analysis in the balance of this chapter. Nevertheless, most of the points raised will also be applicable to other types of budgets.

## Benefits of Budgetary Control

The term *budgetary control* is somewhat misleading because budgets are as much a planning and coordinating device as one of control. In seeking to understand the benefits that may be secured from budgetary control, all three phases should be considered. These will be discussed in terms of:

1. Improvement in planning
2. Aid in coordination
3. Comprehensive control

### Improvement in planning

*Stimulates thinking in advance.* The preparation of a budget tends to make an executive anticipate future operating problems and ways of meeting them. The budget usually covers operations for at least several months or a year in advance; and for this entire period the executive is expected to predict his expenses and operating results.

This assignment when conscientiously done shifts the executive's attention from immediate problems to those that are just appearing on the horizon. This forward look often provides an opportunity to avoid trouble and take advantage of unusual opportunities. To be sure, budgeting has no monopoly on forward planning, but when applied throughout an enterprise, it will force some executives to look more carefully into the future than they otherwise would do.

*Leads to specificity in planning.* For budgeting purposes it is not enough to say that output will probably go up in the last half of the year, or that payroll expenses should go down. These ideas have to be reduced to specific estimates. The increase has to be set at, say, $50,000 per month, and the reduction in payroll at $3,000. Vague and often casual generalities will not suffice; instead, someone has to figure out "how much and when."

The introduction of budgets will not, of course, endow executives with supernatural foresight. Unforeseen events almost always cause actual operations to deviate more or less from plan. The point is that budgeting tends to improve the quality of planning. The necessity of looking ahead for the entire budget period and making specific estimates of results usually refines the quality of planning that is done.

### Aid in coordination

*Promotes balanced activities.* Budgetary control contributes to coordination in several ways, the most obvious of which is the balancing of activities. Estimates of operating results will be received from sales, production, purchasing, and other departments. These can easily be checked one against the other to see if one department is planning on a larger volume of activities than the others.

Moreover, when monthly budgets are prepared, the timing of activities can be checked to make sure that the sales department is not planning to sell goods before the production department expects to make them available, or that similar discrepancies do not exist. The fact that the plans of each department are stated in specific and comparable terms makes it easier to secure unified planning.

*Encourages exchange of information.* The preparation of specific estimates necessary for budgets often leads one executive to seek information from other executives. Especially when the work of one division is dependent upon another, this exchange is likely to take place. For example, the purchasing department must find out what the production department plans to produce, the sales department checks on the time a new product will be available and also gives the production department some idea of prospective demand for the regular products; the training division must find out about plans for additions to the sales force, and so forth.

This interchange of ideas regarding planning contributes significantly to the coordination of the budget plans themselves. It also provides an occasion for voluntary coordination on other matters. As executives of related departments discuss their respective plans, one man has an excellent opportunity to suggest minor revisions that will simplify his work and to make adjustments that will aid the other divisions. Most of this give and take may be on matters that do not show up directly in the budget estimates but that still contribute significantly to harmonious action.

*Discloses unbalance early.* One of the important principles of harmonious action is coordination in the early stages. Mutual adjustments are more easily made if the need for them is known well in advance and particularly if actual operations are not already underway. The emphasis in budgetary control on forward planning means that lack of balance and inconsistencies are likely to be discovered while plans are still in the formative stages; hence, budgeting not only brings to light places where coordination is needed, but it tends to do so early enough for easy remedial action.

**Comprehensive control**

*Provides inclusive standards.* Financial budgets normally include all the important accounts in a profit-and-loss statement. In a large enterprise, these accounts will be broken down for several divisions and departments, but all items of income and expense will appear some place. A comprehensive budget shows what all of these accounts should look like if present plans are carried out. The projected accounts can then serve as standards of performance. They show what the persons preparing the budget think should happen.

One of the chief advantages of such standards of performance is their inclusiveness. They cover every activity of the company recognized in the accounting records. While details and intangibles may be concealed, the coverage is systematic and penetrates into every division. No other single control device is so comprehensive.

*Uses available reports on performance.* Another distinctive feature of budgetary control is that very little special effort is required for the comparison of actual results with the standard. The accounting records will be kept and reports prepared whether or not the budgets exist. Since the control standard, that is, the budget, is classified and expressed in terms of the regular accounts, comparison of the actual results with standards is simple. No additional inspection or reporting system is required. Here, then, is a control device that is at the same time comprehensive in coverage and relatively simple to operate.

In conclusion, budgetary control should be regarded as both a procedural device and a psychological tool of administration. While its concrete form is in tables of figures, much of its benefit lies in the thinking and relationships that it promotes among executives.

## Requisites for Successful Budgetary Control

The benefits of budgetary control which have just been described are impressive. Better planning, coordination, and control are desired by every administrator. Unfortunately, these benefits cannot be obtained by merely adding some reports and accounting procedures. Instead, budgetary control must be made an integral part of the administrative process. The more important requisites for successful budgetary control include: (1) managerial planning in terms of budgets; (2) actual use of budgets as a coordinating medium; (3) effective follow-through on current operations; (4) flexibility in budgeting.

### Managerial planning in terms of budgets

*Plans—not mere predictions.* The figures appearing on a budget statement should represent, as nearly as possible, actual plans rather than informed guesses as to what is likely to happen. There is a marked difference between forecasting the weather and planning to do something about it. Likewise, a forecast of sales volume, perhaps made by someone outside the company, represents a different kind of thinking than the budgeted sales figure based on careful plans for sales promotion, direct selling, and customer service. An estimated cost of production figured from trends in price indexes and expense ratios is a different kind of a figure from a budgeted cost based on planned machine loads, material usage, and specific labor rates.

Of course, a large element of forecasting is present in all planning, but this does not mean that budgeting should rely on forecasts alone. Improved planning as a result of budgeting will occur only if there is insistence that the figures placed in the budget be the anticipated result of actual plans for future operations.

*Clear-cut organization.* The type of planning needed for budgeting cannot take place unless responsibility is clear. For example, some department stores have had difficulty in the use of budgetary control because of confusion as to who determines the number of salespeople to be employed. The departmental buyers have nominal responsibility, but the personnel department makes the day-by-day decisions as to the number of additional people to employ, and the controller sets a monthly maximum figure for selling expense. Under circumstances such as these, it is extremely difficult to know who really does the planning, and there is a temptation to be satisfied with mere forecasting. Not infrequently, organization clarification must accompany the installation of budgetary control.

*Arrangement of accounts parallel to organization units.* Accounting figures serve a number of purposes, such as financial reports and tax records, in addition to their use for internal management. Emphasis on the former uses has resulted in the accounts of some companies being poorly adapted to budgetary control. Inventory figures, for example, may be classified primarily in terms of liquidity because of the significance of these facts to creditors; or, payroll records may be set up primarily to facilitate payroll deductions.

Unless these accounts are also divided according to managerial responsibility, it is hard to take the first basic step in budgeting, namely to translate plans into anticipated accounting figures. Also, it is difficult to assign responsibility for deviation of actual results from the budgeted figures. Thus, if four different department heads are responsible for semiprocessed inventory, close budgetary control requires that separate inventory accounts be established for each department. Similarly, payroll, supplies, and other controllable expenses should be allocated to departments whose decisions determine their amounts. Only as the account classification reflects administrative responsibility can budgets serve as a good planning tool.

*Active participation by executives in budget preparation.* Budget preparation should not be assigned to some central staff unit, nor delegated by operating executives to their administrative assistants. These people can help in the preparation of budgets, but, unless the operating executives themselves take time to think through their future operations and make sure that the figures in the budget reflect this thinking, many of the planning benefits listed earlier in this chapter will be lost. The budget will become "just another set of figures," and it will be a burden rather than an aid to the executive.

Moreover, unless the operating executives participate in the preparation of the budget, they will be loath to accept the budgets as reasonable goals; they will not be so strongly committed to achieving budgeted results; and they will feel free to criticize the budget as "wild guesses" or "stupid mistakes" if actual results are not as favorable as those anticipated in the budget.

*Summary.* Budgeting tends to improve planning because it stimulates thinking in advance and leads to specificity in planning. To obtain these benefits, however, the budget must reflect actual plans and not merely sideline predictions; the organizations should clearly indicate who should be responsible for preparing each part of the budget; accounting classification must parallel organization units so that the plans of the several departments can be translated directly into the appropriate account; and lastly, the operating executives themselves must actively participate in the preparation of the budget if it is to improve their planning and is to be accepted as a reasonable goal for current operations.

### Use as a coordinating medium

*Estimates carefully fitted together.* Whenever over-all budgets are prepared, it is typically assumed that they have been geared together, and hence that they assist in coordination. An executive using budgets should make sure that this is a true assumption, for it is entirely possible to add together unrelated estimates. For example, the purchasing department might estimate disbursements for raw materials based on a sales volume out of line with other plans. The purchase budget should, of course, be synchronized with the need to build up finished goods inventory in anticipation of seasonal peaks, changes in product specifications, decisions to purchase some subassemblies rather than manufacture them, availability of cash to make quantity purchases, and similar factors.

Budgeting provides an excellent *opportunity* to coordinate activities, but the actual fitting together of plans requires specific attention and often hard work. This is one aspect of budgetary control where a central staff unit can be particularly helpful.

*Joint participation in adjustments.* Not only should the original budget estimates be coordinated, but any necessary adjustments should be dovetailed. For instance, if the sales manager grants the request of a customer to postpone delivery of a big order for six weeks, it is not enough for him to inform only the production manager.

Several departments should take part in deciding what adjustments are to be made. The treasurer, concerned about working capital tied up in inventory, may suggest operating short hours; but a decision to delay production will cause temporary layoffs, and this will seriously affect personnel activities. As an alternative to curtailed production, the sales manager may recommend earlier deliveries of other orders, but this requires adjustment of purchasing schedules. Clearly, the sales manager, production manager, treasurer, personnel director, and purchasing agent must all join in the revision of plans. Without this joint participation in the adjustment, the budget may even be dangerous, because some executives, assuming the original budget is still reliable, may proceed to take unwarranted action.

*Top management use and support.* The effectiveness of a budget as a device for achieving coordination of current operations also depends upon the behavior of senior executives. For example, if the general manager orders a curtailment in a plant expansion program without insisting that corresponding adjustments be made in various departmental budgets, the prestige of the budget will drop sharply. Orders from the chief obviously supersede any voluntary agreements as to coordination, and the man who is following orders from the boss is likely to look with contempt upon a now obsolete budget. On the other hand, if the senior executive insists that revisions of the budget be made as soon as major changes are known to be necessary, the budget will soon be regarded as a primary mechanism for interdepartmental coordination.

The initial preparation of the budget contributes to coordination, provided care is taken that the estimates are carefully fitted together. If budgets are to serve as a continuing means of coordination, there should be both joint participation in any adjustments and active use and support by top management.

### Effective follow-through

*Prompt and intelligible reports.* The significance of prompt, clear reports for effective control has already been stressed. Reports comparing actual results with budgets are no exception. Some large companies are able to present operating figures within five working days after the close of the budget period. Even with the use of computers, however, some figures will have to be revised later; nevertheless, the usefulness of the reports is greatly enhanced by this speed in preparation. The sooner the control information becomes available, the easier it is to take constructive corrective action.

A related issue in budgeting is the length of the budget period. For broad planning and control annual budgets may be adequate; but for planning, coordination, and control of internal operations a shorter period is necessary. For most types of enterprise, monthly (or a four-week period) budgets, extending six months or a year ahead, are the most useful. The closer the control desired, the shorter the period that should be used.

*Regular use by executives.* Even well-prepared budgets and prompt reports on actual operations do not assure that budgeting will be a strong control mechanism. They must be regularly used by operative executives to appraise performance. If a subordinate knows that his chief watches budget results closely and that unfavorable results are sure to lead to a request for explanation, he will: (1) try to avoid the occasion for making such explanation by keeping performance up to the budget standard, and (2) when deviations do occur, try to devise corrective action before he is called into conference. On the other hand, if the executive permits unfavorable results to slip by without comment, the subordinate will soon regard the budget as a set of figures not to be taken very seriously.

**Flexibility in budgeting**

One of the principal difficulties in using budgets for control purposes is that operating conditions differ from those assumed in preparing the budget. Sales may be higher or lower, prices may have changed, or other shifts occurred that make it unreasonable to expect operating results to conform to budget. In other words, the standards of performance are no longer applicable. While the budget may continue to be used as a starting point in appraising performance, the troublesome question of how much allowance should be made for these changes in operating conditions always arises. In order to meet this problem, some flexibility is needed. The chief ways of securing such flexibility are alternative budgets, flexible budgets, standard costs, and regular revisions.

*Alternative budgets.* One way of securing flexibility in budgeting is to prepare a separate budget for different operating conditions; then the conditions that actually prevail will determine which one is used as a standard for performance. For example, one company prepares three budgets, one based on very favorable business conditions, a second on poor business conditions, and a third on probable conditions. The middle budget is really used for operating plans while the other two indicate what the company might do in event of unexpected shifts in business activity. If business takes a turn for the worse, the lower budget is, of course, used as the standard of performance.

Alternative budgets are time-consuming to prepare and clumsy to handle. Most companies prefer either to use a single budget or to adopt one of the means of flexibility described below.

*Flexible budgets.* In their simpler form, flexible budgets are simply a means of interpolating between two alternative budgets. Typi-

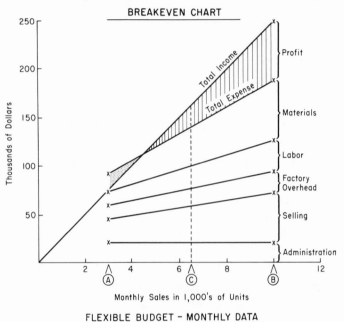

## BREAKEVEN CHART

## FLEXIBLE BUDGET – MONTHLY DATA

|  | (A)<br>Low Volume Budget | (B)<br>High Volume Budget | (C)<br>Computed Budget<br>for May |
|---|---|---|---|
| Number of Units | 3,000 | 10,000 | 6,300 |
| Sales income at<br>$25 per unit | $75,000 | $250,000 | $157,000 |
| Materials | 18,000 | 60,000 | 38,000 |
| Labor | 13,000 | 34,000 | 23,000 |
| Factory Overhead | 15,000 | 22,000 | 18,000 |
| Selling | 22,000 | 50,000 | 35,000 |
| Administration | 20,000 | 20,000 | 20,000 |
| Total expense | 88,000 | 186,000 | 134,000 |
| Profit or (Loss) | $(13,000) | $ 64,000 | $ 23,000 |

FIGURE 37. *Illustration of Flexible Budget with
Corresponding Break-Even Chart*

cally, they are designed to show cost and income figures for different levels of activity. Income and expenses are budgeted for a low level and for a high level; then arrangement is made to estimate what expenses should be for any level of activity in between these two budgeted figures. This can be done mathematically or graphically on what is popularly known as a break-even chart. (See Figure 37.) Once the estimating device is prepared, the executive waits until operations have been completed and the level of activity is known. He then sees what expenses and income should have been for this level and uses these figures as a standard with which to appraise the actual results.

Such flexible budgets have two chief advantages. They provide an operating standard that can be easily adjusted at different levels of activity. Moreover, since they show a condensed picture of the entire business operation, they are convenient devices for analyzing certain types of business problems. For example, it is simple to estimate the additional volume necessary to offset a cut in sales price.

Flexible budgets are, however, subject to a number of severe limitations from the point of view of both technical construction and practical use. They are well suited only to a company or department that makes a single product, or performs some basic operation for which volume of activity can be readily defined. Normally, the only independent variable recognized is volume, and as soon as an effort is made to cover changes in material cost, labor rates, and selling prices (which is often necessary to make realistic adjustments to changes in business conditions), the device loses its great virtue of simplicity. Also, there is usually an implicit assumption that costs will vary with volume at a constant rate, and this often is quite unrealistic. Irregular cost increases can be used, but to do so again introduces complexities into what starts out as a simple scheme.

The operational limitations of flexible budgets are even more significant from the point of view of general administration. In seeking a flexible standard for control purposes, most of the planning and coordinating benefits of budgeting are sacrificed. Flexibility is achieved by evading any question as to level of activity until the period is over, and yet questions of volume lie at the very heart of budgetary planning and coordination.

Flexible budgets, then, are useful as diagnostic tools and as a means of providing flexible standards of expense in relatively simple operating situations. But, for the broad concepts of budgetary control discussed in this chapter, a partial flexibility is achieved at the sacrifice of most of the benefits.

*Standard costs.* Although standard-cost accounting is not used primarily to provide flexibility in budgeting, it deserves at least mention in this connection. Standard-cost accounting is typically used by companies making many different products. A standard, or budgeted, cost for each product is first computed; then, as specific quantities of each of these products are put into production in a given month, the standard costs are picked up and added to find what the total costs should have been that month. These total figures are the standards against which actual performance is compared. In this way standard-cost accounting overcomes one of the limitations of flexible budgets, in that it provides cost standards even though varying quantities of different products go through the plant. Standard costs also permit simplification in accounting procedures—a subject outside the scope of the present discussion.

Unfortunately, the computation of standard costs is open to just as much serious question as the computations in flexible budgets. Also, as in flexible budgeting, over-all control standards are computed only after the close of an accounting period, and, because of this characteristic, standard costs are of limited help in planning and coordination.

*Regular budget revisions.* Each of the foregoing ways of securing flexibility in budgeting is useful in particular situations. Generally, however, flexibility can be secured best through an established plan of regular revision. It is not practical, of course, to revise an entire budget each time some change in operating conditions occurs. To do so would entail a tremendous amount of work, and the numerous revisions would probably be more confusing than helpful.

A more practical plan is to revise budgets regularly at the end of each month or quarter. Often, budgets will be computed for a year ahead, then at the end of a month (or a quarter) the budget for the month immediately following will be revised on the basis of then current conditions, and a new budget for the twelfth month ahead will be added. In this way a company always has a budget for a year ahead and a revised budget for the immediate future.

Such a plan of regular revision retains the single over-all budget and makes an additional contribution to planning and to coordination in the very process of revision. Since fairly accurate predictions of operating conditions can usually be made at the time the revision is made, the adjusted budget should serve as a good standard of performance for control purposes.

## SUMMARY

Budgetary control tends to improve the program planning within an enterprise. It stimulates thinking in advance and leads to specificity of planning. To realize these benefits, however, the budget must be based on actual plans rather than side-line predictions; the organization should be clear-cut and paralleled by an account classification so that the plans of responsible people can be directly reflected in accounting terms; and the operating executives themselves must take an active part in the preparation of budgets.

Budgeting also aids in coordination in that it promotes balancing of operations, a general exchange of information, and a variety of direct contacts early enough to give time for corrective adjustment. Here again, full realization of benefits comes only under certain conditions. Someone must make sure that the estimates of the several departments are, in fact, carefully geared together; there should be joint participation in adjustments to budget figures; and, above all, senior executives must insist that the budget be used as a coordinating medium.

Budgets provide a distinctive control device because they serve as broad, inclusive standards. Moreover, since they are expressed in accounting terms, it is relatively easy to compare actual results with these standards. Like any other control scheme, their effectiveness depends in large measure upon prompt, accurate reports and consistent use by the executive of the budget information. The chief difficulty in using budgets for control purposes is that they are often made for some period in advance and operating conditions may change substantially before the planned activity takes place. The most generally usable means of providing flexibility to meet this condition is a regular revision of budgets shortly before the beginning of each operating period. Alternative budgets, flexible budgets, and standard costs may also be used to secure flexibility, or they may be used to assist in the regular revision process.

Budgetary control is no simple road to administrative success. It can be a very helpful tool, provided the key executives use it as an integral part of their administrative activities. Without this patronage, however, budgetary control will be only partially effective, and the burden of preparing budgets and reports may outweigh the curtailed benefits.

### SELECTED REFERENCES

Dearden, J., *Cost and Budget Analysis*, Prentice-Hall, Inc., 1962.

Heiser, H. C., *Budgeting*, The Ronald Press Company, 1959.

Smith, R. L., *Management Through Accounting*, Prentice-Hall, Inc., 1962, Chaps. 11 and 12.

Welsch, G. A., *Budgeting: Profit Planning and Control*, Prentice-Hall, Inc., 1957.

# 26

# Over-All Control Structure

Many controls are involved in the launching and directing of a satellite. Each control has its particular purpose, but if the satellite is to follow a desired orbit, the *total control system* must function in an integrated manner. Similarly, the various controls in a company should be considered not only in terms of their immediate purpose but also in terms of the combined effect of all controls on over-all company action.

### Significance of total control structure

*Trouble created by narrow viewpoint.* Examples of specific controls that have caused more trouble than they corrected are all too frequent. One firm found itself in serious labor difficulty because a new inventory control plan, coupled with an existing cost control system, led to sporadic layoffs just prior to a union contract negotiation. The new inventory control by itself looked fine; it coordinated production with sales and lowered investment in finished goods. But in terms of the total operations, the effects clearly were bad.

A retail store, to cite another case, placed rigid restrictions on the hiring of new personnel as a part of a general campaign to reduce costs. For most departments this control caused only minor inconvenience. At the same time, however, the maintenance department was responding to another control—budgets—by shifting from contracting-out to in-company performance of some repair work, and this involved adding men to the maintenance payroll. The maintenance manager was caught between two pressures. Since the control over hiring new personnel originated in the president's office, he took the easy way out. He continued to contract-out the repair work—even though this appeared to be more expensive—and met the budget squeeze by scrimping on other work.

In other instances, the *absence* of controls over, say, product development or cultivation of new customers may lead to difficulties if strong emphasis is placed on filling a tough sales quota.

The specific control in each of these examples had a worthy objective, but its effect was undesirable because it was not properly integrated into the total control structure of the company.

*Diversity of controls.* Every enterprise has numerous controls. There will be controls over output—quantity, quality, time—for departments, sections, and probably individuals. Various controls will deal with the methods of work. Cost controls in terms of dollars, physical units, difficulties caused other departments, and the like will surely exist. Controls over the flow of capital into fixed assets and inventories are very common although the degree of detail varies greatly. The protection of assets, ranging all the way from cash to good will, is another area for controls. Most companies have an array of personnel controls dealing with training, compensation, handling of grievances, and similar matters. Even this incomplete list suggests that a total control structure is a complex matter.

Many of these controls will be local, applying only to the activities of one or a few people, whereas others will permeate the entire enterprise. Some will be quite formal in their prescription of standards, measurements, and reports while others will be informal though nonetheless real. Enforcement may be tough, with frequent measurement and severe penalties for deviation, or it may be so casual that the standard is given only sporadic attention. The standards themselves may be easy to maintain by normal activity, or they may represent challenges to the most proficient workers.

The individual controls are so diverse that we frequently fail to think of their combined effect; and they often exert competing—if not conflicting—pressures.

*Structure involves synthesis.* We have already used the concept of over-all structure in regard to planning and organizing. (See Chapters 5, 16, and 17.) In each instance the practical value of fitting various parts into a unified, interdependent whole was stressed. A similar point of view should be taken by an administrator toward controlling.

Most problems of control that demand attention—the squeaky wheels—will be fairly specific and often focused on a narrow issue. These problems should, of course, be treated promptly. But, (a) in solving each such problem its relation to the total control structure should be weighed, and (b) from time to time the administrator should review his over-all control structure in terms of balance, possible omissions, impact, cost, and similar factors. In control, as in organization and planning, the effect of the whole structure should be greater than the sum of its parts.

When appraising the control structure of his company (or his department), an administrator should consider the following:

1. Emphasis and balance resulting from the *combined* effect of all controls
2. Where control is exercised—machine operator, first-line supervisor, staff, higher executives
3. Speed and simplicity of controls
4. Effect of controls on motivation
5. Sensitivity to dynamic forces
6. Provision of useful data for future planning

These are not independent considerations; instead, they are six important features of any single control structure.

**Emphasis and balance in total structure**

The pattern of controls adopted for any one company—or department—should, of course, be suited to the crucial factors for success of that particular operation. Assets in a bank, quality in a food plant, safety on an airline, internal security in a defense plant—are easily recognized examples of such key factors. On the other hand, we cannot control everything; this would be impossible from an administrative standpoint and would create too much rigidity. Moreover, the number of different controls an employee—executive or operator—can respond to is limited. Emphasis on one tends to crowd out attention to others.

Since controls must be selective and also adapted to the needs of each specific enterprise, no standard control system fits all companies or units within a company. Instead, every administrator faces the task of shaping a unique control structure fitted to his particular operations. What factors should be stressed? Which merely kept within acceptable limits? Where can summaries or indicators be relied upon to reflect a whole host of normal activities? Is the precision of one control or the informality of another resulting in an unintended direction of attention? In total, is the combined effect of all controls operating in the manager's domain producing the emphasis and the balance he desires?

Among the difficulties in achieving such a balanced structure, four types of problems arise over and over again.

A. *Easily measurable factors tend to get too much weight, and intangible factors too little.* For instance, a company often watches carefully the expense per mile of its traveling salesmen but makes no check on whether the entire trip was desirable or undesirable. Similarly, an advertising manager may be promptly called in to explain a small deviation from budgeted expenditures, whereas the output of his efforts receives only occasional subjective appraisal. Control over research and development expenditures is in much the same predicament. In the personnel field, turnover figures can easily be watched, but the hiring of men with high potential often is subjected to little direct control.

B. *Short-run results tend to be overemphasized compared with long-run results.* In a typical control system, the annual profit-and-loss statement of a division receives more attention than building for long-run growth. Customer good will, employee morale, product development, and even maintenance of equipment, rarely "pay off" in accounting reports during the period when expense on such items is incurred. Long-run results are uncertain, and even if we withhold appraisal for a period of years, causal relationships are often difficult to trace. Consequently, it is difficult to design a control system that does not overweigh the short-run—or even the past.

C. *The relative emphasis desired in a control structure may shift over time.* For example, at one stage in the growth of a company dependable quality and assured delivery may warrant higher priorities than costs; as competition increases, expense controls may need more emphasis; later, product development may become crucial to survival. At no time should any of these factors be completely neglected, but a shift in emphasis may be very desirable. In practice, the tendency is to leave existing controls intact and not adjust them to new objectives.

D. *The high status and/or the energy of a staff man who is concerned with controlling only one aspect of operations may upset a desirable balance.* One company, for example, promoted upstairs an aggressive executive who had been on the board of directors ever since the firm was a small, single-product enterprise. His new assignment was staff work on manufacturing costs in all plants—a subject dear to his heart. Unfortunately, his corrective action was so vigorous whenever cost reports showed even small margins above tough standards that supervisors engaged in many unwise practices to avoid a blow-up with this crusty character. In another instance, the young son of the company president was given an assignment to control inventories; for some strange reason there was great concern throughout the company about keeping inventory levels low—even though doing so might raise costs or hurt sales.

These four sources of misdirected emphasis, while by no means the only causes, do indicate why an administrator should examine his control structure in terms of its over-all balance and emphasis.

**Who exercises the various controls?**

A second important aspect of a control structure is where in the company organization the control work is actually performed. Depending upon the particular control objective and the activity, this may be done by a machine, operator, first-line supervisor, staff, or higher executive.

To get to the heart of the question of who exercises control, we must recognize that the several steps in a control cycle often are taken by different people. That is, design of a control (picking factors to watch, selecting indexes or other measuring devices, and setting levels of achievement) may be done by one or more persons; actually measuring or testing often is performed by someone else; perhaps evaluation is separated from measuring; and, corrective action is normally reserved for the person being controlled or his immediate supervisor.

This question of who does what is illustrated by a change in the organization for quality control of a paper products company. For many years, a separate quality control staff at company headquarters had designed the controls to be used, and then in each plant a separate quality control group measured, evaluated, and recommended corrective action at four or five stages in the production process. The company later decided to turn over all in-process control to the machine operators. Testing equipment was placed near the machines, and the operators themselves were taught to use the equipment and take corrective action whenever this appeared necessary. The design of the system was still done by the headquarters staff, but the transfer of the remaining control activities to machine operators brought about a significant decrease in defective products. To be sure, an independent sampling of finished products was continued, but this did not interfere with a feeling by the production operators that now they were their own inspectors.

Effective decentralization and control structure are closely linked. An oil company, for example, devoted much effort to "decentralizing" its operations. But it failed to adjust the flow of control information, and older men remaining at the headquarters continued to order corrective action whenever they noted deviations from what they considered to be desirable results. Both confusion and bad feeling arose. Unfortunately, the president was not clear in his own mind how to retain necessary central control while delegating wide latitude to field men, and the net result has been that the decentralization plan never did work.

As these examples suggest, the administractor must decide who should perform each control phase for each of the factors to be watched. This organization of control work should, of course, be consistent with the rest of the organization structure. Such allocation of control work is delicate because the administrator is also concerned with the attention and balance among controls—as pointed out in the previous section—and with motivation of behavior—as indicated in the discussion of budgeting and later in this chapter.

In designing his control structure, then, an executive should recognize that the impact of his controls depends in part upon *who performs various control activities* and how this assignment of work relates to company organization, prevailing attitudes about legitimacy of control actions, actual behavior of executives, and similar factors.

### Speed and simplicity of controls

Thirdly, a control structure should also be appraised in terms of its speed and simplicity of action. An elaborate system that is complex and slow rarely produces satisfactory results.

For day-to-day operations, a servo mechanism—so important in automated production—provides a model of speed of control. Here, results are measured, this information is fed back to an instrument that compares results with a standard, and if significant deviations are noted, the servo automatically sets in motion a predetermined corrective action.[1] Many managerial controls work essentially in this fashion, except that a human being receives the information and decides on the corrective action. The servo mechanism analogy does suggest that the faster control data can be fed back to someone close to operations who knows what corrective action is needed— perhaps the operator himself—the simpler will be the system. In fact, most good control structures have numerous short feedback circuits of this sort. The task of the designer of a structure is to make sure that they exist at the necessary points, that the standards and corrective actions they employ are consistent with the aims of the over-all structure, and that they work promptly and with a minimum of friction.

With such an underlying set of controls, the number and frequency of reports flowing to higher executives and to staff men can be held down. As suggested in the discussion of strategic control points in Chapter 24, some provision must be made for prompt reporting of exceptional conditions and forewarnings of impending trouble. And various types of comprehensive appraisals will be needed from time to time. Even these reports, however, can be made a part of a well-established *system*.

By no means can all controls be reduced to a system, however. Some of the most important long-range and intangible controls will require intensive attention of key executives. But by systematizing the more routine controls, and by encouraging prompt localized action, senior executives have more time to focus on unusual problems. So, when appraising his control structure, the administrator should consider the extent to which speed and simplicity can be introduced by use of systematization—especially local feedback systems.

Simplification can also be obtained through the obvious step of eliminating controls that are no longer needed. Once established, control procedures tend to linger on—even after (a) work habits are sufficiently strong to assure adequate performance without a formal control, (b) a temporary stress such as a war shortage is

---

[1] In a noncontinuous operation, the servo may also detect that a part has been finished, and then it signals, "Stop, remove finished part, bring in new part, start again." Such additional refinements are not central to our examination of basic control concepts.

removed and controls in that area are no longer needed, or (c) some new control provides adequate check on a factor covered by an old system. But note, a decision to eliminate a control mechanism can best be made on the basis of an analysis of the total control structure.

**Effect of controls on motivation**

A control structure, just as a single control, should be appraised in terms of its impact on the motivation of the people it affects. The purpose of controlling is not to create reports; it is to channel the efforts of executives and operators. This means that the human response to the controls we establish is highly significant.

Much of the response to a control system depends upon how the workers feel about the system itself. If workers feel that controls are unreasonable, unfair, or illegitimate, they will resist and resent them. Such resistance, especially when supported by social pressures, can go far toward nullifying the intended results of the controls.

We probably should not expect controls to be popular. Occasionally they will carry grim, unpleasant news, and frequently they are a stern reminder of work to be done. Nevertheless, we can help make controls an acceptable feature of normal, purposeful endeavor by the following methods:

- Relate control to recognized objectives.
- Make measurements as accurately as possible, and quickly admit inaccuracies when they do occur.
- Obtain acceptance of normal levels of performance; use participation in setting standards for each person as one method.
- Release control information to the men being measured as soon as or before giving it to anyone else.
- Distinguish between making measurements and taking corrective action.
- Maintain a dispassionate view when errors crop up.
- In analyzing unfavorable results, seek a cure rather than a culprit.
- Introduce flexibility into the administration of the control system.

Often the measures just listed can be applied to a single control as well as to a control structure. But only an over-all review deals with (a) *inconsistencies* between controls which make a worker feel he is caught between the devil and the deep blue sea; (b) such a *galaxy* of controls that workers just give up trying to meet any of them, or rebel because no direction permits freedom for self-expression; and (c) the possibility that adverse reaction to one or two controls is so strong that *resistance is transferred* to the entire system—even to those parts which otherwise might be acceptable. Negative responses arising from these causes indicate that the control structure itself, not just the manner of its administration, needs revision.

### Sensitivity to dynamic forces

The features of control structures we have discussed thus far—relative emphasis, organization of control work, speed and simplicity, personal response to the control system—are largely concerned with well-established activities and with clearly designed standards. A good control structure should also be sensitive to dynamic forces. Technological and social changes may upset the value of a control mechanism, especially a systematized one. Unless these dynamic changes are recognized, the existence of a venerated control may actually create a false sense of security.

Classic examples include the soap company that kept a close watch on its position in the soap industry only to discover several years after detergents had gotten a good start that a more significant measure of its market position would have embraced all sorts of cleaning agents—not just soap. Many railroads made a similar mistake by watching carloadings instead of all forms of transportation. In another instance, an insurance company had elaborate controls on its clerical and other office costs—based on historical records and time study; but its control failed to reflect the way computers had reduced the cost of its more progressive competitors.

As these examples suggest, a control system may actually be detrimental if it monitors the wrong factors or applies the wrong standards. At a minimum, the control structure should include individuals charged with keeping track of new developments in designated fields of vital interest to the company. They should provide warnings of problems and opportunities, just as a more routine control report calls attention to the need for corrective action.

Another problem area is the difficulty of keeping controls abreast of dynamic changes in external relationships—discussed in Chapter 18. For instance, a company knows about orders it receives, but keeping track of the strength and efficiency of its dealers is much harder. A few firms do extend their control systems to cover the health of their distributing organizations—automobile companies are a notable example—but typically the standards and feedback information are scanty. There is similar difficulty in keeping track of suppliers. A medical products company, for example, found itself in a weak position because a manufacturer that was its sole source of a key material decided to shift his product development efforts into another field. As a result the company found itself with an obsolete product line because a key supplier had lost interest in keeping the product up to date. And, in the field of finance many a company has found itself in difficulty because its bank or other anticipated source of credit had to "realign its lending policies."

External alliances cannot be "controlled" in the same sense as internal operations; business custom forbids it, and the power of sanctions is more sharply restricted. Nevertheless, these outside firms are essential parts of a social organization, and feedback information on their aims and health is very valuable. A formal control system may not be appropriate, but the total control structure should include some avenues of current data about "partners"— even though they are not on the company payroll.

**Provision of useful data for future planning**

Control aids planning (and other phases of administration) in two ways: it draws attention to situations where new planning is needed; and it provides some of the data upon which plans can be based. Clearly, creation of planning data is not a primary function of control, but insofar as useful information can be a byproduct, it should be produced. So, a final question about a control structure is whether an optimum amount of planning information is generated.

Here is a simple example. A folding paper box manufacturer decided its job-order cost system was not worth the expense and trouble of maintaining it. Machine hours for each process provided a simpler and adequate unit for scheduling, measuring efficiency, and the like. The feedback was quick and understandable. Nevertheless, the company did retain simple records of hours spent on each job so cost analyses could be made when needed for such decisions as types of business to be sought or purchase of new equipment. Fortunately in this case, zeal to simplify the cost control system did not eliminate the basic data that could be converted into planning information when needed.

*Integrated data processing*, while much more complex, also provides both control and planning data. A wide range of information is fed into the processing center which then sends out reports for diverse purposes—including control. In most installations, some adjustments have to be made in the control systems, and of course not all kinds of controls are covered by the data center. The concept is mentioned here as another example of modifying the general control structure to some extent in order to aid the performance of other management tasks.

## SUMMARY

Specific control problems can be dealt with by picking strategic control points, setting norms of satisfactory performance, measuring and comparing actual performance against these norms, reporting deviations to all persons concerned, and taking corrective action. Considerable ingenuity may be required to perform effectively each of these steps of a normal control cycle—especially when the purpose is to assure that some intangible or long-run objective is attained. Nevertheless, the basic elements of the process are clear.

In addition to thinking about controlling particular operations, the wise administrator will be sure that his over-all control structure is sound. "Structure" in this context means the *interaction* of the numerous specific controls and their *combined* effect on the results achieved by the company (or other unit of administration). When viewed as a whole, the various controls form a network of norms, reports, and influences that can greatly aid administration— or if poorly fitted together, can create confusion.

When developing a control structure, an administrator should consider: (1) relative emphasis he wishes to give different aspects of his operations, (2) where in his organization control work can best be done, (3) speed and simplicity of controls, (4) effect of his control structure on motivation of people, (5) sensitivity to dynamic changes—both internal and external, and (6) generation of data useful in planning. He should strive for a skillful blending of these features into a control structure suited to the unique needs of his enterprise.

## SELECTED REFERENCES

Malcolm, D. G., et al., *Management Control Systems*, John Wiley & Sons, Inc., 1960.

Newman, W. H. and C. E. Summer, *The Process of Management*, Prentice-Hall, Inc., 1961, Chaps. 27 and 28.

Rowland, V. K., *Managerial Performance Standards*, American Management Association, 1962.

# *VI*
# Conclusion

27. Putting Administrative Principles to Work

# 27

# Putting Administrative Principles to Work

Principles of administration, like principles in any other field of activity, must be adapted to real problems if they are to be of practical use. This adjusting and fitting of a general idea to the specific situation is a very important part of the art of administration.

Throughout this book suggestions are found for applying the principles which have been discussed. Most of the basic ideas have been stated in terms of executive action; this was done to help in the transition from principle to practice. Nevertheless, three broad points deserve particular emphasis here:

1. Be sure to get the facts.
2. Adjust to individual personalities.
3. Consider the whole situation.

**Be sure to get the facts**

Every concrete management problem has its own specific setting. The industry, the company, the people directly concerned, the external forces, the preceding chain of events, and many other aspects vary from one problem to another. Executive action to meet a given problem must take these technical and economic facts into consideration.

Management principles by themselves are as sterile as mathematics; only when the retail clerk or the engineer applies mathematics to actual facts does it give tangible results. Likewise, management principles are useful only when they are skillfully applied

*471*

to the facts in a given situation. In other words, expertness in management *per se* is no substitute for the knowledge and judgment growing out of intimate contact with the operations themselves. Nor, we might add, does a great store of facts necessarily give a man skill as an administrator. Both are essential to effective administration.

This book has stressed basic processes and principles because that is its purpose. We hope that this in no way detracts from the significant of good information, or what the Army calls "intelligence," in practical administration.

### Adjust to individual personalities

A second point that should be made in this brief conclusion is the need to recognize the cardinal importance of individual personalities in actual administration.

*Administration—a segment of human relations.* Administration was defined in Chapter 1 as "the guidance, leadership, and control of the efforts of a group of individuals toward some common goal." While the executive must give attention to technology, physical facilities, capital resources, and the like, his predominant concern— as the definition implies—is with human relations.

The underlying significance of human behavior has been referred to repeatedly. For example, in the discussion of *planning* attention was called to the effect of detailed planning on individual initiative, and later to strategies that are largely concerned with the interplay of personalities. Similarly, in the section on *organization* the need to adjust departmentation to available personnel and informal organization was noted. Other examples in this section include the effect of decentralization on morale, and the necessary adjustment to personalities in the process of delegation and in deciding upon an effective span of supervision. The section on *assembling resources* gives primary attention to executive personnel. Again, under *supervision,* the importance of the human element is illustrated in the application of the concepts of indoctrination and consultative direction; motivation, of course, deals solely with human responses; voluntary coordination is built upon personal objectives and social intercourse. In the final section we noted that administrative *control* is dependent upon guiding the actual behavior of those whose joint efforts are necessary if objectives are to be attained.

These are merely convenient examples of the ever-present need to regard administration as a social process. Unfortunately, our present knowledge of social psychology and other aspects of human behavior is far from exact. To a large extent, administrative principles set forth in this book are pragmatic; that is, they are believed to be sound because executives in a variety of enterprises have found that they work. As the scientists increase our knowledge of individual and group behavior, we will be able to refine these principles so that they will be even more effective.

*Recognize individual differences.* These principles of administration are, of course, based on the common or typical behavior of the employees. We should recognize, however, that the attitudes and behavior of a specific individual will vary to a greater or lesser extent from the common pattern. The physical characteristics and personal history of each individual give him a distinct personality in at least some respects.

In a specific situation, then, the executive deals, not with men in general, but with separate and distinct personalities. He should take account of individual differences. Where there is a sharp variation from the common pattern, it may be necessary to modify the action normally required by a general principle. For example, if an otherwise good subordinate lacks ability to get things done on time, it may not be practical to decentralize as much as the general organization structure provides. Similarly, an individual with an unusual amount of energy may be given a larger span of supervision. Men differ considerably in their response to different types of motivation, and better control often can be secured if the executive is able to adapt incentives to the particular individual involved.

Adjustment to individual idiosyncrasies may have repercussions on other people doing related work, and it may create precedent and habit that will cause inefficiency at a later date. Consequently, care is necessary in making such adjustments. The executive should be ever-alert to individual differences, but the extent to which he caters to them, capitalizes on them, or seeks to modify them, is a part of the art of administration.

### Consider the whole situation

The skillful application of administrative principles requires, in addition to knowledge of local facts and adjustments for individual personalities, a capacity to sense the entire administrative operation. Management of an enterprise must be understood as a whole, as well as in its parts.

*Interdependence of planning, organizing, assembling resources, supervising, and controlling.* In actual practice, management problems rarely fall neatly into a single niche. Two or more of the phases of administration are often involved. For instance, what may appear to be largely a control problem frequently can be resolved only after plans or organization have been improved. Similarly, good executive selection and development starts with organization analysis; the degree of decentralization has a marked effect on the type of direction that is desirable. Many management problems are likewise multi-phase in nature.

Consequently, when applying principles to a particular problem, one should be ever on the alert for the repercussions that a proposed change may have upon other phases of the operation. For purposes of analysis and as a guide to executive thinking, a somewhat artificial separation of administration problems has been presented in this book. Useful as this is as a way of thinking, it does not justify only partial study of a problem. Practical solutions will be found only when the entire administrative operation is brought under review. Perhaps the remedy will deal with only one phase of administration, but it is not safe to assume that this is so until possible interrelations have been carefully considered.

*Web of related decisions and actions.* The need for taking a broad view of a specific administrative situation also arises because planning, organizing and assembling resources, supervising, and controlling are going on at the same time. As pointed out in Chapter 2, it is rarely practical to delay action on a problem until all plans have been completed. For example, once objectives and a broad program have been mapped out, it is often necessary to set up preliminary organization and to hire key personnel, inasmuch as these people will probably do much of the detailed planning. To cite another example, product specifications may be established in detail and orders issued for actual production of an initial run before the sales promotion department begins its task of planning a sales campaign. Furthermore, since a single executive is usually concerned with several different projects, he may be involved in exploratory planning of one, making final decisions with regard to a second, and controlling the actual performance of still a third, all in the same day.

| PLAN | ORGANIZE | ASSEMBLE RESOURCES | SUPERVISE | CONTROL |
|---|---|---|---|---|
| 1. Develop integrated and comprehensive structure.<br>  a. Use all types of plans.<br>    1) Objectives and sub-goals.<br>    2) Single-use plans.<br>    3) Standing plans.<br>  b. Weigh detail and period covered.<br>    1) Benefits of planning:<br>      a) Crises avoided.<br>      b) Better methods.<br>      c) Easier delegation.<br>      d) Basis for control.<br>    2) Limits on planning.<br>      a) Unreliable forecasts.<br>      b) Nonrecurring problems.<br>      c) Danger of inflexibility.<br>      d) Expense of planning.<br>      e) Time required.<br>      f) Effect on individual.<br>  c. Incorporate logistics and strategy.<br><br>2. Use these steps:<br>  a. Diagnose problem.<br>  b. Find creative alternatives.<br>  c. Project consequences.<br>  d. Evaluate and choose.<br><br>3. Aid planning.<br>  a. Simplify scope.<br>  b. Organize for planning.<br>  c. Simplify with logic.<br>  d. Consider operations research.<br>  e. Test choice.<br><br>4. Integrate planning structure. | 1. Establish departments which:<br>  a. Make use of specialization.<br>  b. Facilitate control.<br>  c. Aid in coordination.<br>  d. Secure adequate attention.<br>  e. Recognize local conditions.<br>  f. Reduce expense.<br><br>2. Provide staff and service divisions where needed.<br><br>3. Clarify relations between units and men.<br>  a. Decentralize where practical.<br>    1) Who knows facts?<br>    2) Capacity of men.<br>    3) Need for speed.<br>    4) Need for coordination.<br>    5) Importance of decision.<br>    6) Executive load.<br>    7) Effect on morale.<br>  b. Identify staff responsibility.<br>  c. Use functional authority cautiously.<br><br>4. Build a sound structure.<br>  a. Assign all duties.<br>  b. Avoid dual subordination.<br>  c. Keep spans of supervision workable.<br>  d. Use committees wisely.<br>  e. Provide for top-management.<br>  f. Seek:<br>    1) Even strata.<br>    2) Consistent departmentation.<br>    3) Parallel departmentation.<br>    4) Simple structure. | 1. Build external alliances.<br>  a. Informal agreements.<br>  b. Formal contracts.<br>  c. Partial ownership.<br>  d. Serving on board of directors.<br>  e. Consortiums for projects.<br><br>2. Select key executives.<br>  a. Determine needs through:<br>    1) Job analysis.<br>    2) Man specifications.<br>    3) Promotion programs.<br>  b. Appraise and select using:<br>    1) Group judgment.<br>    2) Performance appraisals.<br>    3) Promotion qualifications.<br>    4) Trial or series of jobs.<br>    5) Psychological tests.<br><br>3. Assist executive to develop by:<br>  a. Learning on the job.<br>  b. Rotation among jobs.<br>  c. Use of committees, courses, etc.<br>  d. Support of personal programs.<br><br>4. Compensate executives wisely.<br>  a. Build a sound salary structure.<br>  b. Recognize individual results.<br>  c. Use bonuses, stock options, etc. for special cases. | 1. Give directions that will obtain desired results.<br>  a. Issue good instructions.<br>  b. Always follow up instructions.<br>  c. Simplify through s. o. p. and indoctrination.<br>  d. Explain why.<br>  e. Use consultative direction in key relationships.<br><br>2. Motivate men through:<br>  a. Financial income.<br>  b. Social status.<br>  c. Security.<br>  d. Attractive work.<br>  e. Opportunity.<br>  f. Worthwhile activity.<br>  g. Power.<br>  h. Personal attention.<br>  i. Participation.<br>  j. Just supervision.<br><br>3. Promote coordination in all phases of administration.<br>  a. Harmonize programs and policies.<br>  b. Organize for coordinated action.<br>  c. Design effective means of communication.<br>  d. Aid voluntary coordination.<br>    1) Instill dominant objectives.<br>    2) Develop customs and terms.<br>    3) Encourage informal contacts.<br>    4) Provide liaison as needed.<br>    5) Use committees.<br>  e. Coordinate through supervision. | 1. Set standards at strategic points.<br>  a. Tie standards to individual responsibility.<br>  b. Concentrate on strategic points.<br>  c. Use integrated budgets.<br><br>2. Check on performance.<br>  a. Use required confirmation sparingly.<br>  b. Concentrate on exceptions.<br>  c. Observe personally.<br>  d. Design reports for action.<br><br>3. Take corrective action.<br>  a. Adjust physical and external factors.<br>  b. Review direction, training, and selection of men.<br>  c. Motivate and discipline.<br>  d. Modify plans where necessary.<br><br>4. Balance control structure.<br>  a. Check relative emphasis.<br>  b. Focus control at suitable organization level.<br>  c. Seek speed and simplicity.<br>  d. Check motivation effects.<br>  e. Detect dynamic changes.<br>  f. Provide data for planning. |

FIGURE 38. *Five Basic Processes in Administration.*

The use of specialized staff units to help plan and control in their respective areas and the varying degrees of decentralization in different departments add still further complexity to the realistic operating situation, particularly in large-scale enterprises.

Improvement in administration will be accomplished only if the executive is able to penetrate through this interlacing of plans and actions. He should recognize it as the mosaic pattern upon which improvement must be built, and at the same time he should not be confused by its complexity.

*Follow analysis with synthesis.* This complexity of actual operations tends to hide the basic principles and processes of administration that are being used. Therefore, when dealing with a concrete problem, careful analysis is a first step toward improvement. The basic outline of this book, which is summarized in Figure 38, provides one approach that may be used in analyzing an over-all management problem.

Analysis, however, is not enough. Having broken the total operation down into parts or stages and designed improvements for at least some of them, the parts must be put back together into a new working whole. The chapters on planning structure, organization structure, and control structure provide guides for integrating each of these phases. But, in addition, the phases have to be fitted together. Here again the outline of the book will be of assistance. The broad headings—planning, organizing, assembling resources, supervising, and controlling—are more than a list of potential trouble spots for the executive. These processes, when considered together, represent a comprehensive and basic view of administration as a whole. They are related together in a logical and realistic fashion. Thus they provide a framework upon which to build an integrated view of administration in a specific situation.

The outline of the book, then, should be regarded as a tool for analysis and for integration when dealing with broad management problems.

# Index